Understanding the Global Experience

Becoming a Responsible World Citizen

EDITED BY

Thomas Arcaro
Rosemary Haskell

CONTRIBUTING AUTHORS

Robert G. Anderson
Thomas Arcaro
Laurence A. Basirico
Anne Bolin
Stephen Braye
Ann J. Cahill
Brian Digre
Chinedu "Ocek" Eke
Mathew Gendle
Rosemary Haskell
Duane McClearn
Jeffrey C. Pugh
Laura Roselle
Jean Schwind
Kerstin Sorensen
Anthony Weston

Elon University

Allyn & Bacon

Boston   Columbus   Indianapolis   New York   San Francisco   Upper Saddle River
Amsterdam   Cape Town   Dubai   London   Madrid   Milan   Munich   Paris   Montreal   Toronto
Delhi   Mexico City   Sao Paulo   Sydney   Hong Kong   Seoul   Singapore   Taipei   Tokyo

Executive Editor: Jeff Lasser
Editorial Assistant: Lauren Macey
Executive Marketing Manager: Kelly May
Production Supervisor: Patty Bergin
Editorial Production Service: Laserwords Maine
Manufacturing Buyer: Debbie Rossi
Electronic Composition: Laserwords India
Photo Researcher: Martha Shethar
Cover Designer: Kristina Mose-Libon

Map identified as: Hobo-Dyer Equal Area Projection (South on Top). Permission for use of this copyrighted image granted to Allyn and Bacon by ODTmaps.com for use on this book's cover. For maps and other related teaching materials contact: ODT, Inc., PO Box 134, Amherst MA 01004 USA; 800-736-1293; Fax: 413-549-3503; Skype: ODTInc; E-mail: odtstore@odt.org, Web: www.ODTmaps.com

Library of Congress Cataloging-in-Publication Data

Understanding the global experience : becoming a responsible world citizen /
Thomas Arcaro ... [et al.].
    p. cm.
  ISBN-13: 978-0-205-70741-6
  ISBN-10: 0-205-70741-6
  1. World citizenship. I. Arcaro, Thomas.
  JZ1320.4.U54 2010
  323.6--dc22

                                              2009022931

10 9 8 7 6 5 4 3 2 1 HAM 13 12 11 10 09

**Allyn & Bacon
is an imprint of**

www.pearsonhighered.com

ISBN 10:   0-205-70741-6
ISBN 13:   978-0-205-70741-6

We dedicate this book to all those who seek to understand the global experience.

Brief Contents

PART I   Approaches to Studying the World Today   1

1   *Beyond the Pledge of Allegiance: Becoming a Responsible World Citizen* / Thomas Arcaro   *3*

2   *The Joy of Culture: A Beginner's Guide to Understanding and Appreciating Cultural Diversity* / Laurence A. Basirico and Anne Bolin   *26*

3   *Reading, Writing, and Researching the Global Experience* / Jean Schwind   *49*

4   *Numbers and the World* / Duane McClearn   *75*

5   *Reading World Literature to Read the World: Literature and the Global Studies Student* / Rosemary Haskell   *109*

6   *Global Media and Global News: A Guide to Decoding and Analyzing Information* / Chinedu "Ocek" Eke   *138*

PART II   Topics in Global Studies   161

7   *Environmentalism Gone Wild: The Great Green Mobilization and Beyond* / Anthony Weston   *163*

8   ***Western Imperialism and Its Legacies*** / Brian Digre   *180*

9   ***Looking at the World through a Gendered Lens: Feminism and Global Studies*** / Ann J. Cahill   *205*

10   ***Use and Abuse: Drugs and Drug Commerce in a Global Context*** / Mathew Gendle   *229*

11   ***Navigating Religion in the Global Context*** / Jeffrey C. Pugh   *252*

12   ***Global Politics and Global Issues: Where Do You Fit?*** / Laura Roselle, Robert G. Anderson, and Kerstin Sorensen   *273*

13   ***"Jihad vs. McWorld": Benjamin R. Barber Revisited*** / Stephen Braye, Rosemary Haskell, and Thomas Arcaro   *294*

Contents

Preface   xv
Editors' Note   xix

PART I   *Approaches to Studying the World Today*   1

1   *Beyond the Pledge of Allegiance: Becoming
a Responsible World Citizen /* Thomas Arcaro   3

Prelude to What May Be a Surprising Chapter   3

Some Preliminary Thoughts on Being and Becoming a Global Citizen   4

*An Inconvenient Truth: We May Be More Racist and Xenophobic
than Is Pleasant to Admit*   6

*Patriotism, Nationalism, Ethnocentrism, and Racism: All Points
on the Same Spectrum?*   8

*One Good Thing about Sputnik: The Unlikely Catalyst Creating
a Global Community*   11

Crushed Chickpeas, Academic Freedom, and the Blind Machine   14

*Does Fire Purge Us of Our Racism? Some Thoughts
from Evolutionary Psychology*   16

A Model for How To Proceed as a Global Citizen   18

How Will the Rest of This Book Help You Embrace Your Role
as a "Global Citizen?"   20

Part I: Approaches to Studying the World Today   20

Part II: Topics in Global Studies   21

2 *The Joy of Culture: A Beginner's Guide to Understanding and Appreciating Cultural Diversity* / Laurence A. Basirico and Anne Bolin   **26**

What Is Culture?: Perspectives and Practices of Daily Life   **26**
The Importance of Understanding and Appreciating Other Cultures   **28**
Culture Change and Global Impacts   **28**
    An Increase in Cultural Diversity: The United States and the World   30
Ethnocentrism and Cultural Relativism   **31**
    Ethnocentrism   31
    Cultural Relativism: A Means of Overcoming Ethnocentrism   33
Further Explorations of Culture: The Disciplines of Anthropology and Sociology   **34**
    Culture Defined in More Detail: The History of a Definition   35
    The Characteristics of Culture   36
    The Elements of Culture   38
Institutions: Culture and Everyday Life   **41**
Putting It All Together: The Web of Culture   **43**

3 *Reading, Writing, and Researching the Global Experience* / Jean Schwind   **49**

Reading for a Global Perspective   **50**
    Exercise 1: Photo Analysis: The Way You Were   50
    Exercise 2: Comparative News Reading   52
    Reading: Listen and Respond   54
"Overstanding" a Nonfiction Text: Reflective Questioning   **58**
Using Tagmemics: Atomizing and Contextualizing   **59**
    Rabbi Arthur Waskow: "Can America Learn from Shabbat?"   59
    Exercise 3: Generating Questions in Responsive Reading   63
    E. Benjamin Skinner: "A World Enslaved"   63
Researching and Writing for a Global Perspective   **68**
Preliminary Research: Finding Books and Articles   **69**
    Reference Books   69
    Catalogues and Databases   69
Fieldwork and Visual Evidence   **71**
    Conducting Interviews   71
    Recording Observations   71
    Administering Questionnaires or Surveys   72
Forming and Arguing a Thesis   **72**
    Exercise 4: Family Immigration Research Project   73

4   *Numbers and the World /* Duane McClearn   **75**

Mistakes Were Made   **75**

The Real World   **76**

Ignoring Numbers   **78**

*Applications: Using Numerical Information
to Help Understand the World*   **79**

Numerical Information: A Limitation   **80**

*Basics: Understanding the Fundamentals
of Nations via Numbers*   **81**
     The Land   81
     The People   82
     The Faithful   84

Power   **84**
     Mighty Economies   84
     Military Muscle   86

Quality of Life   **89**
     Money   89
     Long Life   92
     Increased Complexity   93
     Good Government   94
     Putting It All Together   96

The Environment   **96**
     The Condition of the Planet   96
     A Primary Offender   98
     The Disappearance of Species   100
     People and More People   100
     Environmental Responsibility   101

Observations   **101**

Return to Borat   **104**

Problems   **104**

Concluding Remarks   **106**

5 **Reading World Literature to Read the World: Literature and the Global Studies Student** / Rosemary Haskell   **109**

World Literature and World Affairs: Looking for Parallels   **109**

Globalization: Not Just about Free Trade, Tariffs and Cotton Subsidies   **111**

Navigating the Map of World Literature: Not Continents and Countries, but Genres and Modes   **113**

Interpreting Individual Works: The Historical and Cultural Critic's Broad Perspective on Finding Meaning   **115**

    One Example: *The Tempest*   115

    Other Familiar Examples of Literature as Purveyors of "History" or "Culture": *Huckleberry Finn, Heart of Darkness, A Modest Proposal*   116

The Interpreter's Choice: Being an Intelligent Critic of World Literature   **117**

    Classifying and Theorizing the Various Relationships between Literature and the World   118

        Literature as Mirror   118

        Literature as Commentator   118

        Literature as Participant and Shaper   119

        Literature as Alternative or Subversive History   120

Global Studies Topics in a Novel, a Poem, and a Short Story: The Global Experience through Literature   **122**

    Novel: Khaled Hosseini's *The Kite Runner*   122

    Poetry: Steve Chimombo's "Developments From the Grave"   124

    Short Story: Kojo Laing's "Vacancy for the Post of Jesus Christ"   127

Nonfiction: The Essay, Nature Writing, the Blog   **130**

Conclusion   **131**

6 **Global Media and Global News: A Guide to Decoding and Analyzing Information** / Chinedu "Ocek" Eke   **138**

Introduction: Information Everywhere, but Not a Drop to Drink?   **138**

Defining Mass Communication and the Mass Media: The Great Global News System   **139**

Mass Media: World-Wide Roles and Responsibilities, and the Limits of Freedom   **139**

    Ownership and Ownership Patterns   140

    Ownership, Culture, and Ideological Shaping   141

Gatekeeping in Mass Media   142

The Individual and the System: i-media and u-report   147

The Product Itself: News or Infotainment?   **148**

What Is News?   148

Elements of News   149

Don't Be Fooled: Reading the Mass Media Intelligently   **149**

Steps to Analyzing and Understanding News: Critical Thinking—A Strategy for All Seasons   149

Applying Critical Thinking   151

Conclusion   **156**

PART II   *Topics in Global Studies*   161

7   *Environmentalism Gone Wild: The Great Green Mobilization and Beyond* / Anthony Weston   163

Environmentalism Evolves   **164**

The Mobilization   **165**

Debating the Mobilization   **166**

What Would Thoreau Do?   **168**

Trapped in a System   **169**

Whole-Systems Design   **170**

Earth in Flow   **172**

Yes, We Can!   **174**

Religion Gone Wild   **176**

8   *Western Imperialism and Its Legacies* / Brian Digre   180

Chapter Overview   **181**

The Old Colonial System from the Late Fifteenth to the Early Nineteenth Centuries   **182**

Motives for the New Imperialism in the Late Nineteenth and Early Twentieth Centuries   **184**

Africa Partitioned   **186**

Colonial Policies and Their Legacies   188

Imperialism in Asia   **189**
    India   190
    Southeast Asia   191
    China   192
    Japan   194

Neocolonialism in the Caribbean and Central America   **194**
    The Middle East and the League of Nations Mandates   196

Revolution in Asia and Africa: Dismantling Empires after 1945   **198**
    Asia   199
    Africa   200

9   *Looking at the World Through a Gendered Lens: Feminism and Global Studies* / Ann J. Cahill   **205**

Defining Feminism   **205**

The Conceptual Tools of Feminism and Global Studies   **208**
    The Social Construction of Gender   209
    Gender and Other Social Factors   210
    The Male Generic   211
    The Devaluing of the Feminine   212

Deploying Feminism's Conceptual Tools Around the World: Some Examples   **213**
    Example 1: Female Genital Cutting   213
    Example 2: Agriculture   217
    Example 3: HIV/AIDS   219
    Example 4: Fill in the Blank   222

Conclusion   **223**

10   *Use and Abuse: Drugs and Drug Commerce in a Global Context* / Mathew Gendle   **229**

Drugs around the World: The Challenge of Cultural Relativism   **229**

Drugs Have Shaped Culture, Just as Culture Has Shaped Drug Use   **233**
    Peyote and the Native American Church   233
    Caffeine and the Eight-to-Five Workday   234
    Drug Prohibition in the United States   235
    Race, Social Class, and Drug Legislation   237

Drugs and Relationships Between Cultures   239
   Europeans Discover Coca and Tobacco   240
   China, Great Britain, and Opium   242

U.S. Foreign Policy in the Twentieth Century   **243**
   Drug Proxy Armies and Foreign Policy   248

Conclusion   **249**

11   *Navigating Religion in the Global
        Context /* Jeffrey C. Pugh   **252**

Introduction   **252**

The Disappearing God: Is Religion Relevant in the Western World?   **253**

Shaping Our Inner and Outer Worlds   **255**
   The intersection of religion and culture   255
   Religion's special power: transcendent command and the realm of the absolute   256

When Worlds Come Undone   **258**

Worlds Colliding: When Religions Conflict   **259**
   The Ottoman Empire and the European Powers   260
   Iran and Islam   261
   Iraq and Islam   262

Resistance Is No Respecter of Religions   **263**
   Israel: Judaism, Christianity & Islam   263
   Latin America and Liberation Theology   264

In the African Context: Nigeria and Darfur   **265**

Is There a Way Forward?   **267**
   World religious and secular forces still at odds   268
   The need for negotiation and the example of Northern Ireland   268
   Using the model of the Good Friday Agreement in other parts of the world   269

12   *Global Politics and Global Issues: Where Do You Fit? /* Laura
        Roselle, Robert G. Anderson, and Kerstin Sorensen   **273**

States as Political Actors   **274**

Rules and Organizations for the Engagement of States   **276**

Non-state Political Actors   **277**
   Organizations for Non-state Actors   277

Key Concepts Related to Cooperation and Conflict: Interests, Ideas, Perceptions, and Power   **279**

    International Law—Its Range and Limitations   281

    State Dominance in International Law   282

    International Law and Non-state Actors   282

The Role of Theory in International Relations   **285**

    Realism and Liberalism   285

    Constructivism and Feminism   286

The United States in the World Today   **287**

The Politics of Addressing Pressing Global Problems and Pursuing Global Opportunities   **289**

Communication and Making Connections   **290**

Your Place in Global Politics—or the "Who Cares?" Question   **291**

13 *"Jihad vs. McWorld": Benjamin R. Barber Revisited /* Stephen Braye, Rosemary Haskell, and Thomas Arcaro   **294**

Introduction: Finding Frameworks for the World's Multeity and Unity, Change and Stasis   **294**

    Barber's "Jihad vs. McWorld"   294

    The Presocratics   295

    Friedman, Sachs, Stiglitz, Soros, Ritzer   295

    Hegel   296

    "McDonaldization" and "Flattening"   297

Locating "Jihad" and "McWorld"   **299**

    The Wars in Afghanistan and Iraq   301

    China and the Olympics: Beijing, Summer 2008   303

    Zambia: A Personal Experience   304

    Zimbabwe: Tribalism Dial Set at "Self-Destruct"?   306

    Namibia Since Independence: Beyond Jihad and McWorld?   306

Talking Points   **307**

    Exporting Democracy   307

    The Successes and Failures of McWorld   308

    The Successes and Failures of Jihad   308

Can We Do As Well As Barber, Friedman, et al.? Some Student Voices   **310**

Last Thoughts about Our Need for Other People's Interpretive Perspectives in the Field of Global Studies   **312**

Preface

Look at the cover of this book. What do you see?
Now read on...

On October 19, 1781, Lord Cornwallis surrendered his British forces to the American colonists of George Washington, thus effectively bringing to an end the war for American independence. As the British troops ceremoniously laid down their arms, the military band played the song "The World Turned Upside Down."

For the British, it truly did seem as if the world was "upside down," or, at least in some way, severely out of joint. The most powerful nation in the Western world, Great Britain, had been challenged by a cluster of squabbling American colonial upstarts. In the American colonies themselves, only a minority of citizens actually favored independence from Britain. Many others remained loyal to the mother country, or were neutral. When, against many expectations, the Americans who favored independence prevailed, Britain lost some valuable possessions, and the natural order really seemed to have been turned on its head.

British politicians and others saw the outcome of the Revolutionary War upset their notion of the way things were supposed to be. To adjust to the new world realities, old assumptions had to be questioned, and a fresh way of viewing the world and its political and social forces was called for.

In much the same way, the traditionalist leaders of the Soviet Union (the U.S.S.R.), and of the entire Eastern Bloc, behind the Iron Curtain, were astonished in the late 1980s and early 1990s to witness the collapse of their own political and economic system. The Berlin Wall crumbled in November 1989, and the demolition squads, it must have appeared, just moved on in through all the old Warsaw Pact countries, finally reaching Moscow. To the true believers in Soviet Communism, it was the capitalistic West, with all its corrupt weaknesses, which had seemed to teeter on the verge of collapse. But, with surprising rapidity, the Kremlin saw its own world "turned upside down," as the old Soviet Union broke apart into myriad new states. This was a scene as shocking to the rulers of the Communist empire as the one the British imperialists had watched unfold two centuries earlier. The Soviet military bands probably did not, in 1991–1992, play "The World Turned Upside Down," but the tune would have been appropriate.

History, then—both distant, and more recent—teaches us, apparently, not to get complacent or too comfortable in our own world or in our own world view. Perhaps most citizens of the United States actually don't need that lesson now as much as they did in the years preceding September 11, 2001, the day the United States suffered an attack that caused more casualties than the 1941 bombing of Pearl Harbor. Many of us really did sit up and take notice of "the rest of the world," and our place in it, after the frightening and shocking al Qaeda onslaught of that sunny autumn morning on the East Coast.

Still, it's all too human for us to want to move swiftly away from disorder and the threat of disorder. When our world is turned upside down, as it was on 9/11, we seek to right it. We want to get comfortable again as soon as we can. Well, as university professors, we can't allow you—or ourselves—to do that. In Global Studies courses, as in many undergraduate courses, there are plenty of opportunities for students to be made uneasy about their world. But, more excitingly, there are plenty of occasions, also, to embrace challenging new ideas, alternative perspectives, and new and better methods of analysis and interpretation. This book, *Understanding the Global Experience: Becoming a Responsible World Citizen,* is designed to give you a lot to think about as you work in your Global Studies (or other, related) classes. We want to challenge your assumptions, push you to become critical readers, writers, and thinkers, and provide you with enough enticing and gripping information about an array of topics and ideas so that you will want to study at least some of them on your own. Even if your world doesn't actually turn upside down, it may sway, or shake, as a result of your studies.

But that's not all. The subtitle of the book, "Becoming a Responsible World Citizen," is both very clear and very ambiguous. All of us have some ideas about "world citizenship" and what it means. But these ideas are probably not identical nor, sometimes, even mildly similar. What does it mean to be a world citizen, let alone a responsible one? And what role does a Global Studies course, and this book, or any book, play in helping anyone to become such a thing? The subtitle asks far more questions than it answers. It may even infuriate Global Studies instructors and students, who might wonder why the book's editors and authors think they have the right to lecture their readers on how to become responsible world citizens. Who are they to tell us what to be and how to be it? Even more annoying, some of the authors seem to want to tell us what we should do! Still, in a free country, we don't have to do these things. We might, however, want to consider them seriously.

In the end, each author's chapter or essay in this anthology suggests different ways of defining responsibility, which turns out to have not merely ethical, but also intellectual, practical, and spiritual components. As to "world citizen": well, to belong to the world, as one belongs to one's country, is to know it well; to identify with a majority of its inhabitants' needs, hopes, fears, and desires; and to share its dominant values and beliefs. We cannot do any of those things unless we actually know something about the rest of the world. If there were a "world citizenship" test, as there is a test for would-be new American citizens, what questions would be on it? What language would applicants have to speak? What oath would they have to take to get citizenship on this globe? Yet, to be a *responsible* world citizen, something more would be needed: the intellectual power to interpret and evaluate complex situations, the ability to identify right values and the strength to support them, in word and deed. Further, responsible world citizens learn not only about what *was* and what *is,* but additionally they embrace their potential to make an impact on what *will be:* that is, to be informed agents of positive change.

We like to think that this book would be a good study guide for those aspiring world citizens who present themselves for interview and testing at the Global Citizenship Office.

While sharpening some analytical and interpretive skills useful to any undergraduate anywhere, the thirteen essays in this anthology also push their readers a short way along the path to knowledge, understanding, informed criticism, and sympathy: in other words, toward responsible world citizenship.

Acknowledgments

The editors gratefully acknowledge the support and encouragement of Elon University. We especially thank Provost Gerald Francis, who provided the administrative and financial resources for this book's first incarnation, in 1999–2000; and Dr. Duane McClearn, Associate Professor of Psychology at Elon, the co-editor of that earlier version, without whom the entire project would not have begun. Dr. Janet Warman, Director of General Studies at Elon University, and Coordinator of the Global Experience course there, has been generous with her time and advice, as have our colleagues in the Global Experience curriculum at Elon.

As editors, we want to thank all of the authors who worked with us from the beginning to make this text possible. Their patience, responsiveness, and enthusiasm made our lives easy.

Our warmest thanks go to Ms. Brenda McClearn for her invaluable advice during the early stages of this project.

Ms. Patty Donovan, at Laserwords Maine, deserves a medal for her kind patience with the authors' and editors' endless (and usually illegible) changes to the text.

At Pearson's office in Boston, Mr. Jeff Lasser and Ms. Lauren Macey have enthusiastically advised us and supported our work for many months. We will miss talking to them.

We also thank Ms. Roxane Roberts, energetic and thoughtful sales representative for Pearson, who first connected us with our publishers.

Editors' Note

To the Reader

In this anthology of essays for Global Studies students, we hope to encourage our readers to live intelligent and thoughtful lives, not only as citizens of their native countries, but also as citizens of the world.

If you glance at the book's table of contents, you will see that the anthology has two main sections: Part I, a "Tools" or "Methods" section; and Part II, a "Topics" section. Essays in Part I offer some ways of analyzing, interpreting, researching, reading, and writing within the varied fields that constitute "global" studies. Essays in Part II examine selected topics from that same large interdisciplinary realm.

Because each "topics" essay is written from one or more identifiable disciplinary perspectives—such as sociology, anthropology, history, philosophy, literature, political science, and so on—and also because each author has his or her own individual angle on the subject of the essay, readers should expect to disagree with, question, or even reject, the arguments presented. However, all the authors in this book are writing with the same goals: to enlighten their students about several topics of interest in the world today; to give them insights into the different methodologies which will help them to analyze and interpret those topics; and to show that, through study, all of us can make progress, through the acquisition of information, knowledge, and understanding, toward the goal of responsible world citizenship.

Questions, and suggestions for other activities, appear at the end of each chapter, along with a short list of suggested readings. Some of these questions and activities help to expose the conflicts and points of contention embedded in the preceding chapter, and encourage the reader to explore such complexities in more detail.

We hope you enjoy using this book; but, even more, we hope you enjoy the process of learning about the world and about the things that you might do to help shape its future.

Thomas Arcaro
Rosemary Haskell

Summer, 2009
Elon, North Carolina

Approaches to Studying the World Today

1

Beyond the Pledge of Allegiance

Becoming a Responsible World Citizen

Thomas Arcaro

Prelude to What May Be a Surprising Chapter

This first essay will be unlike most you have read in other texts. First, my words may anger you and challenge you to question some basic assumptions about your—and our—life. Secondly, I will not talk *to* you but *with* you. I will invite you to consider, to question, to observe, to research, to examine, and to reassess. I will invite you to wrestle with ideas and to join me in conversation about those ideas. I will even give you a way to contact me so that we can, indeed, share thoughts together. I will respond. However, I will not give you answers, or the "Truth." That is for you to create for yourself. You can contact me at tarcaro@gmail.com.

I offer you the words of the Spanish philosopher and theologian, Miguel de Unamuno. He conveys everything I want to say by way of introduction to this chapter, only more poetically and powerfully. This statement was in response to those who came to him looking for answers:

> My intent has been, is, and will continue to be, that those who read my works shall think and meditate upon fundamental problems, and has never been to hand them completed thoughts. I have always sought to agitate and, even better, to stimulate, rather than to instruct. Neither do I sell bread, nor is it bread, but yeast or ferment. (1968, p. 8.)

Some Preliminary Thoughts on Being and Becoming a Global Citizen

I am happy for the opportunity to write this chapter, in part because it has caused me to reflect upon—and hence rewrite—my personal definition of "global citizen." I want to share this definition with you as a way of starting a conversation about our place in this world.

Global citizens understand, at a fundamental level, that all humans are born with basic rights; they share one planet, and thus one fate. Further, these individuals embrace an ideology of human growth and potential based upon the assumption that all global citizens, especially those in positions of privilege, should work toward creating a global social structure wherein all humans are not only allowed to reach their full potential—intellectually, physically, and spiritually—but are actively encouraged to do so. This fulfilling of human potential is done in such a way as to honor the fact that humans are only one species among many, and that we must live in sustainable harmony with all life forms on the planet. Further, global citizens understand that just as they have certain rights as global citizens this role entails an array of important responsibilities.

However, although all of us are global citizens by virtue of living together on this planet, not all are equally positioned in their lives to either understand or to act on their responsibilities as world citizens. What I am about to point out may appear elitist, but nonetheless I feel it is valid. I can assume with some confidence that you are reading this chapter because it was assigned as part of a college-level class somewhere in the English-speaking world, most likely the United States. You are literate and, relative to others your age around the world, healthier, wealthier, and, in a word, more privileged. You most likely know from where and when your next meal will come. You don't fear your home will be attacked in the next 24 hours, or the rape, torture, mutilation, or death that might come from that raid. I do understand that, relative to others your age in your country, you may not feel exceptional, but the fact remains you are probably in the upper one tenth of one percent in terms of material wealth among the 6.6 billion people on this planet. As a member of this class of people, your "carbon footprint" is, by a significant factor, larger than most others' around the world. Very likely you consume more resources and create more pollution than 95% of those on Earth. For example, one average 20-year-old in the United States is "equal" to approximately 40 villagers in rural India in terms of their impact on the planet's ecosystem. Among the reasons to stress this point is to present the aphorism that most of you have heard from your parents, your pastor, or from some other authority figure or moral guide: "With great privilege comes great responsibility."

So, yes, though all of us are global citizens, we who have greater resources in terms of time, energy, and raw wealth have more responsibility to do something with our position, to partner with others and continue the struggle to create a more just world. Think about this assertion in terms of Abraham Maslow's hierarchy of needs (see Maslow's *Motivation and Personality*, published in 1954, for the original source) that you learned about in psychology class: Those who are struggling to simply survive have neither the time nor the energy to work as global citizens. But those of us who have our basic needs taken care of and are much higher on the hierarchy can, and perhaps should, embrace our role as global citizens more aggressively.

After I had written the above, I rescanned the Web site of the Bill and Melinda Gates Foundation, the largest private foundation in the world, with assets of 35 billion dollars and grant partners in dozens of countries around the world. I found this under their "guiding values" section:

There are two simple values that lie at the core of the foundation's work:

All lives—no matter where they are being lived—have equal value.
To whom much is given, much is expected.

I can anticipate some of you right now are thinking to yourself: "I have enough trouble keeping my own personal life in order. Where can I find the time or the energy to be a responsible world citizen?" The short answer to that is: yes, your first priority is to stay healthy, both mentally and physically. You are no good to yourself, to your loved ones, or to the larger world if you are unable to function to the best of your abilities. But when you are stable and healthy you need to have your eyes open to the world. To be an engaged, and therefore responsible, world citizen you must be able to dream and to act on your dreams. Nietzsche once wrote, "He who has a why to live can endure almost any how." Put more colloquially, "Where there is a will there is a way." This chapter—indeed this book—is all about telling you how to become a more responsible world citizen. But that is not enough. You must have a *why* in order to act. Why should you care about your role as a citizen of the world? This is an important question you will have to answer for yourself. This chapter, and the others in this book, should give you plenty of stimulating ideas and, perhaps, help you find your personal "why."

Before I end this section, let me pose some questions to you. Are good global citizens liberals or conservatives? Are they religious or are they atheists? Are they idealists or pragmatists? Are they the "elite" or are they the average Joe or Sue? Quite honestly, I see myself fitting, at various times in my life, into all the categories above (well, not the Sue one). Where do you find yourself? To answer my own question—but not to let you off the hook in answering it for yourself—I think a good global citizen can be any of the above. Here are some real-life examples just from the United States:

Liberal
- President Bill Clinton—The Clinton Foundation with a focus on HIV/AIDs

Conservative
- President George W. Bush—President's Emergency Plan for AIDS Relief (PEPFAR) monies, first 15 billion dollars in 2004 and more recently, in 2007, 56 billion dollars more

Religious
- Rev. Dr. Martin Luther King, Jr—Leadership in the Civil Rights movement

Atheist
- Cyclist Lance Armstrong—Global outreach against cancer with the Livestrong Foundation

Idealist
- Anthropologist Margaret Mead—Championing of indigenous peoples around the world

Pragmatist
- Noted academic John Dewey—Educational reformer

Celebrity
- Talk show host Oprah Winfrey—Building a school for girls in South Africa

Average Joe/Sue
- Any of the 3,000 plus individuals who join the Peace Corps each year

These people at some point made the leap—or move, or step, or perhaps they simply stumbled—into global citizenship. Or at least that's the way it looks to the outsider. However, almost all of them probably arrived at their worldview in stages—some short, some long, some sudden, and some gradual. I'm almost certain the journey or transition was not particularly easy or painless and I'm even more certain most people we think of as global citizens endure the tensions, anxieties, and uncertainties that we'll explore in the rest of this chapter.

An Inconvenient Truth: We May Be More Racist and Xenophobic than Is Pleasant to Admit

> *Distance does not decide who is your brother and who is not.*
>
> —Bono

The t-shirt I am wearing now as I write this is from the Diversity Emerging Education Program (DEEP) at the school where I am a professor. Its message is both clear and accepted as fact, I am sure, by almost all of the people reading this book; it states very simply *"NO Human is MORE Human THAN Others."* Indeed, I am sure no person who is vigilant in his or her fight against racism and sexism would disagree at all with this sentiment and could even quickly point to various other iterations. These might be religious as well as secular: for example, "We are all God's children," or "All men are created equal." But before I get to the heart of my argument, let me cite some recent history.

After the Sept. 11, 2001, attacks on the United States, there was a flood of donations to the Red Cross and other relief organizations from both ordinary American citizens and from citizens and governments around the world. In the end, the direct victims of this tragedy and their immediate family members were granted all manner of benefits, essentially securing them—at least financially—for the rest of their lives. Many people who lived in the affected areas of New York City received from the Red Cross cash awards for their inconveniences and many of these awards were in the six-figure range.

In the aftermath of Hurricane Katrina, in the late summer of 2005, there were many commentaries and reports that pointed out the glaring disparities between the relief efforts for Sept. 11 and for Katrina. Specifically, it was argued that because most of those affected in New Orleans and the rest of the Gulf Coast area were poor and of color they did not get the same attention as the victims in Manhattan. To wit, spouses of the victims of Sept. 11 received as much as $1,000,000, whereas in New Orleans those who survived were lucky if they received even minimal relief from our government. Indeed, maybe some of you agree with rapper Kanye West's observation that "George Bush don't like black people." In comparing the reaction to these two events, there is factual evidence that both our government and our nation acted as if some humans' lives were worth more than others, and many media outlets and others were quick to point that out. Kanye West was not the only one to hurl the epithet "racist" at many of those in political power. But can the people of the United States really be racist in this way? Let's think about it. If we were to try to explain "earth behavior" to a Martian, how would we explain the disparity between the aid given to victims of Sept. 11, 2001, and the aid given to victims of Hurricane Katrina in 2005? What might that hypothetical Martian say in response to our explanations? One way we might choose to explain this disparity would be to say that the comparison is between "apples and oranges," and that a natural disaster is different from a foreign terrorist attack.

Let us look, then, at yet another natural disaster and the response that followed. The death toll from Katrina was approximately 1,800, but just over a month later, on Oct. 8, 2005, nearly 80,000 people lost their lives during and after a record earthquake in northern Pakistan. This earthquake made four million homeless and as I write, over three years later, many of those people will probably face another year without adequate shelter from what promises to be a very long and cold winter. By comparison, Hurricane Katrina left about 60,000 without homes, and then only temporarily. It is estimated about 2,000–3,000 Pakistani and Kashmiri people have had arms or legs amputated because they could not get timely treatment for their injuries. To underline: Forty times more people died in the Pakistani earthquake and nearly 67 times more people were left homeless than was the case during and after Hurricane Katrina. But today, the American people—including American college students—continue to respond to the Katrina disaster with effort, aid, research, and rhetoric. At the same time they have forgotten, if they were ever really aware—were you?—of the millions of Asian earthquake survivors and their needs.

Our Martian looking down at Earth attempting to discern our values might be forced to conclude that most Americans—as is indicated by our respective responses to these two events—believe some humans are worth more than other humans. Or, to be more blunt, that some Americans are racist, or at least xenophobic. (Suppose the victims of the earthquake had been Australians.)

But let me push this thesis about racism and xenophobia even further. On Sept. 13, 2007, the United Nations Children's Fund (UNICEF) released to the media its 2007 report. Among the most startling facts contained in this report is this: approximately 9.7 million children under the age of five die each year from preventable causes (such as malnutrition, diarrhea, and diseases such as malaria). Simple math reveals that this number—9.7 million—calculates to nearly 30,000 deaths per day, 1,250 per hour, or about 600 during the time it will take you to read this chapter (just less than 30 minutes). Three thousand people died on Sept. 11 in the United States, which is one-tenth the number of children who die *each day* from preventable causes. (See http://www.unicef.org/childsurvival/ for details.)

So what is the "inconvenient truth" that we must face? Could it be that by our actions we demonstrate that some people are worth more than others? To say, "I know that we are 'all God's children' and are all equal, but I have a right to respond with more passion to those I know better (read: look and act more like me)" is a weak defense. The inconvenient truth is that, though we say we are not, a strong argument can be made that we are definitely racist (or is it xenophobic?) in our behavior. To say we are also very sexist in our behavior—the vast majority of world cultures treat women far worse than they treat men—has perhaps even more convincing evidence. (See Chapter 9 by Ann J. Cahill for a detailed discussion of such discrepancies.)

Finally, let's revisit Bono's comment that begins this section. What would *your* religion say about this statement? Does distance determine who is and who is not your brother or sister? To help you think more deeply about this idea, here is another provocative statement from Bono: "Where you live should not determine whether you live."

Patriotism, Nationalism, Ethnocentrism, and Racism: All Points on the Same Spectrum?

> *The only real nation is humanity.*
> —Paul Farmer

As you read this section, think about the question "Where does being a global citizen fit into my role as an American?"

Consider the word "patriotism." How would you differentiate this term from "nationalism"? Similarly, how would you differentiate "nationalism" from "ethnocentrism"? Finally, how would you semantically distinguish "ethnocentrism" from "racism"? Certainly the dictionary definitions of all these terms will help you clarify some differences but, in the end, you will note there are clear overlaps between these words. One way to think about this is to consider putting this question into the form of a Venn diagram (Figure 1.1).

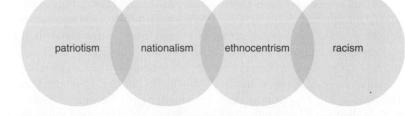

FIGURE 1.1   A Spectrum of Overlapping Attitudes.

Or perhaps the following diagram (Figure 1.2) is a better representation of the relationship between the terms. Which do you think is more accurate?

Although these four terms may overlap in meaning, it should not be argued that they are the same thing: only that they are not as distinct as most of us might have assumed. But let's explore these overlaps and see what we find.

Consider: Can you be patriotic without being nationalistic? Can you be nationalistic without being somewhat ethnocentric? Can you be ethnocentric without being somewhat racist? And in a world where we are forced to generalize and make quick judgment calls, does one term bleed into the next? What kinds of things do "very patriotic" people say? Certainly, for some people, reciting the Pledge of Allegiance with their hand over their heart is an act of patriotism. But what does the Pledge of Allegiance ask us to do? Many of you reading this chapter have recited this one sentence countless times, frequently at the beginning of your school day. But have you ever considered what it means?

> I pledge allegiance to the flag of the United States of America, and to the republic for which it stands, one nation under God, indivisible, with liberty and justice for all.

Does this pledge imply that you will protect and defend your country?

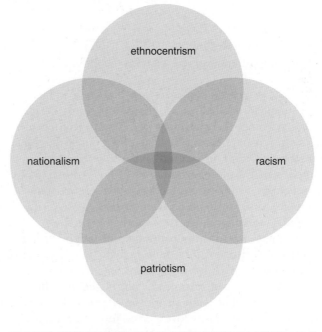

FIGURE 1.2 A Cluster of Overlapping Attitudes.

Here is the Oath of Citizenship we ask new United States citizens to recite:

> I hereby declare, on oath, that I absolutely and entirely renounce and abjure all allegiance and fidelity to any foreign prince, potentate, state, or sovereignty of whom or which I have heretofore been a subject or citizen; that I will support and defend the Constitution and laws of the United States of America against all enemies, foreign and domestic; that I will bear true faith and allegiance to the same; that I will bear arms on behalf of the United States when required by the law; that I will perform noncombatant service in the Armed Forces of the United States when required by the law; that I will perform work of national importance under civilian direction when required by the law; and that I take this obligation freely without any mental reservation or purpose of evasion; so help me God.

As an important side note, let me point out that in 1954 the phrase "under God" was added to the Pledge of Allegiance and the ending "so help me God" was added to the Oath of Citizenship; although technically optional, it is an implied requirement. So does this make a belief in God a requirement for being patriotic? Indeed, is "patriotic atheist" a contradiction in terms? Since the beginning of the Cold War against those whom many in the United States referred to as "godless communists," there has been both an implicit and explicit conflation of the terms "patriot" and "Christian." According to several independent research sources, most notably the Pew Research Center, in the United States there are likely more atheists than Jews or Muslims or Buddhists; they estimate as many as 20% of the American population is non-religious, though many remain closeted because they fear reprisal or ostracism. In a 1987 interview, President George H. W. Bush said, "I don't know that atheists should be considered as citizens, nor should they be considered patriots. This is one nation under God." He failed to restate or change his position on this issue in subsequent interviews. As Jeffrey C. Pugh argues in Chapter 11, religion and culture are interwoven in complex and important ways and we need to be mindful of how religion makes an impact on all cultures.

But back to the basic question for this section: Insofar as these four "ism's" overlap, what does implied parallelism for these four terms mean? For example, if a patriot puts "country first," does that not imply the plight of others around the world should only be tended to after we have taken care of all of our domestic problems? Doesn't humanitarian aid to, for example, Darfur, in western Sudan, rob from the hungry and homeless right here in the United States? Is it unpatriotic—as in not putting country first—to donate to the Red Cross for tsunami victims in Sri Lanka while there are some in your own country that will go to bed hungry tonight? To go one step further, are we not saying that some people—people in our country—are indeed worth more than others?

Then comes the apparent contradiction within our United States culture: Many would assert we are a Christian nation. Indeed, many falsely claim we were founded as a Christian nation (see Boston, 1993, for a very informative discussion of this myth). But if this is true, how is it that our sense of patriotism, "putting country first," is, on its face, un-Christian? A good argument could be made that Jesus Christ was first and foremost a world citizen as in "all God's children are to be loved" (See John 3:2). I'll ask you: Would God "put country first"? Or, perhaps, would He agree with Paul Farmer's observation that "The only real nation is humanity"? Can you be a patriot and a global citizen at the same time?

One Good Thing about Sputnik: The Unlikely Catalyst Creating a Global Community

To say history changed on Oct. 4, 1957, when the Soviet Union successfully launched Sputnik, is no exaggeration. If a basketball-sized satellite could be put into orbit, then so could nuclear weapons, and it was only a matter of time until the two superpowers—the United States and the then-Soviet Union, or U.S.S.R.—realized they now lived in a world where mutual annihilation was possible. This possibility included the likely destruction of all human life on this planet. Rereading some of President John F. Kennedy's speeches and those of others of the Cold War era, one gets a sense that the leaders of the world knew quite clearly that we were now one world and would either live or die together, our fates mutually interdependent. The fact that during the Cold War we were all living under the (il)logic of Mutually Assured Destruction (MAD) seeped quickly into popular awareness and forever changed the way we understood our world. Although on Dec. 10, 1948, the General Assembly of the United Nations had proclaimed the Universal Declaration of Human Rights, and thus spoke of all humans as members of the same community, it took the Cold War to make these idealistic words have a deeper, more personal relevance.

It is certainly true that many years earlier the idea of a "citizen of the world" was expressed. Clearly this concept was discussed in the Enlightenment, for example, at least in its rather limited Eurocentric fashion. Ancient Athens and Rome saw their empires as huge, even global. To be a Roman citizen was to be a citizen of the then-known-world, the Romans, at least, would have claimed. This idea, though, did not have the same reality as it does now, when "citizen of the world" is more *literally* true.

Certainly not unrelated to the beginnings of our sense of global interconnectedness is the rise of the environmental movement, fueled by books like Rachel Carson's *Silent Spring*, (1962), which came to a "formal" point of maturity in the spring of 1970, when the first Earth Day was held in the United States. The image of planet Earth as seen from space has certainly become an icon not only for the environmental movement but also for all those who seek to create a more global awareness.[1] Very simply, my point is that the last several decades of the twentieth century saw a dramatic rise in "global consciousness" for many in the United States, and though this rise was generated from many social and historical forces, there is no mistaking its importance. As a sociologist, I am struck by how globalization (however one chooses to define that word) has created a new entity, namely a global culture. I will not dare place a birth date for this new global culture (perhaps when the World Wide Web was created?), but it certainly did not exist in 1609 or 1809, and it most definitely does exist now in 2009. The real challenge for 21st century global citizens is to describe and understand this new global culture and begin to connect what we know about specific "traditional" cultural entities (like the United States culture) and this new, growing non-national, global entity. Further discussion of this path will have to wait for another essay, but suffice it to say that having a global awareness has become *de rigueur* for those who are in positions of leadership in any capacity.

So, how can we relate this global awareness to the world both you and I are living in right now, namely the academic world of universities, classes, research, and books? Let's consider what *academic* global citizenship might mean.

In the early 1990s, the Carnegie Commission on Higher Education published a report highly critical of American higher education, pointing out that American college and university students were far too insulated and isolated from the rest of the world; they had little global awareness, especially compared to their counterparts in Europe and the rest of the world. Many institutions of higher education responded to the challenge from the Carnegie Commission and reexamined their mission statements and even their core curricula. Elon University (then Elon College) was one of those institutions and in 1994 the faculty and administration at Elon gutted their General Studies core curriculum and, among other changes, added a required course for all first year students called "The Global Experience." Elon, like many other institutions, also redrafted its mission statement; it now reads, in part, "We integrate learning across the disciplines and put knowledge into practice, thus *preparing students to be global citizens* and informed leaders motivated by concern for the common good." My quick Internet review of the mission statements of many other institutions indicates a similar change has happened in colleges and universities all over the United States. In a sense, education is just catching up with a bigger movement that exists in many circles in the larger United States culture and globally: the Bill and Melinda Gates Foundation and the Clinton Global Initiative are great examples of this movement.

Because I am a sociologist by training, I will use my own discipline to make a point. In 2001, Sociologists Without Borders was established with a mission to work "in solidarity with oppressed peoples." Their Web site further states, "Sociologists Without Borders supports the right to peaceful meddling, and opposes States' practices and programs that advance their own sovereignty but diminish peoples' human rights."

Also from its Web site we learn, "Sociologists Without Borders is an academic and professional alliance committed to advancing transnational solidarities and justice." This organization, along with sister organizations such as Doctors Without Borders, Lawyers Without Borders, Engineers Without Borders, Teachers Without Borders, Reporters Without Borders, and even Mothers Without Borders, is reaching more and more people. As a latent—but perhaps not-so-latent—function, these organizations are furthering acceptance of the sentiment indicated in the Paul Farmer quotation that I mentioned previously: "The only real nation is humanity."[2]

However, becoming a global citizen is a stretch for some students (and, frankly, for some faculty, academic disciplines, and universities as well) and the process creates some tensions and contradictions.

One example of the complexities of prioritizing various ways of being a global citizen took place recently at my university when two speakers, invited from different parts of Central America, shared the same table and fielded questions about their projects. One represented "Hope for Honduran Children" and the other "Schools for Chiapas." The speakers had been invited by two different student groups, each very devoted to their respective projects. As the conversation unfolded, it was apparent there was a tension in the room between the Honduran group and the Chiapan (Mexican) group, and this tension boiled down to the fact the Honduran group had trouble understanding why the Chiapan group was spending their energies on a need that was not nearly as acute as theirs. ("The Honduran children are literally starving, while the Chiapans at least have food!") Wisely, the speaker representing "Hope for Honduran Children" pointed out each cause is important and there are many kinds of philanthropy. As the Javanese told the anthropologist Clifford Geertz (1973:53) long ago, "Other fields, other grasshoppers." Being a global citizen means understanding there are many, many injustices in the world and, unfortunately, individual human effort is finite, restricted by a 24-hour day and limited resources.

A second tension exists between being a local or national citizen and a global citizen. If indeed "the only true nation is humanity," what becomes of nationalism and patriotism? Consider an instructive insight from Archbishop Desmond Tutu:

> We realized then, and we need to realize now, that we are bound together by a common humanity, by a common vulnerability, bound together by our common passion for freedom that we can't go it alone, that we are bound up in the bundle of life. We used to say to our white compatriots in South Africa: 'you will never be free until we blacks are free, for freedom is indivisible.' (2004 speech in New York City at the dedication of the Freedom Center)

I would add to his statement that just as freedom is indivisible so also is justice, and just as there can be no freedom until there is global freedom, there can be no justice until there is global justice. To fight for the causes in your own backyard is clearly the right thing to do for many of us, but to modify the argument sociologist C. Wright Mills taught us long ago, we must see the connection between private (local) problems and public (global) issues (1959). Certainly, all of us cannot abdicate our responsibilities as local citizens in order to live our lives as *literal* global citizens, but clearly we must act more consciously and conscientiously to understand our responsibilities as inhabitants of the whole world.

I can think of no better example of simultaneous local and global citizenship than the Zapatista movement in Chiapas, Mexico. In response to the signing of the NAFTA agreement in 1994, the indigenous Mexicans in the state of Chiapas revolted against the Mexican government. Two years later there was an enormous response to the 1996 Zapatista call for a series of continental and intercontinental Encounters that led to a historic gathering in Chiapas in July of that year. Camped out in tents and makeshift accommodations, over 3,000 grassroots activists and intellectuals from 42 countries on 5 different continents came together to discuss the struggle against neoliberalism on a global scale. What is special about the Zapatista movement is that from the very beginning there was an understanding that its members were not just fighting for the rights of property and dignity for the Chiapans, but for the rights and the dignity of indigenous peoples everywhere. Their words and actions reflect the spirit of Desmond Tutu's words and they clearly inspired many outside of Mexico, setting in motion new waves of hope and energy among those engaged in the struggle for freedom and justice all over the world, especially among those fighting for the rights of indigenous peoples.

We must be careful, though, in our desire to be active global citizens. We should never frame our actions as "helping the poor downtrodden" around the world. Rather, we should listen closely to the words of Lilly Walker, an Australian Aboriginal woman, who said, "If you are here to help me, then you are wasting your time. But if you come because your liberation is bound up in mine, then let us begin." To state this differently, we cannot solve the problems of the people in Darfur. We can only solve *our* problems in Darfur. Paternalistic "do-good" behavior done out of guilt or a vague sense of duty is antithetical to the sentiment that Walker is offering because it is based on an assumption that the world is made up of "us" and "them." As global citizens we must reframe our understanding of our relationship with others in this world: We shouldn't give aid to others around the world; rather, we must join with them to solve *our* problems.

Allow me a side note about being a global citizen: Tracy Kidder, Paul Farmer's biographer, notes, "Lives of service depend upon lives of support" (Kidder, 2003, p. 108). The point he makes in this comment is an important one that should not be underestimated: We cannot all "save the world" either as individuals or institutions, but those of us who choose to heavily invest in our role as global citizens must recognize, honor, and value those around us who make what we do possible. In Farmer's case, it is his family (broadly defined) in both Boston and Haiti who provide the necessary support. In my case, it is my wife and children who supply unlimited love and support for my work on HIV/AIDS. Clearly, to be a global citizen is not everyone's calling, but some of us, like Bill Gates, Bill Clinton, Bono, and Stephen Lewis, among countless others who lead the way, will always seek to gently nudge others in our lives toward a greater understanding of our global connectedness.

Crushed Chickpeas, Academic Freedom, and the Blind Machine

> *All evolution in thought and conduct must at first appear as heresy and misconduct.*
> —George Bernard Shaw

Al Lee, one of the founders of the Association for Humanist Sociology, said in *Sociology for Whom*: "In spite of the contrasts between science and religion, social historians can demonstrate how both have gained from the often unsettling contributions of the heretical." And further: "Whether heretics are 'nuts' or 'radicals' or 'brilliant innovators' depends upon current vested interests, propaganda struggles, public opinions, and changing life conditions." He goes on to list various heretics from history, Charles Darwin among them. His book is filled with "...contributions being made to knowledge and social policy by heretical and emancipatory sociologists, persons dedicated to the further development and application of sociology for people" (1986, p. xii). Predictably and appropriately, Lee mentions Thomas Kuhn (1959) and his definition of normal science. I will go further than Lee did and state explicitly that what is needed is nothing less than a paradigm shift within education as a whole and specifically with those who teach about the nature of global citizenship.

You cannot make hummus without crushing a few chickpeas, and, perhaps, you cannot make fundamental change without committing heresy. So here is my heretical suggestion: *As global citizens privileged with a seat (either as faculty or as students) at an institution of higher education we need to reconsider, both individually and collectively, with what values and priorities we set our study, research, and activism agendas.*

The global social problems that exist today cannot be effectively addressed under the old paradigm of academic freedom. I say this for many reasons, but the two most important ones have to do with the accelerating rate of social change and the emerging existence of a global culture. However you measure it, the rate of social change is faster now than it has ever been and there is no reason to believe it is going to slow down. Who among us would be so brave as to predict what technological and social changes will occur in the next 20 years? Who could have predicted 20 years ago the tremendous impact the Internet has had on all of our lives? Intimately linked to this ever-quickening change is the fact, mentioned above, that for the first time in our species' history there is now a global culture, one that has yet to be fully formed and defined, and also yet to be fully understood. The problems we face are more acute, more devastating, more critical in terms of human life on this planet (environmental degradation, anyone?) than ever before, and our global social and environmental problems are only going to become more dramatic. We cannot afford what Thomas Kuhn might call "normal" social science anymore.

I would describe the functioning of education ("science"—both social and "hard") as demonstrably acephalous. It has no "head" or mind for making decisions about its direction. The academy is a "blind machine" moving forward with no clear direction. It was Thomas L. Friedman who, not long ago, observed (with regard to globalization and the future) "No one is in charge" (qtd. Singer, 2002). Peter Singer, reflecting on Friedman's words stated, "For Marx this is a statement that epitomizes humanity in a state of alienation, living in a world in which, instead of ruling ourselves, we are ruled by our own creation, the global economy" (Singer, 2002, p. 11). Indeed, in a free market economy, who is in charge?

Although this varies dramatically between disciplines, to a very real extent our academic journals get cluttered with articles that pad someone's *curriculum vitae* and, taken as a whole, move us little closer to making a purposeful impact on the direction our global culture is headed, that is, to "take charge." We chant the mantra "academic freedom" to justify our individual tastes in research projects and to excuse our unwillingness to take on globally useful projects as if there were no alternative. We are afraid to imagine a world where, as August Comte argued 1849 sociology and the social sciences, governed by objective reason, research, and logic, inform and guide the direction of the discipline. Certainly there is much to disagree with concerning a great deal of what Comte said, but his basic sentiment, that the social sciences must drive social policy and social change, is shared by many other classical social theorists. The heresy I am suggesting is grounded in the history of my discipline of sociology and I would wager that many of our foreparents would lament at the fact that sociology, and most of the other social sciences, now play minor roles in political and social decision-making.

Why does the direction of academic research matter so much? Shouldn't academics be allowed to gather knowledge and draw conclusions as they wish? As indicated by the paragraphs above, I don't think we can afford that luxury any more. As individuals and as global citizens, we should reread Lee's words: "Whatever optimism or pessimism we might have about the future of the human lot depends upon the relative speed with which broader participation may be achieved in the control and employment of social power" (1986, p. xi). I do not believe "broader participation" means proceeding apace the way we have in the past. The human agency of which I speak is one that embraces the fact that together we can make a difference but that, divided by our idiosyncratic and opportunistic research and activism agendas, we are not the effective leaders that we could and should be. I propose, for example, we begin by making study, research, and activism agendas that reflect what is happening globally. We should then imagine how we might start to agree on how to prioritize our efforts and allocate our resources. This means, yes, giving up one kind of "academic freedom." And it means submitting to the collective wisdom of larger, more globally-minded groups and beginning to take more control over our futures. It also means starting to become the global citizens we need to be. I propose we in colleges and universities act as a model for other people and organizations and begin a movement within education. I make the above suggestions in an absolutely sober state; I realize the heresy I am suggesting. But I submit that to remain acephalous (or perhaps *many* headed) is not an option.

As a final note I will point out to the astute reader: you are right in your suspicion that I have been describing the classic "free will versus determinism" dilemma. Restated, the question becomes do we really have control over our future? Read Leslie White's essay (actually the title says it all!) (1948) "Man's Control Over Civilization: An Anthropocentric Illusion." He represents an end of the continuum most of us dare not contemplate too deeply, the end that says history will unfold despite, not because of, purposeful human action. Complex global economic forces beyond the direct control of any group of individuals drive the price of commodities like grains and oil, for example. On the direct opposite end of the pole lies one of White's contemporaries, whose words grace the walls of many undergraduate dorm rooms, namely Margret Mead. Her statement, "Never question whether or not a small group of people can change the world. Indeed, that is the only thing that ever has, " epitomizes the idea of free will and deep faith in human agency. Mead claims indeed, that we are in control of how the future unfolds. What I am proposing is rejecting White and embracing Mead: thus reassessing the false freedom that comes with embracing a social world "left alone" by human acts.

Does Fire Purge Us of Our Racism? Some Thoughts from Evolutionary Psychology

> *Our real desires, our lasting and strongest passions, are not for the good of our species as a whole, but, at best, for the good of those who are close to us.*
>
> —Peter Singer

You see a house on fire and inside, behind one door, is your daughter. Behind another door, right beside it, is another parent's child. You can only save one child. Which do you choose? Now imagine the same scenario except with 10 saveable young children behind the other door. Now which do you choose? Is there *any* number of children behind the second door that would turn your hand away from the door behind which your own flesh and blood cowers and cause you to save the others?

This and other similar gedanken (thought) experiments have been researched and tested by several evolutionary psychologists[3] and the results are consistent and predictable.

With convincingly high regularity, the choices people make are directly correlated to their genetic closeness to the person behind the door. Moral philosophers have written about this tendency for at least a century:

> We should all agree that each of us is bound to show kindness to his parents and spouse and children, and to other kinsmen in a lesser degree: and to those who have rendered services to him, and any others whom he may have admitted to his intimacy and called friends—fellow countrymen more than others: and perhaps we may say those of our own race more than to black or yellow people, and generally to human beings in proportion to their affinity to ourselves.[4]

I immediately need to use Singer's own words to make a critical point: "To say that a certain kind of behavior is universal and has its roots in our evolutionary history does not necessarily mean that it cannot be changed, nor does it mean that it should not be changed." Clearly we are wired to behave in a way that is biased toward those close to us, especially to those who share our DNA. Few things could be more "real" than parental love. But does that mean we cannot focus on and give to those who are separated from us either genetically or geographically, that we cannot be good national or global citizens? Of course not, but we should never take for granted how counterintuitive it is for us to give up family time for activities related to being a better global citizen. Are we racist—or simply patriotic—for caring about Katrina victims more than those affected by the Pakistani earthquake? Earlier I addressed that question and argued that our behavior is racist—or perhaps xenophobic—but now I am not so sure. Perhaps there needs to be a better word to describe the moral dilemma we face. We have several roles that we play daily, so we experience some serious conflict between being a family member, a citizen of a country, and at the same time a global citizen. How do we decide where to put our energies and priorities?

But there is at least one more challenge associated with our Darwinian wiring. Additional wisdom from the field of evolutionary psychology indicates it is not "natural" for people to worry about the long future: We are programmed to get our genetic material passed on in our lifetimes. We care about mating and we care about with whom our children mate, but in terms of life beyond our immediate kinspersons, we are not naturally concerned.[5] It is our culture that allows us to see into the future and plan for lives long after ours and also to urge us toward understanding that we are all now "one world," one global community. Though we can understand this concept intellectually and speak of our futures both in person and in writing, our day-to-day behavior is guided much more than we realize by our unconscious drives, urges, and needs. Indeed, perhaps it can be said, as anthropologist Miles Richardson observed, that "Rather than thinking and proceeding to act, we act and then proceed to explain" (1976, p. 3). My point is simply that it takes great effort and vigilance to stay focused on the long term and on our connection to, and co-dependence with, the other six billion people on this planet. We sociologists enjoy a professional life that demands we stay tuned to cultural trends and look at the world with a keen sociological imagination, but most of those in our families and communities have little regular contact with ideas of this nature. It is our responsibility to not only keep our focus on our global connectedness but to also introduce others to the reality that we are all global citizens.

> *It is important to sound a warning about the habit of conflating the notion of society with that of nation-state. We already live in a global society. Thus, calls of a right to equality must necessarily contend with steep grades of inequality across as well as within international borders. The same holds for analysis of human rights—such as those appearing in, for example, reports from human rights watchdog organizations—that may obscure their fundamental transnational nature.*

—Paul Farmer

A Model for How to Proceed as a Global Citizen

Jeffrey D. Sachs tells us, in fine detail, how to escape the debilitating poverty that grips the developing world in his controversial book *The End of Poverty* (2005). In this book, Sachs recounts his experiences in helping to "fix" economic crises in Bolivia and Poland and argues how what he calls "clinical economics" could work on other parts of the world. The central message of this book is that, "The very hardest part of economic development is getting the first foothold on the ladder. Households and countries at the very bottom of the world's economic distribution, in extreme poverty, tend to be stuck" (2005, p. 24). With the right assistance from the richer nations, Sachs argues, all nations could effectively end poverty, and in doing so help save, for example, the more than 10,000 Africans who die every day of poverty-related health conditions.

Sachs and Bono are, on the surface, an unlikely pair, but they have come together in an effort to end global poverty. Sachs is one of the intellectual forces behind the United Nations Millennium Development Goals. These goals include:

1. Eradicate extreme poverty and hunger
2. Achieve universal primary education
3. Promote gender equality and empower women
4. Reduce child mortality
5. Improve maternal health
6. Combat HIV/AIDS, malaria and other diseases
7. Ensure environmental sustainability
8. Develop a global partnership for development[6]

Bono still works at his "day job" as the front man for the Irish rock band U2, but he has labored tirelessly in the last decade for many global causes. Bono's One campaign[7] perfectly complements the Millennium Development Goals, and that is no accident. Through their energy and drive, these two men have inspired many others to embrace their roles as global citizens. Bono and Sachs are just two examples of many I could have cited; the Clinton Global Initiative focuses on the four interrelated issues of global warming, global health, poverty, and race/religious divisiveness. This initiative is not a replacement of, but an addition to, The Clinton Foundation's global work on HIV/AIDS, especially in sub-Saharan

Africa. My point is simple: The task of identifying and even prioritizing the most significant social issues we face as global citizens has already been substantially started. I propose the question we should ask as concerned students and faculty is: "How can my study, research, publication, and activism agendas begin to more regularly address larger issues, especially those related to the MDG's?"

As an anthropologist and medical doctor, Paul Farmer provides us with a wonderful example of how to function as a professional and global citizen. By establishing Partners in Health[8] and working tirelessly in Haiti for the poor, he has shown it is possible to live as though "humanity is the only true nation." Can we all be Farmer (or, as he is known by many, "Saint Paul")? No, of course not, but as individuals and as leaders in our respective communities we can lead the way, both for our fellow students and for other organizations, to a new paradigm for how to function as global citizens. Yes, this means giving up some freedom, but giving up that freedom may be necessary as we, more and more, become one world. Let me end this section with a passage from President John F. Kennedy's commencement address at American University, delivered June 10, 1963:

> Let us focus instead on a more practical, more attainable peace, *based not on a sudden revolution in human nature but on a gradual evolution in human institutions*—on a series of concrete actions and effective agreements which are in the interest of all concerned. There is no single, simple key to this peace; no grand or magic formula to be adopted by one or two powers. Genuine peace must be the product of many nations, the sum of many acts. It must be dynamic, not static, changing to meet the challenge of each new generation. For peace is a process—a way of solving problems. [Emphasis added]

Let us have the courage to be heretics and respond proactively to the challenges faced by a global culture filled with injustice. First, we can make a gradual change by looking beyond our own families to others within our local communities and then we can move further outward, to the rest of the nation and to the rest of the world.

To put the suggestion above into more intimate, concrete terms, consider your—or your parents'—annual giving, both in terms of money and in service/volunteer hours. Here is a typical list: They buy Girl Scout cookies once a year, make a donation to the American Cancer Society when the solicitation comes in the mail, run in the 5K "fun run" to raise money for the local Women's Shelter, donate some canned goods every so often to the local food bank, and serve meals at the local homeless shelter on Thanksgiving. Your family's list may be significantly longer than this, but this is enough to illustrate my point. In a large number—perhaps a majority—of families, these combined philanthropic outreaches are done with little guiding logic other than to "do good." There is no conscious and overt attempt to meaningfully order these varied activities. In fact, it's just the opposite: Many family acts of giving seem more guided by personal interest, contacts, and sheer serendipity than anything else. But you and your family's resources are limited. Doesn't it make more sense, then, to move forward with some overall explicit plan? I argue that now, in this 21st century global culture where our lives are all bound together, we need—both as individuals and as organizations—to mete out our finite resources according to a meaningful and coherent plan.

How Will the Rest of This Book Help You Embrace Your Role as a "Global Citizen?"

Global citizens lead mindful lives and dole out their time, energy, and resources in a manner that reflects a clear understanding of their connections to the world and their appropriate priorities. This book offers you, in Part I, some conceptual tools for analyzing and interpreting the world of information and ideas that faces you as a Global Studies student. In Part II, it offers you focused study of selected topics from the huge interdisciplinary field of Global Studies.

Part I: Approaches to Studying the World Today

A global citizen is one who understands the basic concept of culture and is able not only to understand the concepts of ethnocentrism and cultural relativism but also to use these concepts as he or she learns of, writes about, and acts upon his or her corner of the world. Laurence A. Basirico and Anne Bolin, in Chapter 2, "The Joy of Culture: A Beginner's Guide to Understanding and Appreciating Cultural Diversity," skillfully present their idea of the "web of culture," effectively communicating the truth that in culture "everything is connected to everything else." They stand on the shoulders of Darwin, who long ago (1859 or thereabouts) observed that although our world is marked by great diversity, all parts of the natural—and social—world are interdependent. Effective global citizens make every effort to understand their own cultures, the larger global culture, and the bonds they share.

To know the world effectively and thoroughly, a global citizen must read from an array of sources. But mere reading is not enough; we must be mindful about what we read and how we read it. Jean Schwind, in Chapter 3, "Reading, Writing, and Researching the Global Experience," articulates how to respond as a thoughtful consumer of the written word, from academic essays to advertising copy. She also provides some provocative and innovative concepts, such as "tagmemics," as tools for how to more deeply read the variety of texts we encounter. Her chapter provides not only lofty and challenging new concepts but also a carefully laid out series of practical activities that teach nascent global citizens how to effectively communicate their developing world views.

Information comes in numbers, as well as in words, however. One of the most chilling lines attributed to the Soviet leader Joseph Stalin, as quoted in Duane McClearn's Chapter 4, "Numbers and the World," is "One death is a tragedy. A million deaths is just a statistic." We all tend to be more swayed by anecdotes than by numbers, but we can never let numbers remain merely figures on a page. Near the beginning of this chapter, you were made aware that every three seconds (on average) another child under five dies from causes directly related to poverty. These are real flesh and blood children, not statistics. This cannot be put too emphatically: A responsible world citizen knows how to interpret and understand numbers—quantified information about the world. This global citizen never forgets that each number represents real people, who feel pain, cling to hope, and beg not to be rationalized into another stat sheet.

Rosemary Haskell, in Chapter 5, "Reading World Literature to Read the World: Literature and the Global Studies Student," argues that the Global Studies student cannot afford to ignore still other kinds of sources: poetry, plays, novels, and short stories, which not only give us information about the world but also about alien perspectives and attitudes we would otherwise not encounter. This chapter explores the links between world literature, culture, and history, and demonstrates the different critical approaches that we might adopt as thoughtful readers of fictional texts.

The sheer number of sources of information about the world we have access to is indeed amazing. The Internet alone provides us with video, audio, and print stories from newspapers around the world, not to mention the vast array of news sites such as CNN, BBC, NPR, and on and on. This bombardment of information raises many important epistemological questions: How do we know—what are the sources of our "knowledge"—about what is going on in, say, Afghanistan? Given that news and commentary have been blurred together in much of the media both in the United States and abroad, how do we know which side is telling the "truth?" Indeed, how can one know the truth about *any* current social, environmental, and political news? In Chapter 6, "Global Media and News: A Guide to Decoding and Analyzing Information," Chinedu "Ocek" Eke, a communications professor teaching in the United States but raised in Nigeria, presents useful "media" guidance for the aspiring global citizen.

Part II: Topics in Global Studies

One extraordinarily sobering question Anthony Weston asks in Chapter 7, "Environmentalism Gone Wild: The Great Green Mobilization and Beyond," is: By what right do we suck the Earth dry to leave a hollowed-out and toxic-waste-laced legacy to our grandchildren?" Think about this for a minute. Or two. Or more. And then consider that you are in the middle of seven generations. You may remember or even still visit your great-grandparents, likely your grandparents, and—in most cases—your parents. You may now—or some day soon—have children; and, after more years, grandchildren; and, if you stay healthy, great-grandchildren. A global citizen understands very clearly that we share one precious and irreplaceable Earth. We owe it to ourselves, our ancestors who passed on to us a healthy planet, and our children who deserve to grow up in one, our very best stewardship. Weston's chapter redefines the "environmental crisis" and suggests some rather unconventional approaches to resolving it.

Consider the statement, "The past is embedded in the present." On one level it may sound abstract and distant, but you have only to look at your grandparents to see the reality of this statement. Their core beliefs, values, and overall outlook on life were formed during their childhood and early adult years, perhaps more than half a century ago. Who they are now cannot be fully understood without understanding their past. In Chapter 8, "Western Imperialism and Its Legacies," Brian Digre takes you on a tour around the world, describing and explaining how a colonial past has profoundly influenced contemporary social and political developments in Africa, Asia, the Caribbean, Central America, and the Middle East.

The danger of what I call "monolithic thinking" is ever present when we try to make sense of the world around us. This type of thinking is, in a very real sense, a defense mechanism we use to endure the increasing complexity of modern life: Just see things as simple "black and white." A synonym for monolithic thinking would be over-generalizing. Such is the case for many people when they hear the word "feminist": They tend to plop all "feminists" into one (typically negative) category and not see the many facets of the term. Since women in many parts of the world still suffer from structured social inequality, an effective global citizen must understand the social dynamics and historical forces that characterize this unjust treatment. The conceptual tools offered in Ann J. Cahill's Chapter 9, "Looking at the World through a Gendered Lens: Feminism and Global Studies," will help you to understand better what it means to view the world from a feminist perspective and—with a new set of tools—to find your own way as a critic of gendered inequality and oppression.

Just now, while you were reading this chapter, I think it is somewhat likely you were using drugs of some sort. Specifically, and most likely, you might have been sipping a soft drink that contained caffeine, drinking a cup of coffee or tea, smoking a cigarette or, perhaps, nursing a beer. In this behavior you are not alone: The use of mild drugs is a cultural universal and has been documented to be a part of cultures worldwide from the earliest recorded civilizations. In many cultures, more extreme drug use—for both recreational and religious purposes—is also very common, though at times counter to the formal laws and norms of the culture. To be an effective global citizen, you must be aware of cultural universals, and the various ways that such universals appear, modified, within different cultures. In Chapter 10, "Use and Abuse: Drugs and Drug Commerce in a Global Context, " Mathew Gendle analyzes the spectrum of official attitudes toward drug use—which he identifies as a cultural universal—around the world and assesses the geopolitical significance of the world drug trade over the last four hundred years.

In the culture wars that characterize much of the dialogue in our modern world, the sacred cow of religion seems to be the single most contentious topic. A global citizen's ability to separate personal belief from objective analysis is more seriously pressed when it comes to religion than perhaps any other topic. But we must try to bracket our religious beliefs for study even more carefully than most other dimensions of our cultural life. The study of religion and the role it plays in our lives as global citizens is, in these early years of the 21st century, critical. This research on religion demands that we examine with clarity, rationality, and reason our most fundamental ontological, epistemological, and axiological assumptions: what is, how we can know what is, and with what values we act upon what is, and is known to us. In Chapter 11, "Navigating Religion in the Global Context," Jeffrey C. Pugh presents rich detail, important background information—particularly about Islam—and effective guidance on how to make sense of the impact religion has on both particular cultures and on the global community.

The personal and the political collided—literally—on Sept. 11, 2001 as large jets smashed into the World Trade Center towers that historic morning, killing roughly 3,000 people. Though it is critical to view that day in a global context—30,000 children also died that day and *every day thereafter* from preventable causes—one lesson we must take from that day is that as much as we may want to isolate ourselves from all matters political, this is just not possible in the 21st century. What happens in the mountains of Afghanistan *does* affect the lives of people all over the world and even in the "bubble" that probably surrounds your university. In Laura Roselle, Kerstin Sorensen and Robert G. Anderson's Chapter 12, "Global Politics and Global Issues: Where Do You Fit?" you will learn how to interpret the ways countries interact on the world stage. For example, just understanding the basic difference between a "nation" and a "state" will provide you with a clearer and more useful perspective from which to rethink African history and, perhaps closer to home, recent events in Iraq. International relations theory provides a framework, the very existence of which encourages the responsible world citizen to draw away from the seduction of isolationism and ignorance and to face head-on the taxing yet rewarding study of geopolitical dynamics.

In a 1992 article entitled "Jihad vs. McWorld," political scientist Benjamin R. Barber said, "The two axial principles of our age—tribalism and globalism—clash at every point except one: they may both be threatening to democracy." Barber later elaborated on this claim in his 1996 book, *Jihad vs. McWorld*. In Chapter 13, Stephen Braye, Rosemary Haskell, and Thomas Arcaro bring the recent developments in global politics, technology, and other important cultural trends into new focus with a reinterpretation of Barber's formulation of the "Jihad vs. McWorld" struggle—a struggle which indeed appears more important now than it did in 1996. Their discussion is an important bridge linking the international politics addressed in Roselle, Sorensen and Anderson's chapter and Pugh's thoughts about religion: both cultural institutions contain globalizing and tribalizing forces, and these forces may affect both national and world governance.

Notes

1. The publishers of Peter Singer's book, *One World*, use this view of earth as the "O" in *One* on the cover of the edition I have on my desk.
2. My humanist colleague Olaf Krassnitzky put it this way, "We are one humanity. That should be at the top of any humanist manifesto or creed. We cannot solve the problems of the Sudan. We can only solve our problems in Sudan" (personal communication).
3. See Matt Ridley's work *The Origins of Virtue* for a good review of the research on this subject.
4. Sedgwick, (1907:246), quoted from Singer, (2002:153).
5. See Richard Dawkins' *The Selfish Gene* for some basic ideas along this line.
6. These were taken directly from http://www.un.org/millenniumgoals/.
7. From the One Web site (www.one.org), "ONE is a new effort by Americans to rally Americans–ONE by ONE–to fight the emergency of global AIDS and extreme poverty. ONE aims to help Americans raise their voice as ONE against the emergency of AIDS and extreme poverty, so that decision makers will do more to save millions of lives in the poorest countries."
8. Go to http://www.pih.org/index.html for more information.

References

Alexander, R. D. (1979). *Darwinism and human affairs*. Seattle: University of Washington Press.

Barber, B. (1992). Jihad vs. mcworld. *The Atlantic*. 269(3). 53–65.

Barber, B. (1996). *Jihad vs. mcworld*. New York: Ballantine Books.

Blau, J., & Moncada, A. (2005). *Human rights: Beyond the liberal vision*. Lanham, MD: Rowman & Littlefield.

Boston, R. (1993). *Why the religious right is wrong about separation of church & state*. Buffalo, NY: Prometheus Books.

Carson, R. (1962). *Silent spring*. Boston: Houghton Mifflin.

Comte, A. (1849, 1957) *A general view of positivism*. New York: Robert Speller and Sons. (J.H. Bridges, Trans.).

Dawkins, R. (1996). *Climbing mount improbable*. New York: W. W. Norton.

Dawkins, R. (1976). *The selfish gene*. Oxford: Oxford University Press.

Farmer, P. (2003). *Pathologies of power: Health, human rights, and the new war on the poor.* Berkeley: University of California Press.

Geertz, C. (1973). *The interpretation of cultures.* New York: Basic Books.

Kidder, T. (2003). *Mountains beyond mountains: The quest of Dr. Paul Farmer, a man who would save the world.* New York: Random House.

Kuhn, T. (1970). *The structure of scientific revolutions.* Chicago: University of Chicago Press.

Lee, A. M. (1986). *Sociology for whom?* New York: Syracuse University.

Maslow, A. (1954). *Motivation and personality.* NewYork: Harper.

Mills, C. Wright (1959). *The Sociological imagination.* New York: Oxford University Press.

Richardson, M. (1976). Culture and the struggle to be human. *Anthropology and humanism quarterly* 1(3), 2–4.

Ridley, M. (1993). *The red queen: Sex and the evolution of human nature.* New York: Penguin Press.

Ridley, M. (1996). *The origins of virtue: Human instincts and the evolution of cooperation.* New York: Penguin Press.

Sachs, J. (2005). *The end of poverty.* New York: Penguin Press.

Singer, P. (2002). *One world: The ethics of globalization.* New Haven, CT: Yale University Press.

Unamuno, M. (1968). *Perplexities and paradoxes.* New York: Greenwood Press.

White, L. (1948). Man's control over civilization: An anthropocentric illusion. *The Scientific Monthly,* Volume 66, Issue 3, pp. 235-247.

Questions for Discussion

1. It is my deepest hope you disagreed with at least some of what I wrote in this chapter and that some of your core assumptions were questioned. What, for you, was the "hardest to swallow" in what you read? Which part(s) questioned some of your basic core assumptions about your role as a citizen?

2. One major assumption asserted in this chapter is that humans, to an extent, are "wired" to act in a certain way. Specifically, I argued that people have an innate drive to save those who are close to them genetically (their children in the "house on fire" example for instance). What evidence can you find to support or refute this argument? What is your understanding of the interaction between "nature" and "nurture" and how does this understanding impact the effectiveness with which you play your role as a global citizen?

3. When I addressed the issue of our priorities as individuals and as members of educational institutions (students or faculty) I came out as a heretic. I asserted that continuing on "headless" was not an option and that we all need to come together, agree on global humanitarian and environmental efforts that most immediately need our attention, and function in a more concerted fashion. Basically, what I am saying is our individual freedom to conduct any research we see fit or to select our philanthropic giving must be relinquished in this time of global crisis. Do you agree or disagree with this position? How would a global citizen—as described in this chapter—decide where to allocate his or her yearly donations? How do you make your decisions?

4. Imagine a scale of "global citizenship" with someone like former United Nations Secretary-General Kofi Annan on one end and the exact opposite—(I will withhold giving an example here; I'll leave that to you) on the other end. If being an "ideal" global citizen is a ten and the other end of the scale is a zero, where would you place yourself? Most Americans? What kinds of learning or experiences push us from one place on the scale to another?

5. There is a difference between "giving" and "partnering." When you give to a cause—for example donate cans of soup to the local shelter or send a check to aid the hungry in Honduras—these are meaningful acts and certainly much better than doing nothing. But partnering is more. More meaningful, more difficult, and more time consuming. Here is a summary of differences and similarities:

	"Giving"	*"Partnering"*
Fast?	Yes	No
Easy?	Yes	No
Helpful to others?	Yes, with qualifications	Yes
A meaningful connection?	No	Yes
Culturally sensitive?	Frequently not	Done right, yes

Write a short essay based on the above, citing and reflecting on examples from your own personal life or the lives of some people you know.

The Joy of Culture

A Beginner's Guide to Understanding and Appreciating Cultural Diversity

Laurence A. Basirico and Anne Bolin

This "methods" chapter answers the questions: "What is culture?" and "How may we study it?" In providing the answers to these two questions, the chapter offers basic definitions of culture and an analytical framework for cultural analysis. It establishes the importance of being able to interpret your own culture and other people's cultures. To understand cultural diversity, it is worthwhile to try and "step into another person's shoes": that is, to attempt to see the world through that person's eyes and cultural context. Responsible global citizens need to be able to approach different cultures from a vantage point of cultural relativism by identifying and circumventing their own ethnocentrism. The chapter provides a methodological tool kit for "reading" and interpreting cultural variation through the matrix, intersection, and integration of cultural elements and institutions. Students will find the analytical toolkit useful in a variety of situations: from reading and interpreting a Maori novel to understanding a family in an industrial city or a rural village.

What Is Culture? Perspectives and Practices of Daily Life

Culture is the concept that anthropologists and sociologists have developed to refer to our shared, all-encompassing perspective about our existence and the means through which we maintain our lives. In recent years the word *culture* has become accepted as part of society's general vernacular. While we will define it in greater detail later, we offer you a basic and preliminary definition of culture as the shared reality—including both ideas and patterned behaviors—of peoples within a geographic region. Please note that anthropologists generally use the plural form of the word people—that is, "peoples"—to refer to the inhabitants of a particular geographic region: for example, the peoples of North America. And the term culture refers to a common worldview—a mental and intellectual climate, if you will—and shared ways of doing what is necessary to maintain a way of life. To say that culture is a shared worldview, or perspective, however, does not mean that everyone in a particular place has the same opinions about how best to organize our reproductive practices, run a government, create knowledge, develop a healthy economy, maintain our health, engage in spirituality, and so on. For example, in the United States we may have differences of opinion about whether or not people should marry outside of their faith, but we generally agree that marriage is an appropriate form of public recognition and demonstration of intimacy and a beneficial structure for reproduction. We may disagree about the appropriate level of taxation, but we agree that we will operate by the rules of capitalism. We may disagree about how much power the government should have, but we agree that we will operate according to democratic principles. We may disagree about whether or not there should be vouchers (government subsidies to individuals) for private school attendance, but we agree that the educational system as we know it is a good way to disseminate knowledge in our society. We may disagree about the results of a scientific study, but we agree that the scientific method is the most appropriate way of discovering and creating new knowledge. We may disagree about whether or not prayer should be allowed in schools, but we agree that our beliefs and values stem from Judeo-Christian ethics. Such disagreements are not necessarily dysfunctional for a society. The diversity in individual response to culture is a source for the creative aspects of culture as well as for culture change.

These overarching commonalities of perspectives and methods that we share—that is, culture—are both manifested in and reinforced by social institutions. *Social institutions* are systems of plans and procedures that are necessary for the maintenance of our existence as we know it. In other words, the systems that we have for regulating reproduction and childrearing (family systems), for insuring that our material and subsistence needs are met (economic systems), for establishing and reaffirming our values, beliefs, and morals (religious or spiritual systems), for caring for our bodies (health care systems), for regulating power and resolving conflicts (political systems, military systems) and for discovering, creating, and disseminating knowledge (educational systems) have both shaped and been shaped by an overarching worldview—that is, culture—that we share, regardless of our differences of opinion on specific issues.

Take, for example, our present North American and European industrialized notions of family, religion, economy, and government. At this point it is too complex to discuss how our worldviews have evolved and how they have been shaped. For now, just consider the common thread that runs between our spiritual practices, our reproductive practices, our production and distribution practices, and our practices of governance. Widely agreed upon practices regarding reproduction, legitimate mates, and extra-marital sex can be traced to a spiritual system strongly rooted in the Judeo-Christian tradition. This tradition exists, despite your own personal beliefs. That same tradition is shared by a system of production and distribution—the economy—that the classic German sociologist Max Weber characterized in his well-known book, *The Protestant Ethic and the Spirit of Capitalism* (1904). Weber explains how a capitalist economic work ethic is intricately interwoven with Christian ethics. Indeed, the entire worldview of our society consists of interrelated sets of rules with which we accomplish all our tasks. Our family, economic, government, health care, education, religious, and knowledge systems, while seemingly independent of one another, co-exist and are reinforced by one another. These systems are the mechanisms for the functioning of culture. The relationships among these systems are extremely powerful in that they represent and reinforce an overall worldview (i.e., culture) that lies at the core of every society. In a very real sense, culture is the basis of reality as we know it. Indeed, culture *is* reality. We will talk more about the relationships between culture and social institutions later in this chapter.

The Importance of Understanding and Appreciating Other Cultures

Why is it important to understand other cultures? If you accept our premise that culture is the basis of a people's reality, the answer is somewhat obvious. To understand peoples throughout the world we must learn to understand the basis of their culture. This understanding of culture is increasingly important. Today's world is a shrinking one. New technologies allow fingertip communication and instant interaction. Peoples as far away from the United States as the Nyoongar of South West Australia are our electronic neighbors. Telephones, television, films, radio, faxes, electronic mail, satellites, the Internet, and other electronic communication transmit cultural information to remote sectors of the earth. The various economies of the globe are becoming increasingly integrated into one global economic system fueled by the forces of modernization and industrialism and the knowledge and the expansion of capitalism. Some social scientists contend that these technologies will lead to global homogenization—that is, a "sameness"—among peoples of the world. Others, including the authors, hold that the reverse may be true. That is, people will have more opportunity to become aware of their cultural differences and it will be all the more important to understand cultural diversity. Cultural diversity must be understood before it can truly be appreciated. If culture is not understood, attempts at appreciation could be misguided and damaging, while any international programs, however well-intentioned, could and do have unexpected, and sometimes problematic, results.

Culture Change and Global Impacts

Even the best intentions can have disastrous consequences if culture is not considered as a central feature in virtually any global or even domestic practice. A good example of this need for an understanding of what culture is and how it varies from place to place is found in some economic development programs for *indigenous peoples* (that is, peoples who are native to a particular geographic region) sponsored by nation states and various international organizations such as Oxfam, The International Committee of the Red Cross, and Médecins Sans Frontières, also known as Doctors Without Borders. Following the end of the colonial era and the rise of non-industrialized and industrializing nation states, industrialized powers have wanted to lend a hand to non-industrialized and industrializing world countries. Industrialized nations have invested time and energy in planning programs to help overcome poverty and increase productivity in the name of "progress." But is this necessarily progress and, if so, according to whom? John Bodley, an anthropologist and an activist advocate for indigenous and other peoples of the industrializing world, argues that progress has "involved the deaths of millions of tribal peoples, as well as their loss of land, political sovereignty, and the right to follow their own life styles" (2007, p. 268). For example, poverty in industrializing countries was thought, by leaders of industrialized nations such as the United States, to be a consequence of "underdevelopment" and primitive technologies.

The "Green Revolution" exported to developing countries by the United States and other major nations—undertaken with good intentions—was regarded as a salvation since it included advancements in plant development through genetic engineering and the use of pesticides, fertilizers, and sophisticated technologies. However, these "advancements," offered by this and other international development schemes, often disrupted the prevailing dietary customs of regions that have slowly evolved over hundreds of years as specific adaptations to the natural environment. Such rapid changes in diet often have resulted in severe protein deficiencies causing malnutrition and serious tooth decay. The Green Revolution development project often increased poverty and poor health rather than diminished them, since its premises were false.

Planners of such global aid programs failed to understand that modern poverty wasn't necessarily caused by "primitive" technologies but, rather, was linked to colonialism and globalization—that is, domination by other countries—and to the imposition of *stratification*—that is, systems of inequality and ranking—upon subsistence economies among bands and tribal peoples. These disempowering trends have escalated through the expansion of capitalism and globalization.

Understanding how the global expansion of commercial economies has affected indigenous, tribal, and contemporary peoples and their societies requires an awareness of the complex relations among the elements of culture and institutions/systems. Globalization is a much more complex process than simple cultural imperialism. Although there is widespread agreement among anthropologists and sociologists that peoples of the industrializing/non-industrialized world have been negatively influenced by globalization, local inhabitants are also active agents in modifying, reconfiguring, and resisting external cultural forms. Indeed the global encounter between dominant or more powerful societies and the local less powerful recipients—whether embedded in historical colonialism or in subsequent modern globalization—may lead to *cultural hybridization*. Hybridization is a process in which something new is created from the mixing of borrowed cultural features with the local culture. It includes active indigenous modification and reappropriation of the cultural borrowings—also referred to as *indigenization* or *localization*. Hybridization may be a positive and culturally creative process "rather than indicating a regrettable loss of original purity" (Lavenda & Schultz, 2008, p. 481). This perspective on the hybridization process emphasizes local peoples as dynamic agents in the indigenization of cultural features from industrialized nations and sees local peoples as resisting Euro-American views that they have been globalized or "westernized" (Lavenda & Schultz, 2007).

Despite the positive aspects of hybridization, it is important to be aware that globalization can, and does, result in harming or worsening the lives of peoples in the name of "progress." It is imperative that knowledge of, and respect for, the adaptive survival mechanisms of inhabitants of industrializing nations be incorporated by nation states in their policies and programs to help the marginalized and disenfranchised better survive in the contemporary world.

An Increase in Cultural Diversity: The United States and the World

The United States is a pluralistic society; it has many ethnic groups within its borders. Prior to European immigration and colonization of North America, Native American bands, tribes, chiefdoms, kingdoms, and states thrived. North, Central, and South Americas were founded by peoples from Asia crossing the Bering Strait, a land bridge between Siberia and Alaska, at least 12,000 years ago. This occurred in prehistoric migrations of different language and cultural groups that evolved over time to become the diverse peoples Europeans encountered upon arriving and colonizing the Americas. European immigrants brought their own traditions that were later influenced by slavery and African peoples. Subsequent wars and ethnic conflicts throughout the world have increased United States diversity even more.

Today, far from achieving a homogenized blend, the forces of economic globalization are increasing the level of heterogeneity more and more. Never has it been so crucial for us to have knowledge about the elements and processes of culture. That knowledge is important not only in international relations, but also in the domestic realm, where culture penetrates a broad spectrum of policy issues and practices in the United States such as health care, education, family planning, ecology, economics, development programs, and political action. For example, an episode of a prime-time television hospital program that aired from 1994 to 2000, *Chicago Hope*, illustrated very well the importance of understanding culture within the context of health-care systems. In the episode, a North American cardiologist treating a Japanese patient in a U.S. hospital discovered that the patient had a form of heart cancer. When the cardiologist explained to the husband of the patient that his wife had cancer and had only about a year to live, he pleaded that his wife's condition be kept secret from her. The cardiologist objected, explaining that she had an obligation to her patient to be honest and that the patient had a right to know of her terminal condition. Again, the husband pleaded and explained that in his culture, finding out such news about one's self would be cause for losing face, a condition to be taken more seriously. Arguments ensued between the husband and the doctor, and the doctor remained adamant in her position. She said that she respected his culture, but in the United States we do it this way. Think of how a full knowledge of cultural variation could have entered into the doctor's decision in this case. Consider the reverse situation. If a North American terminally ill patient were in a hospital in a country whose culture forbade divulging this information to terminally ill patients, do you think the North American patient would have a right to this information? This is an illuminating example of the importance of understanding and appreciating culture in our everyday lives. With such an ethnically diverse population as exists in the United States today, it would be difficult to name even one occupational setting in which an understanding of cultural differences is not essential.

To really understand cultural differences, so that our own work in the world will be shaped by knowledge and understanding rather than by ignorance and indifference, we must approach unfamiliar attitudes, actions, values, and appearances with a non-judgmental attitude, with openness and an appreciation of cultural context. This means we must adopt a culturally relativistic perspective and overcome ethnocentrism. We discuss these ideas in the following sections.

Ethnocentrism and Cultural Relativism

Ethnocentrism

Ethnocentrism is the belief that one's own cultural patterns are superior to others', and that one's own way of doing things is "normal." Ethnocentrism means judging others by one's own cultural beliefs about the good, right, proper, "natural," and "normal" way to do things. Sometimes ethnocentrism entails the outright condemnation of cultural practices different from our own. For example, to say that capitalism and democracy, the particular forms of economic and government systems embraced by many industrialized nations, must be embraced by every nation is ethnocentric. While these economic and government systems may be appropriate for industrialized nations such as the United States, they are not necessarily appropriate for all types of societies. To say that the Judeo-Christian concept of a Supreme Being is the most appropriate belief system for all peoples is a form of ethnocentrism. While a Judeo-Christian religion may be very positive for some peoples, it is not necessarily the best choice for all peoples of the world. For example, disastrous consequences occurred for the indigenous peoples of Australia when Christian missionaries tried to "save" them by imposing Christianity upon them. This occurred in conjunction with government policies of "protection" whereby aboriginal people were relocated to reserves and missionized throughout the 1800s, culminating in the establishment of the infamous Removal Act, in 1905, when children who appeared to be of mixed blood were "stolen" from their parents and placed on missions or with white families.

Yet, while ethnocentric attitudes and behavior may often be obvious and even crude, sometimes they are hidden and rather subtle. An interesting example is found in examining students' responses to the sexual practices of cultures that have very different patterns of sexual behavior from those in the United States. For example, the traditional Mangaians (Marshall, 1971; 1993), a Cook Island people in the South Pacific, like some other Polynesian peoples have generally been described by anthropologists as having a "sex-positive" culture. This means that sex, within that culture, has not been regarded as a negative or even an ambiguous behavior. At the time of the research, there was a focus on sexual pleasure, particularly on female satisfaction and multiple orgasms. Romantic love was not necessarily linked to sex. The restrictions on sex were few, with most restrictions placed upon the royals and the elites in Old Polynesia. In Mangaia, young people were encouraged to have as many partners as possible prior to marriage. (This research occurred before the advent of HIV in industrializing countries, and, particularly, before its arrival among Polynesian peoples, where HIV/AIDS entered the population through tourism.) Mangaian youths did not date. There was no gradual increasing of intimacy beginning with kissing, necking, and petting. In fact, until more recent influences from industrialized cultures, kissing had not been part of traditional Mangaian sexuality. For the Mangaian youth, coitus was the expected outcome of the intimate encounter. According to Donald Marshall, a cultural anthropologist, less than one out of one hundred girls or boys had not had "substantial sexual experience" (1993). Young Mangaian male youths (early teens to early twenties) averaged three orgasms per night, seven nights a week. At twenty-eight years of age the average dropped to two orgasms per night, five to six times a week. The expectation was that the male should strive to have his partner have two to three orgasms to his one.

This situation is very useful to our discussion of ethnocentrism because it is likely to provoke surprised approval, even amusement, in at least some parts of a United States audience. We have used this example to demonstrate that ethnocentrism need not necessarily be in a negative vein. In Anne Bolin's anthropology of sex class, the student response usually has been something along the lines that they are going to pack their bags and move to Mangaia immediately. For some students, the Cook Islands are seen as a sexual fantasyland. But this very positive view is in itself a kind of ethnocentrism. Such a perspective does not consider the cultural context of the Mangaian peoples, their attitudes toward children, marriage, community, and kinship. By looking at the Mangaians as a fantasyland, the outsider detaches one aspect of their sexual system—intercourse—from its cultural context. It is difficult to get past one's Euro-American lens in seeking to understand the Mangaian sexual system. This is because U.S. culture has a strong sex-negative stance toward sexuality, which is linked primarily to its Judeo-Christian heritage. In the United States, sex is sanctioned primarily for only one age and status group: young adults through middle age who are married. Sexuality is culturally denied and discouraged to the young, adolescents and teenagers, and also to the elderly. Therefore, ours is a system that makes the transition to pleasurable sexuality for a young adult a difficult one, especially for females, who are subjected to a double standard. Women are reared to control their sexuality and to confine it to a relationship, preferably a marital one, although these standards have been relaxed somewhat within the past few decades. This gender-linked set of characteristics for women collides with masculine enculturation that traditionally celebrates a recreational approach to sex (Bolin & Whelehan, 2009).

Ethnocentrism can be found in other forms as well, and it can be expressed in seemingly divergent ways when faced with the same phenomenon. For example, indigenous peoples may provoke disparate, but equally ethnocentric responses from members of other groups. One of the most well known examples is that of the "noble savage." In our studies abroad courses in Australia, we have found two prevalent reactions to the indigenous Nyoongar peoples of Australia. One reaction is similar to the United States stereotype about Native Americans: "They are lazy. They drink too much. They could work if they wanted to, but would rather be on welfare." And so on. This is obviously an ethnocentric and uneducated view of the plight of indigenous populations subjected to colonialism—the domination of a region's original inhabitants by more powerful countries—and to ongoing discrimination in a post-modern world.

But a more subtle, yet equally dangerous form of ethnocentrism is voiced by many white Australians and some of our students who have studied in Australia. They have said to us something like this: "Well, those 'aborigines' [sic] in the city are lazy drunks, but the real aborigines [sic], those living in the desert like their ancestors, well they're alright, they're the good ones." This is what anthropologists call a noble savage viewpoint, stereotype, or attitude. It, too, is an ethnocentric construction, as much as the "drunken layabout" stereotype. You may have heard it often in reference to Native Americans. This is not to say that we shouldn't admire aspects of other cultures, as long as we know that you can not simply take a cultural element out of context and incorporate it into your own society with equanimity. Many students in our anthropology courses are particularly drawn to the egalitarian Ju/wasi of Africa who, until the late 20th century, practiced a communal way of life with food sharing and equality among all. Incorporating the Ju/wasi lifestyle into our own culture wouldn't work for a number of reasons, primarily because they were gatherers and hunters living in small autonomous groups. This is not to say, however, that we can't find these elements desirable and find ways to make our capitalism more compassionate and less stratified. So, we can learn much from other cultures, and we can even attempt to change our own in positive ways as a result. But, we can only do this through an understanding of the complexity of the culture concept, which we will discuss in greater detail later.

The noble savage stereotype, which implies a thoughtless, generalizing approach to fellow human beings, can be a most insidious form of ethnocentrism. It romanticizes indigenous populations and their way of life before contact with dominant nations and the impact of colonialism, before the emergence of new nation states, and the birth of international aid and development schemes. Those who adopt this viewpoint of indigenous peoples deny cultures the right to change and grow, to adapt, and yet to persist. One of the authors of this chapter, Bolin, has taught an anthropology course on Native American Spirituality. As part of the course, she required that students attend a pow wow—a Native American cultural festival. Some students, upon first attending a pow wow, usually find it a disappointment. They do not expect to see the United States flag, honoring of Native American veterans of war, drum songs that incorporate Barney and Disney characters into the lyrics, or red-haired and blue-eyed "Indians." They ask where the "real" Native Americans are, just as some of the white Australians think the only "real" aboriginal people are living naked in the desert. This is the ultimate form of Euro-American disrespect—to assign status as real or authentic on the basis of a Euro-American conception of what a "real" indigenous person should be like. Such an attitude is the height of conceit. It is ironic that the nations that deprived the indigenous peoples of Australia and the Native Americans of their lands and traditional ways of survival now elevate the old ways as criteria for being "real." Thus, in Western Australia, for example, where peoples of indigenous descent have the potential, as a result of High Court decisions, to claim native lands and possibly rent them to mining companies, they are criticized by white Australians for wanting to participate in capitalism after having had their traditional way of life dismantled. Somehow, apparently, the aboriginal peoples have violated the romantic boundaries constructed for them by those who rendered them powerless in the first place.

Ethnocentrism exists in many forms. Regardless of the expression that ethnocentrism takes, it always involves a disrespect and lack of understanding and appreciation for other cultures. While most of us are ethnocentric in one way or another, it is important that we continually strive to overcome it. If you are to understand and appreciate cultural diversity, it is imperative that you recognize and overcome your ethnocentrism and learn to use a culturally relativistic approach.

Cultural Relativism: A Means of Overcoming Ethnocentrism

How can you come to understand and appreciate cultural diversity so that you can successfully interact with members of other cultures and nations? The approach that anthropologists and sociologists use is called *cultural relativism*. Cultural relativism is an attitude of openness toward other cultures. It is the opposite of *ethnocentrism*—a belief that one's own cultural patterns are superior to others—and requires that you let go of your own cultural standards.

Another way of saying this is that cultural relativism is a non-judgmental approach that treats the worldviews and practices of peoples in other societies with respect and attempts to understand them within the context of those societies. Cultural relativism does not mean that you should accept in a non-critical way all behaviors and beliefs of another group, or of your own, for that matter. Nor does cultural relativism suggest that "anything goes." If this were the case, then the Jewish Holocaust would be regarded as acceptable as long as we understood how it fit into German culture. This is far from the case. While cultural relativism is valuable in understanding, for example, the Holocaust, being culturally relativistic does not mean that we must necessarily endorse every behavior. This is why cultural relativism is about *temporarily* suspending judgment until knowledge and understanding are gained. Using a culturally relativistic approach is not always easy to do, especially when we are examining cultural behaviors or practices that appear abhorrent to us. However, embedded in cultural relativism is a perspective of ethical relativism. Thus, following the understanding generated by a culturally relativistic stance may come an ethical re-positioning; that, for many of us, includes a humanistic concern for all human rights.

Cultural relativism can broaden your horizons and can lead you to consider new ideas and other ways of thinking about your place in the world and your relationships to others. If we think our culture has all the right answers and we uncritically accept its tenets, our growth and development as individuals and as a nation may be stifled. Conversely, cultural relativism can lead us to understand better those aspects of society that we may feel are desirable, such as democracy.

Cultural relativism is as much a method as it is a perspective. Cultural relativism requires that you have an understanding of what culture means, its characteristics and its elements, and how it is related to social institutions. The remainder of this chapter explores the concepts of culture and institutions further and shows you how your understanding of these concepts can lead you to cultural relativism.

Further Explorations of Culture: The Disciplines of Anthropology and Sociology

Because awareness of and sensitivity to culture are so important, we would like to turn now to a more detailed discussion of the "culture concept." Before proceeding, a warning is in order. We have found over the years in classes and workshops, that many people are surprised at learning that culture is indeed a full-blown concept with well-defined parameters and characteristics. In educating students and teachers alike, we have found most people assume that they know what culture is because—after all—they live in one. This is a potentially dangerous assumption that can inhibit, rather than enhance, our understanding of diverse peoples. The culture concept is really more sophisticated than one might first suspect.

A variety of disciplines within the social sciences and humanities have examined some aspects of culture. However, our definition of culture comes from the one discipline whose central conceptual and research concern is culture. Anthropologists have studied culture as it has been expressed over millions of years and across the globe. As a result, the anthropological definition may be broader and more nuanced than that taken by other disciplines or even than a lay definition. This is because anthropological theory and method are driven by the culture concept.

The other discipline we will use to help guide you through your understanding and appreciation of cultural diversity is sociology. While sociology examines many other topics besides culture, sociology does place considerable emphasis on understanding and explaining the relationship between culture and the means by which societies are organized. *Culture* consists of everything that people do (behavior), believe, know (both consciously and unconsciously), and make, among other things, which we describe in greater detail below. But *society* is usually defined as an organized system of statuses and roles and does not necessarily include a shared worldview. For example, bees and wolves are known to live in societies where there are shared patterns of interaction associated with an individual's status within the group, e.g. the Queen bee. But for humans, a society is defined as a group of people who live in the same area *and* who interact according to certain shared cultural expectations. In fact, culture cannot exist without groups of people who live it and pass it on. Unlike human societies, animal societies do not have culture, although it has been argued by some physical anthropologists that some of the non-human primate groups, like chimpanzees, have proto-culture.

Culture Defined in More Detail: The History of a Definition

Anthropologist Sir Edward Tylor was the first to argue that culture could be studied scientifically because culture was patterned. And he gave us the first definition of culture, in 1871. We offer you his classic definition, which has stood the test of time. Tylor defined culture as "that complex whole which includes knowledge, belief, arts, morals, law, custom, and any other capabilities acquired by man as a member of society" (p. 1). Although there are many definitions of culture, this nineteenth-century formulation continues to serve us well. The most important characteristics of culture are: values, beliefs, meanings, interpretations, knowledge, as well as human behavior and what people make and produce. To reiterate what we said earlier, culture is the shared reality of a people.

Culture is both conscious and out of our awareness. For example, we are aware of what goes on in the United States classroom and we can tell someone who inquires about it. But when we enter a classroom, we unconsciously, without thinking, sit at the desk and expect that the teacher will be the person—standing—at the front of the room. So much of culture is taken for granted that it is difficult for us to see it. This is why in order to "see" our culture we may need to make it alien, a technique you will see utilized in our exercises.

However, other parts of culture are readily available in our consciousness. If you ask United States Americans about marriage, they might still talk about getting married and "living happily ever after." Americans today, however, are becoming increasingly aware that there is a big discrepancy between the *ideal* cultural pattern of monogamous marriage until death do us part, and the *real* culture pattern of a high divorce rate and serial monogamy. The actual pattern of practices may indeed vary from the ideal pattern. This is the "nature" of culture so that culture change, and ideal, and real cultures, are usually in flux. Many other institutions, such as the economy, government, religion, and so forth, as well as marriage and the family, are continually undergoing change. As cultures change, there may often be discontinuities between beliefs and behaviors.

As you can see, the culture concept is multifaceted. It includes what you know about your way of life, *cultural knowledge*, and how you behave. Behavior includes everything you do: for example, the things you say and how you say them, and the act of making or producing things. Those products of society we call *material culture* or *artifacts*. These include everything from the stone axes of the Yir Yoront indigenous Australians and the pottery of the Pueblo peoples to the computers of U.S. college students. What you know about your social world and your behavior are stimulated by the meanings your culture has for you. Virtually all aspects of human behavior, except for involuntary physiological responses, are cultural behaviors.

The Characteristics of Culture

Culture has several common characteristics. It is learned, symbolic, shared, integrated to varying degrees, and ever changing (although the rate of culture change varies). We will discuss each of these characteristics briefly. Culture is *learned*. Humans learn their culture rather than inheriting it biologically. When winter comes, rabbits' fur grows longer and thicker, while humans adapt through cultural means by making clothing and shelter. Culture is an adaptive mechanism that has given humans great survival value for over two million years. Because we don't rely on genetics to provide us a map for living, humans have become incredibly diverse while adapting to various ecological circumstances: modifying the environment, and passing on cultural information for survival to our young. This process of learning one's culture is termed enculturation.

Culture is *symbolic*. A symbol is something that stands for something else. Culture is filled with symbols. In fact, language is our primary symbolic system for transmitting culture. It is difficult to find an aspect of culture that does not have a symbolic dimension. For example, in our society during the nineteen-sixties and seventies, long hair was a symbol of rebellion or non-conformity among men. Another example of the importance of symbols is found in traditional Hopi marriage practices. Among the Southwestern Hopi in the United States, a girl initiated the marriage proposal by presenting a boy with a loaf of *gomi*, a cornmeal cake. There were several occasions when the giving of the cornmeal bread occurred. Acceptance of the proposal was up to the boy and his family, although the boy must always accept the bread so as not to offend the girl (Schlegel 1973). In our dominant Anglo society it is the man who traditionally spearheads the marriage proposal by offering a diamond ring as a symbol of his proposal.

Culture is *shared* among a group of people. As we shall see, although there is diversity among individuals, culture refers to broadly shared symbols, values, beliefs, norms, emotions, technology, and so on, among groups who share, to varying degrees, certain attributes of a culture. For example, United States Americans value individualism while the Mbuti of the Ituri Forest value community and the common good so that individual achievement is not acknowledged. Anthropologist Richard Lee wanted to repay his Ju/wasi friends of the Kalahari Desert by buying them a huge fat ox for Christmas. Upon presenting his gift, not only did he not receive thanks, but the Ju/wasi made fun of the ox, saying it was skinny, had no fat, and that Lee had been taken. Lee knew the cow was fat and meaty so he wanted to find out what was behind their seemingly "ungrateful" (by United States standards) behavior. The Ju/wasi were an egalitarian society in which all people are equal: that is, they all had equal access to resources. If they acknowledged that Lee had bought an unusually large ox, one they could never afford, then Lee would be elevated above the Ju/wasi. This could then lead to envy, which could be very disruptive to a group so communally oriented and egalitarian (Lee, [1969] 2007).

Culture is *integrated* to varying degrees. In this regard, anthropologists Carol and Melvin Ember explain: "In saying a culture is mostly integrated, we mean that the elements or traits that make up that culture are not just a random assortment of customs but are mostly adjusted to or consistent with one another" (2004, p. 26). As we discuss in greater depth later in this chapter, culture can be conceptualized as consisting of a number of elements such as symbols, values, beliefs, and norms; and also by *institutions* such as family, education, economic, and political systems. All societies are cultural systems in which the *non-material elements* such as symbols, values, beliefs, and norms and the *material elements*, which are the things people make (artifacts) and the tools people use (technology), are articulated with the society's *institutions* or systems of adaptation and survival. Anthropologists may call institutions "structures" or "systems" but the two terms mean the same thing. These two concepts, "the elements of culture" and "institutions," are useful tools that allow us to understand cultures, make comparisons, establish patterns, and offer interpretations, analyses, and hypotheses. All cultures possess the elements of culture although the content varies; that is, all cultures have beliefs, although the actual beliefs vary. Many of the institutions or structures are universal; they are found among all peoples as ways to adapt to the cultural and physical environment and to one another. We have already introduced the term *institutions* to describe the social organization of society. The elements of a culture and its institutions are divergently integrated into a cultural whole that has its own internal logic and patterning. Keep in mind that the notion that culture is integrated to varying degrees must be understood as complicated and complex. The culture of a given people is embedded in historical circumstances and consequently contains contradictions and inconsistencies (Middleton, 1998, p. 59). Culture is by no means a smoothly operating system.

To provide an example, we will look at how the institution of marriage is *integrated* with other cultural institutions. For example, if a society practices polygyny, so that one man may marry several women, then this practice will relate to other institutions, such as the institution of food getting and economics. The nature of this relationship varies cross-culturally depending on the subsistence strategy. The traditional Australian Tiwi provide an interesting example demonstrating how institutions are integrated in various ways. The Tiwi were foragers who subsisted on gathering, hunting, and fishing in a particularly rich resource environment. The cultural ideal was polygyny. A man who had many wives strategically located himself in a career trajectory of wealth and prestige. Wives furnished a man with economic assets, thereby freeing him from many subsistence activities and providing him time to invest in public life, including entrepreneurial and ritual activities. These activities then enhanced his standing in his community. Therefore, wives were regarded as an important resource, and we can see how the institutions of marriage and subsistence were integrated among the Tiwi. Institutions are also integrated with the elements of culture. The symbols, values, beliefs, and norms found in a culture provide important ideologies and values supporting institutional practices. It is probably no surprise that Tiwi women had high status and were valued participants in society (Goodale, 1971). The relatively equal status of women and men is a common feature among foragers. Bear in mind that today, for a number of reasons, there are very few remaining foragers. The invention of agriculture, colonization, the development of nation states, and the expansion of capitalism and globalization, among others, have drastically reduced their numbers.

Culture change can have a profound impact on the degree to which a culture is integrated. This is why we say culture is integrated to varying degrees. Change in one part of culture will therefore result in changes in other parts. Culture change occurs through many channels, such as contact with other cultures, through internal processes that include innovation, and as a product of the complexity of peoples and the active agency of individuals. To think about culture change, imagine all the sectors of United States culture that have been impacted by the computer: from education, shopping, recreation, to finding a life-partner, to name only a few.

Culture is *ever changing*. Cultures are not static entities and have always undergone change, as evidenced from our earliest tool traditions two million years ago. However, a strong argument can be made that the rate of change has been dramatically increased as a result of colonialism and contemporary globalization. As mentioned, culture can change as a result of encounters with other societies. These interactions can lead to sharing of ideals, and diffusion of cultural traits, or they can lead to colonial and global imposition. Evidence of this "imposition" is found in the enforced conversion of the Polynesian peoples by various missionary groups, and in the assimilation policy in the United States, where Native American children were taken from their homes and placed in boarding schools so they would lose their native culture and blend into Anglo society.

Cultures are dynamic and even the most traditional culture does not remain static. This is because individuals are not all the same. They negotiate their culture through lived experiences and, as a consequence, change occurs. Thus, human beings are not just blind robots enacting their culture. All cultures have "room to move." Despite individual variation, there are boundaries and limits around the choices available in a society. In the United States, marriage is considered a monogamous institution for heterosexuals only, (until recently); individuals can be married to only one partner at a time. While the marriage pattern of monogamy prevails in our society, there is room for variation, which occurs through divorce and serial marriages. We do not, with the exception of a few small but illegal religious enclaves, sanction polygynous (one husband and several wives) or polyandrous (one wife and several husbands) marriage, as practiced in other cultures.

The Elements of Culture

The various forms that institutions take shape the *elements of culture*. Culture can be analyzed as consisting of a number of elements. As you may recall, our definition of culture included cultural knowledge, behavior, and the products of that behavior. We may think of these elements of culture as *non-material* (i.e., knowledge and behavior) and *material*. The *material* elements of culture include those things that people make, the tangible parts of culture. These are termed *artifacts* and *technologies*. We will focus on those *non-material* elements of culture that are in people's heads. It is this aspect of culture that motivates individuals to act. While we could generate a fairly extensive list, we have chosen to use the following elements as a tool for students to encounter the culture concept: symbols, values, beliefs (includes worldviews, cosmology), norms, emotions, attitudes, laws, perceptions, aspirations, and technological knowledge. These are defined in Figure 2.1, "The Elements of Culture." We have selected three of these elements to discuss and illustrate: symbols, values, and beliefs. Test yourself on the list of elements provided in Figure 2.1 and try to think of examples for each of the elements.

Cultures include beliefs, values, and norms about how people should feel and behave, but people do not always follow the guidelines of their culture. "People use their culture actively and creatively, rather than blindly following its dictates. The *ideal culture* consists of what people say they should do and of what they say they do." *Real culture* refers to their actual behavior that can be observed (Kottack, 2007, p. 47).

Non-Material

Symbols	An object or event that represents another object or event only because people agree as to its meaning
Values	Subjective reactions to experiences expressed in terms of good or bad, moral or immoral. The ideals that people look up to but do not necessarily achieve or pursue.
Beliefs	The ideas people hold about what is true and/or real are considered their beliefs.
Norms	Shared rules that define how people are supposed to behave under particular circumstances
Emotions	Inner reactions to experiences. A society enculturates (teaches) its members to associate certain emotions with specific situations and to experience these emotional states at various intensities depending on the context.
Attitudes	Likes and dislikes, and general preference for certain experiences over others
Laws	Norms defined by political authorities as principles that members of a society must follow
Perceptions	Interpretations of cultural phenomena which may vary from person to person due to his or her unique experience as a member of society
Aspirations	Ambitions and goals that are valued and desired within a culture
Technological Knowledge	Human knowledge of the techniques and methods for subsistence (how one makes a living, acquires the calories for survival) and/or control of and adaptation to the cultural and natural environment

Material

Artifacts	The material products of culture, past and present
Technology	The tools and products used for subsistence and/or control of and adaptation to the cultural and natural environment

FIGURE 2.1 The Elements of Culture

Symbols are defined as objects or events that represent other objects or events only because people agree as to the symbols' meanings. The American flag is an example of a symbol that carries a very powerful meaning to many in the United States, hence the controversy over flag burning. Yet, the arbitrariness of meaning is recognized among those United States citizens who do *not* think it should be illegal to burn or wear the United States flag. All symbols have a history and context and their meaning can change over time. The peace sign was an important symbol in the decade of the nineteen-sixties. However, now, to the younger generation, it just remains a quaint symbol of a time past, with much of its passion and power lost through time. As a symbolic system, language looms large in human lives. The meaning in words is arbitrary: that is, there is no inherent or essential meaning in the word itself—only that which people agree upon. Language is the primary symbolic system through which culture is transmitted and shared.

Values are subjective reactions to experiences expressed in terms of good or bad, moral or immoral. These are the ideals that people look up to but do not necessarily achieve, or even pursue; people think of these as the "good, right, and proper" ordering of the world. One of the phrases politicians have popularized is the term "family values." This phrase has been used by politicians in both major political parties to refer to a valuing of the traditional nuclear family with a stay-at-home mother and a breadwinner dad. This was an ideal cultural value that was actually achieved by the middle and upper classes in an earlier period in United States history—prior to the 1960s. It is an ideal and a value whose economic reality is no longer viable or perhaps even desirable for many living in the United States today. Women have achieved increasing economic independence over time. Statistics indicate that fewer than 20% of all United States households practice this earlier twentieth century arrangement. Dual career couples are now the norm and "today most mothers—even those with the youngest children—participate in the labor force" (Bolin & Whelehan, pp. 507–508, 2009; Department for Professional Employees, AFL-CIO "Professional Women: Vital Statistics Fact Sheet 2008"). Perhaps you can begin to see how values are integrated within the greater cultural system, including economic and political institutions, such as government policies of non-discrimination on the basis of gender.

Ideas people hold about what is true and/or real are considered their *beliefs*. Beliefs are assumptions that underlie worldviews. For example, in societies in which women are unequal and excluded from political activities, a number of beliefs exist to support male domination of women. These may include beliefs that menstruating women are unclean and a source of pollution to men. Such beliefs justify cultural practices in which women are segregated from men. In such cases, men come to dominate the public sector of society where decisions are made and women's voices are excluded.

In our society, we have a belief system that there are "temperamental" or characterological differences between the genders and that these differences are biologically based. Two prominent beliefs about biology are that women are nurturing and caring and men are aggressive and competitive. Yet, cross-cultural research reveals that what cultures call feminine and masculine has virtually no constancy throughout the ethnographic spectrum (Mead, 1963). It turns out that human beings are incredibly flexible and capable of adapting to a variety of cultural circumstances. Although there are some researchers who might disagree with this position (most notably those who subscribe to essentialist perspectives), almost all characteristics that we call masculine or feminine are learned as one grows up in a society.

Institutions: Culture and Everyday Life

What do the following have in common?

- A cashier in a supermarket asks: "Paper or plastic"?
- A president states at the close of the State of the Union address: "Good night, God bless you, and God bless America."
- A television advertisement directs: "Talk to your doctor about solutions for erectile dysfunction."
- A clergy person in a traditional religious ceremony concludes: "I now pronounce you man and wife."
- A political candidate proclaims: "I support immigration reform."
- A political candidate announces at a victory celebration: "Let us now begin the process of restoring traditional values and morals."
- An aphorism appears on national currency: "In God we trust."
- A sportscaster requests: "Ladies and gentlemen, please stand for our national anthem."
- A magazine advertisement reads: "Enjoy the ultimate luxury, high miles per gallon driving experience."
- A sign in a grocery store admonishes: "Recycle."
- An advertisement concludes with: "Visit our Web site."

What do the above have in common? They are all part of a set of expectations and guidelines—rules, if you will—about how we are supposed to accomplish the most essential tasks necessary to maintain our existence as we know it. Every society—every population since the beginning of human civilization—has had to concern itself with meeting certain objectives as a means of attempting to ensure its survival. This is a basic premise of human existence. Some of these essential survival tasks include:

- how we regulate our reproductive practices and ensure that our children are properly cared for;
- how we insure that all of our material needs—such as housing, clothing, food, transportation, and so on—are met;
- how we reaffirm our values, morals, and spiritual beliefs;
- how we regulate power relationships, create laws, govern, and resolve conflicts;
- how we care for the continued well-being of our bodies;
- how we discover and create knowledge that is necessary for maintenance of our way of life and for our capability to adapt to changing circumstances;
- how we disseminate information from generation to generation and prepare people for livelihood and good citizenship.

Of course, the survival objectives may not be exactly the same in every society and there may be additional tasks necessary for maintaining a specific way of life related to various regions of the world. For example, most societies have established gender systems for maintaining certain types of relationships between men and women in the home, in personal relationships, and in the workplace. Some societies have systems related to how people spend their leisure time. Some may have systems of warfare. Sociologists and anthropologists tend to agree, though, that the tasks mentioned in the list above are common throughout most of the world. Regardless of the types of systems of survival used by people in a region, these systems are responsible for maintaining the existence of a people's way of life. The concept that sociologists use to refer to these systems of survival is *"institutions"* (see Figure 2.2), although other disciplines may use terms such as "systems," "structures" or "social organizations." Statements, signs, symbols, admonishments, and other expressions such as those illustrated above fill our consciousness. Such phraseology directly and indirectly, overtly and covertly, subtly and boldly affirms the prevalence of specific forms of health care, development of knowledge, family values, economic policies, defense policies, environmental practices, religious practices, educational achievement, social policies, and other "rules" of social life that we, as a people, generally agree upon. It must be emphasized that, while these examples illustrate the "rules" of social life in American society, other societies may have different symbolic manifestations of their "rules."

The extent to which these manifestations of our "way" of life take place is so vast and all-encompassing that we fail to take notice of them as affirmations of our "reality" and often mistake them for reality itself. This is no accident of social life. On the contrary, a society would be hard-pressed to survive without the fact that its members embrace a taken-for-granted reality that appears to exist independently of the people that make up that society. Indeed, if we did not hold onto these "rules" of social life as being nearly absolute—or at least agree to pretend that these "rules" are objective and absolute in their origin—our way of life would crumble. That is why some of our most deeply entrenched systems—systems pertaining to the family, gender, economy, government, religion, education, health care, the development of knowledge—become battlegrounds when changes to how these systems operate are proposed. In the United States for example, abortion, prayer in schools, government regulated health care, same

---

Institutions/structures are established systems that people within a region have developed that enable them to meet universal adaptive requirements.

The following is a selective list of institutions/structures found among cultures of the world. Although these are generally considered cultural universals, not every culture has a military or a formal education system.

- Family systems
- Educational systems
- Economic systems
- Subsistence systems
- Political systems
- Religious and magical systems
- Health care systems
- Military systems
- Sex and gender systems
- Arts and leisure systems

FIGURE 2.2   Social Institutions/Structures

sex marriages, government regulation of business, school vouchers, and other topics, create intense debate and arouse deep emotions. This intensity occurs not only because of differences in beliefs, but because the challenges to the *status quo* may fundamentally change the systems that maintain necessary societal survival mechanisms for us as a nation.

Putting It All Together: The Web of Culture

It is difficult to separate culture and institutions into parts. They are intertwined. They create each other and they reinforce each other. The symbols, norms, beliefs, values, technology, and other elements of culture shared by a people help to create the social institutions—the patterns a people agree upon for insuring their survival—while at the same time, the social institutions reinforce the elements of culture. It is nearly impossible to look at each element of culture and each institution separately because they obtain their meaning from each other. We use the term *the web of culture* to refer to the interrelationships between the elements of culture and social institutions. To help you conceptualize the web of culture a little more easily, picture, if you will, a rubber-band ball. While the rubber-band ball isn't exactly the same as a cobweb or spiderweb, it does have some of the same properties. We think both the web and the ball are useful metaphors for the intricate links among all parts of any culture: pull on one thread, or one band, and everything will start to move. And every thread of the web, or band in the ball, is integral to the whole structure. The ball itself consists of hundreds, maybe thousands, of separate rubber bands. Each rubber band by itself is simply a single rubber band when apart from the ball. But when they are intertwined, each rubber band is connected to each of the others, holding the others up, supporting one another, creating and giving shape to the whole ball. Together, they form a ball. Yet, separately when not intertwined, all you have is a pile of rubber bands.

Culture, then, is a little like a rubber band ball (see Figure 2.3). Think of the separate rubber bands as elements of culture—values, beliefs, norms, symbols, technology, and so on. Now, think not just of one value, one belief, one symbol, and so on, but think of the hundreds of examples of values, beliefs, norms, symbols, and so forth in a particular place. Imagine that each rubber band represents one value, belief, symbol, norm, etc. Further, imagine that other rubber bands represent social institutions—the family, the economy, politics, religion, education, health care, and so forth. Think of how intertwined the strands of a rubber-band ball are and how they create something solid, real, and tangible that is much more than the individual strands. The relationship between the elements of culture and institutions is a little like that ball in that they create a whole culture that is greater than the individual parts.

Let's use a simple example to try to make this a little more understandable. This example, by the way, serves as an illustration of cultural relativism in action. You can use this exact same method to gain a better understanding of any culture. Suppose you were an observer of one small situation in United States Anglo culture. Let's take a common example that most of us are familiar with—a marriage ceremony. Imagine that you, as an outsider to the phenomenon of church weddings in the United States are simply observing and collecting facts. (Social scientists would call such observations "data.") Here is a list of just a few facts you might observe in such a situation.

- A priest, minister, or rabbi performs the ceremony.
- The bride has on a diamond engagement ring.

FIGURE 2.3   Culture as Rubber-band Ball

- The bride is wearing a white wedding dress.
- Vows are taken that invoke the name of God.
- There is an exchange of gold rings.
- There is a limousine waiting outside the place of worship.
- The wedding vows include serving one another and being faithful to one another in sickness and health until death.
- The father gives the bride away.
- You overhear someone say that the couple is going to take a honeymoon in Bermuda.

What does all of this have to do with culture? Before we explain that, first we need to introduce another idea that will serve as the basis for any culturally relativistic analysis. Remember that at the beginning of this section, we introduced the idea of a web of culture—the interrelationship of the elements of culture and social institutions. Although culture is not always so readily decipherable, consider the following matrix, or web, (see Figure 2.4) as a way of making sense of your observations.

Think of this matrix as a series of boxes (e.g., family symbols, family values, religious norms, economic values, and so on). Now go back to our observations of the wedding ceremony. If you had to categorize each of those observations, think about in which box you would place each of the observations. More importantly, why would you place an observation in a particular box in the matrix? Some observations are easier than others to categorize because they clearly fit into only one box of the matrix. But as you will see when you do this exercise, other observations may fit in a number of places, or boxes. And when you begin to think further about it, there is considerable overlap between how each of the observations can

Structures/ Institutions	*Non-Material Culture*					*Material Culture*		
	Symbols	Values	Beliefs	Norms	Emotions	Laws	Artifacts	Tech.
Family Kinships								
Educational Systems								
Economic Systems								
Government/ Political Systems								
Religious/Magical Systems								
Sex & Gender Systems								
Healthcare Systems								
Military Systems								
Arts and Leisure Systems								
Non-kinship Associations/ Interest Groups								

FIGURE 2.4   The Web of Culture

be categorized. For example, where would you place the observation that the wedding is taking place in a church or synagogue? Would this be an example of a religious norm? That is, does this observation suggest that, as part of our rules regarding how we practice our faith, many of us feel that we are supposed to get married in a place of worship? Or, perhaps this represents a religious belief? That is, by getting married in a place of worship, we are reaffirming that we collectively accept a Judeo-Christian deity as a common source of spirituality. Or, maybe, this is a religious value—that we agree that it is good and right to get married in the eyes of a Judeo-Christian deity. Perhaps, getting married in church has something to do with our family values, suggesting that Judeo-Christianity should be a focus of our family life.

Keep going a little further with your analysis. What about the diamond engagement ring? Does this say something about the value we place upon material goods and thus reaffirm somewhat our economic institution of capitalism? The father walks the bride down the aisle. Does this connect somehow with our views about who is the head of the family, and with our beliefs about the role of men and women in the family? More so, does it suggest that a certain relationship between men and women is sanctioned by the Judeo-Christian God? Does this notion of women as property—after all, the father is "giving away" his daughter—suggest anything about the extent to which gender inequality may also be viewed as part of the United States' economic institution? Look closely again at the matrix and at this one set of observations. Norms, symbols, values, and beliefs support and reinforce one another. They are upheld and shaped by numerous institutions that are mutually supportive and reinforcing. Taken alone, some of these observations—for example, the bride wearing white, symbolizing virginity (as if most brides were virgins)—may seem odd to an outsider looking in at the culture of the United States. But when examined in the context of the interrelationships between the other elements of culture and institutions, this white dress does not quite seem so odd. Indeed, it seems to make complete sense. Take the remaining observations in the list provided above and see if you can place them in the matrix in Figure. 2.4. When you are finished, try writing a few pages in which you discuss weddings in the United States from a culturally relativistic perspective.

Here's another activity you might try: Think of something from another culture that seems strange or odd to you. Try looking at it in the same way as we have just done and see if it still seems that strange in light of the entire culture.

Return, for a moment, to our analogy of the rubber band ball. Does the analogy make more sense to you now? Culture is a whole, consisting of many parts, yet it is so much greater than the sum of the parts, and at the same time, gives meaning to each of the parts. While it is true that the individual rubber bands may serve a purpose apart from the ball—perhaps to hold some things together—when intertwined in a particular way, they form something that is much greater. Anthropologists refer to this as the *"ethos"* of a culture.

We would like to offer a final thought. In everyday life, people often take things as they appear on the surface. As a result, often people fail to appreciate different cultures. Sometimes, individuals suffer negative consequences because their culture is not appreciated or understood. Looking deeper requires effort and can sometimes make us uncomfortable. It is often simpler to take the easy way and not question or look deeper. However, if you persevere, we believe that your life will be much richer and so will the lives of all peoples. We challenge you to use your cultural relativism so that you can fully experience the joys of culture.

References

Bodley, J. H. (2007). The price of progress. In A. Podolefsky & P. J. Brown, (Eds.), *Applying cultural anthropology* (pp. 267–275). Boston: McGraw Hill.

Bolin, A., & Whelehan, P. (2009). *Human sexuality: Biological, psychological and cultural perspectives.* New York: Rutledge/Francis and Taylor Group.

Department for Professional Employees, AFL-CIO. "Professional Women: Vital Statistics Fact Sheet 2008." http://www.dpeaflcio.org/programs/factsheets/fs_2008_Professional_Women.htm#_edn13. Last accessed July 15, 2008.

Ember, C. R., & Ember, M. (2004). *Cultural anthropology.* Upper Saddle River, NJ: Pearson/Prentice Hall.

Goodale, J. (1971). *Tiwi wives.* Seattle: University of Washington.

Kottack, C. P. (2007). *Mirror for humanity.* Boston: McGraw Hill.

Lavenda, R. H., & Schultz, E. A. (2007). *Core concepts in cultural anthropology.* Boston: McGraw Hill.

Lavenda, R. H., & Schultz, E. A. (2008). *Anthropology: What does it mean to be human?* New York: Oxford University Press.

Lee, R. (2007). Eating Christmas in the Kalahari. In A. Podolefsky & P.J. Brown, (Eds.), *Applying cultural anthropology* (pp. 56–60). Boston: McGraw Hill.

Mead, M. (1963, originally published in 1935). *Sex and temperament in three primitive societies.* New York: Dell Publishing.

Marshall, D. S. (1971). Sexual behavior in Mangaia. In D. S. Marshall & R. Suggs (Eds.), *Human sexual behavior.* New York: Basic Books.

Marshall, D. S. (1993). Sexual aspects of the life cycle. In D. N. Suggs & A. W. Miracle (Eds.), *Culture and human sexuality* (pp. 91–102). Pacific Grove, CA: Brooks-Cole Publishing Company.

Middleton, D. R. (1998). *The challenge of human diversity: Mirrors, bridges, and chasms.* Prospect Heights, IL: Waveland Press, Inc.

Schlegel, A. (1973). The adolescent socialization of the Hopi girl. *Ethnology* 12(4) 449–462.

Tylor, E. B. (1871). *Primitive culture.* London: John Murray.

Weber, M. (1977, orig. 1904). *The protestant ethic and the spirit of capitalism.* New York: Macmillan.

Questions for Discussion

1. Think about how life in the United States has been changed by the computer, the Internet, and mobile phones. Consider all of the ways in which your life is different from your parents' lives when they were your age. Analyze those differences by referring to the institutions (Figure 2.2) and the elements (Figure 2.1) of culture in your discussion.

2. For one week, keep a daily record of at least one example of cultural diversity—i.e., an example of variation from what you regard as "normal" culture—observed while in class, at church, at work, in your home; while driving, traveling; in newspapers and magazines, on television, on the radio; in your interactions with friends, at the movies, at a sporting event, at the doctor's office, and so on. Write down the examples of cultural diversity that you observe. After each example, briefly comment on the following. You do not necessarily have to answer each of these in order; rather, they provide a guide about what you can comment on.

   a. Where did you observe the example of cultural difference?
   b. What culture did it reflect?
   c. Describe the example: is it a behavior or a symbol?
   d. What element of culture (Figure 2.1) does your example suggest (values, beliefs, emotions, norms, etc.)?
   e. What institution (Figure 2.2) does your example suggest (family, education, economics, gender, etc.)?
   f. What type of influence has this cultural behavior had—or is likely to have—on United States society or on your life?

3. For one week, keep a record of ethnocentric comments that you observe (or make yourself), in newspapers, political speeches, classroom discussions and lectures, comments from religious

groups and sermons in church, in encounters with friends and family members, and so on. (Examples: blaming Japanese work ethics for problems in the United States auto industry, criticizing another country's economic or political values, condemning people for having values or sexual orientations different from your own, referring to a religion other than your own as weird, and so on.)

4. Think about what you eat. Generate a list of food items: any will do, e.g. steak, chocolate cake, salad, etc.

    a. For each of your food items, refer to the elements of culture (Figure 2.1). For example, you will find that food is more than just caloric subsistence. It has meaning. Apple pie is a dessert, but it is also a symbol, and it carries a value. What is that value? There are also norms around eating it. People in the United States usually eat dessert *after* the "main" course. See how many elements of culture your food items can be related to.

    b. Relate each of your food items to some of the institutions of culture (Figure 2.2). For example, think about the institution of sex and gender. Is food gendered? Is some food sexy? Or, perhaps, does food relate to the institution of religion? See how many institutions you can relate to your list of food items.

5. Identify countries that have experienced the effects of colonization and globalization over the last few hundred years. Make list of what changes have occurred, and discuss who has benefitted and who has been disadvantaged by such changes, and how. Why do you think these developments have occurred? Identify positive and negative changes within particular nations, societies and cultures that have been affected by globalization.

Acknowledgements

We would like to thank Elon University College Fellows student Leigh Lampley for her thorough review of this chapter, including insightful and critical comments, a keen eye for detail and her fine computer skills.

Suggested Readings

Anderson, B. G. (2002). *Around the world in 30 years: Life as a cultural anthropologist.* Prospect Heights, IL: Waveland Press, Inc.

Boulanger, C. L. (Ed.). (2008). *Reflecting on america: Anthropological views of U.S. culture.* Boston: Pearson Education Inc.

DeVita, P. R., & Armstrong, J. D. (2002). *Distant mirrors: America as a foreign culture.* Belmont, CA: Wadsworth Publishing Co.

Gmelch, S. (2004). *Tourists and tourism: A reader.* Long Grove, IL: Waveland Press, Inc.

Grindal, B., & Salamone, F. (1995). *Bridges to humanity: Narrative on anthropology and friendship.* Prospect Heights, IL: Waveland Press, Inc.

Middleton, D. R. (1998). *The challenge of human diversity: Mirrors, bridges, and chasms.* Prospect Heights, IL: Waveland Press, Inc.

Robbins, R. (2008). *Global problems and the culture of capitalism.* Boston: Pearson Education Inc.

Ritzer, G. (2000). *The McDonaldization of society.* Thousand Oaks, CA: Pine Forge Press.

Van Der Elst, D. with Bohannan, P. (1999). *Culture as given, Culture as choice.* Prospect Heights, IL: Waveland Press, Inc.

3

Reading, Writing, and Researching the Global Experience

Jean Schwind

In *Covering*, civil rights scholar Kenji Yoshino describes his friendship in college with a young woman who shared his Asian-American background and his love for British literature: "Our evenings were filled with the happiness of people learning to read, to write. We read to each other from opposite ends of a couch, like a two-headed disputatious literary creature" (121). What's most striking about this account (besides his peculiar notion of a good time) is Yoshino's claim that he learned to read and write in college. A graduate of Exeter, a prestigious prep school in New Hampshire, and Harvard, Yoshino obviously knew how to read and write very well before college. When he claims to have learned these skills at Harvard, he's speaking about a particular type of reading and writing. There are many different kinds of reading and writing because we engage in these activities for a wide variety of purposes. Reading and writing personal texts (such as journals, memoirs, letters, or blogs) can enhance self-understanding and deepen our sense of connection to others. Ad copy creates desire for consumer goods and services. Academic reading and writing—the subject of Yoshino's memories of Harvard—involve a process of active inquiry and meaning construction that's diametrically opposed to passive conceptions of "receiving" knowledge. This kind of reading and writing requires that you morph into a "disputatious" (or questioning) creature as Yoshino did at Harvard. The goal of this chapter is to help you to understand and achieve this metamorphosis.

Reading for a Global Perspective

The challenges of Global Studies for twenty-first century citizens of the United States are considerable. Responsible global citizenship requires that we read and think *contextually*, that we understand the extent to which we're shaped by world events. American culture, however, encourages ideals of self-determination and individual freedom that vastly underestimate the way social and historical circumstances influence our lives. This chapter begins with a brief exercise designed to highlight the difficulty of contextual thinking in our culture. Avoid reading further in this chapter until you've completed this exercise.

EXERCISE 1:   Photo Analysis—The Way You Were

Assignment: Select an interesting, hilarious, or cringe-worthy photograph of your adolescent self. (Although the onset and end of adolescence vary from individual to individual and from culture to culture, in the United States it generally coincides with middle school and high school. You may have limited access to old photos at college: select the best one of those available; if necessary, ask a parent to select and send a digital photo by e-mail.) Write a brief essay in which you: 1) carefully describe the most important details of the picture; 2) analyze the significance of these details by explaining what they convey about who you were at that time—your beliefs, values, hopes, and fears.

This assignment is modeled after a final exam that I give in an interdisciplinary seminar on American adolescence. Students carefully examine the details of a photo of their 11–18-year-old self, and explain how the various sociological, psychological, and historical theories of adolescence and the coming-of-age films and stories that we've studied illuminate the person in the picture. The essays that students produce are insightful, touching, and fascinating. They combine description (of a brightly patterned, "old lady" dress—a grandmother's gift—that provoked a mother-daughter fight before Easter Sunday service and a memorable barb from a peer afterwards: "You look like a big bag of M&Ms!"; of the clownish grin and jaunty wave that masks the embarrassed distress of a chubby boy in a lifejacket who can't hoist himself from the lake into the motorboat beside him) and analysis (theories of parent-adolescent relations, peer relations, and body image used to explain the significance of the details described) in a way that teaches me about my students at the same time that it enables me to evaluate their command of course material.

This year, as I read through the tall stack of exams and studied the photographs that accompanied them, I was struck by what my students left out of their photo analyses. The years in which they had come of age were momentous for our country: 9/11 permanently shattered assumptions about our national security; the Columbine massacre in 1999 made lockdown drills as routine as fire drills in middle schools and high schools; the disputed presidential election of 2000 deepened cynicism about the American political process. My course emphasizes the historical and economic forces that "invented" adolescence in the early twentieth century and the cultural changes that continuously "reinvent" or revise the adolescent experience. Yet not one of my fifty-two students wrote about how the adolescent self captured within the photo had been affected by a national or global event that had occurred outside the frame of the shot. The pudgy boy (now a trim and athletic college senior) dogpaddling in the lake didn't consider himself within the context of the fast-food, junk-food, video game culture that had literally shaped him. The Easter Sunday photo of a thirteen-year old African-American girl in a matronly "M&M" dress was taken in the same spring of 1998 that James Byrd, Jr. was murdered by three white men who chained him by the ankles to their pickup truck and dragged him naked for three miles down a road in Jasper, Texas. Yet in her essay my student blames her fashion-clueless mother and grandmother for her "ugliness." She doesn't consider how racism contributes to her insecurity about her appearance. The Jessica Simpson ideal of beauty, daunting for most women, is utterly unattainable for her.

Examine your own photo analysis. Did you explain who you were at age 12 (or 14 or 16) by referring to specific political, social, or economic forces of the time that influenced your thoughts and actions? Did you consider, for example, how electronic communication shaped the quantity and quality of your relationships with the friends and family who appear with you in the photo? How the global economy represented by the material artifacts in the photo (as I write this paragraph, I'm wearing a t-shirt made in Macao and shorts made in Indonesia) has affected your family life, education, and career plans? Does anxiety about environmental deterioration and reliance on nonrenewable energy sources complicate the hope for the future celebrated in rites-of-passage shots of bar/bat mitzvahs, newly-licensed driving, prom, or high school graduation?

If you're like the students in my adolescence seminar, you wrote about the personal relationships, individual achievements and ambitions, and internal struggles that the photo depicts, without reflecting upon the larger sociohistorical forces that shaped the moment captured in that picture. This failure to examine the self within a larger world context can't be attributed to individual ignorance, however. *No* student in the fifty-plus that I taught described national or global issues that informed the world of their adolescent self and their place in that world. The unanimity of this detached perspective on the self points to a deficiency in our ways of seeing and reading the self that is cultural, and not individual.

In a recent study of the transition from high school to college, sociologist Tim Clydesdale argues that our culture encourages teens to "view politics, national issues, and global issues as important in theory but irrelevant to their present daily lives" (26). According to Clydesdale, this political and social disengagement is fostered by mainstream American culture, which urges us to adopt very narrow and private perspectives on who we are and what we're about:

> The current default settings in the United States install a popular American moral culture that: celebrates personal effort and individual achievement; … values loyalty to family, friends, and coworkers; expects personal moral freedom; distrusts large organizations and bureaucracies; and conveys the message that happiness and fulfillment are found primarily in personal relationships and individual consumption. (3)

The photo analyses written by my students highlight the most important consequence of the hyperindividualistic culture that Clydesdale describes: our belief in powers of self-determination engenders indifference to and ignorance of world forces that determine our identity and destiny.

Within the context of a culture that discounts political and social issues as irrelevant to personal well being, developing an awareness of "what it means to live in the biggest house in the global village" is enormously difficult (Clydesdale 6). Developing this awareness is also imperative, and it should be the aim of all the reading you'll do in an introduction to Global Studies. Peter Singer argues in *One World: The Ethics of Globalization* that self-interest demands that we understand the global village we inhabit, even if we disavow any responsibility to those who live outside the big house. Defending this claim, Singer cites a United Nations report issued just before the September 11 attacks: "In the global village, someone else's poverty very soon becomes one's own problem: of lack of markets for one's products, illegal immigration, pollution, contagious disease, insecurity, fanaticism, terrorism" (7).

Both self-interest and responsible citizenship in the era of globalization explain *why* we must resist cultural pressures to regard what's happening in Myanmar and Zimbabwe as irrelevant and read widely and deeply about the world. Two fundamental questions about reading in a global context remain: *What* do we read? *How* do we read?

Texts of many different types illuminate the global experience, including books and articles by scholars and journalists; documents published by national governments and international organizations; and artistic works (literature, film, ads, music). The interdisciplinary nature of Global Studies virtually guarantees that your assigned readings will reflect diverse disciplinary perspectives. The authors you'll study will employ a variety of strategies and methodologies to discover and communicate knowledge about world issues. To counteract cultural forces that encourage preoccupation with personal consumption and entertainment, required reading in many Global Studies courses begins with international newspapers. An assignment frequently used on my campus, for example, is the "Global News Report." Students in a class are divided into three-member teams, and each team monitors one news source throughout the semester. At the beginning of every class period, each team presents a brief (one or two minute) report on the major headlines from their news source and answers questions about these top stories. Teams select their news source (usually an English-language Web site of a paper from another country) from the long list of international newspapers available online at http://www.world-newspapers.com.

EXERCISE 2:   Comparative News Reading

Assignment: Read Chinedu "Ocek" Eke's Chapter 6, "Global Media and Global News: A Guide to Decoding and Analyzing Information," for an introduction to studying cultural differences in news coverage. Then carefully follow the "top stories" of *USA Today* (http://www.usatoday.com/) and *one* of these international news sources for one week:

Region	News source	Location
Arab world	Aljazeera	http://english.aljazeera.net/HomePage
Africa	allAfrica.com	http://allafrica.com
China	China Daily	http://www.chinadaily.com.cn/english/home/index.html
Cuba	Granma International	http://www.granma.cu/ingles/index.html
Great Britain	BBC	http://www.news.bbc.co.uk/
India	India Abroad	http://us.rediff.com/news/index.html
Japan	Japan Times	http://www.japantimes.co.jp/news.html
Russia	Moscow Times	http://www.moscowtimes.ru/indexes/01.html

Each day, record the headlines of the top stories on each of the two Web sites and perform a brief content analysis of each story by answering these questions in writing: Does the story focus on national or international news? What is its subject: the economy, politics and government, weather, popular culture, or something else?

At the week's end, examine the data that you have collected. What does it suggest about the interests, values, and attitudes of each newspaper's readers? Write a 2–3 page comparative analysis in which you: 1) Clearly present your data on the top stories of the week in the two newspapers that you examined (a table or chart may be the most effective way to do this); 2) Explain the significance of the most important similarities and differences between the headline news in these two papers.

The purpose of the "Global News Reports" and similar assignments is fairly straightforward. They aim to help you to develop lifelong habits of newspaper reading and awareness of how differences in national and cultural perspectives can affect perception of current events. The reasons for reading fiction (Monica Ali's *Brick Lane*, for example, or Dave Eggers's *What Is the What*) to understand our world might be less apparent. In fact, some editors and writers have suggested that reading invented stories is frivolous and irresponsible in a world facing urgent problems. V. S. Naipaul, winner of the 2001 Nobel Prize in literature, has repudiated fiction writing (though he is the author of remarkable novels) because he believes that only nonfiction can represent the complexities of today's world (Donadio "Irascible Prophet"). British novelist Ian McEwen has admitted that after the terrorist attacks on 9/11 he read only history books (especially histories of imperialism) and books about Islam. He found it "wearisome to confront invented characters" at a time when he was desperate "to be told about the world. I wanted to be informed. I felt that we had gone through great changes, and now was the time to just go back to school, as it were, and start to learn" (Donadio "Truth").

Made-up stories do more than entertain, however. Global citizenship is impossible without genuine concern for the welfare of people who are distant from us. And—contrary to the old saying—distance rarely makes our hearts "grow fonder" of those who are historically, geographically, economically, or culturally remote. Distance often weakens human ties. We feel and act compassionately on behalf of those whom we know and care about, and literature can promote identification with those we might otherwise regard as alien and "other." Martha Nussbaum, a professor of law and ethics at the University of Chicago, explains how reading literature—especially realist novels, which provide rich details of the everyday lives, thoughts, and struggles of ordinary people—inspires compassion and commitment to social justice (34). Nussbaum's conclusions about the value of reading Dickens's *Hard Times*, which describes the lives of factory workers in early-industrial England, equally apply to stories about the lives of women in Taliban-controlled Kabul (Khaled Hosseini's *A Thousand Splendid Suns*) or about an illegal immigrant from Nepal working in New York restaurant kitchens (Kiran Desai's *An Inheritance of Loss*):

> Novels ... present persistent forms of human need and desire realized in specific social situations. These situations frequently, indeed usually, differ a great deal from the reader's own.
>
> Novels, recognizing this, in general construct and speak to an implicit reader who shares with the characters certain hopes, fears, and general human concerns, and who for that reason is able to form bonds of identification and sympathy with them, but who is also

situated elsewhere and needs to be informed about the concrete situation of the characters. In this way, the very structure of the interaction between the text and its imagined reader invites the reader to see how the mutable features of society and circumstance bear on the realization of shared hopes and desires. (7)

By helping us to understand, in a very personal, emotional way, how human aspirations are constrained by poverty, religious and racial bigotry, sexism, and other forces, imagined stories encourage us to care about distant and disadvantaged others. While compassion isn't a sufficient response to injustice and suffering, it is a necessary precondition for activism.

Literature has a legitimate and important place in Global Studies, and Chapter 5 in this book, by Rosemary Haskell, focuses on strategies for reading literature from a Global Studies perspective. Much of your reading in interdisciplinary Global Studies courses, however, will be nonfiction investigations of world issues and problems written by economists, political scientists, historians, religious scholars, sociologists, and other experts. Reading these texts well involves more than storing in your head facts and information that they provide. Engaged reading is very different from fact storage, and developing your ability to read critically (as Yoshino learned with his best friend at Harvard) is a principal aim of this course.

An image that provides a vivid metaphor for popular misconceptions of reading is the controversial cover photo by Annie Leibovitz that appeared on the cover of *Vogue* in April 2008. See Figure 3.1 for a parody of this notorious *Vogue* cover. (You can easily find the original photo on the Web, where it's posted on hundreds of sites.) Victor Juhasz's cartoon presents Anna Wintour, editor-in-chief of U.S. *Vogue*, and Si Newhouse, CEO of Condé Nast, the company that owns *Vogue*. Wintour and Newhouse are respectively posed as LeBron James and Gisele Bündchen, who appear in the original Leibovitz photo.

Most of the debate about Leibovitz's photo has focused on the purported racism of its depiction of NBA star LeBron James. James's fierce expression and aggressive stance seem generally to be inspired by King Kong and more specifically to allude to H. R. Hopp's famous World War I recruitment poster (Figure 3.2). "Destroy This Mad Brute" (1916) depicts a Kong-like gorilla wearing a German helmet. He brandishes a bloody club in one arm and bears a ravished woman (the color of her gown suggests that this is Lady Liberty, nabbed from her granite pedestal) in the other as he wades onto America shores. The ruins of Europe appear in the background.

Gisele Bündchen, the Brazilian supermodel who appears on the *Vogue* cover with James, generated little commentary as media analysts and bloggers focused on the racial stereotypes embedded in the photo. Bündchen deserves some belated attention here because she embodies a feminine ideal that shares an important trait in common with traditional notions of reading: passivity. While James is *active* in the photo—dribbling the basketball, embracing a beautiful woman—Bündchen is *acted upon*. She's pulled by James and pushed by a strong wind that sweeps back her hair and dress. James exerts power (he controls the ball and the babe), and Bündchen submits to power. Juhasz's parody calls attention to these stereotypical gender roles by reversing them: Anna Wintour is scowling with menace, driving the ball with manicured nails (in spiked heels, no less), and sweeping her diminutive boss off his feet.

If reading sometimes seems boring or mindless, this is often because of the mistaken assumption that our relationship to the author of a text resembles the dynamic between Bündchen and James. It's no accident that reading has long been stereotyped as a feminine, sissy

FIGURE 3.1 Victor Juhasz's Cartoon of the April 2008
Vogue cover. (*Source:* Illustration by Victor Juhasz for THE
NEW YORK OBSERVER)

pastime favored by those who prefer vicarious experience to the grit and risk of acting in the real world. In this idea of reading, readers mirror Bündchen in the *Vogue* photo: we passively absorb texts like she absorbs manhandling and wind gusts (or like a sponge soaks up water). Engaged reading is the opposite of passive absorption: it requires us to question, challenge, respond, extend, and otherwise interact critically and creatively with an author's ideas. As Yoshino puts it, engaged reading requires us to become "disputatious." The kind of reading that Global Studies requires is more like suiting up and playing with James than submitting to a superior power.

Reading involves two related activities: *carefully listening* to the ideas and arguments of a writer and *thoughtfully responding* to them. We always listen and respond at the same time as we read, and this simultaneity is most apparent when we have an instant or "gut" reaction (either positive or negative) to a text. For example, you might be immediately struck by the brilliance with which Thomas L. Friedman skewers President Bush by extending the President's own metaphor in "Mr. Bush: Lead or Leave" (*New York Times*, June 22, 2008). Or you

0088718   WORLD WAR I: RECRUITMENT.
Credit: The Granger Collection, New York

FIGURE 3.2 "Destroy this Mad Brute": WW I Recruiting Poster. (*Source:* The Granger Collection, New York)

might be put off by the harshness of Friedman's characterization of the President as "our addict-in-chief." Friedman recalls that in 2006 Bush declared that the United States was "addicted to oil." He argues that a new energy policy that President Bush hoped to implement by July 4, 2008—which urges Saudi Arabia ("our chief oil pusher") to lower the cost of oil by increasing supplies and pressures Congress to lift bans on drilling offshore and in the Arctic Wildlife Refuge—increases our addiction to foreign oil at a time when the we should be checking into detox:

> It's as if our addict-in-chief is saying to us: "C'mon guys, you know you want a little more of the good stuff. One more hit, baby. Just one more toke on the ole oil pipe. I promise, next year, we'll

all go straight. I'll even put a wind turbine on my presidential library. But for now, give me one more pop from that drill, please, baby. Just one more transfusion of that sweet offshore crude."

At other times, listening and responding to an author might seem to be sequential activities. When a text is complex or focused on an unfamiliar subject, you'll spend more time reflecting on it before you respond to it.

Rhetoricians Wayne C. Booth and Marshall W. Gregory call these two overlapping stages of reading *understanding* and *overstanding* a text (89–93). *Understanding* is the listening stage, where you analyze the text and work hard to comprehend the author's intent. *Overstanding* is the responding stage, where you evaluate, question, or challenge the text.

To <u>understand</u> a nonfiction text, try to answer these questions as you read:

1. What is the writer's purpose? What does the writer want you to think, feel, or do about the subject of the text?
2. What kind of argument is the author making? (Establishing the type of argument you're examining will help you to evaluate its effectiveness.)
   - Is it an **argument that reports or informs?** For example, "Albanian Custom Fades: Woman as Family Man" by Dan Bilefsky (*New York Times*, June 25, 2008) explains "the tradition of the sworn virgin" that has been practiced in northern Albania for over 500 years. In families without a male head, women would take a vow of lifelong virginity and "swap genders," assuming male dress, demeanor, and authority.
   - Is it an **argument about policy?** In "Strengthening Extremists" (*New York Times*, June 19, 2008), Nicholas D. Kristof argues that U.S. support of Israel's long siege of Gaza has increased regional support for Hamas and Iran.
   - Is it an **argument that defines?** Thomas L. Friedman defines "The New Cold War" between the United States and Iran in an article of that title (*New York Times*, May 14, 2008).
   - Is it an **argument about causation?** Samantha Power contends that Western indifference and inaction were responsible for the massacre in Rwanda, in "Bystanders to Genocide" (*Atlantic Monthly*, September, 2001).
   - Is it an **interpretative argument?** George Will argues in "March of the Polar Bears" (*Washington Post*, May 22, 2008) that the "green left" uses the Endangered Species Act as a "license to intrude" on private enterprise.
   - Is it an **evaluative argument?** Laura Boyes explains why *Outsourced* is a "delightful" romantic comedy about economic globalization in "Undiscovered Countries" (*Independent Weekly*, July 9, 2008).
3. What evidence does the writer offer to support the argument's central claims? Is it convincing? Adequate? Consider graphic evidence (for example, charts, graphs, and pictures) as well as written text.
4. What strategies does the writer use to make the argument clear and persuasive? What strategies seem to backfire by causing you to resist or oppose the argument rather than endorse it? Consider the use of examples, analogies, anecdotes, statistics, and humor.
5. How do the tone, style, and structure of the argument convey the personality, values, and attitudes of the writer? Does the writer come across as engaging and fair? Contemptuous or hypercritical? Reasonable? Emotional?

"Overstanding" a Nonfiction Text: Reflective Questioning

Reading actively requires you to enter into a dialogue or conversation with a writer. This means that "talking back" to a text—whether in classroom discussions or written responses—is as important as considerately listening to what the writer is saying. This "back talk" can take a variety of different forms. It can be adversarial when you disagree with a writer's central position or a supporting argument or affirmative when you endorse or wish to extend the writer's ideas. Back talk sometimes speculates about the validity of a writer's unspoken assumptions; at other times it examines unexplored consequences of a writer's position. Whatever form it takes, back talk always goes beyond summarizing the main points of an argument to question and evaluate those points from your perspective as a reader.

"Back talk" is a term that is often used to describe a disrespectful response to someone in a position of authority, such as a parent, teacher, or coach. When you first attempt it, the response that critical or engaged reading requires might seem like back talk of this impudent, negative sort. How can a college student (or, for that matter, a college English teacher like me) with minimal background in economics presume to question or judge the analysis of global poverty offered by Paul Collier in *The Bottom Billion: Why the Poorest Countries Are Failing and What Can Be Done About It?* Collier directs the Center for the Study of African Economies at Oxford University and is a former director of development research at the World Bank. Talking back to Collier by commenting on his argument is as intimidating (and potentially humiliating) as the prospect of shooting baskets with LeBron James. Responsive reading is actually the opposite of sassy disregard for superior authority or experience, however. Thoughtful response demonstrates respect for writers by acknowledging that their ideas are worth attention and reflection.

Responding to texts in an insightful and original way depends on a fundamental intellectual, professional, and personal skill: asking good questions. The centrality of question-posing to critical analysis is emphasized by Jeffrey D. Sachs in *The End of Poverty*. The "clinical economics" that Sachs practices—and which he advocates as a remedy for world poverty—is inspired not only by his frustration with one-size-fits-all prescriptions of the International Monetary Fund (which requires debtor countries to cut budgets, repay loans, liberalize trade policies, and privatize state-owned enterprises without regard to the specific contexts) but by his wife (83–89). Sachs was struck by the difference between the way the IMF operates and the way his wife conducts her medical practice. She'd ask pages of questions ("Are you taking any medications?"; "Do you have any allergies?"; "Do you have a family history of the following diseases?") before presuming to diagnose a patient's problem and prescribing a cure. Borrowing from the clinical medicine model, Sachs developed a checklist of questions on topics ranging from physical geography (such as "What are the transport conditions in the country?" and "How much of the population is proximate to seaports, airports, paved roads, navigable rivers, and rail services?") to questions about cultural barriers to economic development (such as "Is the society torn apart by class, caste, ethnicity, religion, or gender inequality?") to determine the extent and causes of national poverty, so that remedies might address critical barriers to poverty reduction.

Using Tagmemics: Atomizing and Contextualizing

Asking good questions generates textual "back talk" in the same way that it initiates medical and economic diagnoses. By raising questions about the validity and significance of a writer's claims or about the evidence and persuasive strategies used to advance those claims, you interact with the text in a dynamic and critical way. Learning to ask the "right" questions—questions that promote insight and evaluation—of a medical patient, a national economy, or an assigned text is a skill that improves with practice. A useful tool for acquiring this valuable skill is tagmemics. Originally a linguistic theory developed by Kenneth L. Pike, tagmemics has been adapted by rhetoricians as an invention strategy to help writers explore a subject.

This adaptation of tagmemics (also called particle-wave-field analysis) postulates that all subjects (including texts) can be examined in three ways. First, they can be *atomized*, or examined as complex wholes made up of smaller "atomic" elements or particles. For example, the April 2008 *Vogue* cover is made up of dozens of compositional elements besides the Leibovitz photograph: headlines in various font styles, sizes, and colors surround and overlap the photo; the design layout puts James's crotch at the visual center of the cover and superimposes the photo over the *Vogue* masthead (which is orange to match the basketball); the silver-gray background descends into dark shadows at James's feet. Second, all subjects can also be *contextualized or situated in time*. That is, they can be analyzed within their specific historical context. The historical context of the *Vogue* cover includes the magazine's 116-year publication history. (James is the third man—and the first black man—to appear on its cover; Richard Gere and George Clooney preceded him.) It also includes African-American history and art history (the famous recruitment poster evoked by the photo's composition and celebrity photography). Finally, all subjects can be *contextualized or situated in place*. That is, they can be studied within their cultural context. The significance of the social context of this *Vogue* cover—the politics of race and sex in the contemporary United States, where another black male and another white female were battling for the 2008 Democratic presidential nomination—becomes evident when you compare it to the April 2008 issues of *Vogue* published in Australia, Japan, India, and elsewhere. The Leibovitz photo doesn't appear on the covers of international editions. The UK *Vogue* for April 2008 features a headshot of Victoria Beckham.

To see how atomizing and contextualizing operate as a method of generating questions about a text, read "Can America Learn from Shabbat?" by Rabbi Arthur Waskow. The full essay from which this excerpt is taken appears in a book about "time poverty" in the United States, edited by John de Graaf: *Take Back Your Time: Fighting Overwork and Time Poverty in America.*

Can America Learn from Shabbat?

by Rabbi Arthur Waskow

Several years ago, I went to a folk song festival in Philadelphia. Many of the singers sang labor songs of the 1930s, civil rights songs of the 1960s, and peace songs of many decades. The audience sang along, nostalgia strong in the air. Then Charlie King began singing a song with the refrain, "Whatever happened to the eight-hour day? When did they take it away? ... When did we give it away?"

The audience roared with passion, not nostalgia. This was about our own lives, not something from the past. I was startled. Suddenly I saw that my own sense of hyper-overwork, of teetering on the edge of burnout, was not mine alone. Suddenly I saw that everything I had learned about the joys of Sabbath were not just for lighting private Jewish candles at the dinner table and chanting private Torah in the synagogue.

I began to talk with others, especially with scholars who have studied overwork as a growing problem in American society, and people whose religious and spiritual traditions call for time to reflect, to be calm, to refrain from Doing and Making in order to Be and to Love.

Out of those discussions came an effort that brought Christians, Muslims, Buddhists, Jews, Unitarians, and spiritually rooted "secular" intellectuals together to redress the rhythms of work time and time for family, community, the Spirit. By freeing time, we thought, we could help free people.

Free time. Not just through the ancient practice of the Sabbath, but also through new ways—befitting an industrial/informational economy—of pausing from overwork and overstress. . . .

The Scriptures Say . . .

For all the religious traditions that take the Hebrew Scriptures seriously, there is a teaching we call *Shabbat*. (The word is usually translated into English as "Sabbath," and comes from the Hebrew verb for pausing or ceasing.)

In Exodus 20: 8–11, the reason given for the Sabbath is to recall Creation; in Deuteronomy 5: 12–15, it is to free all of us from slavery. In the Jewish mystical tradition, it is taught that these seemingly two separate meanings are in fact one. Meditate on them, and we can see them that way.

And we are taught not only the seventh-day Shabbat; there are also the seventh year and the seven-times-seven plus one year, the fiftieth year, the Jubilee.

In the seventh year, the land must be allowed to catch its breath and rest, to make a Shabbat for God, the Breath of Life. Since nearly everyone in ancient Israel was a shepherd or a farmer, this meant that almost the whole society rested. Since no one was giving orders and no one was obeying them, hierarchies of bosses and workers vanished.

In this year-long Shabbat, even debt—the frozen form of stored-up hierarchy—was annulled. Those who, because of poverty, had been forced to borrow money were released from the need to repay; those who, out of wealth, had been pressed into lending were released from the need to collect.

And in the fiftieth year, the land could breathe freely once again and not be worked. All land was redistributed in equally productive shares, clan by clan, as it had originally been held (Lev. 25 and 26: 34–35, 43–45; Deut. 15: 1–18). This year was called "yovel," usually rendered in English as the "Jubilee."

These year-long Jubilee observances that the Bible calls "shabbat shabbaton," "Sabbath to the Sabbatical power," or "deeply restful rest" are times of enacting social justice, and times of freeing the earth from human exploitation. They are times of release from attachments and habits, addictions and idolatries.

Indeed, in these socially revolutionary passages of Torah, the text never uses the word "tzedek" (justice), but instead the words "shmitah" and "dror," which mean "release." It is what

Buddhists today call "nonattachment." The deepest root of social justice, according to these biblical passages, is the profoundly restful experience of abandoning control over others and over the earth. And, conversely, the deepest meditation intended to free us from our egos cannot be experienced as long as we are egotistically bossing other human beings or the planet.

Balance

The tradition of Shabbat did not teach that restfulness and utter nonattachment was the only worthy path to walk. Rather, the tradition was rooted in an earthy sense of sacred work as well as sacred rest. Indeed, the tradition taught a rhythm, a spiral of Doing and Being in which the next stage of Doing would always be higher and deeper, because a time of Being had preceded it....

According to Evan Eisenberg's book *The Ecology of Eden*, this rhythm of Shabbat may have emerged from an effort of Western Semitic communities to cope with the emergence of monocrop agriculture in the Sumerian empire. Semitic small hill-farmers, shepherds, and nomads had to face the new high-efficiency agriculture with its emphasis on population growth, ownership, and armies.

The question was what should the communities of Canaan do? They could ignore the new efficiency and go under. They could imitate it and disappear. Or they could learn what was valuable and Godly within it and absorb that into their own lives in ways that kept their culture both sacred and distinctive.

So, one year [out of] every seven, they pretended to become hunters and gatherers again. They would eat only what grew freely from uncultivated land. They re-affirmed their age-old teaching that God alone, and no human being, owned the land. They came through this profound challenge to their sacred life path changed, but intact as a people whose Sabbatical restfulness was precisely a sign of their covenant with God.

The Crisis of Modernity

In the last century, all traditional communities on Planet Earth have been living through an analogous crisis. The great leap in economic efficiency and military mastery that came with Modernity played the same role in shattering the ways of Rabbinic Judaism, Christianity, Islam, and Buddhism that Sumerian efficiency and power played in the ancient Semitic communities.

Thus it is not surprising that just as we realize the extent of today's new Global Gobble of human communities and of the earth itself, just as the Nazi Holocaust and the H-Bomb and sweatshops and the burning of the Amazon basin and the privatization of water supplies and global warming come to pass, the need for rest, reflection, and calm comes back into our consciousness.

Already, in 1951, in the aftermath of those grotesque mockeries of Making—the Holocaust and Hiroshima—Rabbi Abraham Joshua Heschel (who later marched alongside Martin Luther King against racism and the Vietnam War) wrote in his book *The Sabbath*.

> To set apart one day a week for freedom, a day on which we would not use the instruments which have been so easily turned into weapons of destruction, a day for being with ourselves, a day of detachment from the vulgar, of independence of external obligations, a day on which we stop worshipping the idols of technical civilization, a day on which we use no money ... on

which [humanity] avows [its] independence of that which is the world's chief idol ... a day of armistice in the economic struggle with our fellow [humans] and the forces of nature—is there any institution that holds out a greater hope for [humanity's] progress than the Sabbath?

Christianity, Islam, and Rabbinic Judaism all reinterpreted these biblical teachings in their own ways. But all of them, as well as Buddhism and perhaps all the world's other spiritual traditions, taught the necessity of periodically, rhythmically calming oneself for inward reflection, for time to Love and time to Be.

Tagmemics helps us to identify and consider three kinds of questions about Waskow's subject—rest—as we read his essay: 1) atomizing or definitional questions about the distinctive features and component parts of rest; 2) contextual questions about how rest has changed over time; 3) contextual questions about how ideas of rest vary from place to place. See the following list for examples of each type of question. Raising questions like these will focus your response to readings in class discussion and papers.

Atomizing and Contexualizing "Can America Learn from Shabbat?"

Atomizing rest (What are its distinctive features and components parts?)

1. Define rest. How do popular and secular notions of rest compare and contrast to the spiritual conceptions of rest emphasized by Shabbat? Does our culture respect contemplative and spiritual notions of downtime?
2. Describe your last truly restful experience. Extrapolate from this experience to identify the essential characteristics of rest.
3. What is the purpose of rest? Why does Waskow consider it an essential part of human freedom? How does "freeing time ... help free people"? How does it promote social justice and creativity?
4. List a variety of activities that might be considered types or subsets of rest. Does rest vary according to sex, socioeconomic class, age, and other variables? Explain.

Contextualizing rest in time (How has it changed over time?)

5. Answer the questions raised by the chorus of the song that Waskow quotes: "What ever happened to the eight-hour day? *When* did they take it away?... *When* did we give it away?" (emphasis added). Why and when did doing nothing become suspect?
6. What is multitasking? Why is it a late twentieth-century phenomenon? Is it good? Bad? Neither? Both? Explain.
7. What do you know about how your grandparents and parents spent Sundays during their childhood and adolescence? How do their Sundays in the 1930s–1970s compare and contrast to yours? What accounts for these similarities and differences?
8. Waskow argues that Canaanites invented the Sabbath as a means of coping with a cultural crisis. Explain this theory of the genesis of the "day of rest." What "analogous crisis" is being experienced by contemporary cultures? How might reclaiming the Sabbath help us to resolve this crisis?

Contextualizing rest in place (Does it vary cross-culturally?)

9. "Americans are a queer people; they can't rest," according to Canadian writer Stephen Leacock ("Power of Rest" 77). That Benjamin Franklin is popularly credited with inventing the rocking chair confirms this perception: Americans can't even *sit* still. Does your personal experience square with this assessment of our national character? If so, explain why this might be true. If not, explain why.

10. How do American adults typically spend leisure time? What's the difference between these leisure activities and genuinely restful activities?

11. Another contributor to *Take Back Your Time* describes the "growing international work-time gap" (Hayden 203). While average fulltime work hours have fallen dramatically in many European Union countries, South Korea, and Japan over the last thirty years, hours on the job have increased in the United States. Why is this? Do other national cultures seem to value rest more than the United States does? Offer specific cross-cultural examples to defend your answer.

EXERCISE 3:   Generating Questions in Responsive Reading

Read E. Benjamin Skinner's "A World Enslaved" (from *Foreign Policy*, March/April 2008, 62–67). Following the example of the three types of questions raised by Waskow's essay on rest, use tagmemics to pose, in writing, three questions about Skinner's article:

- one "atomizing" question focused on specific detail of Skinner's account of modern slavery that you find especially interesting, important, or puzzling;
- two "contextualizing in time" and/or "contextualizing in place" questions that inquire about historical and/or cross-cultural dimensions of the problem Skinner presents.

Write a brief (1–2 page) response to the question that most interests you.

A World Enslaved
by E. Benjamin Skinner

Standing in New York City, you are five hours away from being able to negotiate the sale, in broad daylight, of a healthy boy or girl. He or she can be used for anything, though sex and domestic labor are most common. Before you go, let's be clear on what you are buying. A slave is a human being forced to work through fraud or threat of violence for no pay beyond subsistence. Agreed? Good.

Most people imagine that slavery died in the 19th century. Since 1817, more than a dozen international conventions have been signed banning the slave trade. Yet, today there are more slaves than at any time in human history.

And if you're going to buy one in five hours, you'd better get a move on. First, hail a taxi to JFK International Airport, and hop on a direct flight to Port-au-Prince, Haiti. The flight takes three hours. After landing at Toussaint L'Ouverture International Airport, you will need 50 cents for the most common form of transport in Port-au-Prince, the tap-tap, a flatbed pickup retrofitted with benches and a canopy. Three quarters of the way up Route de Delmas, the capital's main street, tap the roof and hop out. There, on a side street, you will find a group of men standing in front of LeRéseau (The Network) barbershop. As you approach, a man steps forward: "Are you looking to get a person?"

Meet Benavil Lebhom. He smiles easily. He has a trim mustache and wears a multicolored, striped golf shirt, a gold chain, and Doc Martens knockoffs. Benavil is a courtier [sic], or broker. He holds an official real estate license and calls himself an employment agent. Two thirds of the employees he places are child slaves. The total number of Haitian children in bondage in their own country stands at 300,000. They are the *restavèks*, the "staywiths," as they are euphemistically known in Creole. Forced, unpaid, they work in captivity from before dawn until night. Benavil and thousands of other formal and informal traffickers lure these children from desperately impoverished rural parents, with promises of free schooling and a better life.

The negotiation to buy a child slave might sound a bit like this:

"How quickly do you think it would be possible to bring a child in? Somebody who could clean and cook?" you ask. "I don't have a very big place; I have a small apartment. But I'm wondering how much that would cost? And how quickly?"

"Three days," Benavil responds.

"And you could bring the child here?" you inquire. "Or are there children here already?"

"I don't have any here in Port-au-Prince right now," says Benavil, his eyes widening at the thought of a foreign client. "I would go out to the countryside."

You ask about additional expenses. "Would I have to pay for transportation?"

"*Bon*," says Benavil. "A hundred U.S."

Smelling a rip-off, you press him, "And that's just for transportation?"

"Transportation would be about 100 Haitian," says Benavil, or around $13, "because you'd have to get out there. Plus [hotel and] food on the trip. Five hundred gourdes."

"Okay, 500 Haitian," you say.

Now you ask the big question: "And what would your fee be?" This is the moment of truth, and Benavil's eyes narrow as he determines how much he can take you for.

"A hundred. American."

"That seems like a lot," you say, with a smile so as not to kill the deal. "How much would you charge a Haitian?"

Benavil's voice rises with feigned indignation. "A hundred dollars. This is a major effort."

You hold firm. "Could you bring down your fee to 50 U.S.?"

Benavil pauses. But only for effect. He knows he's still got you for much more than a Haitian would pay. "*Oui*," he says with a smile.

But the deal isn't done. Benavil leans in close. "This is a rather delicate question. Is this someone you want as just a worker? Or also someone who will be a 'partner'? You understand what I mean?"

You don't blink at being asked if you want the child for sex. "I mean, is it possible to have someone that could be both?"

"*Oui!*" Benavil responds enthusiastically.

If you're interested in taking your purchase back to the United States, Benavil tells you that he can "arrange" the proper papers to make it look as though you've adopted the child.

He offers you a 13-year-old girl.

"That's a little bit old," you say.

"I know of another girl who's 12. Then ones that are 10, 11," he responds.

The negotiation is finished, and you tell Benavil not to make any moves without further word from you. Here, 600 miles from the United States, and five hours from Manhattan, you have successfully arranged to buy a human being for 50 bucks.

The Cruel Truth

It would be nice if that conversation, like the description of the journey, were fictional. It is not. I recorded it on Oct. 6, 2005, as part of four years of research into slavery on five continents. In the popular consciousness, "slavery" has come to be little more than just a metaphor for undue hardship. Investment bankers routinely refer to themselves as "high-paid wage slaves." Human rights activists may call $1-an-hour sweatshop laborers slaves, regardless of the fact that they are paid and can often walk away from the job. But the reality of slavery is far different. Slavery exists today on an unprecedented scale. In Africa, tens of thousands are chattel slaves, seized in war or tucked away for generations. Across Europe, Asia, and the Americas, traffickers have forced as many as 2 million into prostitution or labor. In South Asia, which has the highest concentration of slaves on the planet, nearly 10 million languish in bondage, unable to leave their captors until they pay off "debts," legal fictions that in many cases are generations old.

Few in the developed world have a grasp of the enormity of modern-day slavery. Fewer still are doing anything to combat it. Beginning in 2001, U.S. President George W. Bush was urged by several of his key advisors to vigorously enforce the Victims of Trafficking and Violence Protection Act, a U.S. law enacted a month earlier that sought to prosecute domestic human traffickers and cajole foreign governments into doing the same. The Bush administration trumpeted the effort—at home via the Christian evangelical media and more broadly via speeches and pronouncements, including in addresses to the U.N. General Assembly in 2003 and 2004. But even the quiet and diligent work of some within the U.S. State Department, which credibly claims to have secured more than 100 antitrafficking laws and more than 10,000 trafficking convictions worldwide, has resulted in no measurable decline in the number of slaves worldwide. Between 2000 and 2006, the U.S. Justice Department increased human trafficking prosecutions from 3 to 32, and convictions from 10 to 98. By 2006, 27 states had passed antitrafficking laws. Yet, during the same period, the United States liberated less than 2% of its own modern-day slaves. As many as 17,500 new slaves continue to enter bondage in the United States every year.

The West's efforts have been, from the outset, hamstrung by a warped understanding of slavery. In the United States, a hard-driving coalition of feminist and evangelical activists has forced the Bush administration to focus almost exclusively on the sex trade. The official State Department line is that voluntary prostitution does not exist, and that commercial sex is the main driver of slavery today. In Europe, though Germany and the Netherlands have decriminalized most prostitution, other nations such as Bulgaria have moved in the opposite direction, bowing to U.S. pressure and cracking down on the flesh trade. But, across the Americas, Europe, and Asia, unregulated escort services are exploding with the help of the Internet. Even when enlightened governments have offered clearheaded solutions to deal with this problem, such as granting victims temporary residence, they have had little impact.

Many feel that sex slavery is particularly revolting—and it is. I saw it firsthand. In a Bucharest brothel, for instance, I was offered a mentally handicapped, suicidal girl in exchange for a used car. But for every one woman or child enslaved in commercial sex, there are at least 15 men, women, and children enslaved in other fields, such as domestic work or agricultural labor. Recent studies have shown that locking up pimps and traffickers has had a negligible effect on the aggregate rates of bondage. And though eradicating prostitution may be a just cause, Western policies based on the idea that all prostitutes are slaves and all slaves are prostitutes belittles the suffering of all victims. It's an approach that threatens to put most governments on the wrong side of history.

Indebted for Life

Save for the fact that he is male, Gonoo Lal Kol typifies the average slave of our modern age. (At his request, I have changed his first name.) Like a vast majority of the world's slaves, Gonoo is in debt bondage in South Asia. In his case, in an Indian quarry. Like most slaves, Gonoo is illiterate and unaware of the Indian laws that ban his bondage and provide for sanctions against his master. His story, told to me in more than a dozen conversations inside his 4-foot-high stone and grass hutch, represents the other side of the "Indian Miracle."

Gonoo lives in Lohagara Dhal, a forgotten corner of Uttar Pradesh, a north Indian state that contains 8% of the world's poor. I met him one evening in December 2005 as he walked with two dozen other laborers in tattered and filthy clothes. Behind them was the quarry. In that pit, Gonoo, a member of the historically outcast Kol tribe, worked with his family 14 hours a day. His tools were simple, a roughhewn hammer and an iron pike. His hands were covered in calluses, his fingertips worn away.

Gonoo's master is a tall, stout, surly contractor named Ramesh Garg. Garg is one of the wealthiest men in Shankargarh, the nearest sizable town, founded under the British Raj but now run by nearly 600 quarry contractors. He makes his money by enslaving entire families forced to work for no pay beyond alcohol, grain, and bare subsistence expenses. Their only use for Garg is to turn rock into silica sand, for colored glass, or gravel, for roads or ballast. Slavery scholar Kevin Bales estimates that a slave in the nineteenth-century American South had to work 20 years to recoup his or her purchase price. Gonoo and the other slaves earn a profit for Garg in two years.

Every single man, woman, and child in Lohagara Dhal is a slave. But, in theory at least, Garg neither bought nor owns them. They are working off debts, which, for many, started at less than $10. But interest accrues at over 100% annually here. Most of the debts span at least two generations, though they have no legal standing under modern Indian law. They are a fiction that Garg constructs through fraud and maintains through violence. The seed of Gonoo's slavery, for instance, was a loan of 62 cents. In 1958, his grandfather borrowed that amount from the owner of a farm where he worked. Three generations and three slave masters later, Gonoo's family remains in bondage.

Bringing Freedom to Millions

Recently, many bold, underfunded groups have taken up the challenge of tearing out the roots of slavery. Some gained fame through dramatic slave rescues. Most learned that freeing slaves is impossible unless the slaves themselves choose to be free. Among the Kol of Uttar Pradesh, for instance, an organization called Pragati Gramodyog Sansthan (Progressive Institute for Village Enterprises, or PGS) has helped hundreds of families break the grip of the quarry contractors. Working methodically since 1985, organizers slowly built up confidence among slaves. With PGS's help, the Kol formed microcredit unions and won leases to quarries so that they could keep the proceeds of their labor. Some bought property for the first time in their lives, a cow or a goat, and their incomes, which had been nil, multiplied quickly. PGS set up primary schools and dug wells. Villages that for generations had known nothing but slavery began to become free. PGS's success demonstrates that emancipation is merely the first step in abolition. Within the developed world, some national law enforcement agencies such as those in the Czech Republic and Sweden have finally begun to pursue the most culpable of human trafficking—slave-trading pimps and unscrupulous labor contractors. But more must be done to educate local police, even in the richest of nations. Too often, these street-level law enforcement personnel do not understand that it's just as likely for a prostitute to be a trafficking victim as it is for a nanny working without proper papers to be a slave. And, after they have been discovered by law enforcement, few rich nations provide slaves with the kind of rehabilitation, retraining, and protection needed to prevent their re-trafficking. The asylum now granted to former slaves in the United States and the Netherlands is a start. But more must be done.

The United Nations, whose founding principles call for it to fight bondage in all its forms, has done almost nothing to combat modern slavery. In January, Antonio Maria Costa, executive director of the U.N. Office on Drugs and Crime, called for the international body to provide better quantification of human trafficking. Such number crunching would be valuable in combating that one particular manifestation of slavery. But there is little to suggest the United Nations, which consistently fails to hold its own member states accountable for widespread slavery, will be an effective tool in defeating the broader phenomenon.

Any lasting solutions to human trafficking must involve prevention programs in at-risk source countries. Absent an effective international body like the United Nations, such an effort will require pressure from the United States. So far, the United States has been willing to criticize some nations' records, but it has resisted doing so where it matters most, particularly in India. India abolished debt bondage in 1976, but with poor enforcement of the law locally, millions remain in bondage. In 2006 and 2007, the U.S. State Department's Office to Monitor and Combat Trafficking in Persons pressed U.S. Secretary of State Condoleezza Rice to repudiate India's intransigence personally. And, in each instance, she did not.

The psychological, social, and economic bonds of slavery run deep, and for governments to be truly effective in eradicating slavery, they must partner with groups that can offer slaves a way to pull themselves up from bondage. One way to do that is to replicate the work of grassroots organizations such as Varanasi, India-based MSEMVS (Society for Human Development and Women's Empowerment). In 1996, the Indian group launched free transitional schools, where children who had been enslaved learned skills and acquired enough literacy to move on to formal schooling. The group also targeted mothers, providing them with training and start-up materials for microenterprises. In Thailand, a nation infamous for sex slavery, a similar group, the Labour Rights Promotion Network, works to keep desperately poor Burmese immigrants from the clutches of traffickers by, among other things, setting up schools and health programs. Even in the remote highlands of southern Haiti, activists with Limyè Lavi ("Light of Life") reach otherwise wholly isolated rural communities to warn them of the dangers of traffickers such as Benavil Lebhom and to help them organize informal schools to keep children near home. In recent years, the United States has shown an increasing willingness to help fund these kinds of organizations, one encouraging sign that the message may be getting through.

For four years, I saw dozens of people enslaved, several of whom traffickers like Benavil actually offered to sell to me. I did not pay for a human life anywhere. And, with one exception, I always withheld action to save any one person, in the hope that my research would later help to save many more. At times, that still feels like an excuse for cowardice. But the hard work of real emancipation can't be the burden of a select few. For thousands of slaves, grass-roots groups like PGS and MSEMVS can help bring freedom. But, until governments define slavery in appropriately concise terms, prosecute the crime aggressively in all its forms, and encourage groups that empower slaves to free themselves, millions more will remain in bondage. And our collective promise of abolition will continue to mean nothing at all.

Researching and Writing for a Global Perspective

Active reading not only develops critical thinking skills but also facilitates good writing. Absorbent-sponge conceptions of reading (wherein you passively soak up the author's words) result in writing that merely parrots or regurgitates an author's views. When you read actively, however, you are constantly questioning a text and testing its claims against your own knowledge and experience. Your written responses to assigned texts in papers and exams will reflect this: they will present your voice and your views interacting with those of the author. Reading for both understanding and overstanding greatly reduces the possibility that you'll have nothing to say when you're writing about a text.

Other writing assignments in Global Studies will require you to research environmental, political, social, and economic issues or problems. A popular, semester-long assignment on my campus, for example, is a "Global Citizen Project" that combines scholarship and activism. This project has two major components: an analysis of a current world problem and a practical plan for addressing that problem. A shorter research assignment requires students to write the "back story" of a current news event. The back story of Ingrid Betancourt's dramatic rescue in Colombia after six years of captivity in July 2008, for example, would involve an investigation of recent Colombian history and politics and information about the Revolutionary Armed Forces of Colombia, the guerillas who held Betancourt hostage. Research assignments often reflect the interests and expertise of particular Global Studies instructors. A class taught by a child psychologist, for instance, investigates children's rights issues (such as child sexual abuse, child soldiers, child labor, and juvenile prisons). Global Studies students in a class taught by a neuroscientist write a position paper on an aspect of the international drug trade. The assignment requires them to "step into the shoes" of someone from a non-Western culture (for example, an opium farmer in present-day Afghanistan or a contemporary health official in Thailand reacting to increased tobacco sales by U.S. companies) and examine the drug trade from their perspective.

Thanks to electronic search engines and databases, information on Global Studies research topics is abundantly available. The challenge you'll face is identifying the *best* information: the information that is most current, authoritative, and relevant. Because the quality of a scholarly investigation depends on the quality of its research sources, instructors often caution students against using Wikipedia and information gathered using commercial search engines such as Google and Yahoo! Publishing on the Internet is extremely democratic: it provides a forum for perspectives and opinions that would otherwise never be communicated. The downside to Wikipedia's "anyone can edit" policy is a high risk of inaccurate information: "anyone" includes misinformed and wrong-headed contributors. Works published by journalists and scholars in books, magazines, newspapers, and journals tend to be more reliable because they are more likely to be subjected to fact-checking or review by scholarly experts (this is called "peer review") before publication.

Preliminary Research: Finding Books and Articles

Reference Books

For essential background information about the history and culture of a country or region that you're examining, start with your library's **reference collection.** Books in the reference collection do not circulate and are centrally located in the library, so they are dependably available and easily accessible. Annuals in this collection provide important data about population, economy, government, and geography. Specialized encyclopedias contain short articles by experts in a field of study. These articles often conclude with a bibliography that recommends books and articles for further reading. Randall Bowman, reference and instructional librarian at Elon University, recommends these reference books for preliminary Global Studies research:

> *Countries and Their Cultures,* eds. Melvin Ember & Carol R. Ember (New York: Macmillan, 2001)
> *CultureGrams* (Provo, Utah: ProQuest Information & Learning Co., 2006)
> *Encyclopedia of World Cultures* (Boston: G.K. Hall, 1992)
> *Encyclopedia of the World's Nations,* George Thomas Kurian (New York: Facts on File, 2002)
> *The Statesman's Yearbook* (New York: St. Martin's)
> *Worldmark Encyclopedia of Cultures and Daily Life,* ed. Timothy L. Gall (Detroit, MI: Gale, 1998)

Catalogues and Databases

Use your library's electronic catalog to find books on your research topic. If you come across a reference to a book that sounds interesting or useful in your daily reading or preliminary research, you can see if your library has it through an **author** or **title search.** If you wish to find all the books in your library's collection on a particular subject, start with a **keyword search** or a **subject search** in the online catalog.

To do a keyword search, type in the word or words that are most likely to appear in the titles or descriptions of materials about your subject. For example, to research a paper in which you're writing from the perspective of Thailand's chief health official about that country's increasing use of American tobacco products, you might type in the keywords "smoking and

Asia." (In Boolean logic, which is used by most research databases, the connective "and" indicates that you want sources that deal with both smoking and Asia. See your library's Web site for more information about Boolean operators and about strategies for advanced keyword searches.) This search yields two sources in my university's library: *Tobacco in History and Culture: An Encyclopedia* edited by Jordan Goodman (Detroit, MI: Gale, 2005) and *Smoke: A Global History of Smoking* edited by Sander Gilman and Zhou Xun (London: Reaktion, 2004).

Subject searches can be a bit trickier because they require that you use Library of Congress information classification headings. On the topic of the marketing and sales of U.S. tobacco in Asia, relevant Library of Congress subject headings include "Smoking Social Aspects"; "Smoking Economic Aspects"; "Tobacco Industry Advertising" and "Antismoking Movement." If you attempt a subject search using a term that is not a Library of Congress subject heading, you'll come up empty handed. For example, a subject search for "Myanmar" yields no results because the Library of Congress uses "Burma" as the classification heading for this Asian country. Ask a reference librarian for help if you strike out in a subject search.

To find articles in newspapers, magazines, and journals, use an **electronic database.** Most databases focus on particular subject areas. **EconLit** is a top database in economics, for example. **PsycINFO** is a database of choice in psychology. The interdisciplinarity of Global Studies means that you'll frequently explore topics from multiple disciplinary perspectives. Investigating the recruitment and use of child soldiers in Chad, for example, involves an understanding of nineteenth-century colonialism and its legacy, the physical and psychological effects of violence on child development, and the correlation between dire poverty and tribal conflict. Hence, relevant articles will come from many different fields: history, psychology, economics, and cultural anthropology.

To select the databases most relevant to your topic, list the questions that you need to answer about it and identify what disciplines are most likely to provide answers for those questions. Suppose, for example, that you are investigating the "internationally contested issue of whether Muslim women should have to remove their veils or head scarves" in schools, identification photos, and other places (Yoshino 178). The questions you'd need to answer through research might include the following (the subject area or areas of each question are indicated parenthetically):

1. What are the religious and historical reasons for the custom of female veiling? (world religions, history)
2. How have 9/11 and increased international concern about radical Islam influenced views of this custom? (history, international studies)
3. How do feminists regard this practice and prohibitions against it? Does either veiling or prohibitions against it disadvantage women? (women's studies)
4. What specific national or state laws have prohibited or limited this practice? How have these laws been defended and challenged? How have courts interpreted them? (law, political science)

Use a computer linked to your college library's Web site to access the database services to which your library subscribes. **General databases** contain articles on a wide variety of subject areas. Popular general databases are ***EBSCOhost, ProQuest,*** and ***LexisNexis Academic.*** The first page on the **EBSCOhost** site will ask you to indicate the subject areas of the databases you wish to search: the most comprehensive one is **Academic Search Premier,** a multi-disciplinary database that provides full text for more than 4,500 journals. *LexisNexis* includes articles on current events, law, business, and medicine; **ProQuest** enables you to access major newspapers, magazines, and journals.

To answer questions within a specific disciplinary field, limit your search to a subject area database. A list of subject databases appears on the first page of the **EBSCOhost** site. Included on this list is the **ATLA Religion** database, described as "the premier index to journal articles, book reviews, and collections of essays in all fields of religion." **ATLA Religion** will lead you to materials that explain why traditional Islam requires female veiling. To find out more about national laws that prohibit veiling (France, for example, prohibits it in public schools), you might limit your search to the legal database on **LexisNexis.** Many college and university library Web sites provide quick links to "databases by subject" to facilitate searches for information within specific disciplinary and interdisciplinary fields. Elon University librarian Randall Bowman recommends these interdisciplinary databases for introductory Global Studies courses:

- **CIAO** (Columbia University's International Affairs Online, a "comprehensive source for theory and research in international affairs")
- **Europa World Plus** (for political and economic information about more than 250 countries and territories)
- **Library Press Display** (online access to over 500 newspapers from 70 countries)
- **Military & Government Collection of EBSCOhost** (current news pertaining to all branches of the military and government)
- **United Nations Security Council** (includes news, mission reports, and resolutions)
- **World Development Indicators Online** (sponsored by the World Bank; offers data and statistics about hundreds of development variables for countries across the world)

Fieldwork and Visual Evidence

Through secondary source research, you learn from the work of experts in a field. Primary research enables you to contribute new information to existing knowledge about your subject. One type of primary research that is particularly important in interdisciplinary Global Studies is *fieldwork*, which involves gathering original data outside the library. Fieldwork in Global Studies usually takes one of three forms:

- **Conducting interviews** (For an investigation of child soldiers in Sudan, you might interview a staff member of Invisible Children—an organization devoted to ending the use of child soldiers in Uganda—or interview an African Studies expert on your faculty.)
- **Recording observations** of real-world phenomena (To examine city ordinances against chicken raising and allegations that these laws reflect hostility toward Hispanic immigrants, you might visit some urban chicken coops to determine the legitimacy of complaints about the noise and pollution they generate. Exercise 2: Comparative News Reading in this chapter is another example of observational-record fieldwork.)

- **Administering questionnaires or surveys** (To investigate peer attitudes toward feminism in connection with Ann J. Cahill's chapter on global feminism, you could conduct a survey to see if current students believe that women in our culture are "systematically disadvantaged" economically, educationally, politically, or in other ways.)

Well designed and executed fieldwork enhances an investigation of global issues and problems because it builds upon the work of previous researchers by generating new information on your subject of inquiry.

Visual images can sometimes convey or illustrate points that are central to your written arguments more powerfully than words. Color photographs of melting glaciers and shrinking mountain snow caps dramatically enhance Al Gore's presentation of the "inconvenient truth" of global warming, for example, just as the bar graph William Easterly presents in *The White Man's Burden* vividly captures the correlation between average incomes within a nation and its level of governmental democracy (130). Computer technology has made it easy to transmit and reproduce images, and software enables us to incorporate graphics into the text of a paper or PowerPoint presentation with a few clicks of the mouse. As you research and write about a subject, be attentive to ways in which visual evidence—pictures, charts, tables, maps, cartoons, and so on—might advance your argument. Be careful to incorporate graphics into your text only when they serve a clear and explicit purpose, however. Otherwise, they'll simply distract readers and waste space. The sources for reproduced images must be credited using the documentation form required by your instructor.

Forming and Arguing a Thesis

Once you've gathered sufficient evidence from primary and secondary sources to answer your main research question, carefully evaluate that evidence. What ideas or facts address your question insightfully and convincingly? What information seems extraneous or dubious? What are the most serious disagreements between the experts on your subject? What's the significance of these points of conflict? Your goal in sifting through and weighing your evidence is to form the **thesis** of your argument. A thesis is essentially a clear and informed answer to the question that has been the focus of your research. An effective thesis not only presents your position on this focal question or issue, but also explains your principal reason for taking this stand (Callaghan & Dobyns 238). For example, "The French law that prohibits head scarves in public schools unfairly discriminates against Muslim women" is an incomplete thesis. It states a position, but offers no rationale to justify it. A better, more complete thesis might be: "The French law that prohibits head scarves in public schools unfairly discriminates against Muslim women because in Western cultures Islamic practices are more likely to be perceived as unusual and 'ostentatious' displays of religion, which French law explicitly forbids." Your paper will then present and support this argument in detail.

The conceptual structure of a research argument resembles a table or desk. The table top is your thesis (which you present in the first page or so of the paper), and your supporting arguments provide "legs" for the table. A sturdy working surface needs at least three legs (in a tripod formation) to support it; four legs are better yet. To form your argument, identify the three or four major supporting points that best explain or defend your thesis. (If you can't do this, you'll need to consider the possibility that your argument is flimsy and inadequate to support your thesis.) Then organize your evidence into subsections (legs for your table) that correspond to these supporting arguments. For example, my current research investigates representations of foreign-exchange students in films about high school (for example, Asian nerd Long Duk Dong in *Sixteen Candles* [1984] and Euro-vixen Nadia in *American Pie* [1999]). My thesis answers my central research question about the significance of these representations: Foreign-exchange students in popular high school movies dramatize the historic xenophobia of the majority culture in the U.S., adolescent anxiety about insider/outsider status, and ambivalence about human sexuality. The first pages of my paper present this thesis and explain why this subject is worth exploring. This is the table top. The three subsequent sections of the paper put legs on my table by explaining in detail the three parts of my thesis about how these characters reflect American xenophobia (section 1); teenage status anxiety (section 2); and the values of a "sex-negative" culture (section 3; for an explanation of "sex-negative" and "sex-positive" cultures, see Chapter 2 in this book by Laurence A. Basirico and Anne Bolin).

You must carefully cite sources for all information gathered through research by using a standard method of documentation. Paraphrased references to research sources as well as direct quotations must be credited to acknowledge your indebtedness to the ideas and work of others. APA or MLA documentation styles are both used in interdisciplinary courses: APA is generally favored by the social sciences (for example, psychology, sociology, economics, and political science); MLA is used by humanities disciplines (such as English, religion, philosophy, and art history). The other chapters in this volume use APA documentation; this chapter provides a model of MLA citation style. Ask your instructor about the preferred citation method for your course, and take care not to mix documentation styles within a single paper. An excellent online guide to APA and MLA source citation is provided by the University of California at Berkeley: http://www.lib.berkeley.edu/instruct/guides/citations.html.

EXERCISE 4:   Family Immigration Research

Use field work and secondary source research to answer two questions:

1. Who was the first of your ancestors to immigrate to the United States? Interview family members to find out as much as possible about this first immigrant. When and why did s/he come to the United States?
2. What social and historical circumstances in your ancestor's home country motivated this immigration? Use secondary sources to research the reasons (social, economic, political, religious, and other) why your relative left his/her native country.

Present your research findings in a story that captures both the personal experience and the historical context of your ancestor's immigration. Cite sources using MLA or APA documentation style.

Note: I am indebted to Elon University colleagues who have generously shared assignments, classroom exercises, and teaching strategies with me, especially Jeffrey Coker, Mathew Gendle, Tom Mould, Janet Warman, and Linda Wilmshurst.

Works Cited

American Pie. Dir. Paul Weitz. Universal Pictures, 1999.

Bilefsky, Dan. "Albanian Custom Fades: Woman as Family Man." *New York Times* 25 June 2008. 23 July 2008 <http://www.nytimes.com/2008/06/25/world/europe/25virgins.html>.

Booth, Wayne C. and Marshall W. Gregory. *The Harper & Row Rhetoric: Writing as Thinking, Thinking as Writing.* 2nd ed. N.Y.: Longman, 1998.

Bowman, Randall. Research Guide for GST 110: The Global Experience. 2007–2008. Library, Elon U. 7 July 2008 <http://www.elon.edu/e-web/library/research_guides/gst110.xhtml>.

Boyes, Laura. "Undiscovered Countries." *Independent Weekly* 9 July 2008: 57.

Callaghan, Patsy, and Ann Dobyns. *A Meeting of Minds: Strategies for Academic Inquiry and Writing.* 2nd ed. N.Y.: Pearson Longman, 2007.

Clydesdale, Tim. *The First Year Out: Understanding American Teens after High School.* Chicago: U of Chicago P, 2007.

Collier, Paul. *The Bottom Billion: Why the Poorest Countries Are Failing and What Can Be Done About It.* NY: Oxford UP, 2007.

De Graaf, John, ed. *Take Back Your Time: Fighting Overwork and Time Poverty in America.* San Francisco, CA: Berrett-Koehler, 2003.

Desai, Kiran. *The Inheritance of Loss.* N.Y.: Grove, 2006.

Donadio, Rachel. "The Irascible Prophet." *New York Times* 7 Aug. 2005. 23 July 2008 <http://www.nytimes.com/2005/08/07/books/review/07DONADIO.html>.

_____. "Truth is Stronger than Fiction." *New York Times Book Review* 7 Aug 2005: 27.

Easterly, William. *The White Man's Burden: Why the West's Efforts to Aid the Rest Have Done So Much Ill and So Little Good.* N.Y.: Penguin, 2006.

Friedman, Thomas L. "Mr. Bush: Lead or Leave." *New York Times* 22 June 2008. 23 July 2008 <http://www.nytimes.com/2008/06/22/opinion/22friedman.html>.

_____. "The New Cold War." *New York Times* 14 May 2008. 23 July 23, 2008 <http://www.nytimes.com/2008/05/14/opinion/14friedman.html>.

Gore, Al. *An Inconvenient Truth.* Emmaus, PA: Rodale, 2006.

Hayden, Anders. "Europe's Work-Time Alternatives." De Graaf 202–210.

Hopps, H. R. *Destroy This Mad Brute.* 1916. 28 July 2008 <http://www.hrc.utexas.edu/collections/art/holdings/poster/images/hopps_mad_brute_large.jpg>.

Hosseini, Khaled. *A Thousand Splendid Suns.* N.Y.: Riverhead, 2007.

Juhasz, Victor. Cover illustration. *The New York Observer.* April 1, 2008.

Kristof, Nicholas D. "Strengthening Extremists." *New York Times* 19 June 2008. 23 July 2008 <http://www.nytimes.com/2008/06/19/opinion/19kristof.html>.

Nussbaum, Martha. *Poetic Justice: The Literary Imagination and Public Life.* Boston: Beacon, 1995.

Pike, Kenneth L. *Linguistic Concepts: An Introduction to Tagmemics.* Lincoln: University of Nebraska Press, 1982.

"The Power of Rest." Cover Story. *Utne Reader* Jan./Feb. 2004: 77–85.

Power, Samantha. "Bystanders to Genocide." *Atlantic Monthly* 288: 2 (Sept. 2001). 23 July 2008 <http://www.theatlantic.com/doc/200109/power-genocide>.

Sachs, Jeffrey D. *The End of Poverty: Economic Possibilities for Our Time.* N.Y.: Penguin, 2006.

Singer, Peter. *One World: The Ethics of Globalization.* New Haven, CT: Yale UP, 2002.

Sixteen Candles. Dir. John Hughes. Channel Productions, 1984.

Skinner, E. Benjamin. "A World Enslaved." *Foreign Policy* March/April 2008: 62-67.

Vogue. Cover with photograph by Annie Leibovitz. April 2008.

Waskow, Arthur. "Can America Learn from Shabbat?" De Graaf 123–132.

Will, George. "March of the Polar Bears." *Washington Post* 22 May 2008: A25.

Yoshino, Kenji. *Covering: The Hidden Assault on Our Civil Rights.* N.Y.: Random, 2006.

4

Numbers and the World

Duane McClearn

Mistakes Were Made

Let's start with a little tale. Long ago a brave and loyal subject performed a great service for the king of a rich and mighty nation. In gratitude the king offered to reward the subject. "Choose anything I can give," said the king. "A carriage of gold, a basket of jewels, even a fine palace. Anything you desire is yours." Pointing to a chessboard that was at hand, the subject responded, "Today place a single penny on the corner square of that chessboard. Tomorrow place double that amount, two pennies, on the next square. On the third day put double *that* amount, or four pennies, on the next square. Proceed in this manner of doubling the previous day's pennies each day until you reach the last (64th) square. Each day I will come to collect my reward until such time as the last square is filled. This is my request."

The king was taken aback at this strange request, but figuring that this would be simple enough to comply with, he agreed. "Why would he not prefer something of greater value, such as a box of jewels?" the king wondered.

As stipulated, each day the subject showed up at the king's palace to collect his due. Soon it became difficult to fit all the requisite coins on the chessboard square, but the subject graciously consented to the heaping of coins nearby. After several days, it was observed that obtaining enough pennies for the following day was going to be difficult. The subject agreed to allow the use of gold coins to equal the value of the pennies. A bit later, the king's servant, who was in charge of gathering the loot to place on the appropriate chessboard square each day, informed His Majesty that the once-overflowing treasury was nearly depleted. Soon it became clear that long before the 64th square was filled, the king would have to give away the total value of his entire kingdom. There was no possible way, even by putting his kingdom up for sale, that he could keep his word to his subject. In despair he called the subject to him.

The story's ending has two versions. In one, the king, deciding to keep his word of honor as best as he is able, gives his kingdom to the subject. In the other version, the king, irritated at being tricked by his subject into agreeing to his request and not willing to part with all he possesses, has the subject executed.

Now for a true story. In 1999, a very costly spacecraft was sent to Mars. Its purpose was to land on the surface of Mars and transmit information regarding environmental conditions on the planet back to curious scientists on Earth. The mission failed. The vehicle was not able to signal its presence. Apparently, its landing was done incorrectly and it was damaged or destroyed.

What had happened? The calculations needed to shoot the vehicle onto Mars were complicated. Precise timing and trajectory were required for success. As it turned out, the mistake was a minor one, yet also a very expensive and very human one. The hundred million dollar vehicle was lost because somebody in one of their calculations had not made the correct conversion from inches to centimeters.

Both of these stories demonstrate the importance of proper knowledge of numbers and the calamities that may arise when this knowledge is lacking or goes unused. In one case, by his hasty promise based on ignorance of numbers, a king lost his kingdom (at least, in one version of the tale). In the other, because of an error in using numbers, scientists lost an expensive vehicle and an opportunity to make some exciting discoveries about a neighboring planet.

The Real World

As with other realms of interest, I believe that characteristics of national and global problems cannot be firmly understood unless information about them is rendered into numerical form. Can experts really talk intelligently and deeply about the issues of hunger and sickness, wealth and power, the state of the environment, the potential for future progress without recourse to numbers? I really think not.

Suppose, for example, that somebody maintains that there is tremendous and widespread poverty in Zimbabwe and that United States aid should be sent there to alleviate the problem. This person tells stories of suffering and starvation of Zimbabwe's people and paints a very grim picture indeed. But somebody else could describe the miserable living conditions of this or that family in, say, Switzerland, and paint an equally bleak picture. So does that mean that Zimbabwe and Switzerland are equally plagued by poverty? Who wins the argument? The person with the most vivid story? Should the United States give financial aid to both nations? Without using number information about the depth and extent of poverty of these, or any other, nations, we are left to trade anecdotes and have our decisions based on them.

Or take a real and rather humorous example. The main character of the 2007 movie *Borat: Cultural Learnings of America for Make Benefit Glorious Nation of Kazakhstan* presents his supposed native country, Kazakhstan, as poor and backward, its people crude and

*"That's the gist of what I want to say. Now get
me some statistics to base it on."*

FIGURE 4.1 *Source:* © *The New Yorker Collection 1977*, Joseph Mirachi from cartoonbook.com. All Rights Reserved.

ignorant. The actual government of Kazakhstan objected to this depiction, stating that the nation was modern and prosperous. In fact, the government of Kazakhstan brought a lawsuit against Sacha Baron Cohen, the British actor who portrays Borat. So what is the real nature of Kazakhstan? Is the country as presented by the movie *Borat* or as it is argued by its government? Number information can easily shed light on this curious dispute.

And while we're at it, why not examine this country? How does the United States stand as far as living conditions are concerned? Many Americans are prone to proclaim that the United States is "Number One." Presumably, a lot of them are referring to quality of life. Does their view withstand the scrutiny of numerical analysis?

Ignoring Numbers

A problem for purveyors of number information is that people may be naturally prone to ignore it or, at least, minimize it. Evolutionary psychologists have suggested that the human brain is set up to be most receptive to information given in story or picture form, not numerically. It is widely reported in the psychological research literature that people will assign more weight to a pithy anecdote about a subject than a group of numerical facts about the subject. And studies have shown that charitable giving is much higher in response to a *picture* of a sad, hungry child than to a message that indicates with words alone that *thousands* of children are in need of help. Soviet dictator Josef Stalin once remarked: "One death is a tragedy. A million deaths is a statistic." At least in terms of the typical person's response, this would seem to be true.

Of course, the typical engaged citizen is bombarded by various numbers, but often these numbers are not put into the proper context, nor are they accompanied by enough explanation. We regularly hear about the rise or fall in the Dow Jones Industrial Average, the latest unemployment figures, the rise of the national deficit, and the amounts of money that are going to be spent to address this or that social woe. But if we are tempted to tune out these numbers, as many people choose to do, we ignore crucial components of the matters being discussed.

Even people in positions of great influence often do not possess enough knowledge of numbers to make well-reasoned decisions (or they choose not to use this knowledge). Take, for example, something quite basic: large figures. John Sununu, former White House chief of staff in the administration of the first President Bush, criticized the lack of number sense among the members of Congress. He noted that these policy makers "all too often do not have an intuitive sense [of the difference] between a million and a billion … It is not a trivial change of one letter to write [an environmental] regulation in terms of parts per billion instead of parts per million." In referring to dealing with huge amounts of tax money, David Stockman, President Reagan's budget director, said, "None of us really understands what's going on with all these numbers" (Qtd. Dewdney, 1993, p. 14 and p. 95; A. K. Dewdney (1993) *200% of Nothing*. New York: John Wiley and Sons).

Actually, this sort of failing is quite common. Many people, when confronted with figures on the national debt or Gross Domestic Product, or the amount of tax money to be spent on this or that problem, are likely to say, "A million or a billion or a trillion dollars. These all seem like such huge amounts of money. Why bother trying to keep track?"

Take a specific example. The current national debt, that is, the amount of money that the United States Government owes to various lenders, stood in 2007 at slightly over $9 trillion. Of course, the amount has to be paid back from tax revenues. Since taxes are collected from the American people, it is they who are ultimately responsible for paying the national debt. It is easy to figure out how much is owed on a per person basis. Dividing the total United States debt ($9 trillion) by the number of United States citizens (about 300,000,000) yields $30,000 per citizen. Thus, if the United States Government were to decide to repay its debt all at once, it would have to demand an average of about $30,000 from each citizen, including you, the reader.

Let us suppose that the national debt were only $9 billion instead. Then your share would be only $30. And suppose further that the national debt were only $9 million. In that case your share would be a paltry 3 cents. So size really does matter. John Sununu is correct in saying that there is a substantial difference between a million and a billion (and a trillion, I would add), even though all these numbers seems so large. To be quite specific, a trillion is a thousand billions; a billion is a thousand millions.

Here is another way of conceptualizing the difference between these amounts. If you counted out dollars at the rate of one per second, 24 hours per day, it would take you almost 32 years to reach one billion. To count to a trillion at this rate would take almost 32,000 years. To count to a million would take only about 12 days.

Let's return to the example of the king, the subject, and the chessboard. It demonstrates the importance of the concept of geometric, as opposed to arithmetic, progression. Arithmetic progression occurs when the *difference* between a number in a series and its predecessor is always the same. If the subject asked the king to put one penny on the first square and then simply add one penny for each square, he would be asking for an arithmetic progression (1, 2, 3, 4, 5, 6, ...) and the final square would end up with a mere 64 pennies. Geometric progression (also called growing geometrically) occurs in a sequence in which the *ratio* of a number to its predecessor is always the same. What the subject requested, a doubling with each square (1, 2, 4, 8, 16, 32, 64, ...), is an example of a geometric progression and resulted in the bankrupting of the kingdom. This difference has important ramifications for our understanding of world affairs. Through much of the 1980s, the national debt of the United States was growing in a geometric progression. Certain diseases spread in a geometric progression. For the past few decades, the world's population has been growing geometrically. Imagine the difference if these processes had, instead, been arithmetic.

Applications: Using Numerical Information to Help Understand the World

So how can we go about applying numbers to national and global issues in a systematic way? I have chosen an approach that I hope will facilitate an understanding of the process and the issues, as well as produce a broad appreciation for at least some of the complexities of world affairs.

First, in the section titled **Basics** we consider some fundamental characteristics of nations, specifically land size (area) and population. We also consider an aspect of culture that transcends national boundaries, that is, religion (more specifically, numbers of adherents of various religions).

Next, in the section titled **Power,** we look at a dimension of nations that is constantly on the minds of governmental leaders and politicians, namely national strength. Nations are constantly vying for influence with their neighbors and the world at large. A particular nation may want to increase its exports to other countries, or decrease immigrants from other countries, or grab territory or resources from neighboring nations, or prevent a nation from expanding its seemingly threatening military forces, or stop a nation from sponsoring terrorism, or press a nation to allow its citizens more human rights. There are dozens of reasons that a nation may want to exert influence on the world stage. This section deals with currently accepted methods of defining and measuring that influence, or power.

After that, we turn to an issue that is more likely to be of personal concern, which is commonly called "quality of life." There are many dimensions to the term "quality of life." I have whittled down the list of measures to a manageable few—ones that are widely used and accepted. These measures take on great importance when nations and charitable organizations set about determining how to target aid, whether in the form of money, medicine, or food, or in the form of pressure on oppressive regimes to extend greater rights to their citizens.

Next, in the section titled **The Environment** we consider a characteristic that, in some ways, could be considered an extension of the **Quality of Life** section. Here we deal primarily with the scope of environmental problems. By far the majority of experts on the environment (scientists, primarily) agree that human-produced changes to the environment, most of them deleterious, are occurring on a vast scale. There is serious concern among these experts about the health—or sickness—of the planet and the ramifications of its condition for its people.

Numerical Information: A Limitation

Before proceeding, the reader should be made aware of a certain limitation regarding the use of number information. No single measure is perfect, of course, in depicting a characteristic of a population, a nation, or a global problem. So a choice has to be made about which measure is the best for the particular issue at hand. Experts are often at odds about which numerical measure best captures the characteristic under investigation. To use a mundane example: Imagine a professor who is trying to measure students' ability in a college course. Suppose further that the professor uses class participation, homework, oral presentations, and exams for this purpose. The professor is likely to have many sub-measures within each measure, such as essays, fill-ins, and multiple choice questions on exams. So for the seemingly simple task of trying to determine the ability of the students, the professor uses a variety of measures in a fairly elaborate set-up (and one that is almost certain to rely on numbers, by the way). Still, reasonable people may argue that different measures should be used, such as pop quizzes or class debates, or that different weights should be placed on the measures (maybe class participation should count for less, for instance) in determining the students' final grades.

Now imagine the difficulties that beset politicians, policy makers, scholars, and such, who are trying to determine the overall power of a nation or the quality of life of a nation's people. Which measure is best? Should several measures be used in combination (in much the same way as a professor uses several measures to determine student ability)? Different experts will have reasonable disagreements on the value and appropriateness of the various measures that are put forth.

Somebody who is interested in examining world issues from a numerical standpoint should be aware of what the numbers signify and what they do not. Just as a critic of a professor's grading system may argue that a strong emphasis on multiple-choice exams ignores other important student abilities, such as critical thinking and writing, so should the analyst of world affairs be aware that no single measure can perfectly capture the essence of a particular feature of a nation. Take, for example, the question of health. How might we define the overall health of a nation's citizenry by use of numerical measures? We might choose the amount of money that a nation spends on the health care of its people. A nation that spends a lot in this regard (on a per person basis) might be judged to have more healthy citizens on average than a nation that spends less. On the other hand, it could be the case that the nation with high healthcare spending has a *less* healthy citizenry and that is precisely *why* it is spending so much on health care: its citizens are in more need of expensive treatments. Or perhaps the nation with higher healthcare spending is using the money in an inefficient way, so its people are receiving worse care than they otherwise might; in this case the amount of money spent is not a good indicator of the quality of the health of the people. Even with something so seemingly straightforward as a number, a bit of interpretation is in order.

Similarly, for this chapter's main sections, choices had to be made regarding the measures to be discussed. The section called **Basics** could have looked at population density or the numbers of speakers of the main languages. The section **Power** could have made an examination of different measures of military strength, or of soft power (essentially, the ability to influence others by the attractiveness of a nation's culture). In the section **Quality of Life**, numerous relevant measures could have been used in addition to, or instead of, the ones that were included, such as infant mortality, access to clean water, average number of calories consumed per day or month or year, or numbers of hours in the typical work week. In the section titled **The Environment**, more could be made of individual species loss, or different kinds of pollutants, or of the adverse health effects of pollutants (such as lead exposure in children). I tried to select measures that are relevant, interesting, and accepted among experts.

Thus, although there are difficulties with respect to the use of number information in understanding the world (more of which are discussed in a later section of this chapter), we shall forge ahead.

Basics: Understanding the Fundamentals of Nations via Numbers

The Land

Perhaps the most obvious characteristic of the nations of the world that can be indicated with numbers is size. The largest nation in the world is Russia, with an area of about 6,591,000 square miles. (The old Soviet Union, of which Russia was the largest part, was substantially larger.) Coming in at a far second place in size is Canada, at about 3,854,000 square miles. Table 4.1 shows the ten largest nations of the world in physical size. This group of the "Big Ten" accounts for almost half of all the national land (i.e., excluding Antarctica) on this planet. (See the section called Notes at the end of the chapter for an explanation of the sources used throughout.)

At the other end of the spectrum are the very small nations. Famous for its fairy tale castles and postage stamps is the tiny European nation of Liechtenstein, comprising a mere 62 square miles. Nauru, a speck of an island in the South Pacific and made rich (for a time) by its tremendous deposits of bird droppings, is a paltry 8 square miles. Minuscule Monaco, famous for its fabulous casinos and the jet-set crowd that flocks there, is only 1.2 square miles in area. The smallest nation of all is the Vatican, also known as the Holy See, residence of the Pope and the spiritual center of the Catholic Church. Located in downtown Rome,

TABLE 4.1   *Largest Nations of the World (in square miles, rounded)*

1. Russia	6,591,000
2. Canada	3,854,000
3. United States	3,793,000
4. China	3,704,000
5. Brazil	3,286,000
6. Australia	2,967,000
7. India	1,269,000
8. Argentina	1,068,000
9. Kazakhstan	1,049,000
10. Sudan	967,000

(Source: CIA, *The World Factbook, 2008*)

Italy, the Vatican (yes, it really is a sovereign nation) is only a fraction of a square mile in size (0.17 to be precise).

Some idea of the relative sizes of nations of the world can be obtained by making comparisons to entities that are generally more familiar to the typical reader, such as states in the United States. Most people would be surprised to learn that France (at about 248,000 sq. mi. in area), Japan (146,000 sq. mi.), Germany (138,000 sq. mi.) and the United Kingdom (or U.K., comprising England, Scotland, Wales, and Northern Ireland, at 95,000 sq. mi.) are substantially smaller than Texas (267,000 sq. mi.), the second largest state in the Union. Japan is close in size to California, and the United Kingdom to Oregon. North Carolina is larger than nearly half the nations of the world. Yellowstone National Park, at close to 3,500 sq. mi., is larger than over two dozen nations of the world. Incidentally, the land masses of the Earth are overshadowed by bodies of water. The Pacific Ocean (largest of the oceans) has a greater area than all of the continents combined.

The People

Another feature of nations (other than area, that is) that can be easily addressed with numbers is population. As with considerations of area, there is a great variation in population for countries. The most populous nation in the world is China, having an enormous population of 1,330,000,000, or about 1.3 billion (according to a 2008 estimate). Second largest is India, with 1,148,000,000, rounded to 1.15 billion. Having 304,000,000, the United States is third largest in population. Other nations plentiful with people are shown in Table 4.2.

This group of the 10 most populous nations has a combined population of 3,940,000,000 or about 3.9 billion. Since the population of the world is about 6,678,000,000 or about 6.7 billion, this set of nations contains about 6 out of 10 humans (59% to be more exact).

China itself has one-fifth of all the people in the world. Put another way, one person in five is Chinese. China, with about the same amount of land as the United States, has over four

TABLE 4.2   *Most Populous Nations (2008 estimates, rounded, in millions)*

1. China	1,330
2. India	1,148
3. United States	304
4. Indonesia	238
5. Brazil	192
6. Pakistan	168
7. Bangladesh	154
8. Russia	141
9. Nigeria	138
10. Japan	127

(Source: CIA, *The World Factbook, 2008*)

times its population. China's population is greater than that of all the nations of the Americas (that is, North America and Latin America, with a combined population of over 900 million). China's population is greater than that of all of the nations of Europe combined, with a total of about 728 million. China has more people than all of the nations of Africa put together (with over 950 million). In fact, China's population is only a bit smaller than that of all of the three continents of North America, Latin America, and Europe combined.

India, the second most populous nation in the world, dwarfs all nations in population except for China. There are eight times as many Indians as there are Russians. India has more people than the continents of North America, Latin America, Europe, Africa, or Oceania. There are more Indians than people of the Americas.

The population of China and India combined is approximately 2,478,000,000, or about 2.5 billion, which amounts to about 37% of the world's total. Together, China and India have almost as many people as the five continents making up the Americas, Europe, Africa, and Oceania combined. Obviously, the huge populations of these nations are very relevant when it comes to questions about future population growth in the world.

And what might these predicted figures be? Estimates vary, but one source places China's population in the year 2025 at 1,445,000,000. In spite of China's policies that aim to curtail population growth, it is set to *add* more than 100 million people over the next 20 years. India is expected to have about 1,369,000,000 people in 2025, an increase of over 200 million. Thus, these two huge nations are likely, by the year 2025, to add an amount of people equal to the current population of the United States. Incidentally, the population of the United States is predicted to grow to 358,000,000 by 2025, an increase of over 50 million.

Germany currently has about 82 million people. France and the United Kingdom have about 64 million and 61 million, respectively. Nigeria has the most people of any African nation, with about 138 million.

Nations with very small populations include Liechtenstein, with about 34,000 people, Monaco (33,000) and San Marino (30,000). Nauru has about 14,000. The smallest

TABLE 4.3   *Religious Adherents (rounded, in millions)*

1. Christians	2,200
2. Muslims	1,387
3. Hindus	876
4. Buddhists	386

(Source: *Time Almanac, 2008*)

population of any nation belongs to the Vatican, which has fewer than 1,000 people (824, according to a 2008 estimate).

The Faithful

One fundamental human characteristic, and one that is discussed in the media and government circles ever more frequently, is commitment to religious faith. The religions with the most adherents are shown in Table 4.3.

Christians make up one-third of all religious believers in the world. It may be surprising to learn that there are more Christians in Europe, Latin America, Asia, or Africa than in North America.

The second largest faith is Islam, with about one-fifth of the world's total. The nation with the largest number of Muslims is Indonesia (with about 207 million), followed by Pakistan (with about 163 million), India (with 149 million), and Bangladesh (with 128 million). Although most United States Americans probably imagine that the bulk of Muslims are Arabs who live in the Middle East, this is, in fact, not true. Of the four nations with the most Muslims, none is in the Middle East and none has a substantial Arab population. (It is difficult to imagine demonstrating this point with information other than that of a numerical nature.) A distant fifth in the nations with high populations of Muslims is Egypt. It has about 74 million Muslims and fits the common impression of a Muslim country by being in the Middle East and being composed of Arabs. The next nations are Turkey (with 72 million Muslims), Nigeria (with 69 million), and Iran (with 65 million). None of these nations has a population that is predominantly Arab.

Other religious affiliations have varying members. There are about 15 million Jews worldwide. The countries with the most Jews are the United States (with close to 6 million) and Israel (with about 5 million). The group composed of non-religious and atheists has about 930 million worldwide.

Power

Mighty Economies

Politicians and diplomats the world over are keen to know the extent of their country's power, as well as the power of any nations they are likely to deal with (which may mean virtually all other nations of the globe). Decisions about dealing with another country are made with due consideration of that country's power. Ways of measuring power are paramount in the minds of many analysts at governmental think tanks. As with other problems of definition of globally-significant phenomena, there is no consensus on which measure of power is the best. Each measure has its value, as well as its limitations.

One measure that interests many national leaders, and with good reason, is Gross Domestic Product, or GDP. The GDP of a nation is the total value of all the goods and services produced by that nation for a particular year. Thus, the value of all the food, furniture, shoes, gasoline, computer games, as well as dry cleaning, taxi rides, stock broker fees, and so on are added up to determine a nation's GDP. Most economists and politicians would agree that the size of GDP is a good indicator of a nation's power on the world scene. Some experts would argue that it is the single most valuable piece of information about a nation's overall strength.

Incidentally, some sources use Gross National Product, or GNP, when measuring economic activity. GNP and GDP measure largely the same thing. Also, many experts in the last few years have turned to using GDP Purchasing Power Parity (GDP/PPP) as a more accurate reflection of the value of what countries produce. Purchasing Power Parity involves the use of standardized international dollar price weights; thus, it takes into account the fact that prices may be substantially higher in one nation compared to prices in another. (*GDP/PPP figures will be used from here on in this chapter.*) Much is made in the news of rises in the GDP each year for this country. The booming economy of the United States is manifested in reports showing an ever-growing GDP (at least, until quite recently).

I have occasionally asked students which nation they thought had the highest GDP. The answers were varied. Many said Japan, others Germany, yet others the United States. Some believed it to be oil-rich Saudi Arabia. It was even remarked that Saudi Arabia was "buying up" the United States.

The reality is this: the nation with the largest GDP by far is the United States, with a figure of $13,860,000,000,000, more easily expressed as $13.86 trillion, or rounded to $13.9 trillion. Second is China, with a GDP of about $7 trillion. Other nations with high GDPs are shown in Table 4.4.

TABLE 4.4 *Nations with the Highest GDP/PPP (in trillions of dollars, rounded, 2007 est.)*

1. United States	13.9
2. China	7.0
3. Japan	4.4
4. India	3.0
5. Germany	2.8
6. United Kingdom	2.1
7. Russia	2.1
8. France	2.1
9. Brazil	1.8
10. Italy	1.8

(Source: CIA, *The World Factbook, 2008*)

We can draw several inferences from these numbers in Table 4.4. As noted, the United States has, by far, the largest GDP of any nation. Japan, although it has a very powerful economy (in spite of several years of recent stagnation), does not have even half the GDP of the United States. China, even though it has about 4 times the number of people as the United States, has a GDP that is about half that of this nation's. Russia, which was the primary antagonist of the United States during the decades of the Cold War (from the mid-1940s to the early 1990s), currently has a GDP of $2.1 trillion, or about one-seventh that of the United States. In fact, the United States produces about one-fifth (21%) of the total world GDP (which stands at about $65.8 trillion), that is, the combined GDPs of all the nations of the world. The other countries on the list of the top ten are the European powerhouses and countries that, largely by virtue of their huge populations, are able to produce a lot of goods and services.

Two nations whose names are nearly synonymous with oil wealth are Saudi Arabia and Kuwait. Saudi Arabia has a GDP of $572 billion, or $0.6 trillion. The United States has a GDP that is about 24 times larger than Saudi Arabia's. (Thus, fears that Saudi Arabia is buying up America seem quite unfounded, although, of course, individual wealthy Saudis may buy many expensive American properties or stakes in United States companies.) Kuwait has a GDP of $139 billion, or 0.14 trillion. The United States has a GDP that is about 100 times that of Kuwait.

A nation can have a low GDP either because its people are not producing much in the way of goods and services (as is generally the case in very poor nations), or because its population is small, or both. Haiti has a GDP of $16 billion. A large percentage of its people live in grinding poverty. On the other hand, while tiny Liechtenstein has a GDP of less than $2 billion, the small dollar amount in this case signifies that this country has very few, but prosperous, citizens.

Some information about United States spending may further serve to put these numbers on GDP in context. Citizens of this nation spend about $9.5 billion on movie tickets each year. This is more than the entire GDP of Niger (about $9 billion), a country in north-central Africa. In other words, Americans spend more in a year going to the movies than the 13 million people of Niger spend on food, shelter, clothing, cars, medicine—in short, everything. In fact, United States citizens spend more per year on movies than the people of dozens of nations around the world produce in their annual GDP dollar amounts.

United States citizens spend about $18 billion on chocolate each year. This amounts to more than the GDP of many countries, including Haiti (with a GDP of $15.8 billion), Republic of the Congo (at $14 billion), and Tanzania (at $13.5 billion).

Military Muscle

When considering the power of nations, most people would look to their military establishments. Generally, nations with a potent military are able to influence international affairs to their own advantage. Many is the time that a bellicose government has engaged in "saber rattling" (using the threat of military force) to intimidate a neighboring country into submission. Famously, Adolf Hitler was able, in 1938, by such threats, to cow European leaders, specifically, those of France, Britain, and Italy, into surrendering part of the territory of then-Czechoslovakia to Germany without a fight. (Interestingly, if the leaders of these nations had been in possession of more accurate number information on the size of Germany's military forces, they might not have capitulated so readily.)

TABLE 4.5 *Nations with Largest Active Military Forces*

1. China	2,555,000
2. United States	1,426,000
3. India	1,325,000
4. North Korea	1,106,000
5. Russia	1,037,000
6. South Korea	687,000
7. Pakistan	619,000
8. Iran	545,000
9. Myanmar	492,000
10. Vietnam	484,000

(Source: CIA, *The World Factbook, 2008*)

All other things being equal, a nation with a large military establishment in terms of number of personnel (soldiers, sailors, etc.) is more powerful than one with a small military establishment. By this standard, China currently stands out as being the most powerful nation (see Table 4.5). It has about 2,555,000 personnel in its active military force (i.e., excluding reservists). This is substantially larger, by several hundred thousand, than the next largest force, that of the United States.

When strategists consider the position of the United States in the world, they note that several nations traditionally or presently hostile to this country are on the list of the top ten military forces by number. These are China, North Korea, Russia, Iran, and Vietnam. And many experts are worried that Pakistan may be slipping from the status of ally to adversary, especially with regard to the war on terror. The combined strength of these countries is 6,046,000, which dwarfs the forces of the United States. So from this perspective, the world looks very dangerous for this nation.

On the other hand, it is quite unlikely that all, or most, of these nations would band together to wage war against the United States. Most of these nations are rivals or adversaries of each other. Vietnam has more to fear from China (even though both regimes are communist and, supposedly, allies) than the United States. Russia and China eye each other with suspicion, and both worry about the instability of neighboring North Korea. So things are probably not so bleak for the United States after all.

As stated above, a large military force is more powerful than a small one, *all other things being equal.* But, of course, in the real world, all other things are not equal. With relatively minor losses, tiny Israel utterly devastated the military forces of Egypt, Syria, and Jordan in the Six Day War of 1967. During a variety of nineteenth-century clashes between British soldiers and native forces around the British Empire, in which the Imperialist forces were greatly outnumbered, they were able to inflict casualties on the order of 50 or 100 enemy killed for every British death. During the two recent (1991, 2003) wars that the United

States has fought against the Iraqi army, American forces completely trounced their opponents while suffering relatively low casualties themselves.

What the victors lacked in manpower in these cases they more than made up for in other ways—extensive training, quality of military equipment, and so on. Although a sizable force has its advantages, these other factors can more than compensate for a small number of troops. Generally, what high quality of equipment, extensive training, etc., have in common is expense. It costs a lot of money to train and supply a group of combatants and then project them into the desired area to engage the enemy. So a way to consider the strength of a military establishment is to determine how much money goes into equipping and maintaining it. This economic measure defines and illuminates "military might" in way that differs from the "total personnel power" measure used above. Table 4.6 shows the nations with the highest military expenditures.

An examination of the table is revealing. The United States comes out clearly in first place, without even a close second. This one country spends more than the next nine nations on the list *combined*. In fact, the United States spends almost half (48.6%) of the total amount (about $1.2 trillion) spent on military forces by all nations of the world!

China, which figured as most powerful in terms of number of people in its military, spends only about one tenth that of the United States' total on its armed forces. China is outspent by France and the United Kingdom, as well. And the United States spends about 15 times as much as its primary erstwhile Cold War nemesis, Russia.

A pair of nations that are currently causing consternation in Washington, D.C. are Iran and North Korea. Iran spends about $6.3 billion on its armed forces, or about one ninetieth that of the United States' total. North Korea spends about $5.5 billion, or only about 1% of the total for the United States. Thus, in terms of military spending, the United States vastly overshadows its rivals and adversaries. To the extent that money spent translates into real military power, then, the United States is in a very enviable position relative to any would-be enemies.

It should also be noted that whereas the list of the ten largest military forces in terms of number of personnel contained several nations antagonistic to the United States to a greater or

TABLE 4.6   *2007 Military Expenditures (in billions of U.S. dollars)*

1. United States	583
2. France	75
3. United Kingdom	69
4. China	59
5. Germany	46
6. Japan	42
7. Russia	40
8. Italy	33
9. Saudi Arabia	31
10. South Korea	29

(Source: CIA, *The World Factbook, 2008*)

lesser degree, the list of the ten biggest military spenders is mostly composed of nations friendly to the United States. France, the United Kingdom, Germany, Japan, Italy, and South Korea, despite fluctuations in amicability, figure prominently on the list of the United States' best friends. The friendship of Saudi Arabia, although normally a close ally of this nation, is now being questioned. In any case, it appears that based on money spent, the United States has the most powerful military establishment (by far), and other big spenders are mostly its friends.

Yet we might do well to examine these dollar expenditure numbers with a critical eye. Is there something that these numbers on military expenditures leave out? First: Obviously, it matters how the money is spent. A government could choose to spend heaps of money on weapons systems that ultimately do not work or on training for its soldiers in outmoded techniques. For example, in the years before World War II, the French spent the lion's share of their military budget on a defensive fortification known as the Maginot Line. The Germans negated this in 1940 by invading France through Belgium and avoiding the Maginot Line completely. The money spent on the Maginot Line was thus largely wasted.

Second: Money spent on the military is money which is not being spent elsewhere, such as on education, healthcare, and in other realms that are dear to a nation's citizens. Many people argue that the government of the United States, by devoting so much money to the military, is shortchanging other needy endeavors, to the detriment of American society overall. Indeed, it has been argued that when a nation spends too much on its military (and underfunds the rest of its society's needs), it actually undercuts that society and eventually weakens it. Thus, a nation that spends overly much on its military machine might actually, in the long run, defeat itself.

So what about the United States in these regards? With the benefit of more complex numerical information, most analysts would argue that, in spite of cost overruns and various fits and starts with specific weapons systems, the money spent by the United States really has produced, by far, the most powerful and effective force in the world today. It remains to be determined whether the expense has been so great as to be undermining the health of this nation overall.

Quality of Life

Of course, what most individuals care about is the quality of the life they lead. Clearly, nations differ in the general quality of life of their citizens. But to a large extent, this rather nebulous-sounding term can be rendered into numerical form. As with other characteristics of nations, one must realize that no single measure captures the essence of the overall quality of life of a nation's people. "Quality of life" is itself a rather complicated construct. When we say "quality of life," do we mean financial security (or abundance)? Or physical health? Or personal freedoms? Bearing in mind the complexity of the concept of quality of life, we proceed.

Money

One measure that can be used to determine the overall well-being of a nation is an indicator of individual wealth. This indicator is typically arrived at by calculating per capita (or per person) GDP. (Recall that we are really using GDP/PPP figures throughout this chapter.)

TABLE 4.7   *Per capita GDP/PPP (2007)*

1. Luxembourg	$81,000
2. Qatar	75,900
3. Norway	55,600
4. Kuwait	55,300
5. United Arab Emirates	55,200
6. Singapore	48,900
7. United States	46,000
8. Ireland	45,600
9. Equatorial Guinea	44,100
10. Switzerland	39,800
11. Iceland	39,400
12. Austria	39,000
13. Andorra	38,800
14. Netherlands	38,600
15. Canada	38,200

(Source: CIA, *The World Factbook, 2008*)

Per capita GDP is calculated simply by dividing the GDP figure for a nation by the number of its people. Thus, for example, the United States, with a GDP in 2007 of about $13.9 trillion and a population of approximately 300,000,000, had a per capita GDP of $46,000. This amount puts it squarely in the list of nations with the highest GDP (see Table 4.7).

What might come as a surprise to many Americans is that the United States, with all its signs of ostentatious wealth, is not in first place on the per capita GDP list. According to this measure of quality of life, the United States is surpassed by two European countries (Luxembourg and Norway) and four Asian ones (Qatar, Kuwait, United Arab Emirates, and Singapore).

Still, the United States does fare very favorably in the world. Its per capita GDP is somewhat larger than that of our neighbor to the north. Canada's per capita GDP is $38,200. The United States' per capita GDP compares even more favorably to those of our Western Hemisphere neighbors to the south. Mexico has a per capita GDP of $12,500. Poor nations of this hemisphere include Cuba (with a per capita GDP of $4,500) and Haiti (at a miserable $1,900). What this means is that people in the United States in 2007 produced on average $46,000 worth of goods and services, and spent (or saved, or invested) $46,000 worth of earnings. Each Haitian had, on average, only $1,900 to last the same year. In other words, the typical United States citizen had about 24 times as much income as the typical Haitian.

The per capita GDP of the United States is fairly close to that of most of the western European nations, such as France ($33,800), Germany ($34,400), and the United Kingdom ($35,300). Nations of Eastern Europe are, on average, poorer. Russia has a per capita GDP of $14,600, while Poland has one of $16,200.

In Asia, there is a mixed bag of per capita GDP figures. As noted, four of the top six nations are Asian. Japan has a figure of $33,800, while that of Saudi Arabia is $20,700. For all its recent economic success, the per capita GDP of China (at $5,300) still lags far behind that of the United States. The per capita GDP of India is lower still, at $2,700. The people of Bangladesh and Cambodia are seeking out a meager living, with per capita GDP figures of $1,400 and $1,800, respectively.

The African continent, for the most part, is plagued by low per capita GDP. The people of Nigeria (with a per capita GDP of $2,200), Mali ($1,200), and Zimbabwe ($500) all suffer from widespread economic hardship. South Africa does substantially better by comparison—$10,600.

One problem with using per capita GDP as a measure of the quality of life of a nation is what this measure fails to tell us. Specifically, the *distribution* of wealth is not taken into account. Suppose we have two groups of 10 people. Group A has one person who earns $491,000 per year and 9 people who earn $1,000 each. Group B's members all earn $50,000 each. Group A, then, has one individual who can afford to lead a luxurious lifestyle and 9 who are destitute. In group B, however, all individuals have the earnings to live a reasonably comfortable life. Yet the average (per capita) income for the two groups is the same—$50,000.

In the same way, we see a disparity in the way income is spread in various nations. The United States has been home in the last several years to many thousands of millionaires and dozens of billionaires. Meanwhile, the United States has a higher percentage of its people living below the poverty line than any other Western industrialized nation.

Luckily, and usefully, a method has been developed for quantifying the extent to which a nation is equitable in terms of the incomes of its people. The resulting measure is called the Gini index. A *high* Gini score for a nation indicates a society in which there is great disparity in incomes, such as the hypothetical Group A above. A *low* Gini score indicates a society in which income is more evenly distributed. Nations with the lowest Gini scores are shown in Table 4.8.

TABLE 4.8   *Gini Index*

1. Sweden	23
2. Denmark	24
3. Slovenia	24
4. Iceland	25
5. Czech Republic	26
6. Slovakia	26
7. Finland	26
8. Austria	26
9. Luxembourg	26
10. Bosnia and Herzegovina	26
57. India	37
78. Russia	41
93. United States	45
101. China	47

(Source: United Nations, *UN Development Report, 2008*)

The nation with the greatest equality in incomes (lowest Gini score) is Sweden. It is followed by several other European countries. By way of comparison, the rankings and scores of several other nations are listed at the bottom of the table.

It is noteworthy that the United States, with a rank of 93, is far from the top in terms of income equality for its people. Only about 40 nations have a higher Gini score. China, which as a communist state is supposed to have extremely high equality of incomes, actually scores worse than the United States. China's richest citizens have an even greater share of their nation's wealth than those in the United States have of theirs. Perhaps the most extreme example of disparity of incomes occurs in Equatorial Guinea. Until relatively recently, this tiny African country had a lot of poor citizens and very few that could be called wealthy. Hence, it had a low per capita GDP. But it appears on the 2007 list of nations with the highest per capita GDP—a remarkable $44,100. The reason for this change in status has to do with oil. Recently developed oil fields have meant a huge influx of money to Equatorial Guinea. But virtually all of this money has been lining the pockets of a handful of politicians while the bulk of the people remain in excruciating poverty. It is a nation of billionaires and paupers, with virtually no middle class. (Unfortunately, a Gini score has not been calculated for this nation, but I imagine it would be one of the highest, if not *the* highest, in the world.)

Long Life

One indicator of the quality of life (some would say the bottom line for measuring life) is longevity. People with inadequate food, shelter, and medicine tend to have, on average, short lifespans. Thus, we can use average life expectancy of a nation's people as a measure of quality of life. As an example, the life expectancy for a baby being born in the United States is now estimated at 78 years. That is, given current conditions in the United States, a baby born today can be expected to live 78 years. Of course, variation does exist. Females can expect to live longer than males. Whites, on average, can expect to live longer than blacks. Nonetheless, overall, the life expectancy stands at 78 years. Nations with the greatest life expectancy are shown in Table 4.9.

TABLE 4.9   *Life expectancy (years)*

1. Andorra	83.5
2. Japan	82.0
3. (tie) San Marino	81.8
3. (tie) Singapore	81.8
5. Sweden	80.6
6. Australia	80.6
7. Switzerland	80.6
8. France	80.6
9. Iceland	80.4
10. Canada	80.3

(Source: CIA, *The World Factbook, 2008*)

The people who live the longest, on average, are citizens of Andorra, a tiny nation wedged in the border between Spain and France. As noted above, the United States has an average life expectancy of 78, which gives it a rank of 29. The rank for India is 116 and for Russia 128. Many African nations fall toward the bottom of the rankings, partly because of the widespread and pernicious effects of AIDS. The nation in last place is Swaziland, with a life expectancy of only 39.6 years.

Increased Complexity

Noting the limitations of measures that take into account only one feature of the human condition, many experts prefer the use of measures that combine several facets of life into one number, referred to as a *composite measure*. One such composite measure is the Human Development Index (or HDI), which is based on a combination of the life expectancy, literacy rate, and per capita GDP of the people of a nation. The highest possible score is 1.000. Not surprisingly, once again there is a huge variability among nations. Table 4.10 shows the nations with the highest HDI scores.

European nations dominate the list of highest human development. The United States is 12th, lower than Canada, its North American neighbor. Russia, China, and India score substantially lower, ranking 67, 81, and 128, respectively.

TABLE 4.10   *Human Development Index (2007)*

1. Iceland	.968
2. Norway	.968
3. Australia	.962
4. Canada	.961
5. Ireland	.959
6. Sweden	.956
7. Switzerland	.955
8. Japan	.953
9. Netherlands	.953
10. France	.952
11. Finland	.952
12. United States	.951
13. Spain	.949
14. Denmark	.949
15. Austria	.948

(Source: United Nations, *UN Development Report, 2008*)

TABLE 4.11   *Child Well-being*

1. Netherlands	4.2
2. Sweden	5.0
3. Denmark	7.2
4. Finland	7.5
5. Spain	8.0
6. Switzerland	8.3
7. Norway	8.7
8. Italy	10.0
9. Ireland	10.2
10. Belgium	10.7
11. Germany	11.2
12. Canada	11.8
13. Greece	11.8
14. Poland	12.3
15. Czech Republic	12.5
16. France	13.0
17. Portugal	13.7
18. Austria	13.8
19. Hungary	14.5
20. United States	18.0
21. United Kingdom	18.2

(Source: Child Poverty Action Group, 2008)

A United Nations team of researchers recently conducted a study of the well-being specifically of children of several nations of Europe, as well as of Canada and the United States, for a total of 21 nations. Nutritional status, access to health care, and quality of education were some of the measures taken. These measures were combined to produce a child well-being score for each nation. The results are shown in Table 4.11.

For this survey, a low score indicates a high level of child well-being. The Netherlands (also called Holland), Sweden, and Denmark top the list. Out of 21 nations, the United States falls in 20th place.

Good Government

One important aspect of quality of life is the condition of the nation in which one lives. A nation that is high in crime and corruption and whose government cannot provide public services is a nation whose people are likely to suffer. A measure exists that takes these attributes and several others into account. It was developed primarily as a way to track

TABLE 4.12 *Most Stable Nations (Measured by Failed States Index, 2008)*

1. Norway	16.8
2. Finland	18.4
3. Sweden	19.8
4. Ireland	19.9
5. Switzerland	20.3
6. Iceland	20.9
7. New Zealand	21.4
8. Denmark	21.5
9. Australia	24.6
10. Austria	25.9
11. Canada	26.3
12. Netherlands	27.3
13. Luxembourg	27.9
14. Belgium	29.0
15. Japan	29.7

(Source: Fund for Peace, 2008)

governments that were faring very poorly, and posed a threat to their people and other nations. The measure was given the name the Failed States Index. A very *high* score on the Failed States Index indicates a nation bordering on collapse and anarchy. A *low* score indicates a stable nation, and hence a desirable place to live. The nations with the lowest scores are shown in Table 4.12.

The United States is not on the list of the top 15. With a score of 32.8, it ranks as 17th in the world. China ranks 68th, while Russia comes in at 72nd place. India ranks 98th. Incidentally, nations that score the highest (i.e., very poorly) on the Failed States Index are as follows:

Somalia
Sudan
Zimbabwe
Chad
Iraq
Dem. Rep. of the Congo
Afghanistan
Ivory Coast
Pakistan
Central African Republic

TABLE 4.13   *Quality of Life Index*

1. Ireland	8.33
2. Switzerland	8.07
3. Norway	8.05
4. Luxembourg	8.02
5. Sweden	7.94
6. Australia	7.93
7. Iceland	7.91
8. Italy	7.81
9. Denmark	7.80
10. Spain	7.73
11. Singapore	7.72
12. Finland	7.62
13. United States	7.62
14. Canada	7.60
15. New Zealand	7.44

(Source: The *Economist* Intelligence Unit, 2008)

Putting It All Together

Perhaps the most ambitious measure of the overall quality of life is the aptly named Quality of Life Index, another of the composite measures that experts find so useful. Nine factors enter into the determination of a nation's score. These are health, family life, community life, material well-being, political stability and security, climate and geography, job security, political freedom, and gender equality. The survey included 111 nations. The highest scoring nations are listed in Table 4.13.

By the standards of the survey, Ireland's citizens have the highest quality of life of any in the world. The United States comes in 13th. Not shown on the list are China (ranked 60), India (ranked 73), and Russia (ranked a miserable 105). The lowest score of all belongs to Zimbabwe—3.9, which gives it a rank of 111. Incidentally, several nations were not evaluated; some of these were countries that would have performed quite badly, maybe even worse than Zimbabwe.

The Environment

The Condition of the Planet

Everybody has heard of air and water pollution, the degradation of the world's forests, global warming, and so on. Some argue that the problems are relatively minor, while others argue that they are huge. Some number information might help here.

Take, for example, the case of tropical rain forests. This particular type of vegetation covers about 2 billion acres (somewhat over 3 million square miles) of the Earth's land surface. Although this may sound like a great amount, it actually equals only about 5% of land. In recent years, the rate of destruction of the forest in the tropics, largely a result of logging and burning to clear the land for crops, has been estimated at close to 50 million acres annually. In recent years, Brazil alone has been losing forest at a rate of 12.5–22.5 million acres per year. India has been losing approximately 3.7 million acres per year. Between 1990 and 2005, Indonesia lost about 24% of its forests, and Nigeria about 36%. Every year, rain forest equivalent to the area of North Carolina is lost.

If the estimate of 50 million acres of rain forest being destroyed per year is accurate (and this, incidentally, does not include other types of forest), this means that about 2.5% of the rain forest is lost annually. If this rate of loss continues, it would seem that the rain forests have only about 40 years or so before they cease to exist altogether. Citizens may be complacent in the knowledge that various replanting projects are underway across the globe. But these come nowhere close to offsetting the yearly losses. Overall, for every tree being planted, 10 are being cut down. In Africa, 29 are cut for every one planted. In any case, the kinds of reforestation being done are frequently haphazard and not conducive to the long-term environmental health and stability of the areas involved. For those who do not particularly care about the natural beauty being devastated as the rain forests succumb to human encroachment, or about the multitudes of animal species quickly being rendered extinct, perhaps the loss of valuable medicines and other products derived from the trees will strike a note of concern. One especially valuable product manufactured by the plants of the rain forest is oxygen. Some estimates of the amount of oxygen that is produced by all the rain forests range as high as 50% of all oxygen emitted by all sources on earth. It may be that oxygen will become a scarce commodity in our children's lifetime.

Other natural resources are being depleted. Water is becoming progressively scarcer in many areas of the globe. Increasingly, water is being taken from natural underwater reservoirs, or aquifers—i.e., from groundwater—to meet the needs of people for farming and drinking. Water removal from these underground sources is occurring much faster than it can be naturally replenished. Currently, close to 500 million people live in areas of water stress (where it is difficult to meet even the basic water requirements of humans). It is predicted that by the year 2025, approximately 3 billion people will live in such areas. This shortage is likely to lead to massive starvation, migration to other, more water-rich areas, and to wars between countries for access to water. Already, tensions have risen between many nations of the Middle East over access to water.

There are many other areas of concern. Topsoil, needed for the growing of crops, is being lost at 40 times the rate that it is being replaced by nature. Because of overuse and poor management, many regions are turning into deserts. As a result of pollution and global warming, itself most likely caused by pollution, coral reefs are being destroyed at an unprecedented rate. It is estimated that 70% of the coral reefs in the Indian Ocean have been destroyed in the last several years. The waters of Australia are witnessing similar destruction. Not only do the coral reefs provide the natural habitat for a huge number of ocean species, but they also help protect land areas from the ravages of storms.

Pollution of various kinds has far-reaching effects. Currently, air pollution in the United States costs at least $40 billion per year in health care costs and lowered worker productivity. Destruction of European forest caused by the effects of air pollution alone is costing over $30 billion per year. These losses come as a result of damage to wood that otherwise might be cut and sold, increased flooding, and lost soil. As air pollution contributes to global warming, the world can expect even more problems. By 2025, for example, it is predicted that global warming will cause a high increase in heat stress and drought throughout the world. Farming will become less productive, electricity use will soar (due to an increase in needed air conditioning), and coastal areas will be damaged by a rise in sea level.

A Primary Offender

One of the primary pollutants, and one of the so-called greenhouse gases that contribute to global warming, is carbon dioxide. It is worthwhile to make a close examination of this pollutant. Carbon dioxide is released into the environment primarily through car exhaust and various industrial processes. Leading contributor nations to carbon dioxide emissions are shown in Table 4.14.

The United States is first on this list of polluters. It is accountable for about 22% of the world total of carbon dioxide for 2004, i.e., 27,044 million metric tons. (Note: a metric ton is 2,204.62 pounds). Annual carbon dioxide emissions in the United States have increased about 24% since 1980. China, which is undergoing an astonishingly rapid industrialization and modernization, has seen its annual emissions rise 224% between 1980 and 2004, propelling it to second place on the list of polluters. Environmental scientists predict that it will overtake the United States within the next few years. India has also experienced a huge increase in emissions since 1980—271%.

Rather than merely considering overall levels of carbon dioxide emissions, we might want to consider how much CO_2 individual nations are releasing in proportion to their population.

TABLE 4.14 *Top Nations Producing Carbon Dioxide Emission (in millions of metric tons, 2004)*

1. United States	5,912
2. China	4,707
3. Russia	1,685
4. Japan	1,262
5. India	1,113
6. Germany	862
7. Canada	588
8. United Kingdom	580
9. South Korea	497
10. Italy	485

(Source: U.S. Dept. of Energy, *International Energy Annual, 2007*)

TABLE 4.15 *Per capita Carbon Dioxide Emissions (in millions of metric tons, 2004)*

United States	20.2
China	3.6
Russia	11.7
Japan	9.9
India	1.0
Germany	10.5
Canada	17.8
United Kingdom	9.7
South Korea	10.1
Italy	8.4

After all, a nation with a huge population might be expected to produce more pollution simply because it has more people engaged in activities that emit this gas. If we want to assign blame for creating pollution, we should probably take into account the amount of carbon dioxide each nation emits based on its population. These numbers are shown in Table 4.15.

Looking at the top carbon dioxide polluters, we can see that the United States is responsible for releasing 20.2 metric tons *per capita* (or *per person*). This puts it in the unenviable position of being first among these nations. Canada is second in this regard, and Russia third. Although China as an entire nation produces a huge amount of carbon dioxide, on a per-person basis it produces less than one-fifth as much as the United States. The least egregious on this measure is India, which releases one ton per person, or about one-twentieth that of the United States. The United Kingdom, which led the world into the Industrial Revolution, creates substantially less carbon dioxide than the United States on a per-person basis—about one-half of the United States' amount.

Yet there is another way of looking at the question of carbon dioxide pollution. Perhaps the amount of emissions has to do with the amount of economic activity that occurs in a nation. After all, a country that produces a lot of goods (cars, shoes, computers, etc.) is likely to create more pollution in doing so. Table 4.16 lists the same nations but this time shows the amount of carbon dioxide emission per thousand dollars worth of GDP created.

In looking at the top overall carbon dioxide polluters in the light of GDP, we may note that the worst offender is Russia. It creates 1.2 tons of this pollutant for every thousand dollars of GDP it generates. This is twice the amount of China, the second greatest polluter in this regard. The United States, Canada, and South Korea are quite close on this measure.

In these days of increasing concern about the state of the planet and amid initiatives to "go green," it becomes pertinent to know which nations are responsible for creating the most pollution, certainly a task requiring numerical information. But which numbers are the most relevant? Are they those reflecting the overall amount of pollution that nations produce, or the amount of pollutants *per person*, or the amount of pollutants *per $1,000 GDP?* Or is there another way of measuring pollution that is even more illuminating and helpful?

TABLE 4.16 *Carbon Dioxide Emissions (in tons, 2004) per $1,000 GDP*

United States	.50
China	.65
Russia	1.20
Japan	.34
India	.34
Germany	.36
Canada	.57
United Kingdom	.33
South Korea	.54
Italy	.30

The Disappearance of Species

The trashing of the planet by humans has placed many of the world's animal species at risk of extinction. One recent (2006) estimate considers close to 8,000 animal species threatened with extinction. This includes about 20% of mammal species and 12% of bird species. Yet as the researchers themselves note, this is bound to be an underestimate, as it doesn't consider species that remain to be identified (which may be the majority of them). People tend to lament the possible loss of great animals such as the polar bear, tiger, elephant, and rhinoceros, all of which are threatened by extinction. As unfortunate as their passing may be, extinction of less noticeable (to humans) species may ultimately be more devastating. For reasons that are unclear (but that are likely due to human contamination of the environment), the population of bees in the United States and Europe has in recent years dropped dramatically. With stunning rapidity, once-thriving hives have become bereft of bees, a phenomenon termed "sudden colony collapse." Scientists and farmers realize the tremendous importance of this: bees are responsible for pollinating a substantial proportion of crops. If the current crisis continues, we could be facing a drastic reduction in crop yields, which will undoubtedly raise food prices. Already the damages are estimated in the billions of dollars.

Meanwhile, naturalists have observed the rapid decline in population of a group of species of frogs in Central America. The frogs are considered to act as a sort of sensor for the quality of the overall environment, much as canaries were once used by miners to indicate the quality of air in coal mines. The massive reduction in frog population may be a warning of widespread environmental destruction in the making.

People and More People

What is behind all the environmental damage and the predictions of much worse to come? To a large extent the answer is human population. In terms of food, water, and so on, the Earth is unable to meet the needs of its current inhabitants. As the population grows, the problems will become ever more acute. And the tricky thing is that the population is growing in geometric progression, much like the coins on the king's chessboard. It took the world thousands of years to reach a grand total of 2.5 billion people in 1950. By the year 2000, a mere fifty years later, the population had more than doubled, to 6.1 billion. Currently, the world is adding about 80–90 million people (about the population of Germany) annually. The population stands at about 6.7 billion as of July 2008.

Actually, the rate of growth may be slowing. The more optimistic estimates predict that the population of the world will be about 9 billion by the year 2025. If it continued to grow at the rates of the last few decades, the number would be closer to 20 billion. Of course, it is doubtful that the Earth will be able to support 9 billion people in 2025 any better than it can support 6.7 billion at present.

As population increases, many people are demanding a better life. Attention should be focused on the two most populous nations: China and India. As noted above, China is currently undergoing a massive program of economic and industrial development. It is estimated that the amount of carbon dioxide that it will produce by 2025 will be greater than the current combined total of the United States, Japan, and Canada. Referring to global warming, one expert commented, "Just how hot the planet ends up getting will be largely determined by the actions of China." India, too, hopes to increase its people's standard of living. But in the long run, as more industry leads to more pollution, more drought, and more starvation, this approach to economic progress is likely to end up causing more harm than good.

Environmental Responsibility

Individual nations differ with regard to the amount of damage they do to the environment and the steps they take to restore the environment. Researchers have recently developed a measure for national responsibility, which is termed the Environmental Performance Index (EPI). This measure takes into account such indicators as natural resource endowments, present pollution levels, contributions to the protection of the global environment, and a society's ability to improve its environment in the future. The nations scoring the highest, indicating greater environmental responsibility, are shown in Table 4.17.

Switzerland takes top honors in this category. Other high scores go primarily to wealthy European nations. But the existence of Costa Rica and Colombia on the list indicates that a nation does not need to be wealthy to be environmentally responsible. The United States ranks 39.

Observations

So how does the preceding information help us to understand the nations of the world and global affairs? Some hypothetical examples might prove instructive. Suppose you are witnessing an argument between two people on the national strength of the United States.

TABLE 4.17   *Environmental Performance Index (2008)*

1. Switzerland	95.5
2. Norway	93.1
3. Sweden	93.1
4. Finland	91.4
5. Costa Rica	90.5
6. Austria	89.4
7. New Zealand	88.9
8. Latvia	88.8
9. Colombia	88.3
10. France	87.8
11. Iceland	87.6
12. Canada	86.6
13. Germany	86.3
14. United Kingdom	86.3
15. Slovenia	86.3

(Source: Yale Center for Environmental Law and Policy, 2008)

One maintains that it is a declining power and has become a second-rate nation. The other person states that the United States is still a great power, in fact the only superpower, and has little to worry about. Suppose further that the two people rely on general statements and anecdotes to support their positions. What could your response be, just using the information gleaned from this chapter? First, you could ask what measure of strength should be used here. If you choose economic strength as indicated by GDP, then the clear answer is that the United States is the world's most powerful nation. At $13.9 trillion, its GDP is twice as large as that of China (which has the second largest GDP in the world), three times as large as that of Japan (third in terms of GDP), and over four times as large as that of India (fourth in GDP). If, instead, you decided to measure power by military strength, a somewhat more complex picture emerges. China has a substantially larger military force than the United States in terms of number of personnel. On the other hand, looking at military expenditures, the analyst observes that the United States is without peer. It outspends every other nation by far. It currently spends on its military establishment about six times as much as Russia and China, two of its likely future adversaries, combined. Thus, from the information in this chapter, it would be difficult to conclude that the United States is *not* a very powerful nation. It would make more sense to conclude that it is *the* most powerful nation on Earth. (Of course, how the United States chooses to use this power is another issue altogether.)

TABLE 4.18

Measure	United States' rank
Per capita GDP	7
Gini Index	93
Life expectancy	29
Human Dev. Index	12
National stability	17
Child well-being	20 (out of 21)
Quality of Life Index	12

What about the quality of life? Once again, by examining number information we can make some reasoned judgments. Although the United States tends to score quite well on some of the measures, it doesn't come out in first place on any (see Table 4.18).

On these measures, the United States is outclassed by several nations. It appears in the top ten on only one list—per capita GDP. By comparison, Sweden, Switzerland, and Ireland each appear in the top ten on six lists. Norway appears five times, while Iceland, Denmark, and Australia appear four times. In terms of quality of life, then, the United States is certainly not "Number One."

What about the comparison put forth toward the start of this chapter, that between Switzerland and Zimbabwe? (See Table 4.19.)

On every measure, Switzerland scores better (sometimes by an enormous margin) than Zimbabwe. The people of Switzerland have more money to spend and live longer lives. The earnings equality is greater for Switzerland, as is human development, and stability of the nation. By recourse to numbers, we see that Switzerland provides its citizens with better lives than does Zimbabwe. If the United States is to consider giving economic aid to a nation in need of help (based on the plight of its people), then clearly it should assist Zimbabwe, and not Switzerland.

TABLE 4.19

Measure	Switzerland	Zimbabwe
Per capita GDP	$39,800	$500
Gini Index	33.7	57
Life expectancy	80.6	39.5
Human Dev. Index	.955	.513
National stability	20.3	112.5
Quality of Life Index	8.07	3.89

TABLE 4.20

Measure	Kazakhstan
Per capita GDP	$10,400
Gini Index	40
Life expectancy	67.2
Human Dev. Index	.794
National stability	72.4
Quality of Life Index	5.08

Return to Borat

And what about the controversy surrounding the film *Borat* and the lifestyles of the people of Kazakhstan? (See Table 4.20.)

Kazakhstan scores substantially worse than Switzerland on all the dimensions of quality of life used in this chapter. The average citizen of Kazakhstan has less money and a shorter lifespan than the typical Swiss citizen. The people of Kazakhstan live in a society that is less stable and less economically equitable than the society of Switzerland. On the other hand, the quality of life in Kazakhstan is far superior to that in Zimbabwe. Kazakhstan stands pretty much in the middle of the pack (that is, of all nations of the world) in terms of the quality of life that its citizens enjoy. So perhaps it is safe to say that Kazakhstan is in reality about halfway between the portrayals put forth by Borat and the real Kazakhstan government. (Borat's portrayal is, of course, much more humorous.)

Problems

As much as numbers can be of great assistance in shedding light on important world matters, certain problems in use of those numbers can arise.

1. We should be careful in the use of our sources and the numbers they provide. For instance, there is a problem in dealing with numbers when they lead us to imagine a level of precision that simply does not exist. Let's use an example. One source gives the 2007 population of Indonesia as 234,693,997. For one thing, it is simply impossible to know the exact population of a any nation at a given point in time. (Perhaps some of the extremely small nations are exceptions.) Beyond that, a nation's population is constantly changing through births, deaths, and migration. So even for 2007, Indonesia's population had many values other than 234,693,997.

2. There can be problems in data gathering. For example, the official statistics of the FBI show a great increase in the murder rate of the United States throughout the 1970s and 1980s. There was much anguish among politicians and the public about this alarming trend. But it turned out to be a false alarm. The murder rate just *appeared* to be increasing. This was due to improved reporting. The FBI relies on local police departments to report the numbers of various crimes. These numbers are added together by the FBI. In the early 1970s many police departments did not bother to report to the FBI. The number of complying police departments rose throughout the 1970s and 1980s. So what looked like an increasing murder rate was in reality an increase in the *reporting* of murders. In fact, the murder rate remained stable throughout this period.

3. Faulty comparisons can be made. In recent years many observers have indicated concern about the high United States murder rate, comparing it to the relatively low murder rates of other Western democracies. For example, the United Kingdom, Japan, and Germany all have lower murder rates than the United States. A particularly striking comparison has been made between the United States and Sweden. That is, Sweden's murder rate has been shown to be much lower than the rate of the United States. But a little investigating reveals why the comparison is a bit inappropriate, somewhat akin to comparing apples and oranges. Traditionally, United States law enforcement officials have been prone to categorize deaths of unknown causes as murder. If a man is found dead in an alley, it is likely to be considered a case of murder and is recorded as such. If it is later found to be a suicide, or death by illness or accident, it remains in the FBI records officially as a murder.

On the other hand, in Sweden, a death is not considered officially a murder until a suspect has been tried and convicted for it. Thus, even an obvious homicide, if the culprit is never caught, never gets counted as such. Because of national differences in the standards for the counting of murders, the rate appears grossly higher for the United States than for Sweden. As it happens, even when these factors are ruled out and a reanalysis is done, the murder rate of the United States is found to be higher than for Sweden, just not hugely higher.

4. Problems of definitions arise in other contexts. Every nation desires having a high literacy rate. But different sources (sometimes countries) use different definitions of literacy. Adult literacy is used to mean, by some analysts, the ability to write one's name. Others take literacy to mean the ability to read at a certain grade level, say 3rd grade. (And, of course, what is meant by 3rd grade reading level is open to different interpretations.) Thus, a particular country may have a 98% adult literacy rate if the first standard is used, but only a 20% rate by the second. Comparing different countries with respect to literacy is actually quite difficult to do accurately. The numbers become very misleading if different definitions are applied to different countries.

The same is true for standards of poverty. One definition of poverty is living below the level required to sustain food intake necessary for long-term survival. Another definition of poverty is to be in the lowest 10% of incomes of your nation. Using this definition, if your nation is Switzerland, you are—as a "person living in poverty"—likely to be much better off than if your nation is Ethiopia. And a person living in the lowest 10% of incomes in Switzerland is still likely to have enough food to sustain life.

5. Of course, accuracy can be quite difficult and even respectable sources can disagree. An inspection of several popular almanacs would reveal that there are discrepancies, sometimes substantial, among different sources, for population estimates (even for the same year), for the GDP of various nations, and even for something seemingly so fixed as national geographic area. It is hard enough to come up with an accurate GDP of the United States. It is much more difficult to estimate the GDP of many third-world nations, where record keeping of financial transactions is not as precise as it is elsewhere. And some nations are very secretive about their national statistics. During the Cold War, the Soviet Union did not publish reliable figures for its economy, including its GDP. In the United States the CIA was given the responsibility for estimating the GDP of the Soviet Union (USSR) during these years. It is now recognized that those estimates grossly exaggerated the economic power of the Soviet Union. This was no trivial matter. The highest reaches of the United States government based their dealings with the Soviet Union on these inaccurate estimates. The huge increase in United States defense spending during the 1980s was partly a response to the CIA's faulty estimates of the Soviet Union's GDP. Even today the estimates made by the CIA of the GDP of China are recognized as very likely being 25% too high (which accounts for almost $2 trillion of China's economy).

Concluding Remarks

Many people do not like dealing with numbers, as mentioned at the beginning of the chapter, because they think that it is too mentally taxing to do so. But other people deliberately avoid paying attention to numbers for other reasons. They are aware of the errors that can creep into arguments which employ numbers. They are also aware that unscrupulous people may, for various reasons, at times willfully distort number information. So they turn a blind eye when numbers are presented. Their attitude seems to reflect the disparaging adage, variously attributed to Mark Twain and the nineteenth-century British Prime Minister Benjamin Disraeli: "There are lies, damned lies, and statistics."

But I would argue that even though number information has its drawbacks and people may at times try to deceive you with numerical distortions, your best defense is *not* ignorance of numbers. Rather, you should learn how to use numbers correctly and how to recognize deceptive maneuvers. After all, people may lie using the written word. But nobody would argue that the best way to prevent yourself from being hoodwinked in print would be never to learn to read.

It is my hope that the reader has gained an appreciation for the ways in which number information can be used to describe fundamental aspects of a nation, its strengths and weaknesses, and its people. As I indicated in the beginning of this chapter, I believe that a complete picture of a national or a global problem cannot be had without recourse to numbers. But I do not believe that subjecting every nation to a quantifying analysis is sufficient for a full understanding of it or its problems. As valuable as numbers are, they do not tell the whole story. No one would deny that personal accounts, descriptive studies, art, and literature are all relevant to gaining insight into the state of a nation. But just as an analysis that relied completely on numerical methods would paint a distorted picture, so any analysis that excluded numbers from consideration would give us but partial truth.

Notes

I tried to choose sources for the tables in this chapter that are widely used and respected. One main source was the United Nations, which collects gigantic amounts of data on hundreds of characteristics of nations and peoples, and makes it available to the public. Its Web site is www.un.org. The interested student should find the section on Indicators for a detailed look at political, economic, environmental, and social aspects of nations. Another main source was the Central Intelligence Agency, whose Web site is www.cia.gov. Like the UN, the CIA gathers huge amounts of information about countries and makes it available to the public. This can be found in its *World Factbook*. Generally, when the UN and the CIA are examining the same feature of nations, such as life expectancy, their numbers are fairly close in agreement. Insofar as they sometimes use different methods to gather their data, it should not be surprising that their numbers are not identical. Often when I chose one of these sources over the other, it was because the chosen one included more nations in its calculations. If you were to look in several common almanacs for figures on GDP, longevity, population, and such, you would probably find that the almanacs use the CIA and the UN as their sources.

Other sources were used. The Failed States Index, which I used to discuss national stability, is produced jointly each year by the think-tank Fund for Peace and the magazine *Foreign Policy*. The Quality of Life Index was developed by the Intelligence Unit of the magazine *The Economist*. The Environmental Performance Index was developed by Yale University, Columbia University, the World Economic Forum, and the Joint Research Center of the European Commission. It can be accessed at www.epi.yale.edu. L. R. Brown's *Plan B 2.0* (2006) provided other environmental data.

Questions for Discussion

1. Switzerland and Zimbabwe (and Kazakhstan) were highlighted in this chapter during discussion of "quality of life." It became clear that the people of Switzerland have, by all measures used, a higher quality of life than the people of Zimbabwe (and the people of Kazakhstan are somewhere in between the two). Pick two nations outside the United States for which you already have a strong impression or prediction. By the measures used in this chapter, examine and assess their quality of life. Which nation "wins"? How do your two choices compare to the United States? Does your investigation give you any surprises?

2. What ways other than the measures used in this chapter can you think of to use number information to examine, and measure, national power, quality of life, and environmental status? Can you find measures for your new ways? Are they better or worse than those provided in this chapter? (*Hint.* Try these to start: Corruption Perceptions Index, Freedom House Ratings.)

3. Find examples in the media in which number information is being used to argue a point about nations or the world at large. Does the number information provided by the media help you understand the topic? Can you provide other number information to make the argument about this topic better? Can you provide other number information to counter the claim being made? What do various kinds of number information lead you to conclude about the point under consideration?

4. Suppose you were advising a large charitable organization that wished to spend money to improve the lives of the people who were most desperately in need of help. Which nation(s) would you recommend to receive that aid? How would you use number information to argue for your choice(s)?

5. Choose one of the charts from this chapter and write a 500-word interpretation of the figures it contains. Compare your interpretation with those of other students. How do you account for the differences among the explanations?

Suggested Readings

Brown, L. R. (2006). *Plan B 2.0*. New York: W. W. Norton.
Huff, D. (1954). *How to lie with statistics*. New York: W. W. Norton.
Kennedy, D. (2006). *Science magazine's state of the planet, 2006–2007*. Washington, DC: Island Press
Novacek, M. J. (2001). *The biodiversity crisis*. New York: The New Press.
Paulos, J. A. (1988). *Innumeracy: Mathematical illiteracy and its consequences*. New York: Vintage Books.
Prescott-Allen, R. (2001). *The wellbeing of nations*. Washington, DC: The Island Press.

5

Reading World Literature to Read the World

Literature and the Global Studies Student

Rosemary Haskell

World Literature and World Affairs: Looking for Parallels

Becoming a responsible world citizen sounds weighty and difficult. Sometimes it sounds as though you have to get out there right now and build houses, drain swamps, distribute medicines and run schools in remote villages in order to get the title. These are necessary and praiseworthy activities. But there are other ways also of being a responsible world citizen.

Understanding—analyzing, interpreting and evaluating—different facets of the global experience so that you can participate in it more usefully and intelligently can happen through the medium of imaginative literature—poetry, plays, novels, and short stories. Non-fiction genres such as the essay, journal, biography and autobiography, and the electronic versions of these—the blog, for example—can illuminate the world. Reading about other places and people, and imaginative identification with the perspectives of people half a world away, may uncover not only new geographic worlds but also new ways of thinking. Imaginative literature has, in addition, complex and various connections with the culture, and the history of the culture, it emerges from. As we'll see, novels, poems, and plays can operate on many planes and at many levels in relationship to the world we call "real." By the end of the chapter, you should see that the real concrete tangible world may be no more (and no less) important than the world you can experience through imaginative literature.

English teachers in particular believe that literature explains the world, the inner life, and even the after life. We've all been there, usually with our own English teachers. But you don't have to be an English teacher to know how to use novels, poems, and plays to illuminate the ways of the world, past or present. Global Studies students can learn that literature may help us analyze and interpret all facets of culture, including politics, economics, religion, and our attitudes toward material culture and nature. Literature gives us vicarious experiences and allows us to adopt for a while other people's viewpoints and understandings of their own parts of the world. Literature can unpack big topics into some surprising components. It can be a kind of alternative or additional history—something as valuable as a history book or archival document or news broadcast. But literature is certainly different from other discourses in our culture; and it requires us to hone our interpretive and analytical skills if we are to make the most of it as a facet of our total global experience.

Knowledge of literature—its major types, or genres, and its principal modes, or styles—can also help us to analyze and interpret so-called real-world people, events, and situations. An actual event may have an illuminating literary parallel: is an ageing despot of a fragile state a little like Shakespeare's King Lear, with a family of potential successors, some loyal, some treacherous? Is a war-torn land like the battlefield of an ancient epic such as Homer's *Iliad?* Is an army general more like Achilles than is good for him—or for us? Is a formerly prosperous country in economic free fall—with empty supermarket shelves, empty granaries and unplanted fields—like the untended farms referred to in Virgil's *Georgics?* Is a state beset by a parallel world of invisible enemies—perhaps they are labeled as "terrorists"—like the universe depicted in J. K. Rowling's Harry Potter books, where a war is intermittently waged against the subversive and ambitious Lord Voldemort and his hidden minions? Such parallels will always break down at some point—but, perhaps, not before illuminating some component of an otherwise puzzling world situation.

In addition to these particular texts, there are what we might call "literary events": occurrences involving novels, poems, plays, and their authors which tell us something about the state of the world. Box 5.1. gives us a selection of these so-called "literary events." Think of your own examples, also, and what they say to us about the world today.

BOX 5.1 • *Literary Events that Tell Us about the State of the World*

The story of Kenyan writer Ngugi Wa Thiong'o, is a kind of parable or microcosm of east/west relations during the early postcolonial period. Ngugi published novels and plays in English until 1978, at which point he declared he would write only in Kikuyu. He took the risk of limiting his readership: if no translator stepped forward, the whole English-speaking readership would be lost to him. His choice of his native tongue, rather than the colonizers' English, was inextricably personal, political, and public. After publishing the novel *Petals of Blood*, in 1977, a critique of postcolonial Kenyan government, Ngugi was imprisoned by that government. Reversion to Kikuyu involved a turning away from the corruptly-westernized leadership of his own country. But the story of this author's language journey, told in his 1986 work *Decolonising the Mind* (Ngugi, pp. 4–33), also explains facets of international economic and political relationships: between Kenya and the UK, Kenya and the West, and between the former African colonies and their reliance on the publishing houses and the language of their former colonial masters. Ngugi's decision also moved literature in Kikuyu forward. Ngugi's position was opposed to Nigerian novelist Chinua Achebe's 1964 view: "I have been given the language and I intend to use it." Achebe regarded English as a language to be freely used by former colonies as a way of reaching a broader audience. (qtd. Ngugi, *Decolonizing*, p. 7).

****

Writers who don't get translated into English are writers that those of us in the United States and the rest of the English-speaking world will miss. David Damrosch notes (12) that when Gao Xingjiang won the 2000 Nobel Literature prize, western publishers had to scramble madly. Nobody had translated this author's works and so he was essentially invisible to most western eyes. The Prize was the catalyst that made Gao's work available to millions more readers. In 2008, the Nobel Literature winner, Jean-Marie Gustave Le Clezio, unknown to most Americans and also to many Europeans, also achieved—among other things—the opportunity to become internationally read, in translation as well as in his native French.

****

Very occasionally, a novel, or poem, or play, will appear on the national stage with a flash and a bang—a sign of the kind of importance we normally associate with political, or economic, or even military phenomena, such as a fall in the stock market, or the election of a government, or some raid or invasion. One such literary event was the publication of Salman Rushdie's novel *The Satanic Verses* (1988)—which brought the *fatwa*, edict of condemnation to death—upon the author from Ayatollah Khomeini, then the leader of Iran. Rushdie's novel was read by many as an ironic, even derisive, treatment of Islam, and was denounced by the Ayatollah as such. In

hindsight, the *fatwa*, which drove Rushdie into hiding for many years, looks like a border skirmish conflict between Islam and "the West," defined by most of us only after the 9/11 attacks on the United States. But in 1988, the "Rushdie affair" appeared as a coda to the hostage taking of United States citizens in Tehran in 1978. In those late-Cold-War days, the American media weren't thinking very much about Iran, or about Islam.

****

Nigerian novelist Chinua Achebe had to run for his life after publishing his 1966 novel *A Man of the People*. Nigerian military powers thought it was the prediction of a coup which had just taken place: and, if it was a prediction, how did the novelist know it was coming? As noted elsewhere, the Nigerian government was forced into the position of literary critic: Was the novel a work of imagination or an actual call to arms? Or both? (Haskell, Lee, and Crenshaw p.101).

****

The death in summer 2008 of Soviet novelist Alexander Solzhenitsyn reminded the world of something that they had almost forgotten—or would like to. The great Russian novelist's life spanned the entire history of the Soviet Union from its emergence after the 1917 Revolution right up until the devolution of the USSR in 1992 into the "Commonwealth of Independent States," and into the Yeltsin, Putin, and post-Putin years. Most U.S. readers of a certain age suddenly remembered their youthful interest in his 1968 novel *The Cancer Ward*, a bitter denunciation—through the metaphor of a clinically sick society—of the grim and brutal Stalinist era and in *The Gulag Archipelago* (1974), a chronicle which revealed the terror and oppression of Soviet totalitarianism.

Globalization: Not Just about Free Trade, Tariffs, and Cotton Subsidies

The examples in Box 5.1 show that the Nobel Prize—and other prestigious awards—can boost the globalization of literature, just as the engines of economic globalization—the IMF (International Monetary Fund), the World Bank, the WHO (World Health Organization), the UN (United Nations), the WTO (World Trade Organization) and the ILO (International Labor Organization)—play their part in energizing, financing and legislating the flow of goods, capital, and labor around the world. Translators and publishers and booksellers—including online sellers such as Amazon.com and other smaller firms—are the engines of this literary globalization or internationalization. The flow of literature as part of any model of globalization—its very existence, and then its dissemination to its readers—has, like the transmission of other kinds of information, been enormously helped by the progress of the means of production, transmission, and distribution. Ever since Gutenberg and Caxton brought us the printing press, poets and playwrights, and then novelists, have had a much easier time getting a readership of more than their immediate social circle. Movable type was a big help, as was the mass production of cheap books and weekly and monthly periodicals that came with the high-volume, low-cost manufacture afforded by the machinery of the industrial revolution. Cheap mass-market paperbacks seem like a way of life to us, but they are relatively recent arrivals on the shelf. Finally, in the late twentieth century, the advent of the Internet, in addition to making the mere transmission of ideas and information dramatically easier and cheaper, allowed publishing itself to become more feasible for the individual, and more likely to get into the hands of nonprofessionals and out of the sole control of the professional publishing houses.

But, like the flow of goods, services, capital, and labor, the circulation of literature can be interrupted, impeded, or stopped—either mischievously or unintentionally. Some countries essentially subsidize the production of poems, plays, and novels: through state-funded education, through organizations such as the United States' NEH (National Endowment for the Humanities), and through grants and prizes for people who produce literature. Though some would argue that government funding of the arts may create political problems for the artists, the absence of such central support can indeed be a hindrance, both to the production and the dissemination of literature. Lack of translators also presents a problem; lack of publishers with a national or international reach—or lack of any publishers—is another barrier; censorship—official or unofficial—dams up the flow of ideas. And, of course, illiteracy is a huge obstacle. Cultures where "orature,"[1] or spoken-word "texts," predominate face still other problems if they wish their stories to be transmitted to the rest of the world. Homer's *Odyssey* and *Iliad* were originally performed as dramatic speech by court poets or bards—but it was the poems' commitment to paper that ensured their survival for more than 2500 years.

Just as in the globalization of political and economic life, so, in the literary world, too, there will be winners and losers. Some literature is marginalized, while other texts flourish. In the industrial western world, which has until recently been much devoted to print and reading, oral literature, or orature, has struggled for notice. But with a collage of multimedia texts—video, still pictures, recorded voice—gaining ground in the hands of so many, this traditional folk medium might find its place again, for audiences around the world. It's also clear that the new electronic media have helped to give birth to some new types of literature, or modified versions of old ones.[2]

Understanding the way that literature "goes global," or fails to do so, is one way to grasp at least some of the history of global society and global culture. World literature, past and present, can also function like a map or chart of world affairs, or as a political drawing of the globe.

Navigating the Map of World Literature: Not Continents and Countries, but Genres and Modes

Mapping, and then navigating, this literary terrain is relatively simple. Genre is the name of the broad category to which a literary text belongs. The main categories are: novels, short stories, poems, plays, and essays. Within each of these categories, a text may be presented in a certain style, or manner, usually called a "mode." "Mode" is almost like a tone of voice, a way of speaking. Knowledge of genres and modes can help us to organize our approach to literature: we know, after all, what to expect of—and what to look for in—a novel, poem, play, essay, or short story. And, if we think we have grasped the mode of a play, story, novel, or poem—whether comic, tragic, gothic, or epic—we are able to be pragmatic, to limit our interpretive range and avoid wasting energy looking for characteristics which simply aren't there. Finally, a knowledge of genre and mode can help us to make connections among different texts: even apparently dissimilar works may share family resemblances that can be mutually illuminating.

In Global Studies, in particular, a knowledge of literary genres and modes allows us to interpret world events within a literary framework. Turning from the page to the real world, and back again, we can ask if an event, or even a person, is—or is behaving—in gothic, or pastoral, or tragic, or comic, or even magical fashion—or some combination of these.

Here then, is a brief list of literary genres and modes:

GENRES: These terms indicate a type, or category, or class of texts, with distinguishing characteristics.

Novel and Short Story: Continuous prose fiction; has plot, character, setting, narrator, point of view; narrator separate from author; short story can be very very short—"flash fiction"—or quite hefty: perhaps up to fifty pages. Novellas are short novels, or long short stories.

Play or Drama: Text consists of dialogue, stage directions, indications about setting for the guidance of the actors; plays have character, setting, and plot, but rarely a narrator or narrative viewpoint; may be in prose or poetry; usually meant to be performed on stage.

Poetry: Verse, not prose; may be closed or open form; huge variety of lengths—from seven-line haiku and fourteen-line sonnets to ten-thousand-line epics; condensed language, relying heavily on imagery, metaphor, and symbol. Speaker in the poem may or may not be associated with the author.

Essay: Nonfiction prose text of short to moderate length; transmits author's personal viewpoint on one of a huge range of topics.

Blog, Weblog: Electronic prose text resembling a mix of diary, letter, essay, and journal; can be interactive; may have links to other texts or pictures.

MODES: These terms indicate a "manner of speaking," a way of delivering and framing the text of a given genre.

We should note, to begin with, that—for example—a drama can be tragic, or comic, or satiric; that novels, poems, plays, and short stories alike may each show gothic, satiric, pastoral, and elegiac features. Many, if not most, literary works demonstrate the characteristics of more than one literary mode.

Comic: The story ends well, with loose ends tied up, mistakes ignored or forgiven; emphasizes inclusion and harmony, but also focuses on absurd or hilarious discrepancy or incongruity, to provoke laughter; e.g. Shakespeare's *A Midsummer Night's Dream*; William Wycherley's *The Country Wife*; Ben Jonson's *Volpone*.

Tragic: The story ends badly; characters suffer disproportionately to their misdeeds; provokes (Aristotle says) pity and fear; e.g. Shakespeare's *Hamlet* and *Macbeth*; Tennessee Williams's play *A Streetcar Named Desire*; Theodore Dreiser's novel, *An American Tragedy*.

Satiric: Close relative of the comic mode; author homes in on a target to reveal its ridiculous or evil characteristics. Provokes laughter, sometimes unkind; and can have a shock value; e.g. Jonathan Swift's essay *A Modest Proposal*; Jamaica Kincaid's essay *A Small Place*; Alexander Pope's poem, *The Dunciad*.

Gothic: Reads like a horror story or horror movie; contains blood, death, ghosts, imprisonment, live burial, tombs, graveyards, damsels in distress; e.g., Mary Shelley's novel *Frankenstein*; Stephen King's novel *The Shining*; Erich Maria Remarque's novel *All Quiet on the Western Front*; Toni Morrison's novel *Beloved*; and William Faulkner's short story, *A Rose for Emily*. Steve Chimombo's poem "Developments from the Grave," (see pp. 124–125) has many Gothic features.

Pastoral: A story or setting of country life, with shepherds, sheep, other rural features or pursuits; implies sharp contrast with city life, and overlaps with satire as it does so; e.g., Virgil's four-book poem the *Georgics* (about farming); the poetic *Idylls* of Theocritus; William Faulkner's short story "The Bear." Annie Dillard's prose nature writing (e.g., *Pilgrim at Tinker Creek*) (see p. 130) is essentially pastoral.

Elegiac: A solemn and melancholy lament for the dead; often includes **eulogy,** praise for the dead; e.g. Walt Whitman's poem, "When Lilacs Last in Dooryards Bloom'd"; President Ronald Reagan's lament and praise for the Challenger astronauts who died in the space shuttle explosion of 1986. John Milton's poem, *Lycidas*, combines elegy and pastoral in a lament for a young poet, dead before his time.

Realistic: Often means documentary fidelity to the material world as perceived through the five senses; can mean fidelity to the viewpoint of a chosen character, as in "psychological realism." J. D. Salinger's novel, *The Catcher in the Rye*, is psychologically realistic; Daniel Defoe's novel, *The Life and Strange Surprising Adventures of Robinson Crusoe*, has many elements of documentary realism. Khaled Hosseini's novel, *The Kite Runner* (see pp. 122–3) is written in broadly realistic mode.

Fantastic/Magic(al):   Text abandons Newton's laws of the physical universe; things happen strangely and unrealistically. **Magical Realism** mixes the fantastic with elements of documentary realism, with no overt acknowledgment of the strangeness created by their proximity and disparity. Kojo Laing's short story, (see pp. 127–9) "Vacancy for the Post of Jesus Christ," is in this mode, as are Toni Morrison's novel *Song of Solomon*, the novel *One Hundred Years of Solitude* by Gabriel Garcia Marquez, and the short stories of Jorge Luis Borges, such as "The Aleph," "The Library of Babel," and "The Garden of Forking Paths."

Cyberpunk: Science fiction "with elements from cybernetics, robotics, and advanced computing…and punk rock culture" (Harmon p. 135); e.g., William Gibson's *Neuromancer* and the movie *Blade Runner*.

Interpreting Individual Works: The Historical and Cultural Critic's Broad Perspective on Finding Meaning

In a single chapter, however, beyond sketching the outlines of the map of world literature, we can look at just a few texts to show how literary study can be helpful in the Global Studies classroom. The message here is: don't ignore so-called creative writing—poetry, plays, novels, short stories, and essays—as sources of knowledge and understanding about world affairs, past and present.

Using broadly historical and cultural brands of literary criticism, which include traditional Historical Criticism, New Historicism, Gender/Feminist Criticism, Marxist Criticism, and Postcolonial Criticism, readers can take texts of many kinds and use them as routes into other parts of the world and other lives. On pp. 118–122, you can read more about these types of literary criticism. But the chief assumption that all these literary critics share is that literature can deliver its full meaning *only* if it is connected by the critic or interpreter—in some way or ways—to the time and place from which it emerged.

One Example

Shakespeare's 1608 drama, *The Tempest*, provides a helpful example of how the historical and cultural literary critic can illuminate some of our own concerns in Global Studies: principally, in this case, colonial activity and its moral, cultural, and spiritual implications. *The Tempest*—which also has many fantastic and fairy tale qualities—tells the story of a group of European sailors shipwrecked on an island in the New World. Their encounters with the natives of that island—the sprite Ariel, the "monster" Caliban, offspring of the witch Sycorax—are often interpreted as blueprints of the quintessential "colonial encounter." The magician Prospero, deposed Duke of Milan, from a historical critic's perspective, becomes the technologically-sophisticated colonizer, imposing his will on the naïve and helpless natives and dispossessing them of their rightful inheritance. The other side of the "colonial coin," the idea that colonizers save the soon-to-be-colonized natives from their own undesirable and disadvantaged condition, is embedded in Prospero's "rescue" of Ariel, who had been imprisoned in a tree by Sycorax. Prospero reminds Ariel of this, and shows that he expects something in return:

> *Thou best knowst*
> *What torment I did find thee in. Thy groans*
> *Did make wolves howl, and penetrate the breasts*
> *Of ever angry bears. It was a torment*
> *To lay upon the damned, which Sycorax*
> *Could not again undo. It was mine art*

When I arrived and heard thee, that made gape
The pine and let thee out.

Ariel: I thank thee, Master

*(**The Tempest**, Act I, Scene ii, 340–348).*

Questions of ownership of the island and of its governance are also recurrent problems in the play, while the depiction of the native Caliban as monstrous—"a freckled whelp, hag-born" (I, ii, 336)—and threatening, particularly to the beautiful Miranda, daughter of Prospero, appears to the same historical critics as a sign of the racism inherent in the earliest days of the European colonial venture.

Caliban's anger at the visitors' treatment of him springs from his loss of ownership and dominion—"This island's mine by Sycorax my mother,/Which thou tak'st from me" (I, ii, 331)—and from his deprivation of a native tongue. No longer master of his own words, he must use those of Prospero and the other outsiders. Caliban says to Prospero:

You taught me language, and my profit on 't
Is I know how to curse. The red plague rid you
For learning me your language!
(I, ii. 437–39).

Shakespeare's play thus illuminates the "legacies of western imperialism" (see Brian Digre's Chapter 8 in this volume) by showing us something of their early-sixteenth-century origins.

Other Familiar Examples of Literature as Purveyors of "History" or "Culture"

It would be easy to point to other familiar books from the standard Anglo-American high-school curriculum in order to show how literature might be said to explain particular places at particular times. For example, most of us remember at least some of the following: Virgil's *Aeneid*, Mark Twain's *The Adventures of Huckleberry Finn*, Jonathan Swift's *A Modest Proposal*, Joseph Conrad's *Heart of Darkness*, Toni Morrison's *Beloved*, Richard Wright's *Native Son*, Harper Lee's *To Kill a Mockingbird*. The list goes on.

It seems only reasonable to regard these works as parts of a particular time and place. Their meaning is, we argue, partly historical and cultural. Who needs to be told, after all, that Mark Twain's 1884 novel, *Huckleberry Finn*, is about the expanding, but soon to be closed, American frontier? Or that Virgil's epic poem, *The Aeneid* (19 B.C.), is both the story of Rome's foundation, and, simultaneously, a justification for, and an astute critique of, its vast imperial power? Or that Jonathan Swift in his *A Modest Proposal* of 1729 didn't *really* want the wretched Irish peasantry to sell, cook, and eat their babies? (What he really wanted his prosperous English readers to realize was that British colonial policy in Ireland was so brutal that the ironically proposed baby-eating program might actually be an improvement—or at least be no worse—for the indigent and oppressed Irish people. Joseph

Conrad's novella, *Heart of Darkness*, (1899) terrifies us with a look into the corrupt, powerful heart of the European imperialist Kurtz, but it also reinforces, and helps to give birth to, the racist stereotype of a generic "African savagery"—which, according to the text's narrator—threatens the sanity of the "civilized" European. Some critics and historians argue that Conrad's book, by justifying the need in "darkest Africa" for Europe's civilizing power, helped to fuel the "second wave" of imperialism referred to by Digre, in Chapter 8 of this volume.

All of these works, then, might be said to convey cultural and historical messages from their own times and places. They also allow the reader to "thematize" particular places, events, or series of events, and to understand them in ways that nonfiction texts—histories, journalists' reports—cannot provide. Literature, with its highly-structured plots, characters, settings, points of view, symbols, metaphors, and verse forms, offers us enrichment and illumination of the meanings, or themes, of world events and the ways that human beings experience them.

Still, these dense and complex texts won't yield all their meanings immediately to the casual reader. The discipline of literary study, like all academic fields, has its range of theoretical perspectives, which are useful to all of us as we grapple with new and sometimes difficult works. These perspectives spring from assumptions that different scholars make about what's valuable in literature and important in the world, about how texts work, and about how they deliver their meanings to their readers. What follows is a brief analysis of the theoretical perspectives most useful in Global Studies: those based on historical and cultural criticism.[3]

****

The Interpreter's Choice: Being an Intelligent Critic of World Literature

Here's a preliminary disclaimer or caveat: we won't do much with those critical theories which detach the text from its cultural and historical context. Mythical or Jungian criticism, Psychoanalytic, Deconstructive, or Structuralist criticism are not our focus. Here, we need the critical theories which assume that the text's meaning can be fully delivered only when that text's relationship to the time and place which produced it is fully explored.

We might also say that, as a general rule, all fictions—whether poetic or prosaic or dramatic—are means for the reader to get vicarious emotional, intellectual, spiritual, and moral experience of other lives. Fictions also provide knowledge of other places, and points of view on those places, unavailable elsewhere. Poems, plays, novels, short stories, essays, and blogs allow us to—almost—*be* other people in other places. Global Studies students usually want to know more about the rest of the world—its politics, economics, religions, material culture, home life, and so on. Since we are unlikely to visit all those other places, we should value the role of imaginative literature in taking us to them. If we do visit those places at some point, reading about them beforehand in imaginative literature perhaps will give us a head start in grasping their material reality.

Classifying and Theorizing the Various Relationships between Literature and the World

The examples of the preceding familiar texts can be worked through almost instinctively, as you probably realized. Think of a novel, poem, play, or short story that you know well and explain it to yourself; you'll find that you're telling yourself something about the inside of the text, its outside, its connections with your own experiences and with the world you know, and the world the text seems to represent or to which it refers.

Because literature can produce meaning in so many ways, it might be useful to try to categorize or classify the ways in which texts connect with, or, more indirectly, comment on, the so-called real world.

What *is* the range of relationships between literature and the real world? For the purposes of this chapter, it's enough to divide the many relationships into a few rather broad categories. In a book on literary theory or literary criticism, the terminology and the subcategories would get a bit more complicated, but the basic assumptions about the way literature works and delivers its meaning would still be the same.

Relationship I: Literature as Mirror of Society or Nature.   Literature is sometimes seen as a mirror of nature, reflecting what is there in an almost documentary fashion. Traditional, or "Old" Historical critics work on this premise and argue that, for example, J. D. Salinger's 1951 novel, *A Catcher in the Rye*, is "about" the early 1950s in the United States and that Harper Lee's *To Kill a Mockingbird* (1960) is "about" the pre-Civil Rights era South. Still, we know that literature is not actually life and it doesn't take long to say, "Well, yes, but the novel, or play, or poem doesn't merely reproduce the world photographically as a documentary film, or as an interview transcript might do. Literature must be saying something *about* the times, even in its selection and inclusion of material. What is it saying? What is it not saying? What kind of commentary is occurring?" These questions bring us to Relationship II.

Relationship II: Literature as Commentator on, and Interpreter of, Society or Nature. Questions about what literature says, or does, about culture and history open the door to exciting considerations of symbolic, metaphoric, and even magical treatment of real life. What *is* Harper Lee's mockingbird, after all? What does it stand for? In Arthur Miller's 1953 play, *The Crucible*, who are the Salem witches? What do they and their accusers stand for? Most critics are willing, we know, to agree that they are prototypes of the McCarthy HUAC (House Unamerican Activities Committee) hearings: part of the so-called Communist "witch-hunts" of the 1950s in the United States.

We are used to this kind of symbolic, or parable-like, reading of imaginative works, which produces commentary on actual events that transcends the detailed and particular reportage of the journalist or historian. Aristotle's ancient insights in his "On the Art of Poetry" show us how this works. Poetry he says, "is more philosophical and more worthy of serious attention than history; for while poetry is concerned with universal truths, history treats of particular facts" (Aristotle, pp. 43–44).

Examples abound of literary works which incorporate the specific yet go beyond it to generalize, or to create a theme *about* the specific, which the reader can step back and examine.

For example:

- Anchee Min's *Red Azalea* (1994)—hybrid novel and autobiography—comments upon China's Cultural Revolution in the nineteen-sixties and seventies by purporting to unfold the experience of a young woman who lives through it. We not only see, hear, and feel the regimented life of a totalitarian regime; we are also allowed to hear the book's commentary about that "collective" life, through the author's management of key symbols—the mosquito net, the red azalea, and the motif of filmmaking. These symbols undermine the standard Communist party claims of the collective joyful experience of work by suggesting separation, fragility, and pretence. The book analyzes the private— rather than the public—reality of the People's Republic of China at this period.
- Khaled Hosseini's 2003 novel, *The Kite Runner*, explores a boy's experience of the world of Afghanistan before and during the war with the old Soviet Union.
- Mariama Bâ's novella (1981), *So Long a Letter*, explains as no newspaper report ever could what it means to be the first wife in a polygamous Muslim marriage in a Senegalese household.
- Ama Ata Aidoo's 1964 play, *Dilemma of a Ghost*, explores life in newly-independent Ghana, with its immense possibilities brought by a growing Westernization which brings with it elements of consumerism, feminism, secularism, and individualism. The play also identifies the threats to native culture signaled by those same potential gains. And, through the character of the returned "been-to," and his new African-American wife, the play comments from a distance upon 1960s United States events: the movements toward Civil Rights and Women's Rights in particular.

But, say some critics, surely the poet, or playwright, or novelist is more than the interpreter of, and commentator upon, the world? Isn't literature more than the handmaid of history? Relationship III takes us a step further, to characterize a more dynamic link between literature and the real world.

Relationship III: Literature as Part of History and Shaper of History. New Historicism, a critical movement starting in the early 1980s, with Stephen Greenblatt's studies of English Renaissance literature, says that the relationship between literature and history is certainly more complex, and more than one-way: it's reciprocal and dynamic. And, in the end, it denies any marked differences between literature and history. New Historicists, according to literary and cultural critic H. Aram Veeser, say that literature both shapes and is shaped by history and that historical texts and literary texts have a lot in common. As Veeser says, "'Expressive acts' cannot be separated from 'material' conditions; the boundary between 'literary and nonliterary texts' is a false one; [and] neither 'imaginative' nor 'archival' (historical) discourse 'gives access to unchanging truths nor expresses inalterable human nature'"(Veeser, quoted in Murfin & Ray, p. 296).

What is the difference, New Historicist critics ask, between a play and a nonliterary cultural ritual, such as a coronation, or a trial in court, or a religious ceremony? Both are dramatic, with fixed roles and words, and a preordained sequence of actions. Trials presented on television—the "reality TV" *Judge Judy*, for example, and the "dramas" of *Law and Order*, or

Boston Legal—make very clear the difficulty of separating "real" trials from "dramatic"—i.e., fictional, ones. And, if literature is so like history—so like the story of what we call *reality*—can literature not also influence or shape real life? Is it actually *part* of real life? Some people certainly believe so. Think of the times when authors' books have been banned or burned, and the writers themselves imprisoned, or worse. Enlightenment figures such as Voltaire, Rousseau, and Diderot, for example, found that their ideas were just too advanced for the rulers of eighteenth-century France, and faced imprisonment or exile—sometimes both. Kenyan writer Ngugi Wa Thiong'o, was imprisoned by his country's authoritarian regime for the supposedly subversive impact of his novels and plays. After *Petals of Blood*—a satiric treatment of Kenya's postcolonial rulers—was published in 1977, Ngugi was imprisoned by his own government. And Russian novelist Alexander Solzhenitsyn had to live abroad after exposing, in *The Gulag Archipelago*, the brutal penal system of the Soviet Union to the non-Soviet world.

Relationship IV: Literature as Alternative, Unofficial, Minority, or even Subversive, History.

If literature is indeed on a par with history, we may then wish to ask what *kind* of history it tells. Scholarly historians may have their own political bent: the Whig historians, for instance, famously interpret English history from their own clearly-defined ideological perspective. Novels, poems, and plays may similarly tell their own kind of history from a definite political, or moral, or emotional point of view.

New Historicists, often allying themselves with the attitudes and ideologies of the Marxist[4] critics, see history as the story of struggle, or of power relationships, which are almost inevitably portrayed as unequal. Some New Historicists argue that literature is often on the side of those who are disempowered by traditional politics and economics. Literature, for these critics, may then be an alternative, even subversive history of the disempowered—which flies under the radar. Useful to these critics are the theories of Soviet critic Mikhail Bakhtin (1895–1975), whose work on what came to be called "Dialogic Criticism" included the theory that novels, in particular, are "polyphonic" or "polyglossal" texts. They contain, Bahktin argued, many tongues, or voices, from different strata of the culture of the author's world. These voices "talk to" one another in a kind of dialogue. The work of fiction, in Bakhtin's view, is thus inclusive, containing the voices of both the powerful and the powerless.[5]

Chinese author Anchee Min's book *Red Azalea*, (see p. 119), a mix of autobiography and fiction, might be seen as an alternative—and subversive—history of the great Cultural Revolution of Communist China, in the mid-to-late 1960s and early seventies. The narrator's story of her experience of life on the collective farm, where so many young Chinese were sent to practice the theory of Maoism and the Chinese Communist party, is certainly not the account that the People's Republic of China would then wish to have published. Min's account turns the public symbol of collective labor for the good of the state inside out, by focusing on the most intimate parts of human life: human sexuality. She presents the heroine's sexuality as an alternative to the enforced uniform externality of the totally politicized life of the Cultural Revolution. If Communist totalitarianism is a power play of government over every facet of human life, then the claim this young woman makes to define her own sexuality is the way to rebel.

Just as in George Orwell's 1949 novel *Nineteen Eighty-Four*, Winston and Julia's love affair is their private refuge from and protest against the totalitarian world of Big Brother, and just as Margaret Atwood's heroine of *The Handmaid's Tale* (1990), conducts an illicit affair in Gilead, the Neo Puritan dystopia of the future, so Anchee Min's heroine strikes back at authoritarian rule. She does this not only through her unsanctioned relationships with men—which would be "bad enough"—but also through her affair with a woman. This bisexuality represents a double transgression against orthodox Communist Party rule, and is part of Min's alternative (fictional) history of the years of the Cultural Revolution.

George Orwell's dystopian novel itself, published in 1949, far from being only a futuristic fantasy, might also be seen as a subversive, alternative, and unpopular history of actual life in Britain during and soon after World War II (1939–45). The novel depicts a grimy, wretched, rationed, blitzed, and bomb-strewn country known as Airstrip One, which is ruled by the totalitarian system embodied in the figure of Big Brother. This fictional government resembles, in some limited ways, that of wartime Britain, with its new and unprecedented control over what work its citizens did, what food they ate, and where they could travel. In addition, the British government could, during the war years, invoke the notorious clause "18-B" and detain "suspects" without trial. Instead of reflecting or mimicking the tenor of Winston Churchill's heroic—and now near-mythical—accounts of a valiant "island race," whom Churchill, in 1940, exhorted to "fight on the beaches…and…never surrender,"[6] Orwell's novel transmits a view of Britain in the war and postwar years which may have been much closer to the truth than Churchill's propagandists would have wanted enemies and allies—and posterity—to know. The novel can, then, be seen as a minor, subversive, or alternative history of a particular time and place, in competition with dominant orthodoxy and even myth.[7]

Some other kinds of Historical Critics also look to literature for its specific focus on particular facets of history and culture. For example, *Gender* critics, *Marxist* critics, and *Postcolonial* critics all do a kind of "narrow focus" cultural and historical criticism. They look, respectively at the way that men and women are portrayed; at the way money, class, and property are addressed; and at how the lives of people living in cultures once controlled by colonial powers, but now independent, are explored. These three critical perspectives, along with New Historicism, share assumptions that history and culture are "about" power differentials, power struggles and the results of the disempowerment brought about by the disadvantages of gender, class, race, and geopolitical status.

For example, Mariama Bâ's short novel *So Long a Letter*, originally published in French as "*Une Si Longue Lettre*," (1981), invites a gendered perspective, which examines the novel's differentiation of men's and women's experiences of the world. The story of a first wife's experience of polygamous marriage in Senegal, a former French colony in West Africa, Bâ's novel provides insight into not only women's, but men's, experiences of a marriage pattern with which most United States students are not familiar. More than that, *So Long A Letter* elucidates the mixed messages of the hybridized postcolonial culture—both African and European—which has been one result of French imperialism. A Postcolonial critic will look at this syncretic or hybridized culture and note its impact on the personal and cultural identity of the characters in the novel. A Gender critic will note that men and women may be differently or separately affected by imperial and colonial forces. Marxist critics will note that the significance of the possession of money and property is also affected by gender and by politics: women's wealth is closely associated with their marriages, while the sources of the men's wealth are limited by the postcolonial economy of the former French colony.

Global Studies Topics in a Novel, a Poem, and a Short Story: The Global Experience through Literature

The following paragraphs analyze the genres and modes of selected texts and show how various critical approaches can help to unravel each text's treatment of topics of interest to Global Studies students.

Novel

The 2003 novel by Khaled Hosseini, *The Kite Runner*, which tells the first-person narrative of a young man's childhood in an initially peaceful Afghanistan, and then of his flight from a war-ravaged country to refuge and exile in the United States, illustrates one approach to the novel genre. It is one which, here, is written in a broadly realistic mode.

The Kite Runner, then, is a rather traditional novel, presenting in a broadly documentary *realistic* mode, a large array of people, places, and actions. When examined from various angles, Hosseini's text turns out to be a useful tool for understanding at least part of the world today. This novel about Afghanistan opens the door for the average United States citizen, and other outsiders, so that they may look closely at a quite mysterious place. *The Kite Runner* is certainly a rare glimpse of a world both closed (since 2001) and distant for the average Western reader.

If literature is indeed like a mirror, this novel shows a reflection of places people and events which are usually hidden from us in the West. Also, the novel does what all imaginative literature does: it provides vicarious experience for the reader. *The Kite Runner*, in particular, with its first-person narrative method, allows us detailed analysis of one person's experiences and his reactions to those experiences. We can imaginatively engage with the characters' emotional and moral gauges, which register guilt, sorrow, happiness, loneliness, alienation, terror, hatred, and disgust—and the list is incomplete!—in ways unavailable to us outside the realm of the novel.

The novel is also both a commentary upon real life and a kind of historical account in itself. It addresses the history of Afghanistan from before the war with the U.S.S.R. until December 2001, when the U.S./NATO military campaign began as the post 9/11 "hunt" for Osama bin Laden and his al Qaeda organization. Hosseini's fiction is also an alternative history, something other than a standard public version of U.S./NATO military policy in Afghanistan. Like that policy, the novel is "anti-Taliban," but it's also a critique of the Pashtoun and Hazari ethnic and racial conflict, which predates the rule of the Taliban and the 2001 United States invasion. Ronny Noor, in a review article in *World Literature Today*, moves to the very extreme point of the literature-as-history spectrum, by appearing to treat the novel not as art, or fiction, or a work of imagination, but as a work with an almost journalistic obligation to specific and local political fact:

> As far as the Afghan conflict is concerned, we get a selective, simplistic, even simple-minded picture. Hosseini tells us, for example, that 'Arabs, Chechens, Pakistanis' were behind the Taliban. He does not mention the CIA or Zbigniew Brzezinski, the national security advisor to President Carter, "Whose stated aim," according to Pankaj Mishra in the Spring 2002 issue of *Granta*, "was to 'sow shit' in the Soviet backyard."

> Furthermore, says Noor, "Hosseini also intimates that the current leader handpicked by foreign powers, Hamid Karzai … will put Afghanistan back in order," a conclusion that Noor emphatically rejects. (Noor, p. 148)

Finally, the novel itself, according to the New Historicists mentioned above, might be interpreted as a cultural artifact that a historian or even an archaeologist might examine. From this point of view, the novel is part of culture, is part of history and on a par with history. It shares in the general culture's characteristics and should be available for cultural analysis. *The Kite Runner*, with its global reach between the United States and Afghanistan, is perhaps like a map, a passport, a visa, or an atlas. Thinking about the title—which refers to the children who run to pick up fallen kites during the Afghan kite-fighting festivals— we might even see the book and its story as a fallen kite. The reader follows its flight or trajectory until the end, picks it up, and carries it away as a prize. The idea of "reader as kite runner" is a suggestive one and connects readers with the characters of the book, furthering the readers' identification with people otherwise far beyond their ken. A good kite runner judges where the kite will fall, and strives to be the first at the scene of its landing: similarly, a good reader follows the story attentively and looks to see where it will end, or land. The good reader, however, doesn't just want the end of the story, but the whole story: he or she runs to pick up the entire kite, or story, and carries it away—a prized and delightful object.

After reading *The Kite Runner*, we may understand better than we did before some facets of Afghan culture, some parts of its relationship to the United States, and parts of Afghan history. Indeed, the New Historicist critic, who believes that literature is part of history and on a par with history, would say that *The Kite Runner is* history, in its own way: it recounts an identifiable sequence of events in an identifiable place. Furthermore, the novel itself is a historical event, and even an artifact, or economic product, which may shape or affect the course of events in the United States, Afghanistan, and elsewhere. The book itself enters the causal chain that we sometimes see as "history," or perhaps simply "current events." Who, as these critics would ask, is to say that a novel does not create its own ripple effect—in thinking and in action? Knowing something of the relationships between Shia Hazara and Sunni Pashtoun in Afghanistan might affect Westerners' (or Afghanis') understanding of the Shia and Sunni interaction in Iraq and elsewhere. And seeing the Soviet invasion described from such an individual perspective—that of the novel's main character— might balance our much more general and external understanding of the later US/NATO invasion and subsequent overthrow of the Taliban, in 2001–2002.

Poetry

What about poetry, though?—Students and nonstudents alike may shy away from poetry, which seems so different from other kinds of discourses. At least the novel, however dauntingly long, with its wide-ranging prose narrative, has a realistic and familiar air. Still, we should not discount the usefulness of poetry as an illuminator of Global Studies topics. The highly condensed, often figurative language of poetry can make it a challenge. But those very same properties can make poetry an incisive anatomizer of world events, exposing dimensions and relationships that the prose writer leaves unaddressed.

Take Malawian writer Steve Chimombo's poem from the early 1990s, "Developments from the Grave." It's not the most difficult poem in the world, but it's got some puzzling lines, some startling images and some dense metaphoric comparisons. It is certainly not in the realistic mode of *The Kite Runner*. But these tough metaphoric comparisons are revealing and enriching. A thoughtful reading of the poem reveals it to be about, among other things, aspects of foreign aid, or "development," and facets of life in a Postcolonial African nation.

Steve Chimombo (b. 1945, Malawi)

"Developments from the Grave"

1.
We have come full circle,
it seems: burying our dead
right in the homestead now,
on the sites the living had built.   4

We no longer bury our corpses
over there and away from us,
overhung by weeping nkhadzi *trees*
just as the missionaries advised us.   8

We have come full circle,
at last: burying our dead
deep in the soil beneath us;
we climb over the mounds daily.   12

We no longer hang the cadavers
high in the trees away from scavengers
hyenas, ants, beaks and talons;
just as the colonials instructed us.   16

2.
We brought the dead to the homestead,
revived them as ndondocha*   *zombies
cut off their tongues and tamed them
to live in our granaries for ever.   20

Bumper harvests come out of them
and we know who keeps the most,
organising them into one task force
to labour in the tobacco, tea and cotton estates.   24

We unearthed the youth for msendawana*   *purses made of human skin
to skin them for their precious leather
and made purses out of the tender skin
for the most potent charm of them all.   28

We know who has the largest purse
accumulating wealth and more.
Out of the mounds of our youth
sprout palaces, fleets and monuments.   32

3.
Development did not catch us
by surprise, asleep or unprepared:
We knew about space exploration;
we had our own flying baskets.   36

The greenhouse effect is not news;
we know how to heat or cool the land:
Drought comes from a society on heat;
rain comes from a cooled nation.   40

But development came from the graves,
too full and closely packed to grow any more.
The protective nkhadzi trees fenced
Each effort to force the grave boundaries.   44

We have now come full circle,
rightly so: living with our dead,
Not only in nsupa or spirit houses
But in granaries, purses and coffins.   48

Analysis: Steve Chimombo's poem "Developments from the Grave" as a lesson about western imperialism and the postcolonial African state. Why should the Global Studies student be concerned with this poem? It is, after all, apparently unrealistic, even magical. It barely inhabits, apparently, the stern material worlds of politics and economics. Scanning the lines of the first verses, we might ask, "Can the speaker *really* mean that he lives with dead bodies, to say nothing of zombies? Have the young *really* been skinned, so that their soft skin can be used to make purses? Do 'palaces, fleets and monuments' *really* 'sprout' from the 'mounds of our youth'?" It all sounds rather unlikely, but this densely metaphoric and symbolic text can indeed illuminate our understanding of the way others understand and experience their part of the world. In this text, the "other view" is the view from the receiving end of colonial and imperial power, mutated into the modern allotrope, "international development," or "aid."

The broadly historical critic will, of course, look for links between the poem and its time and place. But before we go to "history," we should ask: what's actually *in* the poem?

The Text Itself: In Gothic mode? Reading through the poem a couple of times, we can see a persistent motif: death. Modifications of this motif include disposing of the dead; graves; coffins; living with the dead, the half dead, half alive "zombie"; and the uses of the dead bodies themselves. It appears that we have a poem in *Gothic* mode, with elements of *Magical Realism*.

What do these death images say about the characters, plot, and setting of the poem? The reader gathers that "We" were told by the missionaries not to bury our dead in the trees; this injunction has been obeyed, but the consequences have been very sinister. Now, the dead have been brought "home."

But the dead may not be quite dead. Speechless, but still active, these *ndondocha*, or zombies, are productive workers[8] and they are identified somewhat mysteriously with another set of characters—the "young," whose "soft skin" is made into purses of soft leather.

These purses bring us to another group of images, which are related to wealth and prosperity: purses, bumper crops, granaries, fleets, and palaces. These reassuring images oppose the images of death, and we wonder how the two groups will connect.

One answer we might offer is: They connect through the term "development." Development, or foreign aid—certainly from the donor's perspective—can be a bringer of necessary goods and services; it can feed, clothe, and house. But the speaker of the poem does not see it that way: it "comes from the grave." Some countries are called "developing," or even "underdeveloped." This is perhaps problematic, since it implies that these countries have not yet reached some desirable point of "mature" completeness. After all, we talk about development of embryos, and of early childhood development, for example.

Perhaps the poem is about some part of what it means to be "developing," and to be the recipient of "development" from the "first world," the sender of missionaries in colonial times and now of the technology that addresses such things as space travel and global warming.

Pretty clearly, then, given the deathly imagery which pervades the poem, "Development," in the eyes of the speaker, is not healthy or beneficial: it diminishes or even destroys its recipients, giving them a zombie-like half-life rather than a fully human one. It includes greed and exploitation. It brings redundant knowledge: "We had our own flying baskets."

Still, far from being merely a critique of western aid policies, this poem exposes also the wrongdoing of the "native" population, particularly its elite. They are responsible for allowing foreign money to create brutal exploitative practices: "We unearthed our youth/To skin them for their precious leather." Can it be that this poem is also in *Elegiac* mode—a lament for these dead youth?

The Poem and History.   The above analysis started out as purely textual, but it swiftly started to connect the poem with actual global policies and practices. It is both reflection of and commentary upon real life.

If the reader looks at Steve Chimombo's life and career, she or he might infer a more specific reference point—Malawi, in southeastern Africa, a former colony of Britain. For more than 30 years after independence, it was run corruptly and inefficiently and even heartlessly by a single party government and a single man: Hastings Banda. Malawi continues to be the object of western "development aid," for better or worse. Should we then read this poem as both a reflection, and a critique, of the colonial and postcolonial polices which have shaped life in Malawi for so many years? As noted above, the speaker indicts not only the outsiders, but himself and his fellow countrymen for their complicity in heartless politics and economics.

The poem might even be seen as an alternative history of some part of Malawi: not the kind you get in a text book, but an account—or indictment—of the moral and economic and spiritual fabric of a nation. Perhaps the poem is also a cultural artifact: given the theme of the poem, it might be seen to resemble an epitaph written on a gravestone: "Here Lieth Malawi: Died of _____; RIP." The poem explains why everyone is "dead," spiritually, if not physically. It might even be an epitaph for the colonized native culture, which had its own flying baskets and knew about global warming, even though the colonizers ignored that knowledge and made it irrelevant. Can that native culture ever be revived?

We might also add that Postcolonial and Marxist critics would see the poem as an analysis of the disempowerment brought by both imperialism and capitalism: someone is always being used—and abused—to benefit those with the political and economic power.

Short Story: Kojo Laing's "Vacancy for the Post of Jesus Christ"

We probably expect poetry to be figurative, metaphoric, weird, unreal, and unbelievable in that documentary sense we expect of novels. Poems can be super-condensed and thus very tough to analyze. We're more surprised, however, when we find the same "poetic" effects in novels or short stories. One mode of literary development, or style, popular in the last thirty or forty years has just these qualities—and more! The style or mode is *Magic,* or *Magical, Realism:* a fantastic and unrealistic quality pervading or appearing intermittently and without surprise or comment, within an otherwise realistic context. Probably born in South America, and now characteristic of literature in West Africa and of the works of British authors such as Salman Rushdie and Angela Carter, Magical Realism is seen by many critics as a response to the disparities in power, and to the curious mixes or hybridities of culture, which can be produced by colonial rule and linger a long time into the Postcolonial era. When two cultures collide, strange things can happen. In Global Studies, Magical Realism isn't just an arcane literary mode: it's a way of understanding the impact of those key global forces, imperialism and colonialism. Some critics would say that globalization should also be added to this list of world forces.

Brenda Cooper (1998), in *Magical Realism in West African Fiction: Seeing with a Third Eye,* says:

> Magical realism arises out of particular societies—postcolonial, unevenly developed places where old and new, modern and ancient, the scientific and the magical views of the world co-exist. It grapples with cultural syncretism and accepts it to a greater or lesser extent. Where syncretism is rejected, it is usually the result of pressure arising out of national disaster, which insists on the writer's obligation to engage in national liberation. In other words, as elsewhere in the third world, the unevenness of Western capitalist development, the co-existence of disparate ways of living and of seeing life, have fundamentally determined African fictional politics and aesthetic choices. Among these choices is that of the magical realist mode with its strange relationships, weird linkages, and multi-dimensional spaces. This mode contests boundaries, seamless unities and ethnic purities and can therefore co-exist only very uneasily with cultural nationalism. (Cooper, p. 216)

Global Studies students, analyzing many world cultures, often find themselves trying to interpret formerly colonized spaces. Still in their postcolonial phase, many of these cultures are yet subject to oppressive one-party rule, characterized by a patchwork of western and indigenous cultural features, both institutional and material. Neo-colonialism may still be casting its net over these places, adding to the tension between the domestic culture and the web of international relations within which it is caught.

Magical Realism's mode illuminates the resulting disparities and hybridities of postcolonial cultures, and questions the *status quo* more incisively than the documentary mode found in nonfiction such as history or journalism. *Magical Realism* can span a wider—or different—range of meanings, also, than a novel or short story in traditional *Realistic* mode, such as *The Kite Runner*.

For example, Ghanaian writer Kojo Laing's (b. 1946) short story "Vacancy for the Post of Jesus Christ" reveals the special conflicts and weird disparities which some critics associate with colonial and postcolonial cultures. Historical critics are likely to read Laing's story as an account of a country such as Ghana (independent in 1957) which continues to be shaped by its experience as a British colony (then called the Gold Coast). Such a mix of Western and non-Western features, characteristic of colonial and postcolonial hybridization, emerges with almost *Gothic* garishness through the *Magical Realists'* use of fantastic plots and settings. These cultural qualities are some of the *other* legacies of Western imperialism addressed in Chapter 8 by Brian Digre. Indeed, Digre's description of his own encounter in Zaire (now the Democratic Republic of the Congo, and formerly The Belgian Congo), with road signs to places whose names had changed, in a language (French) that most natives did not speak, has all the makings of a narrative in *Magical Realist* mode. Digre says that these signs were "surrounded by tall elephant grass, on a footpath listing distances that were really only meaningful if you were driving, to places that no longer bore the names on the sign" (Digre pp. 180–181). He has apparently entered the Twilight Zone. Colonial and postcolonial cultures really are bizarre, and Magical Realism can expose that bizarre quality to us.

In Kojo Laing's *Magical Realist* short story, then, the author exposes the extreme illogic of post-independence politics, the puzzling variety of cultural artifacts, the huge division between rich and poor, and the existence of wildly divergent interpretations of the same event. At the beginning of the story, a mysterious vehicle descends from the skies. Crowds of people greet it, and provide different responses to it:

> When the small quick lorry [truck] was being lowered from the skies, it was discovered that it had golden wood, and many seedless guavas for the hungry. As the lorry descended the many layers of cool air, the rich got ready to buy it, and the poor to resent it. The wise among the crowd below opened their mouths in wonder, and closed them only to eat. They are looking up while the sceptical looked down. And so the lorry had chosen to come down to this town that shamed the city with its cleanliness. The wheels were already revolving and, when they shone, most of them claimed they were the mirrors of God. The lorry was quick but the descent was slow. So many wanted to touch it. … And when the great gust of African rain came down, the wise still kept their eyes up, the poor huddled, and the rich shut their purses small. But nobody left. Come down, lorry of golden wood, with your cleanest exhaust ever seen, they said. … At first no one saw the gigantic message being lowered from the wheels of the lorry. The message on the big card … opened out with the sun: VACANCY FOR THE POST OF JESUS CHRIST. The consternation among the crowd spread even at its different

intensities: the sceptical felt vindicated and snorted at the sky, saying that the eternal laws never favoured the wonder-prone, nor the innocent, and that if the heart was closed today, it would be closed tomorrow. And what was joy anyway, but a movement of brain energy. What a pity the African scientists were no different, they said! And the wise grew in stature in their own eyes, for the coming of mystery increased the questions and decreased the answers, thus leaving the space between for them to move confidently in. The poor waited and the rich wrote hundreds of cheques. They were preparing. And the old woman said as she grew in remembrance for them, "Look at the shame of the children dancing when they should be kneeling, they don't train them to respect these days." (Laing, pp. 185–86)

Laing's paragraphs above are a mix of the mundane and the fantastic. The heavenly lorry–or truck—brings food and opportunity, and an announcement of need: the "vacancy for the post of Jesus Christ." Those who see the lorry react in different ways, some with doubt, or "scepticism," and some "with wonder."

Historical critics of any stripe will ask if this apparent fantasy connects to an actual time and place. Putting historical and cultural interpretive pressure on the images and actions contained in the scene above, we might ask:

- Is this a place where the necessities of life—"seedless guavas"—are arbitrarily dispensed?
- Why does food arrive out of the clouds, and not out of the ground?
- Do some people here have far-reaching (godlike) powers (because the lorry descends from the clouds)?
- Is this a place where the rich and the poor have divergent reactions to events? (Why do "the rich get ready to buy it" and the "poor to resent it"? Why do the "poor wait" and "the rich [write] hundreds of cheques in advance"?)
- Is this a place where the need for help of some kind—perhaps salvation?—is so great that the "vacancy" is for no less a person than "Jesus Christ"?
- Does the narrator's complete acceptance of the 'magical' event in a 'realistic' world suggest that this otherwise weird juxtaposition of events and actions is somehow normal?

Specific types of Historical critics—*Postcolonial* and *Marxist* critics—who share with *New Historicists* an interest in history as the story of power and power relationships—might argue that the heavenly lorry which elicits such divergent reactions represents one government for the rich and another for the poor. In addition, they might argue that this mix of fantastic and mundane images is an effective means for conveying the illogic of a place where two vastly different cultures—European and West African—have clashed to produce some very mixed—and often arbitrary-seeming—cultural patterns. The story itself plays out as a parable about political power, and the difficulty of assessing the validity of claims to that power. The lorry's driver, a "bronze-black giant," tours the area, to see the mortuary, the courtrooms, and the "governing rooms" (p. 193), which Laing presents as the incongruous sites of the town's identity. The closing scene shows the people asking a mysteriously-appearing Christ-like figure for validation of his ruling credentials: "Please O son of the universal Controller, can you please show us your appointment letter from God?" (Laing p. 196). Such is the urgency of their quest for a legitimate ruler, and, such, apparently, is its futility.

Nonfiction: The Essay, Nature Writing, the Blog

Literary nonfiction, a broad category which contains the essay and now the blog, is also worth the attention of the Global Studies student. Longer—sometimes booklength—nonfiction pieces may include travel writing and nature writing.

Essays about politics, the environment, economics, all aspects of culture, appear in journals, periodicals, and books. Famous English language essayists include Thoreau, Emerson, E. B. White, and George Orwell. Nonfiction writers also include travel writers and nature writers, such as Paul Theroux and Annie Dillard. Close as essays are to journalism, they are, for Global Studies students, an especially direct route to, or window on, the world. Good essays are personal reflections, yet they address—usually—current events of general interest. They go beyond—or in a different direction from—the impersonal journalistic report, and often beyond the kind of analysis and interpretation of even the best op-ed piece.

Michel de Montaigne, sixteenth century French author, pretty much invented this genre, called the 'essai,' or 'a sally, an attempt' upon a topic. His 1580 essay "On Cannibals" for example, addresses the often-ethnocentric judgments of his fellow countrymen on the peoples and places encountered by Europeans as they explored, and started to stake claims to, the world beyond their shores. Montaigne embraces what we now call a kind of cultural relativism, in order to argue that "every man calls barbarism whatever is not his own practice" (Montaigne p. 422). In his analysis of the cannibalism practiced by non-Europeans, Montaigne contends that the so-called "savage" cannibalism of the New World is probably less cruel and brutal than the so-called "civilized" punishments of the Old World, which he describes in rather harrowing detail.

Jumping forward about 400 years, we can read a modern iteration of the same essay genre, with a very different topic. Annie Dillard's "Stalking" is an essay in her long prose nature narrative *Pilgrim at Tinker Creek* (1974). "Stalking" describes the author's long campaign to observe the elusive muskrats in the local river. This essay, categorized also as *nature writing*, analyzes—through her hard-won encounter with one of these creatures—a relationship between humans and the natural world which presents animals with parallel but completely separate lives. These lives run alongside our human existence, indifferent to it. Dillard concludes that we must treat these independent animal lives with the respect that every sovereign being deserves:

> The great hurrah about wild animals is that they exist at all, and the greater hurrah is the actual moment of seeing them. Because they have a nice dignity, and prefer to have nothing to do with me, not even as the simple objects of my vision. They show me by their very wariness what a prize it is simply to open my eyes and behold. (Dillard, p. 192)

Dillard, watching the muskrats, is overwhelmed by a sense of the muskrat's otherness and separateness, and is humbled by this privilege of connecting briefly with the nonhuman. Her examination of just one facet of her encounter with nature illuminates a part of the huge environmental discussion addressed by Anthony Weston in Chapter 7 of this volume. Our planet's future well-being may depend on such thoughtful analysis as Dillard's essay provides.

Blogs, the (relatively) new electronic genre or subgenre, sometimes seem closer to journalism than to the more literary essay. Nevertheless, the blog also resembles the essay, although its illusion of solitary privacy, its potential for personal interaction, and its hyperlink connections, unite to create a hybrid of journal, diary, and letter. Blogs may incidentally provide information of the kind we normally associate with the newspaper or television report, but they are also vehicles for personal interpretive and reflective thinking about the whole range of Global Studies topics: politics, economics, environmental questions, international relations, facets of culture, and the media itself, for example.

One recent example of the blog, published now in book form, is Riverbend's (a pseudonym or screen name) *Baghdad Burning: Girlblog from Iraq* and *Baghdad Burning II: More Girlblog from Iraq*, both of which immerse the reader in Riverbend's life in wartime Iraq after the start of the 2003 invasion. The diary, or journal, of this young Iraqi woman explores the limits of life under the siege of the insurgency and of life with the attacks by U.S. and British forces. It is also a window into different aspects of Iraqi culture—family, work, education, sex and gender systems, and the increasingly difficult economy. As Miriam Cooke (2007) notes, the new electronic medium offers new opportunities to the young, to women, and to others who might not easily have found an outlet in the traditional publishing world. In countries where normal business life is limited, or has been suspended by war or politics, the electronic medium truly can be a lifeline:

> The chaos and mayhem of the U.S. invasion and occupation of Iraq found a new literary outlet, the blogosphere. This medium made room for new writers: young women and men comfortable with the Internet, fluent in English, and anxious to communicate with the outside world. Several women have chosen to chronicle their lives in war. Coming from different backgrounds…most use pseudonyms.…Keenly aware of her foreign readers, for whom she provided local and cultural information, Riverbend wrote in idiomatic American English. Her blog was eloquent testimony to her enthrallment with American culture, and it provided an important alternative perspective to the one projected by world media and their embedded journalists. With time and a growing readership, her blog became a lifeline. (Cooke, p. 24)

Conclusion

This chapter has attempted to show how literature of all kinds has a place in Global Studies. Poems, plays, novels, short stories, blogs, and essays can indeed teach us a lot about the state of the world. They can bring us closer to other peoples and to the cultures they inhabit; they can help us to see the world as other people see it; and they can also allow us to step away from a particular world event or cultural situation and to "thematize" it in ways that journalism, histories, and other nonfiction texts, do not always invite.

However we achieve it, one goal of the responsible world citizen is surely to find as many different paths as possible toward a fuller and richer encounter with the rest of the world. Literature is one of those paths. Reading world literature in a self-consciously critical fashion, with a knowledge of our own assumptions about what literature is and what it can do, is, ultimately, to read the world itself.

Notes

1. An example of "orature," or spoken-word text, now preserved in print, is *Sundiata: An Epic of Old Mali*, which, its editors say, was "received" by historian D. T. Niane from Djeli (griot) Mamoudou Kouyate (*Sundiata*, vii). See Suggested Readings. The "griot" is the name given to the storyteller in some African cultures.
2. The blog—the electronic hybrid of the journal, diary, and opinion column, is the most well-known of these new forms. Its interactive quality particularly distinguishes it.
3. For more information about literary critical theories, or perspectives, a number of useful texts exist, including: *Texts and Contexts*, by Steven Lynn; *Text, Mind and World*, by Rosemary Haskell, Richard Lee, and Paul Crenshaw; and *The Bedford Glossary of Critical and Literary Terms*, by Ross Murfin and Supryia M. Ray. See *Secondary Texts* under References.
4. Marxist critics believe that literature reveals the economic structure of the culture which produced it. Authors from capitalist cultures, these critics believe, embody in their texts—directly or obliquely—the class struggle between property and business owners, and the proletariat, who own little or nothing. Moreover, capitalist novels, poems, and plays also invite analysis which reveals the dehumanizing "reification," or objectification, of personal relationships, regarded by these critics as characteristic of materialist and consumer societies.
5. See Murfin and Ray, pp. 107–108, for a fuller explanation of Bakhtin's "dialogic" critical theory. See *Secondary Texts* under References.
6. These phrases come from Winston Churchill's House of Commons address, 4 June, 1940.
7. For an alternative view of the historical significance of *Nineteen Eighty-Four*, see Haskell, Lee, and Crenshaw, pp. 99–100.
8. The glossary entry (in *Napolo and The Python*) for *ndondocha*, or the zombie, states that: "It is believed that the owner of the zombies resuscitates the dead, cuts off their tongues, maintains them in this life-in-death state to do different chores for him" (Chimombo p. 180).

References

Primary Texts: The Literature Itself

Achebe, C. (1964). *Arrow of God*. New York: Anchor.
Achebe, C. (1989). *A man of the people*. New York: Anchor.
Achebe, C. (1994). *Things fall apart*. New York: Anchor.
Aidoo, A. A. (1987). *Dilemma of a ghost; Anowa: Two plays*. London: Longman.
Aristotle. (1965). On the art of poetry (T. S. Dorsch, Trans.). In *Aristotle Horace Longinus: Classical literary criticism* (pp. 31–7). Harmondsworth, England: Penguin Books.
Atwood, M. (1986). *The hand maid's tale*. Boston: Houghton Mifflin.
Bâ, M. (1981). *So long a letter* (M. Bode-Thomas, Trans.). Oxford, England: Heinemann.
Borges, J. L. (1998). The Aleph (A. Hurley, Trans.). In *Collected fictions* (pp. 274–286). Harmondsworth, UK: Penguin Books.
Borges, J. L. (1998). The garden of forking paths. (A. Hurley, Trans.). In *Collected fictions* (pp. 119–128).Harmondsworth, UK: Penguin Books.
Borges, J. L. (1998). The library of Babel. (A. Hurley, Trans.). In *Collected fictions* (pp. 112–118). Harmondsworth, UK: Penguin Books.
Chimombo, S. (1994). Developments from the grave. In *Napolo and the python* (pp. 167–168). Oxford, England: Heinemann.
Conrad, Joseph. (1987). *Heart of darkness*. Harmondsworth, UK: Penguin Books.
Defoe, Daniel. (2001). *Robinson Crusoe*. New York: The Modern Library.
Dillard, A. (1974). *Pilgrim at Tinker Creek*. New York: Harper's Magazine Press.
Faulkner, William. (1973). The bear. In *Go down Moses* (pp. 191–331). New York: Vintage Books.
_____. (2006). A rose for Emily. In Richard Abcarian & Marvin Klotz (Eds.), *Literature: The human experience* (9th ed.) (pp. 696–703). Boston, MA: Bedford/St. Martin's.

Gibson, William. (2000). *Neuromancer*. New York: Berkley Publishing Group.

Hosseini, K. (2003). *The kite runner*. New York: Riverhead Books.

Kincaid, Jamaica. (2000). *A small place*. New York: Farrar, Straus and Giroux.

Laing, K. (1985). Vacancy for the post of Jesus Christ. In C. L. Innes & C. Achebe (Eds.), *The Heinemann book of contemporary African short stories* (pp. 185–196). London: Heinemann.

Le Clezio J-M. G. (2002). *The round & other cold hard facts* (C. Dickson, Trans.). Lincoln: University of Nebraska Press.

Lee, H. (1999). *To kill a mockingbird*. New York: HarperCollins.

Miller, A. (1953). *The crucible: A play in four acts*. New York: Viking.

Min, A. (2006). *Red azalea*. New York: Anchor.

Montaigne, M. de. (2004). Of cannibals (Donald Frame, Trans.). In J. Tylus & D. Damrosch (Eds.), *The Longman anthology of world literature: The early modern period* (Vol. C, pp. 420–428). New York: Pearson Longman.

Montgomery, J. (1986, first published 1809). The West Indies. In P. Burnett (Ed.), *The Penguin anthology of Caribbean verse in English* (pp. 113–115). London: Penguin.

Morrison, T. (1977). *Song of Solomon*. New York: New American Library.

Morrison, T. (1988). *Beloved*. New York: Penguin Books/Plume Fiction.

Ngugi Wa Thiong'o. (1978). *Petals of blood*. New York: Dutton.

Ngugi Wa Thiong'o. (1986). *Decolonising the mind: The politics of language in African literature*. London: J. Curry.

Orwell, G. (1992). *Nineteen eighty-four*. New York: Knopf.

Riverbend. (2005). *Baghdad burning: GirlBlog from Iraq*. New York: Feminist Press of City University of New York.

Riverbend. (2006). *Baghdad burning II: More GirlBlog from Iraq*. New York: Feminist Press of City University of New York

Rowling, J. K. (1999). *Harry Potter and the sorcerer's stone*. New York: Scholastic Press.

Rushdie, S. (1989). *The satanic verses*. New York: Viking.

Salinger, J. D. (1951). *The catcher in the rye*. Boston: Little, Brown.

Shakespeare, W. (1994). *The tempest*. B. Mowat & P. Werstine (Eds.). New York: Washington Square Press.

Solzhenitsyn, A. (1968). *The cancer ward* (R. Frank, Trans.). New York: Dial Press.

Solzhenitsyn, A. (1974). *The gulag archipelago, 1918–1956* (T. P. Whitney, Trans.). New York: Harper & Row.

Swift, Jonathan. (1996). A modest proposal. In *A modest proposal and other satirical works*. (pp. 52–64). Toronto: Dover Publications.

Twain, M. (1958). *The adventures of Huckleberry Finn*. Boston: Houghton Mifflin.

Secondary Texts: Criticism

Bakhtin, M. (1984). *Problems of Dostoevsky's poetics* (C. Emerson, Trans.). Minneapolis: University of Minnesota Press.

Cooke, M. (2007, November). Baghdad burning: Women write war in Iraq. *World Literature Today*, 81:6, 23–27.

Cooper, B. (1998). *Magical realism in west African fiction: Seeing with a third eye*. London & New York: Routledge.

Damrosch, D. (2004). Introduction. In D. Kadir & U. K. Heise (Eds.), *The Longman anthology of world literature: The twentieth century* (Vol. F, pp. 1–15). New York: Pearson Longman.

Haskell, R., Lee, R., & Crenshaw, P. (2007). *Text, mind and world: An introduction to literary criticism*. Dubuque, IA: Kendall Hunt.

Harmon, W., & Holman, C. H. (2003). *A handbook to literature* (9th ed.). Upper Saddle River, NJ: Prentice Hall.

Lynn, S. (2007). *Texts and contexts: Writing about literature with critical theory* (5th ed.). New York: Pearson Longman.

Murfin, R., & Ray, S. M. (2003). *The Bedford glossary of critical and literary terms* (2nd ed.). Boston: St. Martin's Press.

Noor, R. (2004, Sept./Dec.). Review of *The kite runner*. In *World Literature Today*, 78:3–4, 148.

Questions for Discussion

1. Read the poem below. Write or talk about the questions that follow it.

From James Montgomery (1771–1854), ***The West Indies*** (first published in 1809)

[EXCERPT]
Dreadful as hurricanes, athwart the main
Rush'd the fell legions of invading Spain;
With fraud and force, with false and fatal breath,
Submission bondage, and resistance death,
They swept the isles. In vain the simple race   5
Kneel'd to the iron sceptre of their grace,
Or with weak arms their fiery vengeance braved;
They came, they saw, they conquer'd, they enslaved,
And they destroy'd—the generous heart they broke,
They crush'd the timid neck beneath the yoke;   10
Where'er to battle march'd their grim array,
The sword of conquest plough'd resistless way;
Where'er from cruel toil they sought repose,
Around, the fires of devastation rose.
The Indian, as he turn'd his head in flight,   15
Beheld his cottage flaming through the night,
And, midst the shrieks of murder on the wind,
Heard the mute blood-hound's death-step close behind.

The conflict o'er, the valiant in their graves,
The wretched remnant dwindled into slaves;   20
—Condemn'd in pestilential cells to pine,
Delving for gold amidst the gloomy mine,
The sufferer, sick of life-protracting breath,
Inhaled with joy the fire-damp blast of death:
—Condemn'd to fell the mountain-palm on high,   25
That cast its shadow from the evening sky,
Ere the tree trembled to his feeble stroke,
The woodman languish'd and his heart-strings broke:
—Condemned in torrid noon, with palsy'd hand,
To urge the slow plough o'er the obdurate land,   30
The labourer, smitten by the sun's fierce ray,
A corpse along the unfinish'd furrow lay.
O'er whelm'd at length with ignominious toil,
Mingling their barren ashes with the soil,
Down to the dust the Charib people pass'd,   35
Like autumn foliage withering in the blast:
The whole race sunk beneath the oppressor's rod,
And left a blank among the works of God....

Thus, childless as the Charibbeans died,
Afric's strong sons the ravening waste supplied   40
Of hardier fibre to endure the yoke,
And self renewed beneath the severing stroke;
As grim oppression crush'd them to the tomb,

Their fruitful parent's miserable womb
Teem'd with fresh myriads, crowded o'er the waves,   45
Heirs to their toil, their sufferings, and their graves.

Freighted with curses was the bark that bore
The spoilers of the west to Guinea's shore,
Heavy with groans of anguish blew the gales
That swell'd that fatal bark's returning sails;   50
Old Ocean shrunk as o'er his surface flew
The human cargo and the demon crew.
—Thenceforth, unnumber'd as the waves that roll
From sun to sun, or pass from pole to pole,
Outcasts and exiles from their country torn,   55
In floating dungeons o'er the gulph were borne…

Captives of tyrant power and dastard wiles,
Dispeopled Africa, and gorged the isles
Loud and perpetual o'er th' Atlantic waves,
For guilty ages, roll'd the tide of slaves;   60
A tide that knew no fall, no turn, no rest,
Constant as day and night from east to west;
Still widening, deepening, swelling in its course,
With boundless ruin, and resistless force.

Questions about *The West Indies:*

a. What significance do you attach to the 1809 date of composition?
b. What are Montgomery's main themes? To find out, interpret the poem from various theoretical perspectives. Consider also the various modes of expression employed by the poet. Are they Gothic, Tragic, Comic, Elegiac, Satiric, or Pastoral, for example?
c. What "Global Studies" themes are involved in the text?
d. Compare this early-nineteenth-century text with Steve Chimombo's late-twentieth-century poem earlier in the chapter. What does each poem tell us about the relationships between two or more distinct cultural, racial, and geographical groups?
e. James Montgomery was born in Scotland. To what extent is his nationality significant to your reading of the poem?

2. Find a list of Nobel Literature Prize winners for the last 25 years. Tap the list for meaning and information by reading more about the winner, the losers—or near-winners—and the controversy (if any) surrounding each year's award. For example, does the list tell you something about:

- international relations
- hotspots or problem areas of the world
- western attitudes toward the nonwestern world
- language and translation
- the publishing business
- the impact of prizewinners on the global scene, both literary and nonliterary
- the rationale or rationales for awarding the prize
- the relative "prize value" of different literary genres and modes
- other?

3. Pick one of the chapter topics from this book—environment, international relations, globalization, imperialism, drugs and the drug trade, religion, feminism—and find a poem, play, novel, short story, or essay which would help you and your classmates understand that chapter's topic better, or differently. Write a short paper about the role of your chosen literary text in explaining the topic.

4. In what respects is literary study an important part of the life of the citizen of the world?

5. Read a novel, play, poem, or short story originally published in a country outside the "industrialized west." (Try browsing the booklist at the site www.readingtheworld.org for a start on finding a title.) Then take the diagram of the web of culture from Basirico and Bolin's chapter, "The Joy of Culture" (Chapter 2), and use the web as an analytical tool to explore the culture described or implied in your chosen book. In other words, identify the fictionalized systems or institutions—economics, family, religion, law, government—and then identify the values, attitudes, beliefs, aspirations, and so on, within each institution.

Suggested Readings: Primary and Secondary Texts _____

South American Continent

Allende, I. (1985). *The house of the spirits.* M. Bogin, Trans. New York: A. A. Knopf.
Felints, M. (1994). *The women of Tijuopayo.* Lincoln: University of Nebraska Press.
Garcia Marquez, G. (1970). *One hundred years of solitude* (G. Rabassa, Trans.). New York: Harper and Row.
Pinto, C.F. (Ed.). (1999). *Urban Voices: Contemporary short stories from Brazil.* Lanham, MD: University Press of America.
Scliar, M. (2003). *The centaur in the garden.* Madison: University of Wisconsin Press.

African Continent

Armah, A. K. (1969). *The beautyful ones are not yet born.* London: Heinemann.
Chukwumerije, Dike-Ogu Eqwuatu. (2008*). The revolution has no tribe: Contemporary poetry on African history, culture and society.* London: Afriscope Publishing.
Coetzee, J. M. (1983). *The life and times of Michael K.* Harmondsworth, UK: Penguin Books.
Gordimer, N. (1981). *July's people.* Harmondsworth, UK: Penguin Books.
Innes, C.L. & Achebe, C. (Eds.). (1985). *Heinemann book of contemporary African short stories.* London: Heinemann.
Magalasi, M. (Ed). (2001). *Beyond the barricades: A collection of contemporary Malawian plays.* Zomba, Malawi: Chancellor College Publications.
Moore, G. & Beier, U. (Eds.). (1998). *The Penguin book of modern African poetry* (5th ed.). Harmondsworth, UK: Penguin Books.
Naipaul, V. S. (1989). *A bend in the river.* New York: Vintage Books.
Paton, A. (1987). *Cry, the beloved country.* Ed. and intro. Edward Callan. New York: Macmillan.
Schreiner, O. (1998). *The story of an African farm.* Mineola, NY: Dover Publications.
Soyinka, W. (1976). *Collected plays.* Oxford, UK: Oxford University Press.
Sundiata: An epic of Old Mali. (1965). Transcribed by D. T. Niane. Translated by D. G. Pickett. London: Longman.
The unsung song: An anthology of short stories and poetry from Malawi. (2001). R. Chirambo, M. J. Iphanoi, & Z. Mbano (Eds.). Zomba, Malawi: Chancellor College Publications.

Asia

Der-wei Wang, D. & Rojas, C. (Eds.). (2007). *Writing Taiwan: A new literary history.* Durham, NC: Duke University Press.

Der-wei Wang, D. & Tai, J. (Eds.). (1994). *Running wild: New Chinese writers.* New York: Columbia University Press.

Khan, N. (2005). *The fiction of nationality in an era of transnationalism.* London: Routledge.

King, B. (Ed.). (2001). *Modern Indian poetry.* Oxford, UK: Oxford University Press.

Lau, J. S. M. & Goldblatt, H. (Eds.). (2007). *Columbia anthology of modern Chinese literature* (2nd ed.). New York: Columbia University Press.

McGrath, J. (2008). *Postsocialist modernity: Chinese cinema, literature and criticism in the market age.* Palo Alto, CA: Stanford University Press.

Mee, E. (Ed.). (2002). *Drama contemporary: India.* Oxford, UK: Oxford University Press.

Narayan, R. K. (1982). *The painter of signs.* Harmondsworth, UK: Penguin Books.

Caribbean Countries

Burnette, P. (Ed.). (1986). *Penguin anthology of Caribbean verse in English.* Harmondsworth, UK: Penguin Books, 1986.

De Loughrey, E. M., Gosson, R. K., & Handley, G. B. (Eds.). (2005). *Caribbean literature and the environment: Between nature and culture.* Charlottesville: University of Virginia Press.

Kincaid, J. (1985). *Annie John.* New York: Farrar, Straus and Giroux.

Kincaid, J. (2002). *Lucy.* New York: Farrar, Straus and Giroux.

Rhys, J. (1982). *Wide Sargasso Sea.* New York: W.W. Norton.

Scott, H. (2006). *Caribbean women writers and globalization: Fictions of independence.* Farnham, UK: Ashgate Press.

Globalization and Literature

Cook, D. (Ed.). (2005). *Contemporary Muslim apocalyptic literature.* Syracuse, NY: Syracuse University Press.

Dimock, W-C. & Buell, L. (Eds.). (2007). *Shades of the planet: American literature as world literature.* Princeton, NJ: Princeton University Press.

Krishnan, S. (2007). *Reading the global: Troubling perspectives on Britain's empire in Asia.* New York: Columbia University Press.

Reading the world. http://www.readingtheworld.org/ [Reading list of international titles in English translation.] January 1, 2009.

Scott, H. (2006). *Caribbean women writers and globalization: Fictions of independence.* Farnham, UK: Ashgate Press.

Words without borders. The online magazine for international literature. www.wordswithoutborders.org January 1, 2009.

6

Global Media and Global News

A Guide to Decoding and Analyzing Information

Chinedu "Ocek" Eke

Introduction: Information Everywhere, but Not a Drop to Drink?

The world is increasingly interconnected, thanks in great part to new communications technologies such as the Internet, satellites, short wave radio, cell phones, and the overall digitization of information. It is amazing that these technologies have all but erased national boundaries as we know them, and with this erosion, pressure is put on authoritarian regimes around the world that in the past have used all sorts of means to control the flow of information. On the other hand, businesses, particularly those in the West, have taken advantage of Internet-based media platforms to create global markets, thereby making their products available to all who have access to the Internet. Furthermore, students, educators, and researchers have also taken advantage of the seemingly-limitless amount of information that can be found on any given topic. In short, information is readily available at the press of a button, but still we misunderstand one another and lack information about important matters. Therefore, while it is apparent that we have lots of information on demand, we are still quite ignorant about world affairs and our role in them. Why should that be? Let's look at the mass media's effect on our knowledge, and ignorance, of world affairs. Let's see if—as Global Studies students—we can become better users of these sources of information so that we may transform that information into knowledge and understanding. Global Studies demands that we be good users of the media for several reasons. The mass media have strong actual and symbolic power; they have immense persuasive and agenda-setting force; they are our windows, moreover, into other cultures; and they allow other cultures to look in at us. Increasingly, and perhaps most intriguingly, the mass media bring us together from the four corners of the earth to read the same text, see the same picture, and hear the same voice. Such powerful phenomena certainly deserve the attention we will give them in this chapter.

Defining Mass Communication and the Mass Media: The Great Global News System

To begin, let us ask a few questions: who—and what—are the mass media? What do we mean by "mass," and what do we mean by "media"? How does the term "communication" relate to "mass media"?

First, some basic definitions: The term "mass" denotes great volume, range, or extent (such as people or production), while "media," the plural of the Latin word "medium," denotes "methods of transmission." Television, radio, newspapers, and the Internet are all examples of mass media because they are the means of conveying information of various kinds to many people, or "the masses."

"Communication" refers to the giving or taking of meaning, to the transmission and reception of messages. "Mass media," according to Denis McQuail (2005), collectively refers to "the organized technologies that make mass communication possible." However, "the process of 'mass communication' is not synonymous with the mass media" (p. 55). Mass media can be used for individual, private, or organizational purposes. As McQuail notes, "the same media that carry public messages to large publics for public purposes can also carry personal notices, advocacy messages" and other targeted communications (p. 55). But "when an organization employs a technology as a medium to communicate with a large audience, mass communication is said to have occurred" (Baran & Davis, 2006, p. 6). The basic vehicles used to accomplish communication to a mass audience include books, newspapers, radio, film, television and, more recently, the Internet.

Mass Media: World-Wide Roles and Responsibilities, and the Limits of Freedom

With these basic definitions in mind, let us ask a few questions: how do the mass media function to fulfill their social responsibility roles, domestically and globally? Because our focus here is on global media, let's first define international or global communication to give a context for how information is managed and how it is transmitted across national boundaries. According to McPhail (2002), "international communication refers to the cultural, economic, political, social, and technical analysis of communications patterns and effects across and between nation states" (p. 2). To this, Thussu (2000) adds that the word 'communicate' is taken from the Latin word *communicare*, 'to share.' Hence, international communication "is about sharing knowledge, ideas and beliefs among the various peoples of the world, and therefore it can be a contributing factor in resolving global conflict and promoting mutual understanding among nations" (p. 3). Unfortunately, Thussu (2000) also points out that "more often channels of international communications have been used, not for such lofty ideals, but to promote the economic and political interests of the world's powerful nations, who control the means of global communications" (pp. 2–3). Ideally, we might say, the mass media *should* be clear channels for sharing knowledge, but somehow they aren't. Why not? This is a big question, but we may find some of the answers in a closer analysis of the various mass media. Some features of the mass media are indeed complex and problematic. For example, features such as ownership and ownership patterns; methods of, and channels of, distribution; ideology; and control; are important components of the mass media global picture. All these components are connected with one another. For example, ownership is accompanied by, or is a result of, economic power, which in turn generates ideological power. This ideological power is part and parcel of the values, attitudes, and beliefs of the culture within which a particular medium operates, and will help to shape media content. Other connections between these components will become apparent.

Ownership and Ownership Patterns

First, let's consider briefly the historical pattern of information ownership and distribution around the world. For the most part, although this pattern is changing, it is evident that information flows mainly from the global north to the global south, and mainly from west to east. The four major news agencies—the Associated Press (AP), Reuters, Agence France Presse (AFP), and United Press International (UPI) —are all based in the West. The West also dominates in television and international broadcasting with cable and satellite outlets such as CNN, Fox News, BBC, and MSNBC. There is also a Western dominance in international radio broadcasting, with such stations as the Voice of America (VOA), the British Broadcasting Corporation (BBC), Radio France, and others. And, of course, Hollywood studios (Paramount, Disney, Warner Bros, 20th Century Fox) and American-made movies (*Titanic, Batman, Spiderman, Shrek, The Little Mermaid*) dominate the global film industry. Nor should we forget the global music and book publishing industries that are also dominated by Western conglomerates and artists. It is not uncommon to hear artists such as Beyoncé on the radio in the remotest part of any developing country, but even more interesting is that the locals can recite the lyrics of her song even though they can barely speak the English language.

This pattern of the global flow of information has been labeled as a new form of imperialism or what McPhail (2002) refers to as "electronic colonialism." According to McPhail:

> Electronic colonialism represents the dependent relationship of less developed countries (LDCs) on the West established by the importation of communication hardware and foreign produced software, along with engineers, technicians, and related information protocols that established a set of foreign norms, values, and expectations, that, to varying degrees, alter domestic cultures, habits, values, and the socialization process itself. From comic books to satellites, computers to fax machines, CDs to internet, a wide range of information technologies make it easy to send and thus receive information. (p. 14)

This domination of information by the West was a key subject of polarizing debate at UNESCO between the LDCs (Less Developed Countries) and the West in the 1970s. In the debate called New World Information and Communication Order (NWICO), developing countries identified the imbalances that existed in the current of international information, and called for a "balanced flow" of information instead of the "one-way flow." In response, the West insisted on a "free-flow" of information, where market principles, backed by democratic ideals such as freedom of speech and expression, ruled the day. Clearly, an agreement could not be reached in this debate, especially with the withdrawal of the United States, the United Kingdom, and Singapore from UNESCO in 1980. But while the NWICO debate did not result in the realignment of global media institutions, we should note the key points raised in the debate, such as the dangers of concentrated media ownership or even of a monopoly, the impact on culture of the English language as the global lingua-franca, and the fact that Hollywood features dominate theaters around the world. When was the last time, indeed, that you saw an African or a Latin American film in major United States theaters? Or have you ever anticipated speaking another culture's native language—that is, going without a translator—in a remote village in a developing country? These directions of the stream of information and ideas, with patterns of media ownership, are parts of a much bigger topic: globalization.

Ownership, Culture, and Ideological Shaping

To fully understand how information and news are shaped and transmitted within and across national boundaries, one has to understand the extent to which ownership implies ideology: i.e., a coherent system of connected values, attitude, beliefs, and aspirations. The owner of a medium, in concert with the culture within which the medium operates, is likely to shape its ideological fingerprint. As the wise man once said: "He who pays the piper calls the tune." Generally speaking, mass media messages will reflect the cultural values and sociopolitical and economic ideologies of the nations in which they (the media) are established (Hachten & Scotton, 2007). And, as Philip Seib (2008) notes in *The Al Jazeera Effect*, "Politics is pervasive, and media organizations that say they will deliver ideologically neutral news and wholesome entertainment are unlikely to be truly apolitical" (p. 29). So for example, there is a distinct difference between the United States press and the press in Egypt, based on the factors listed. The United States press and its journalists enjoy the protection of the First Amendment of the United States Constitution, while the Egyptian press has no such protection under the law in Egypt. The content of each culture's or country's messages will reflect that political and constitutional distinction.

A profound difference between these two countries' media set-ups is further exemplified by the existence of the Ministry of Information in Egypt, and by the absence of such a ministry in the United States. Also, to practice journalism in Egypt, one needs to have a license issued by the government, and the government can dictate what it wants published. In Egypt, journalists face harsh sanctions if they do not comply with directives from the government or if they are accused of "crossing the line." For instance, Ibrahim Eissa, the editor of the independent daily *al-Doustor*, was sentenced to six months in prison for writing "bad" things about Egyptian president Hosni Mubarak's health.[1] This type of incident rarely happens in the United States. We might also note, however, that even this limited comparison may change its significance fairly quickly in the volatile world of Middle Eastern media. Philip Seib comments that "the growth of the new media has been explosive. In the Middle East, Al Jazeera has plenty of company on the airwaves. From a mere handful of stations a few years ago, more than 450 Arab satellite channels are now on the air and most are privately owned, bringing an end to the dominance of government-run media in the region" (Seib, 2008, p. x). The censoring power of, for example, the Egyptian government is, then, perhaps much less effective than it used to be, because other, non-government owned media, may be beaming information to the people, straight over the heads of the government. A medium—and a reporter—originating outside the censoring country will not face the same threat as a journalist working in (e.g.) Cairo. Indeed, Al Jazeera journalists in the Cairo bureau have been arrested at various times in recent years.[2]

New media growth in other parts of the world can also undermine the dominance of corporate-owned (or government-sponsored) media with an international reach. According to Seib, "In Latin America, Venezuelan president Hugo Chavez is the moving force behind Telesur, a regional channel on the model of Al Jazeera. Chavez says Telesur is a means of 'counteracting the media dictatorship of the big international news networks.' Similar ventures are being planned for sub-Saharan Africa and elsewhere. In each instance the new arrivals are wresting influence away from CNN, the BBC, and other Western news organizations on which much of the world has relied for many years" (Seib, 2008, p. x).

Media scholars Hachten and Scotton (2007) offer us a way to categorize, and make sense of, the ways in which different cultures worldwide exert "ideological shaping" on their own mass media. Different political institutions, globally, put their mark on the form and content of television, radio, the press, and the Internet. Table 6.1 provides the basic components of their classification.

While these press categories are useful in generally explaining some key features of the media systems of the world, they are not without limitations. For instance, Yin (2008), has suggested the development of press theories especially in the Asian context that would be a lot more comprehensive than existing ones in addressing the profound cultural and social realities that distinguish Asia from the West. Yin points out: "Western societies are democratic and horizontal, emphasizing public participation in government, while Confucian societies are hierarchical and vertical, believing in meritocracy instead of democracy" (p. 43). Overall, any attempt to categorize the vast and varied global mass media must consider carefully a range of distinctive cultural institutions—religion, economics, politics, sex and gender systems, among others—which help to characterize these media and their messages.

Gatekeeping in Mass Media

Hachten and Scotton's classification (see Table 6.1) shows us that we have to be very aware of how individuals, corporations, governments, and other cultural institutions, such as the church, can act as gatekeepers, or filters, of the information we receive. Mass media can shape our perception of events—both expanding and limiting it. Earlier in this chapter, we listed as problematic features of the mass media such things as their ideological bias, their owners and ownership patterns, and the related topic of their control. Let's return to these features now as possible causes of the extraordinary power of the mass media to act as gatekeepers which help to form the world we inhabit.

TABLE 6.1 *Five Basic Theories of the Press.*

Theory	Concepts and Examples
Development Concept Describes systems in which government and media work in concert to ensure that the media aid the planned, beneficial development of a given nation.	*Concept*: Press used in nation building; No guarantee of freedom of press *Example*: Most of the developing world and global south
Western Concept Combines aspects of Libertarianism and social responsibility theory.	*Concept*: Freedom of the press; Right to talk politics *Examples*: United States, Australia, New Zealand, Western European countries
Revolutionary Concept Describes a system in which media are used in the service of a revolution or change of the existing government.	*Concept*: Press as an instrument for political and social change; temporary *Examples*: 1979 Iranian revolution where audio cassettes played an important role in the overthrow of the Shah
Authoritarian Concept Advocates the complete domination of media by a government for the purpose of forcing those media to serve the government.	*Concept*: Government controlled media *Examples*: Myanmar, Egypt
Communism Concept Advocates the complete domination of media by a Communist government for the purpose of forcing the media to serve the Communist Party.	*Concept*: Media serve to propagandize and agitate the public *Example*: Cuba, N. Korea, U.S.S.R. prior to the collapse of Communism in 1992

(Table created by Eke from Hachten & Scotton, 2007)

Information is critical in every society, and as such, it has been suggested that those who control the flow and content of information ultimately will shape the opinion of the public. Mass communications theories, such as the one often called "Agenda-setting," have, in fact, postulated that the media do not necessarily tell people what to think, but what to think *about*. If this is true, the role of the "gatekeepers" becomes very significant to the domestic and international news arena, mainly because readers and viewers—according to this theory—have their "thinking agenda" set by others.

Gatekeepers in news media are those individuals (editors, producers, news directors, and other media managers) who function as message filters. They make decisions about what messages actually get produced for a particular audience (Campbell, Martin, & Fabos, 2005), slamming doors or opening them to block information or to let it flow through. Ultimately, according to Baran and Davis (2006, p. 140), the role of the gatekeeper, from a critical theory perspective, is to screen information and to pass only items that will help others to share the gatekeeper's own point of view. Critical theories in mass communications research challenge the *status quo* in society by "seeking emancipation and change in the dominant social order" (Baran & Davis, 2006, p. 32). Agenda-setting, discussed above, is an example of a critical theory.

Gatekeepers themselves may be seen as products of various political, economic, religious, and other cultural institutions. One gatekeeper's agenda may be different from another's. So it's important for readers and viewers to understand how and why certain news items have arrived, or failed to arrive, on the national or international page or screen.

To gain insight into the influences of "gatekeepers" on news, one has to consider the global media ownership patterns, especially in the United States, where most of the world's media information is generated. The 1996 Telecommunications Act passed by the United States Congress deregulated the telecommunications industry and thus has permitted a few major corporations to own most of the mass media accessible to the public. Previous ownership legislation, such as the 1934 Telecommunications Act, prevented such concentration of ownership by prohibiting one entity from owning multiple media outlets in one market. For example, individuals or companies that owned a television station could not own the newspaper or the radio station in the same market. The rationale for such restriction was that in order to have a vibrant democracy, different points of view should not only be expressed but also be readily available to the general public. Having a diversity of media ownership can ensure that one owner of multiple outlets does not monopolize content or opinion. On the other hand, the argument by the telecommunications industry that ultimately led to the 1996 Act was that by deregulating the industry, Congress would permit more entrants into the sector, thereby spurring competition. This competition, in turn, would lead to better products at lower costs, a trend, it was argued, that would benefit the consumer. Unfortunately, the opposite happened right after the passage of the Act. It became apparent in subsequent months and years after 1996 that the corporations who were supposed to compete with one another started merging with and acquiring one another, thereby creating what we have today: an industry whose ownership is highly concentrated in the hands of a few powerful multinational corporations such as Time-Warner, Viacom, Disney, and News Corporation. Figure 6.1 shows the ownership pattern that we have today in our United States media landscape.

It is common to hear people say, "If you don't like the channel, change it." But what most people don't know is that even when you "change it," you're still likely to be tuning in to the same content provider. If you decide to pick up a magazine, or go to a movie, you may find that these too are products of the same provider. In short, even though it may seem as though there is diversity in media content, if you scratch the surface, you'll realize that this is not the case. The sources of content are very limited indeed. This limitation, or narrowing, of actual discrete sources of material has serious implications for the range, prevalence, and nature of the "news product" itself.

Corporate control of the mass media has shifted programming, particularly on television, to *entertainment* as opposed to coverage and analysis of civic, political, and other public affairs. It is, therefore, not uncommon that many of us recognize, and can give detailed information about famous athletes or singers, but we cannot name a member of the United States Supreme Court. For instance, Begley and Interlandi (2008) have noted "one quarter of 18–24-year-olds in a 2004 survey drew a blank on Dick Cheney, and 28 percent didn't know William Rehnquist" (p. 43). This finding is further exemplified by a little "experiment" I conduct in my classes at the beginning of each semester. In one version

FIGURE 6.1 Corporate media ownership in the United States. (2007). (*Source: CJR.org*)

Viacom

CBS Network, UPN Network, MTV, Nickelodeon, TV Land, CMT, TNN, VH1, Showtime, Movie Channel, Sundance Channel, FLIK, BET, Comedy Central

Paramount pictures, MTV Films, Nickelodeon Films, Contentville.com, The Free Press, MTV Books, Nickelodeon Books, Simon & Schuster, Famous Music Publishers, Pocket Books, Star Trek Franchise, Scribner, Touchstone, Spelling Entertainment, Big Ticket TV, Viacom Productions, Kingworld Productions

180 Infinity radio stations: Concentrated in 41 cities. In 1999 had 6 of top 10 stations

34 TV Stations: Duopolies in Philly, Boston, Dallas, Detroit, Miami, Pittsburg. Stations in 15 of top 20 TV markets

Labels: TV Stations, Radio Stations, TV Networks, Content

Disney

10 TV stations: NY, LA, Chic., Philly., S.F., Houston, Raleigh, Fresno, Flint, Toledo

53 radio stations: including 6 in Minn., 5 in Chicago, 5 in Dallas, 3 in Wash., 3 in Detroit, and 3 in Atlanta.

ABC Network, Disney Channel, ESPN, A&E, SoapNet, History Channel, Lifetime, EI

Disney Pictures, Touchstone, Hollywood Pictures. Caravan. Miramax. Buena Vista Magazines: Discover, Disney, ESPN, Talk, US Weekly.

Books: Disney, Hyperion, Talk/ Miramax.

Newspapers: County Press (MI), Oakland Press (MI), Narragansett Times, St. Louis Daily Record.

Music: Buena Vista, Hollywood, Lyric Street.

Sports: Anaheim Ducks and Angels. Internet: NFL.com, NASCAR.com, ABCNews.com

Labels: TV/Radio Stations, TV Networks, Content/Production

Clear Channel

Clear Channel is world's leading event promoter; 66 million tix in 26,000 events in 2001. SFX represents hundreds of athletes: Jordan, Kobe, Clemens, Pedro.

36 TV stations in 28 cities in NY, CA, WA, OH, AK, duopolies In Memphis, Pensacola, Little Rock, Jacksonville, Harrisburg (w/CMA)

More than 1,200 radio stations.
- In all 50 States and D.C.
- More than 110 million listeners
- Reach 54% of all 18–49 yr. olds

Premier Radio Network: Syndicates over 100 programs including Limbaugh, Laura Slessinger, Rick Dees, Carson Daly, produces Clear Channel promoted concerts.

Labels: Content, Radio/TV stations, Production/Promotion

AOL/TW

AOL: Largest ISP in world, 37 million customers Internet users; CompuServe, Netscape

Time Warner Cable: 10.8 million cable households

HBO, CNN, WB Network, Cinemax, TBS, TNT, Court TV, Cartoon Network CNN Headline News, TW Sports

Production: Warner Brothers Studios, Castle Rock Entertainment, HBO Productions, New Line Cinema and TV. Turner Productions

Magazines: Time, Life, Fortune, Sports Ill., Money, People, Entert. Weekly, In Style, Southern Living, Popular Science.

Music labels: Atlantic, Rhino, Elektra, Warner Bros., London-Sire, Tommy Boy, Columbia House, Time Life Music.

Books: Time Life, Book-of-the-Month Club, Little, Brown & Co.., Bulfinch Press, Back Bay Books, Warner Books.

Labels: Internet, Cable TV, TV Networks, Content/Production

News Corp

22 TV Stations: Including duopolies In NY, L.A., Chicago, Dallas, Wash. Minn., Houston, Orlando, Phoenix

Fox Broadcasting, Fox News Chan., Fox Kids, Fox Sports, Health Netw., fX, Nat'l Geographic, TV Guide Chan For Sports Radio, Golf Channel

Newpapers and magazines: NY Post, TV Guide, The Weekly Standard.

Books: Harper Collins, Regan Books, Amistad Books, William Morrow & Co.

Sports: LA Dodgers, LA Kings, LA Lakers, NY Knicks, NY Rangers,

Music: Festival Records, Mushroom Records

Marketing: News America Marketing

Labels: TV Stations, TV Networks, Content/Production

of this "experiment," I asked the class who Kobe Bryant was: and the majority of the students identified him—correctly—as the then-star forward of the NBA's Los Angeles Lakers; on the other hand, when I asked who Elaine Chao was, I was greeted with stunned silence. After further discussion, the class came to an agreement that in the overall scheme of the way we live and work, Ms. Chao is a more important figure to know, as she is (or was, at the time of asking) the United States Secretary of Labor.

The ignorance exhibited by many of us about local and global issues is not a sign of our intrinsic dullness, nor even of our lack of interest in national and world affairs. Rather, we might infer that the diversion of our attention to entertainment has minimized our interest in knowing, say, who governs us or makes policy decisions that will have long term effects on our lives.

Media activists and critics see this trend of media ownership concentration in the hands of a few multinational corporations, with its resulting narrowing and homogenizing of the stream of information, as a threat to democracy. For example, the former editor of the *Chicago Tribune*, James Squires, wrote in 1993 that "The corporate media are primarily concerned then not with the preservation of the free press or the conduct of democracy but with the development of the information business in its most profitable form, whatever that may be. Anything else, under the rules of their ownership is a betrayal of their stock holders" (qtd. McChesney & Scott, 2004, p. 3). Moyers (2008) also points out that:

> Across the media landscape, the health of our democracy is imperiled. Buffeted by gale force winds of technological, political and demographic forces, without a truly free and independent press, this 250-year-old experiment in self-government will not make it. As journalism goes, so goes democracy.
> Mergers and buyouts change both old and new media. They bring a frenzied focus on cost cutting, while fattening the pockets of the new owners and their investors. The result: journalism is degraded through the layoffs and buyouts of legions of reporters and editors. (p. 2)

Media historians and activists McChesney and Scott have—even more emphatically—observed that "corporate ownership and commercial pressures have gone a long way toward destroying journalism as a democratic public service" (p. 2).

However, somewhat in contrast to McChesney and Scott's position, we might also note the differently-shaded arguments about global media ownership, media outlets, and the fate of democracy, which have arisen in the wake of the emergence of Al Jazeera, the most well-known (in the United States, at least) of the recent arrivals on the world media scene. A reviewer's note on the cover of Seib's 2008 *The Al Jazeera Effect* says the following about the political significance of the "new" mass media today:

> The emergence of new media, concomitant with new democratic potentials and new forms of violence and terrorism worldwide, is not accidental. In the *Al Jazeera Effect*, Philip Seib provides a thoughtful and sophisticated account of these salient political and media trends and how they interconnect. (Scheuer, 2008)

Overall, no matter how complex this world media scene, it is important to remember, as we analyze the information it brings us, that most of the dominant media outlets are also businesses, whose goal is, of course, to make a profit. This pressure to make money inevitably affects the scope and type of the issues that are covered. For example, major United States news media outlets have cut back on their expensive foreign bureaux and on their funding for foreign correspondents. (How much *does* it cost, we might ask, to maintain a permanent correspondent in Damascus, or Moscow, or Quito? How much *is* the train or plane fare—for a journalist and a translator—from Istanbul to Ankara?) As a result of these economies, the range, if not the actual intrinsic quality, of international news coverage has diminished. Domestic news coverage also continues to suffer, of course, as United States newspapers, in particular, hit hard as they are by the shift to electronic media and by generally gloomy economic trends, cut back on pages and reporters. Some major newspapers—such as (in Spring 2009) the *Rocky Mountain News*, in Denver, Colorado—simply cease to publish.

The Individual and the System: i-media and u-report

Generally, however, in spite of the limitations placed on the mass media by authoritarian, hierarchical, capitalist, and communist cultures, and by the related ownership and gate-keeper patterns discussed here, we can argue that the *individual* has become empowered to a large extent by the democratizing protocols of the Internet. Some newspapers cut back, or disappear, but the story is not only about reduction. New technology has made other, more positive, differences, to the media scene. On the Internet, you can easily read newspapers from different parts of the world, and more importantly, the same technology allows you to participate, so that you're no longer a passive reader but an active participant in the process, through on-line forums, feedbacks, and even blogs. Seib's 2008 study of Al Jazeera, referred to above, sums things up by saying:

> The world of new media is fascinating. It is dynamic and growing, and it offers much more than a collection of high-tech curiosities. New media are also contributing to changes in how the world works, altering the shape of the traditional political structures on which the international system is based. (Seib, 2008, p. 63)

An example of some of these media-driven political changes occurred around the deadly cyclone in Myanmar—known by some as Burma—in 2008. Pictures of the disaster were posted by ordinary people who took pictures with their cell-phone cameras and posted them on the Internet. Such vivid evidence of human suffering in the face of clear government inaction helped to pressure the Myanmar government to accept outside aid into its otherwise closed society. And before this natural disaster occurred, we in the West also "saw" the Burmese government's response to protest as it cracked down on dissenting Buddhist monks, in September 2007.

Our ability to literally *see* occurrences in otherwise "closed" states like Myanmar is a direct result of the pervasiveness of modern mass media, which now include hand-held media technologies such as cell phones equipped with cameras.

The outcome of this pervasiveness can be positive or negative for the local population. The positive, as in the case of Myanmar, is that international public opinion encouraged the government to allow more aid workers into the country to assist those in need. On the other hand, the negative can be a further crack-down on journalists and freedom of expression, as we saw from the murder of the fifty-year-old Japanese photo-journalist Kenji Nagai by a soldier during the protests for democratic reform in Myanmar on September 27, 2007.[3]

Furthermore, new technologies, especially hand-held devices such as the i-phone and cell phones generally, also make it possible for individuals to frequently be updated by alerts or short bulletins from news organizations as the "news" breaks.

This ability to reach us anywhere through our mobile devices is used by businesses, but also, notably, by politicians. For example, candidates in the 2008 United States presidential election used text messaging to alert their supporters to campaign events, and to solicit funds. The candidate-electorate communication street runs both ways, however, as Lowell Feld and Nate Wilcox say in the introduction to *Netroots Rising: How a Citizen Army of Bloggers and Online Activists is Changing American Politics* (2008):

> During the last decades of the twentieth century, politics was largely a commercial, mass media phenomenon. Candidates were foisted upon voters by small cabals of political insiders, financial backers, and campaign 'experts.' The tools of mass marketing were used to 'sell' those candidates to the voters, just like one would sell a bar of soap or a car. In contrast, in the first decade of the twenty-first century, hundreds of thousands of citizen activists are now taking advantage of newly available communications tools to revolutionize American politics. (Feld & Wilcox, p. xix)

In the "news world," too, new technologies have also given the individual the opportunity to participate in the gathering and disseminating of information and opinion in the form of blogs or other social media, such as vblogs and podcasts. Also, cable networks like CNN (*i-report*) and Fox News (*u-report*) have segments in their newscasts that encourage viewers to report news.

Blogs, in particular, continue to attract the attention of many media watchers and scholars. Their interactive quality, their easy dissemination, their position in the hands of many non-professionals, all make them unpredictable and fascinating. Feld and Wilcox, (2008), agree that this new media product has stirred the pot of political activity: "We agree with Jon Henke," say Feld and Wilcox, "that 'there will always be a place for the amateur blogger who can get good information and write with a unique voice.' And we believe that once people get a taste of activist, netroots democracy it will be difficult—if not impossible—to convince them to return to mass media passivity" (pp. 171–172).

The Product Itself: News or Infotainment?

What Is News?

News is not easily defined, partly because one person's news can be another person's propaganda. But generally speaking, news, according to Postman and Powers (1992), "is what news-directors and journalists say it is" (p. 12). This can range from UN Security Council meetings on Iran to the latest U.S. celebrity's visit to a rehab center. It has been observed that, increasingly, news has become "infotainment," a term which suggests "the melding of media roles as purveyor of information and entertainment" (Vivian, 2006, p.8). Again, the concept of "gatekeeping" comes into play in what is selected as newsworthy or simply ignored. But in general, the following criteria indicate standard agreed-upon factors that determine how particular issues or topics are selected as news.

Elements of News

Metz (1985) offers an extremely useful list of factors that influence decision making of editors and other news gatekeepers. Few stories will encompass all of these elements, but they provide us with analytical aids when we are trying to figure out why and how a certain "news" item is covered—or not:

1. Timeliness: When an event took place helps determine whether or not it is reported as news.
2. Consequence: This refers to the importance of an event; for example, political events and natural disasters. Audience response and feedback can help to determine if an event is newsworthy.
3. Prominence: When something happens to famous individuals it is worthy of attention, while the same thing happening to someone else would not be newsworthy.
4. Rarity: Unusual events are often considered newsworthy. Events that may have been rare lose their newsworthiness as they become more common.
5. Proximity: This term refers to the geographical location of an event. The closer the event, the more newsworthy it will be for a local audience.
6. Change & Conflict: An event that may trigger changes in society is likely to be of interest to individuals, either because they will oppose or support the changes.
7. Action: A story about people engaged in activities has more news potential than does one about people merely considering these activities or merely complaining about a topic. Action includes acts of violence, deliberate or accidental.
8. Concreteness: The tangible always take precedence over the abstract on the scale of news value. For example, HIV/AIDS death is more newsworthy than the discussion of the etiology of these conditions. Actual death has human interest.
9. Personality: These are human-interest stories. They are written or aired in order to affect the feelings and sensibilities in some way. They can be about famous individuals, or about everyday people involved in everyday situations. (Metz, 1985, pp. 3–6)

Don't Be Fooled: Reading the Mass Media Intelligently

Steps to Analyzing and Understanding News: Critical Thinking—A Strategy for All Seasons

To be an effective consumer of news, one has to think critically. Critical thinking is the active, skillful deployment of those general principles and procedures of thinking which are most conducive to truth or accuracy in judgment. To understand critical thinking better, consider some of the things that *uncritical* thinkers do. An *uncritical* thinker:

- Accepts things purely on faith.
- Thinks that a person's beliefs are "true for them" and can't be mistaken or criticized.
- Is not disposed to seek evidence or challenge beliefs.

By contrast, a *critical* thinker asks questions like:

- What am I being asked to accept?
- Should I accept it or not?
- Why? What are the arguments and how strong are they?

Basically, the foundation of critical thinking is understanding how claims are supported or opposed by evidence: i.e., how information is relevant to whether a claim is true or false. Therefore, a critical thinker can identify the main contention in an issue, look for evidence that supports or opposes that contention, and assess the strength of the reasoning ("Argument Mapping," a technique you can review at http://www.rationale.austhink.com, provides useful guidance on analyzing other people's arguments.)

According to Paul and Elder (2007), "Egocentric thinking results from the unfortunate fact that humans do not naturally consider the rights and needs of others." Egocentric thinking works against critical thinking, because those kinds of thinkers "do not naturally appreciate the point of view of others nor the limitations in their own point of view. They become explicitly aware of their egocentric thinking only if trained to do so.... They do not naturally recognize their self-serving perspective" (p. 9). Paul and Elder go on to categorize five types of egocentric thinking, as follows:

Types of Egocentric thinking:

"IT'S TRUE BECAUSE I BELIEVE IT."
Innate egocentrism: What I believe is true even though I have never questioned my beliefs.

"IT'S TRUE BECAUSE WE BELIEVE IT."
Innate sociocentrism: Beliefs in the group I belong to are true even though never questioned.

"IT'S TRUE BECAUSE I WANT TO BELIEVE IT."
Innate wish fulfillment: Does not require a change in my thinking and belief in what "feels good."

"IT'S TRUE BECAUSE I HAVE ALWAYS BELIEVED IT."
Innate self-validation: Strong desire to maintain beliefs that have been long held.

"IT'S TRUE BECAUSE IT IS IN MY SELFISH INTEREST TO BELIEVE IT."
Innate selfishness: Beliefs that justify getting more power, money, or personal advantage even though there's no evidence to support such beliefs (p. 9).

For articles in the news, or really for any text at all, thoughtful analysis can begin by responding to several key, but unspoken, questions. Paul and Elder suggest that we have the following headings in mind as we read:

The main purpose of this article is…
The key question that the author is addressing is…
The most important information in this article is…
The main inferences/conclusions in this article are…
The key concepts we need to understand in this article are…
The main assumptions underlying the author's thinking are…
If we take this line of reasoning seriously, the implications are…
The main points of view presented in this article are…(p. 13).

Readers who can fill in the blanks above are on the right track to becoming astute interpreters of the news, or, indeed, of any texts. But good news readers also need:

1. Understanding of how news is made; and
2. Identification of biases inherent in many news reports. Unfortunately, most people tend to think of the news media and their reports as merely liberal or conservative. However, such simple classifications detract from our understanding of the deliberateness and complexity of news construction.

Applying Critical Thinking

Recognizing and Interpreting News Appeals.   The identification and evaluation of news appeals is a method of analysis that is used to understand how the construction of news reports invites political response from citizens or discourages further discourse on issues (Barton, 1990).

Steps in Analysis:

1. Separating the various appeals made to publics.
2. Accounting for the larger international political context of which the appeals are a part.
3. Associating appeals with voices from which appeals emerge.
4. Postulating a political use of appeals on the basis of comparative orientations of the audience.

These steps of analysis take into consideration who the actors are and how they are legitimated as players in the international or domestic scene.

Types of News Appeals
   a. Appeals to Authority—News appeals to uncontested authority, which may close off or limit political discourse. For example, appeals to nationalism.
   b. General Public—News appeals to unseen, generalized, non-discursive public. For example, vague reference to public opinion.

    c. Community Guardian—News appeals to the sense of community needs and values. Depending on the context, it can refer to local neighborhoods or to the idea of international community.

    d. Groups—News appeals that are invitational to groups with highly organized goals and roles constituting a distinctive political culture with high levels of knowledge about specific issues. For example, environmental activists.

    e. Individuals—News appeals to individuals' political conscience, and sense of political commitment perceived as the requisite obligation for participating in society at large. For example, voter registration campaigns.

    f. Ideal Social Order—News appeals that involve an open participatory democracy, distinct from appeals to authority. Encourages discussion of issues across audience orientations and across national boundaries.

    g. Conventional Conception—Appeals that oversimplify news. For example, the subjects of the news reports lack individuality. Media form or re-enforce stereotypes and symbols concerning particular events.

    h. Morality—News appeals in which the media act in establishing certain concepts of deviance. News is framed in terms of guilt or innocence, and emphasis is placed on negative characteristics that define the deviant group. (Barton, 1990, pp. 18, 19)

Recognizing and Interpreting Bias in the News.   One of the basic tenets of journalism and news reports is the idea of objectivity. This idea implies that the news source is neutral, fair, and unbiased. However, a closer look will reveal that most news reports are influenced by the context in which they are produced. Examining, for instance, the attitudes, background, social affiliations, and the political and religious leanings of reporters, editors, photographers, and interviewers can help us to better understand this context. Certainly not all bias in the news is deliberate; however, according to the Media Awareness Network (2009), one can become a more effective news consumer by watching for the following journalistic techniques that allow bias to 'creep in' to the news:

    1. Bias through selection and omission: An editor can express a bias by choosing to include or exclude a specific news item. Within a given story, some details can be ignored, and others included, to give readers or viewers a different opinion about events reported. If, during a speech, a few people boo, the reaction can be described as "remarks greeted by jeers" or they can be minimized as "a disturbance from a handful of dissidents." This kind of bias is difficult to detect. Only by comparing news reports from a wide variety of sources can it be observed.

    2. Bias through placement: Front-page stories are more important than those buried in the back. Radio and television newscasts lead with the most important story of the day and less significant stories are broadcast later. Therefore, where a story is placed influences what the reader or viewer thinks about its importance.

    3. Bias by headline: Headlines are the most read part of the paper. Many people read or scan only the headlines of a news item. They can convey excitement where none exists; they can express approval or condemnation, and thus, can present carefully-hidden biases and prejudices in a summary.

4. **Bias by photos, captions, and camera angles:** Some pictures flatter a person; others make the person look unpleasant. A paper can choose to influence public opinion about, for example, a candidate for election. On television, the choice of which visual images to display is extremely important. The captions newspapers run below photos are also potential sources of bias.

5. **Bias through names and titles:** News media often use labels and titles to describe people, places, and events. A person can be called an "ex-con" or be referred to as someone who "served time twenty years ago for a minor offense." Whether a person is described as a "terrorist" or a "freedom fighter" is a clear indication of editorial bias.

6. **Bias through statistics and crowd counts:** To make a disaster seem more spectacular (and therefore worthy of reading about) numbers can be inflated. For example, "a hundred injured in air crash" can be the same as "only minor injuries in an air crash." The words used reflect the opinion of the person doing the counting.

7. **Bias by source control:** To detect bias, always consider where the news item "comes from." Is the information supplied by a reporter, an eyewitness, police or fire officials, business executives, or by selected or appointed public officials? Each may have particular bias that is introduced into the story. Companies and public relations directors supply news outlets with puff pieces through news releases, photos, or videos. Often, news outlets depend on pseudo-events (demonstrations, sit-ins, ribbon-cuttings, speeches, and ceremonies) that take place mainly to gain news coverage.

8. **Word choice and tone:** Showing the same kind of bias that appears in headlines, the use of positive or negative words with distinctive connotations can strongly influence the reader or viewer. For example, ABC News reported on June 24, 2008 that an Israeli soldier *had been killed* instead of reporting that the soldier *committed suicide* during a farewell ceremony for French President Sarkozy. (Media Awareness Network, 2009)

Recognizing and Interpreting Propaganda Techniques. It has been said that the first casualty of war is the truth. We are constantly bombarded with information that seeks to persuade us to believe or trust in something, or to buy a product, or to take a certain course of action. Remember that these attempts to convince you to think or act in a certain way are carefully planned, studied and tested to improve their effectiveness and get the desired results. For a global news consumer, it is important to understand how people are manipulated, or persuaded to think about or respond to certain events. To this end, understanding propaganda techniques is invaluable to becoming a critical consumer of mass media materials: specifically, the news, public relations statements, and advertising.

Propaganda is defined as the "no-holds-barred use of communication to propagate (or express) specific beliefs and expectations" (Baran & Davis, 2006, p. 73). According to Baran and Davis, there are four types of propaganda. These include: White propaganda, disinformation, black propaganda, and grey propaganda:

> White propaganda is the intentional suppression of potentially harmful information and ideas, combined with the deliberate promotion of positive information or ideas to distract attention from problematic events.
> Disinformation is false information spread about the opposition to discredit it.

Black propaganda is the deliberate and strategic transmission of lies.

Grey propaganda is the transmission of information or ideas that might or might not be false. No effort is made to determine their validity. (pp. 74–75)

These propaganda techniques can be observed at different times in society, especially during wars or after large natural disasters. For example, it is becoming clearer from books that have been recently published by former members of President George W. Bush's administration, principal among them, Scott McClellan, the former press secretary, that the Bush administration used propaganda to convince the American public of Iraq's possession of Weapons of Mass Destruction (WMD). Fenton (2005) says that the American "public was offered one shifty rationale after another for the invasion of Iraq: The prospect that Iraq had Weapons of Mass Destruction (WMD), then the urgency of the war on terror, then the policy of 'regime change,' then the noble goal of bringing democracy to the Mideast" (p. 84). Fenton's comments match those from other political analysts, but as good students of the media we should always evaluate the origin of such judgments, and be alert to possible bias. We should also be aware that one administration's "propaganda" may be another administration's "astute use of the media."

A final example of commentary on this topic comes from The Center for Public Integrity, which concluded in its research that:

The Bush administration led the nation to war on the basis of erroneous information that it methodically propagated and that culminated in military action against Iraq on March 19, 2003. Not surprisingly, the officials with the most opportunities to make speeches, grant media interviews, and otherwise frame the public debate also made the most false statements. President Bush, for example, made 232 false statements about weapons of mass destruction in Iraq and another 28 false statements about Iraq's links to Al Qaeda. Secretary of State Powell had the second-highest total in the two-year period, with 244 false statements about weapons of mass destruction in Iraq and 10 about Iraq's links to Al Qaeda. Rumsfeld and Fleischer each made 109 false statements, followed by Wolfowitz (with 85), Rice (with 56), Cheney (with 48), and McClellan (with 14).

For example, [in a speech on] August 26, 2002, [Vice President] Dick Cheney flatly declared "there is no doubt that Saddam Hussein now has weapons of mass destruction." . . .

Central Intelligence Agency Director George Tenet recalled Cheney's statement "went well beyond his agency's assessments at the time." Another CIA official . . . later told journalist Ron Suskind: "Our reaction was, 'Where is he getting this stuff from?'" (http://www.publicintegrity. org/WarCard/)

One of the primary reasons propaganda techniques are successful is that information, as indicated above, frequently comes from "official sources." Such sources are often legitimated in the readers' minds as representative of the people. "Official sources" are generally believed—in most Western democracies, at least—to have the best interests of the people at heart. However, we have seen over and over again, historically and in the present, that almost all governments are willing to manipulate information using various techniques. Emotional appeals—to fear, love, anger, or hate—and master symbols, such as the flag, may all be used in what Walter Lippmann in his *Public Opinion* (1922) called the "manufacture of consent" of the people. Lippmann noted that this "manufacture of consent" by society's "leaders" was "capable of great refinements," thanks, among other things, to—yes, even in 1922!—"modern means of communication" ([1965], p. 158).

The moral complexities of this media-management of public opinion are explored extensively, and in an international context, in *Control Room*, a 2004 documentary about coverage of the early days of the U.S.-led 2003 invasion of Iraq. Directed by Jehane Noujaim, this film, as *Boston Globe* reviewer Ty Burr notes, while focusing on Al Jazeera, "the Qatar-based independent news network that functions as the controversial CNN of the Arab Speaking world," also examines "the American network news corps and the press offices of the U.S. military at Central Command in Qatar" (Burr, 2004). In notable scenes, says Burr, we see senior Al Jazeera producer Samir Khader declare that his network's reporting of the war—with all its images of wounded, crying children—is not "incitement," but, rather, "the only true journalism in the world." On the other side of the media coin, we see Lieutenant Josh Rushing, the "earnest young U.S. army press officer at CentCom," moving from "adamantly insisting the Arab network is biased in favor of Hussein's regime to admitting to the distortions of both Al Jazeera's nationalism and Fox News's patriotism to confessing to his own horror when he realizes footage of dead Iraqis doesn't outrage him the way similar pictures of US casualties do" (Burr, 2004).

Apparently, then, one person's news—or "true journalism"—can be considered by another to be less than the absolute truth. But the film's portrayal of Khader's and Rushing's shifting and mixed feelings indicates that the line between "good journalism" and "propaganda" is not always absolutely clear, even to those in the business. Readers and viewers must be vigilant interpreters of news and information in order to correct for this—perhaps inevitable—bias.

Misinformation or propaganda is not limited to international news, however. It can be found domestically, both locally and nationally. For example, in the aftermath of 2005's Hurricane Katrina, the news media at times appeared to blame the victims of the storm for their own suffering. People who had not left in time were somehow culpable. In addition, some press reports appeared to use negative racial overtones to describe the events in New Orleans. One report on the Yahoo news Web site in September 2005 showed two pictures. One was a picture of a young black boy chest deep in water and dragging what appeared to be a case of Pepsi. The caption under this picture read: "A young man walks through chest deep flood water after *looting* a grocery store in New Orleans on Tuesday, August 30, 2005." The second picture showed a white male and a white female also chest deep in the flood water and the caption read: "Two residents wade through chest-deep water after *finding* bread and soda from a local grocery store after Hurricane Katrina came through the area"[4] In other words, white residents were *finding* food while black residents were *looting* food. [All italics added.]

In this instance *finding* food is not a crime under the circumstances but *looting* food has a criminal connotation and hence perpetuates the stereotype of blacks as criminals, and of whites as innocents who are struggling heroically to survive.

To avoid becoming a thoughtless consumer of propaganda, one must apply the critical thinking skills that were introduced earlier. *Critical thinkers* are intellectually empowered to defend themselves against misstatements and misinformation because they ask the right questions and are not afraid to seek the truth.

Conclusion

Overall, understanding international and domestic news requires an effort. The effort is to be what we might call "media literate." Media literacy is a skill acquired through a life time, but all of us can make a start. By way of illustration, a popular website, published by the Annenberg Public Policy Center, in Washington, D.C., called FactCheckEd.org, provides us with some simple, yet vital, steps we should take as we read, watch, or listen to, the myriad products of today's mass media. They are:

1. Keep an open mind. Most of us have biases, and we can easily fool ourselves if we don't make a conscious effort to keep our minds open to new information. Psychologists have shown over and over again that humans naturally tend to accept any information that supports what they already believe, even if the information isn't very reliable. And humans also naturally tend to reject information that conflicts with those beliefs, even if the information is solid. These predilections are powerful. Unless we make an active effort to listen to all sides, we can become trapped into believing something that isn't so, and we won't even realize that we are being manipulated.

2. Ask the right questions. Don't accept claims at face value; test them by asking a few questions. Who is speaking, and where are they getting their information? How can I validate what they're saying? What facts would prove this claim wrong? Does the evidence presented really back up what's being said? If an ad says a product is "better," for instance, what does that mean? Better than what?

3. Cross-check. Don't rely on one source or one study, but look to see what others say. When two or three reliable sources independently report the same facts or conclusions, you can be more confident of them. But when two independent sources contradict each other, you know you need to dig more deeply to discover who's right.

4. Consider the source. Not all sources are equal. As any *CSI*—or any other "procedural drama"—viewer knows, sometimes physical evidence is a better source than an eyewitness, whose memory can play tricks. And an eyewitness is more credible than somebody telling a story he or she heard from somebody else. By the same token, an Internet Web site that offers primary source material is more trustworthy than one that publishes information gained second- or third-hand. For example, official vote totals posted by a county clerk or state election board are more authoritative than election returns reported by a political blog or even a newspaper, which can be out of date or mistaken.

5. Weigh the evidence. Know the difference between random anecdotes and real scientific data from controlled studies. Know how to avoid common errors of reasoning, such as assuming that one thing causes another simply because the two happen one after the other. Does a rooster's crowing cause the sun to rise? Only a rooster would think so. (FactCheckEd.org, 2009)

By incorporating or taking into account all the topics and *caveats* discussed above, we can start to *read in between the lines* and be better able to discern what is truth and what is not; what is infotainment and what is news; what is good journalism and what is not. And, even more importantly, through such thoughtful analysis, we will find it easier to become responsible and thinking members—and critics—of this media-saturated society.

Notes

1. For more about Ibrahim Eissa's case, see "Journalists' syndicate petitions to freeze Eissa sentence," by Sarah Carr, 29 September 2008. http://www.thedailynewsegypt.com/article.aspx?ArticleID=16812 4 January, 2009.
2. See, for example, the report of 28 January 2008: "Al-Jazeera journalist arrested in Egypt," ABC News Online, by Nadia El Abou Magd. http://www.abcnews.go.com/International/wireStory?id 4 January, 2009.
3. "Japanese journalist killed in Myanmar," in *The Japan Times Online*. September 28, 2007. http://search.japantimes.co.jp/cgi-bin/nn20070928a1.html 4 January, 2009.
4. For a discussion of these two photographs and their captions, see "Hurricane Katrina and the 'two-photo controversy'" in *Teachable moments: Media awareness network*. http://www.media-awareness.ca/english/resources/educational/teach 4 January, 2009.

References

Argument mapping: http://www.rationale.austhink.com/learn/critical-thinking 28 May 2009.

Baran J., & Davis, D. (2006). *Mass communications theory: Foundations, ferment, and future*. Belmont, CA: Wadsworth.

Barton, R. (1990). *Ties that blind in Canadian/American relations: Politics of news discourse*. Hillsdale, NJ: Lawrence Erlbaum Associates.

Bagdikian, B. (2004). *The new media monopoly*. Boston, MA: Beacon.

Begley, S., & Interlandi, J. (2008, June 2). Dumbest generation? Don't be dumb. *Newsweek*.

Burr, Ty. "A Lucid Look at Al-Jazeera." 11 June, 2004. Review. *The Boston Globe*. www.boston.com/movies/display?display=movie&id=6776. 15 June 2009.

Campbell, R., Martin, C., & Fabos, B. (2005). *Media and culture: An introduction to mass communications*. New York: Bedford/St. Martin's.

Center for Public Integrity: http://www.publicintegrity.org/WarCard 28 May 2009.

Columbia Journalism Review: http://cjr.org/ownership.

FactCheckEd.org. (2009). A process for avoiding deception.

Feld, L., & Wilcox, N. (2008). *Netroots rising: How a citizen army of bloggers and online activists is changing American politics*. Westport, CT: Praeger.

Fenton, T. (2005). *Bad news: The decline of reporting, the business of news, and the danger to us all*. New York: HarperCollins.

Hachten, W., & Scotton, J. (2007). *The world news prism: Global information in a satellite age*. Malden, MA: Blackwell.

Jones, A. (2002). *Beyond the barricades: Nicaragua and the struggle for the Sandinista press, 1979–98*. Athens, OH: Ohio University Press.

Lippmann, Walter. [1922] (1965). *Public Opinion*. New York: Free Press.

McChesney, R., & Scott, B. (2004). *Our unfree press: 100 years of radical media criticism*. New York: The New Press.

McPhail, T. (2002). *Global communication: Theories, stakeholders, and trends.* Boston: Allyn and Bacon.

McQuail, D. (2005). *McQuail's mass communication theory.* 5th Ed. Thousand Oaks, CA: Sage Publications.

Media Awareness Network: http://media-awareness.ca/english/resources/educational/handout/crime/detecting_bias_newscfm 28 May 2009.

Metz, W. (1985). *News writing: From lead to "30."* 2nd Ed. Englewood Cliffs, NJ: Prentice-Hall.

Moyers, B. (2008). Is the fourth estate a fifth column: Corporate media colludes with democracy's demise. *Keynote address at the National Conference for Media Reform.* Minneapolis, MN. June 7.

Noujaim, H. (Director). Salama, H., Varela, R. (Producers)(2004). *Control room.* [Videorecording].

Paul, R., & Elder, L. (2007). *Critical thinking: Concepts and tools.* Dillon Beach, CA: The Foundation For Critical Thinking.

Postman, N., & Powers, S. (1992). *How to watch TV news.* New York: Penguin.

Scheuer, J. (2008). *Review of Philip Seib's* The Al Jazeera Effect. *Cover note.* Washington, DC: Potomac Books.

Seib, P. (2008). *The Al Jazeera effect: How the new global media are reshaping world politics.* Washington, DC: Potomac Books.

Siebert, F., Peterson, T., & Schramm, W. (1957). *Four theories of the press.* Urbana: University of Illinois Press.

Thussu, D. (2000). *International communication: Continuity and change.* London: Arnold.

Vivian, J. (2006). *The media of mass communications.* New York: Pearson.

Yin, J. (2008). Beyond the four theories of the press: A new model for Asian & world press. *Journalism & communication monographs* (10:1). Columbia, SC: Association for Education in Journalism and Mass Communication.

Questions for Discussion

1. **Comparative News Exercise:** To access newspapers from around the world, go to Internet Public Library (ipl.org/div/news). In the Reading Room section, click on "Newspapers." This link will take you to a directory of different countries and links to newspapers in each country. Now find a major news story that has global implications in a major U.S. newspaper such as the *Wall Street Journal, New York Times, San Francisco Chronicle, Chicago Tribune,* or the *Washington Post.* If, for example, the story is about nuclear weapons proliferation in Iran, then go to Iran on the IPL (Internet Public Library) and compare how the same story is being told in the *Tehran Times.* Some points to consider:

   - What are the similarities and differences?
   - What types of news appeals are used in both publications?
   - Do you see any biases in the news reports?
   - What effect, if any, do you think these reports will have on the intended audiences?

   (Be sure that the news stories are written by the publications' own correspondents and not reported by news agencies such as AP, Reuters, or AFP.)

2. Pick a columnist from the op-ed page of a daily newspaper. Read several of that writer's columns. Then discuss (or write about) the columnist's authorial image: his or her political, ethical, spiritual, and emotional make up. Provide as much detailed evidence for your conclusions as you can.

3. Focus on new and relatively recent media outlets outside the United States, such as Al Jazeera and Telesur. Find out more about how, when, and why one or both of these (or other overseas) outlets were established. Write up your findings in a short paper.

4. Take the front page of any daily newspaper. Re-read "Recognizing and Interpreting Bias in the News," pp. 152–153. Then, analyze and evaluate the text and graphics on your front page. What does your analysis tell you about the newspaper's political, ethical, and economic identity?

5. Go back to the front page you chose for question four. Now rewrite the headlines, the captions for photographs, or other graphics, and even key sentences or paragraphs in the stories. How do your rewrites change the overall impact of that front page?

Helpful sources of information:
Media Awareness Network: http://www.media-awareness.ca/english/index.cfm
The Center for Public Integrity: http://www.publicintegrity.org
Librarians' Internet Index: http://lii.org/
http://www.telesurtv.net

Topics in Global Studies

7

Environmentalism Gone Wild

The Great Green Mobilization and Beyond

Anthony Weston

I was driving my fourteen-year-old and her friend to a party when I mentioned the latest discoveries of possibly Earth-like planets orbiting other stars. Great, they answered—more planets for us to screw up.

They left their cynicism in the car when they got to the party, but it stayed with me. There is truth to it, for sure. I have no wish to deny that we are threatening nature and even our own survival on a planetary scale. I recognize too that cynicism can be a form of self-protection: to hope for anything else may not only be too audacious but may also render us too vulnerable. And yet might even a committed environmentalist beg to differ? From even a slightly broader historical perspective, we are talking about one culture here, not somehow the human soul as such. We are looking at just one moment in that culture's history, too, not all of the past or future; and it is arguably too backward-looking a picture even of this very moment, when things are already shifting, already diversifying, as we work out multiple new paths in the face of the emergency. Emergencies are also times of emer*gence*, after all. In the face of the great global crisis, something dramatically new and equally sweeping may only now be taking shape. So could we not advance environmentalism in a celebratory, visionary, transformative key? What are we waiting for?

"*All I'm saying is <u>now</u> is the time to develop the technology to deflect an asteroid.*"

FIGURE 7.1   *Source:* The New Yorker Collection 1998 Frank Cotham from cartoonbank.com. All Rights Reserved.

Environmentalism Evolves

The first Earth Day was quite recent—1970—but twenty years passed before serious environmental awareness became mainstream. Specific and dramatic threats prompted it: killer smog; massive oil spills; pesticides like DDT that threatened all manner of animals including American icons such as bald eagles and pelicans; burning rivers, such as Ohio's Cuyahoga River, whose toxic waters actually caught fire one day in 1969. An enduring memory from my youth is seeing on TV the Cleveland Fire Department hosing down the river.

Those threats were not small—by no means—but they proved to be manageable with political will and economic pressure. The Environmental Protection Agency was a bipartisan creature of an overwhelmingly Democratic Congress and Republican President Richard

Nixon. Pollution controls followed, along with the Clean Air and Clean Water Acts, the Endangered Species Act, fuel economy standards for motor vehicles, and a host of other measures. Two years after the Cuyahoga burned, we had a Clean Water Act with teeth. DDT was quickly banned, though it is still widely used in the less advantaged world, and other toxins were banned or sidelined. And now, forty or so years later, we inherit a world in which recycling bins are omnipresent, eco-tourism, renewable energy, and hybrid cars are all the rage, and everything seems to be going green.

Yet all of this was still really only a beginning. The current areas of concern now are much deeper, more systemic, harder-to-visualize challenges: greenhouse-gas-induced climate change, ozone depletion, species loss and habitat destruction, fisheries collapse, looming fall-offs in the availability not just of oil but also of water, soil, and key minerals, all framed by worldwide hyper-consumption patterns that are deeply entrenched and expanding. Most of these issues are global in their interconnections. All of the clean-air gains made in the United States and Europe may soon be eclipsed by the vast surge in emissions coming from China as it massively expands coal-fired electrical plants and automobile use. Spiralling oil prices affect food costs around the world (oil is used to make fertilizer and process and ship and store food), reshape land use (the biofuels boom is accelerating the destruction of tropical rain-forests to grow soybeans, corn, palm oil), and draw boundaries and even battle lines in inter-national politics and war. Most of the old problems haven't gone away either, really: they've just morphed. The flammable rivers are just in less visible parts of the world now, while the toxins in our own water have subtler, longer-term, or just plain unknown effects.

And it's getting worse. Global warming, in particular, prompts nightmares: massive disruption of agriculture and water supplies worldwide, loss of the glaciers, monster storms, surging species loss, tropical disease vectoring into temperate areas, and waters rising over the fields and into the homes of half a billion people. Already it is coming to pass. Today more than ever, environmentalism speaks the language of catastrophe.[1]

The Mobilization

Urgency is upon us once again. After a decade in which oil, coal, timber, and cattle interests rewrote the nation's environmental laws, and despite millions of dollars invested by the petrochemical industry to stir up climate-change "skepticism," the global scientific consen-sus is finally winning out.[2] Vehicle fuel economy standards that had not improved for an astonishing thirty years were finally raised in 2007. Even "moderate" Republicans are sign-ing onto massive climate-change legislation. And from the environmental camp a new and radical bio-geo-economic-political program is taking shape: nothing less than a rapid and full-scale mobilization to fend off environmental collapse. Leading environmentalists—most famously Al Gore, in his book and film *An Inconvenient Truth*, and Lester Brown of the Earth Policy Institute—are laying out emergency action programs: "A Global Marshall Plan for the Environment" (Gore) and *Plan B 3.0* (Brown's latest book title; Plan A is "busi-ness as usual"). Brown's book is subtitled nothing less than *Mobilizing to Save Civilization.*[3] Adapting his terms, I will call the emerging program simply *The Mobilization*.

The Mobilization will demand huge changes across the board. We must dramatically reduce our use of energy and convert to clean and renewable energy sources: wind, solar, and geothermal power. Transportation must be weaned from dependence on oil, and far more efficient mass transit systems, buses and trains, must be vastly expanded. Super-insulated buildings, both new and "retrofitted," can scale back heating and cooling demands not just a few percentage points but by half, or 90%, or even 99%, slashing pollution and resource loads as well as the bills. Water must be used far more efficiently: we need exact metering everywhere (so we actually know how much we are using and for what—how many of us have a clue right now?), low-flush or waterless toilets, in-ground irrigation, drought-tolerant crops. We must save our soils by doubling or quadrupling land productivity; save endangered species by re-establishing large and connected enough protected habitat; scale our meat consumption way back to use water and primary crops more efficiently; lower our birth rate enough to stabilize and then begin to ease back human populations to more sustainable levels; and on and on.

Some of these goals call for direct legal mandate: straight-out bans, for example, on extremely wasteful practices like above-ground crop watering, and dramatically raised efficiency requirements across the board (cars, appliances, manufacturing, etc.). Others call for price incentives and true-cost pricing. Right now we pay only a tiny fraction of the true costs of water, for example, and the vastly higher gas taxes already in place in Europe likewise reflect at least more (still not all) of the actual costs of road-building, environmental and health damage due to driving. "Cap-and-trade" systems, already in use in the European Union for greenhouse gases, and in the United States for pollutants that contribute to acid rain, may go global for carbon emissions. These systems have been proposed all the way down to the individual level. Each polluter gets a certain set—though progressively more limited—allowance for emissions: that's the "cap." More emissions then require buying extra allowances (the "trade"), thus creating major profit incentives for new technologies that significantly reduce pollution.[4]

You see already that the Mobilization will be massive. Yet in a way its very massiveness is also an attraction. One could argue that it is precisely what "gloom and doom" environmentalism needed all along: not half-hearted half-solutions, but big and serious change, a kind of "can-do" optimism instead. By way of analogy, Gore invokes the Marshall Plan, which gave massive United States aid to a war-ravaged Europe after World War II. Others recall the Apollo project that put astronauts on the Moon in 1969–1972, and the Manhattan Project in the early 1940s that built the atomic bomb. Brown proposes another analogy, recently picked up by *Time* magazine: "the overnight conversion of the World War II-era industrial sector into a vast machine capable of churning out 60,000 tanks and 300,000 planes, an effort that not only didn't bankrupt the nation but made it rich and powerful beyond its imagining and—oh yes— won the war in the process."[5] An immense challenge, yes, but not just a forced, painful, profitless redirection: we can rise to it, also expecting that it will be an immense step forward.

Debating the Mobilization

Naturally the Mobilization has its critics. *Time* is responding to those who fear that going green on such a scale will put the economy into a tailspin. In fact, however, the economy may be far more supple. Huge adaptations and changes go on all the time, though of course there are also costs. On the whole, going green should actually be cost-effective and probably *more* profitable than "business as usual." Dupont, for example, one of the world's biggest chemical manufacturers, has reduced its carbon emissions a massive 65% from 1990 levels and *saved*

$1.5 billion as a result.[6] The financial crisis and the economic recession of 2008–09 only intensify the need to find such cost savings.

Critics doubt that we really can mobilize so massively in time. Environmentalists respond that we already are. Most European countries are already working to slash carbon emissions by half or better in an astonishing twenty years, and many intend to be "carbon neutral" (that is, to reduce *net* carbon emissions to *zero*) in forty. Australia is leading a number of countries, quickly phasing out incandescent light bulbs in favor of the far more efficient fluorescents. Nearly all of the United States' trading partners have embraced the Kyoto Protocols for greenhouse gas limits, which means that American products marketed in signatory countries must meet international standards, despite the Bush Administration's refusal to join Kyoto—which is why Ford and GM are scrambling to offer hybrid vehicles worldwide. (Globalization has some points after all.) With gas prices volatile—sometimes skyrocketing, sometimes falling quickly—Ford now is desperate to phase out truck and SUV production lines and, ironically, bring their fuel-efficient European models back to the United States. Even lowering our birth rate may be more realistic than we may think. Thirty-six countries, including the most developed and heaviest resource-users, already have stable or declining populations, mostly as results of economic growth and security and the education of women. No government, not even the most fanatical, still promotes large families.[7]

Critics worry that the threats are not definitively established. Climate science, like weather reporting, is anything but exact. Suppose the Mobilization turns out to be unnecessary? Shouldn't we wait until the science is clearer? Environmentalists respond, again, that there are huge benefits as well as costs, even if the threats unaccountably turn out to be less dire. Pollution is, among other things, a waste—think of it as not-yet-well-used by-products—and thus a potential resource. Moreover, it is precisely when we don't know exactly what is happening that we must be *especially* careful. Rather than requiring proof that our current track will end in disaster before we agree to get off it, we ought to insist on proof that it will *not* end in disaster before we get (or rather, stay) on it. This is the so-called "precautionary principle." With our one precious and irreplaceable Earth at stake, the only responsible path is to give ourselves the largest possible margin of safety.

Quite different critics of the Mobilization argue that it does not go far enough. Some climate-change models suggest that it is already too late to prevent catastrophic climate change and extreme population loss and dislocation. Change in complex systems is not necessarily gradual or "linear." A system may maintain itself at a constant level under increasing stresses for a long time—nothing seems to be happening, there seems to be no cause for alarm—but then it may quickly collapse, or flip to some very different and much less desirable or liveable state. James Lovelock, the British geoscientist who originated the "Gaia Hypothesis," argues in his 2007 book, *The Revenge of Gaia*, that current projections hugely underestimate the global warming to come because they don't take into account global self-balancing processes that currently help to keep temperatures steady but will have the opposite effect as their limits are exceeded.[8] The oceans can absorb huge amounts of carbon dioxide, for instance, but once they're full, the extra carbon dioxide keeps circulating in the atmosphere, accelerating warming and prompting the release of still more carbon dioxide now stashed in the waters.

If civilization is to have any chance to survive at all, Lovelock argues, we need vastly more higher-tech and politically drastic measures, such as orbiting sunshades, to reduce the sunlight that arrives on Earth, and total conversion to nuclear power, to eliminate carbon dioxide and particulate emissions from fossil fuels. Forget organic farming and lower-impact agriculture, too: we need *no*-impact food growing, such as lab-grown animal flesh and other synthetic foods, taking the pressure off the land entirely. Even with these, Lovelock is not hopeful for anything more than a pitiful and warlord-wracked remnant of humanity eking out a bare existence in a tropical Antarctica.

Traces of a sort of grim satisfaction appear in this sort of apocalypticism: in the title of Lovelock's book for example, the *Revenge of Gaia*, it's clear that he thinks we have had it coming to us for a while. It would not be the first time that fantasies of destruction played out an underlying and not fully-articulated sense of guilt. And we can certainly hope the predictions are wrong. The current consensus of scientists is less grim—but then again, the science is far from exact, much remains unknown, and the accelerating tempo of recent ecological deterioration, especially warming trends and glacial melting, has shocked even the experts. We can only note that the immediate practical implications do not differ so greatly from the Mobilizers' in the end. All we can do, in any case, is move ahead as fast as possible. Gore is now seriously proposing to phase out fossil fuels entirely in a mere ten years. Lovelock and others want to move still faster and farther. We may not have a chance anyway, but we certainly won't have a chance if we don't try. And as Winston Churchill said in England's darkest hour, we might as well be optimists—there is not much use being anything else.

What Would Thoreau Do?

Yet despite the scale and urgency of the Mobilization, there is a way in which it does not represent the emergence of a new environmental vision at all. For the aim of the Mobilization, to put it baldly, is to maintain our current way of life as far as possible, while substituting greener energy sources and productive processes for currently dirtier and more wasteful ones. We picture ourselves driving hyper-efficient hybrids or hydrogen cars, for example—but still, obviously, driving. We picture ourselves getting our electricity from renewable and clean sources—but still flipping the same electrical switches to turn on the same stuff. We expect food grown and delivered without such spectacular waste of water and fuel—but still expect to eat the same things in the same way. "Eco-tourism" may replace regular tourism, but we still want a lot of it, especially in exotic, far-away places. We expect to continue to live as we do now in coastal cities and in challenging climates, just more efficiently and better fortified.

Once I test-drove a Prius. As we hummed along the salesman held forth on the cleverness of the design. It's a radically different engine, he said, but "really it doesn't change anything" except your gas bill. I guess he meant that the driving experience is no different from what you would have in a regular car: from a design point of view the only real change is under the hood. What he brought to my mind instead was Henry David Thoreau's biting complaint in *Walden* about how we preoccupy ourselves with "improved means to unimproved ends."[9] A more efficient car will not give us back the time or the lives that we lose to it, or restore the lands or the public treasuries drained by roads, or slow us down, or make us wiser or even happier. "Really it doesn't change anything!" But change, in fact radical change, is what we *need*.

Of course, to some extent, we need to continue to drive and to use electricity too, and eat industrial food, live in nuclear-family, stand-alone houses, and all the rest. Then, for sure, the greener the better. Still, for almost all of human history, people managed to live without any of these things—or rather, more precisely, they lived with something *different*. Most of the human race still does. Isn't it just possible that we too might actually be better off without, say, fast food, or fast travel, or even tourism or, God forbid, television? If so, then simply "greening" these things is no answer. We could green anything, in principle—even a concentration camp or a chemical-weapons plant. Green alone is not enough.

Thoreau would not let us get by with mere "sustainability" either. Certainly we should try to live in such a way that others who come after us can do the same. Sustainability, so defined, may already make more radical demands than we may think: one plausible implication would be that we should use finite resources only at or below the same rate that nature replenishes them, which would mean using the tiniest fraction of the oil and coal that we presently use, just for one notable example. Still, however much it is a simple demand of justice and act of care for the generations to come, sustainability (also) seems like a forced self-limitation under external duress. Thoreau's challenge goes deeper. We cannot think sensibly about "sustainability" without asking *what* it is that we are seeking to sustain. We want a life that is not merely sustainable but, as the philosopher Aidan Davison puts it, sustain*ing*: good for the soul, good for the world.[10] And the truth is that right now we have barely a clue about how such a world would look. We live in the most spectacularly wealthy and commodious society in human history—a stunning accomplishment that all too often we take for granted—but most of us are nonetheless overwhelmed with busyness, noise, worry, and stress, and are significantly more unhappy, by most measures, than people whose economic poverty we are taught to pity. This is stunning too, actually. Again, though, it has an unsettling implication. Merely greening a dysfunctional society is no way to usher in a new millennium. We are still in need of a genuinely new environmental vision.

Trapped in a System

The Prius story has another unsettling implication as well. Even the Mobilization's *means* may be, in Thoreau's terms, "unimproved." Once again, to put it baldly, the Mobilization invites us to respond to the crisis of the industrial system with, essentially, more of the same. What is mobilized is more industry, more technological ingenuity, more complicated systems with farther-flung vulnerabilities. Hybrid cars, for instance, essentially have two motors rather than one, with a computer layered on top to coordinate things. Complexity more than doubles. Not to mention the toxic lithium or nickel in the batteries (much less toxic than the lead in the usual car battery, but still…) which, like the high mercury in fluorescent bulbs, is so far an unaddressed problem. Think, too, of the dependence of hybrid component manufacture on certain rare earths that come only from China and are about to run out.[11] If this kind of story sounds familiar, that's just the point—it is. We're still trapped in the same old system.

Hydrogen is supposed to be the fuel of the future. Certainly it burns cleanly—the only by-product is water. Hydrogen itself, however, doesn't occur naturally in ways we can simply harvest, like oil. It needs to be produced. It takes electricity, for example, to electrolyze water. But then of course the electricity needs to be produced in some (other) way.

There are certain advantages in this: hydrogen production might be in a few specific locations, say power plants whose pollution could be much more rigorously and efficiently controlled than the emissions of ten or a hundred thousand individual cars. Wind or solar power might help in a few places. But, for the most part, we'd still need oil or coal burning plants—or nuclear power. Hydrogen can also be extracted directly from—you guessed it—oil. Actually, then, hydrogen fits perfectly with a high-fossil-fuel, high-nuclear-energy mind-set. But arguably, for just that reason, it's no solution. It only passes the problem around to another sector of the economy, another technology, another fuel.[12]

New Orleans shows us another example of people running faster to keep the same old wheels turning. The ravaged city is becoming a metaphor for another late-industrial dead-end. Cities profoundly vulnerable to hurricanes and flooding call for higher dikes, stronger flood-gates, bigger pumps, better weather forecasts. These are the answers that seemed to work in the past. But in the end they don't. The fates of more and more people and even of the city's and region's economy and culture are made to depend on more and more complex technological systems, inevitably prone to breakdowns and unforeseen failures. More and higher dikes extend farther and farther out and therefore multiply vulnerabilities. Failure at any point means ever-greater catastrophe. Dikes also exacerbate the original problem, cutting the land off from the flow of water and sediments that regenerated the land level itself. It's not just that the seas are rising—New Orleans is also sinking. Keeping it dry at ever more spectacular costs will also cause it to sink faster.[13]

Technological overconfidence on the one hand, ecological heedlessness on the other: the same lethal combination appears in still starker form when we consider some of the extreme measures to combat global warming proposed by Lovelock and others, such as launching orbiting sunshades or pouring trillions of Styrofoam balls into the oceans to stop them from absorbing so much heat.[14] What larger effects such moves will have elsewhere in the system; how to be at all confident that we even know whether the intended effects will really occur; how to modulate or reverse or get rid of them (*trillions of Styrofoam balls?!*) if and when we need to: these are huge and barely-asked questions.

In short, the Mobilization imagines much cleverer and more strategic use of resources. But it does still envisage a use of resources, deployed on a massive and still-more-intensive scale, coordinated in an increasingly high-tech way, inattentive to nature's own workings and only concerned with forcing its way, which it may or may not succeed at doing. It is exactly the style of response you'd expect from the system that produced the problem in the first place. Conversely, if we truly want to address the problem at its core, we need to consider the possibility of responding *in an entirely different style*. Albert Einstein famously said that it is a hallmark of a real problem that it cannot be solved within the same framework that generated it. That's exactly it: what we really need in the end is not a still cleverer or more massive or better-funded application of an existing framework, but a *new* framework. We need to re-imagine the world from the very ground up.

Whole-Systems Design

Take the question of recycling—seemingly the most boring and everyday of "environmental issues." It is not that re-use is a bad idea. It is a fine and even necessary idea. But it cannot be left simply as a matter of re-smelting aluminium soda cans or keeping used syringes out of the oceans so that they will not eventually float back up on the beach. It is certainly not simply a matter of adding a collection burden to consumers and municipalities while manufacturers keep on making cans, and papers, and packaging just as they always have. All of this is, at best, only an add-on, minimal, piecemeal change within the system we already have. It's the "same old framework" all over again. We need to ask what a truly *different* framework would look like.

One starting-point would be this: the entire system must be redesigned as a whole, and precisely *as* a system, that is, as one interconnected whole. Thinking in an integrated and holistic way is now vital. The real solution to a problem like recycling may therefore not seem to directly address recycling at all: it may intervene at a very different point in the system. Suppose, for example, that our real task is systematic *pre*-cycling: that is, the design of things with their future use and lives already accounted for and built in, making *re*-cycling mostly unnecessary.[15] This probably means using no more plastics whatsoever, just for one example, or maybe only plastics that totally and quickly biodegrade (and into something that's good for the soil; certainly not just plastics that biodegrade into smaller pieces of plastic, like many of the present so-called "green" plastics). Imagine edible containers, say in dessert flavors, so you could end your picnic by just eating the plates and glasses. (This is not so far-fetched, actually: think of ice-cream cones, and tacos, and even pizza, where the "wrapper" is already part of the food.) Buildings, in the same spirit, could be made of durable parts that can be easily disassembled and rebuilt in other ways, or of natural materials, maybe even still living, that can go their own ways afterwards, no worse for the wear. Maybe even better. In these transitional times, too, we really need buildings made of the currently most accessible and cheap raw materials. That is, well, trash: old tires, cans, bottles, auto parts…and if you think this is some kind of impossible dream, check out the film *Garbage Warrior*, a documentary about the "Earthship eco-architect" Michael Reynolds, who in forty-odd years already has built hundreds of ecologically self-sufficient homes completely out of (what everyone else considers) garbage.[16] Two steps down this road and we are designing tires and bottles from the start *as* building materials…and who knows what else? *There's* whole-system design for you.

In some form, everything we use will be with us forever. The law of the conservation of matter actually does have meaning. There is really just no such thing as a "disposable." The upshot is that everything we use must be something that we would welcome whenever or however it shows up again. That sounds commonsensical enough, maybe—in the new age it *will* be the "common sense"—but for us it ultimately requires rethinking everything. Look around right now and ask yourself how many of today's most familiar things could meet such a standard. Not that Styrofoam cup, keeping our coffee warm for five minutes, whose crumbly useless shreds will still be more or less the same even when our bones have long turned to dust. Not those paints and glues and hairsprays all over our houses and hardware stores: specialized, long-lived, and often toxic chemicals (if not to us, elsewhere in the system), all of which will eventually return to the air, and water, and soils to pass through the bodies of our grandchildren, through the bodies of Indonesian cows, and into the depths of the sea. The other side of this question, though, is a design challenge: how *could* we make things so that we would welcome them, whenever or however they show up again? It's not an impossible challenge, but it does take a dramatically different kind of attention.

Or again: mass transit figures heavily in the Mobilization plans. We're beginning to realize that however much we redesign cars themselves, we will not even touch the systemic problems associated with automotive transportation: the endless traffic and traffic jams, death and mayhem on the roads, parking lots everywhere, omnipresent traffic noise, junked cars, spectacular highway construction and maintenance costs, global resource wars, degraded land, and dysfunctional cities. The best hybrid or hydrogen car in the world will not make a dent in these problems. In truth, though, even buses and trains, though vastly more efficient than the equivalent number of cars, and safer and more compact to boot, will not make a huge dent in most of these problems either, and meantime they still require fuels and massive and continuing investments in tracks, roads, stations, and rolling stock, not to mention time, just to get people around. Mass transit is still, after all, transit.

Again, a shift of "frameworks" is necessary. Our commitment both to cars and to mass transit rests on the assumption that people will and should continue to need to travel in the way we do now. But suppose that this assumption itself is the fundamental problem? Maybe in the end we need neither better cars *nor* better alternatives to cars, but alternatives to transportation itself. The real solution is not another kind of car, not another kind of fuel, not even another kind of vehicle—but "re-localization": a system in which we simply do not need to travel so constantly and where there is no serious need for any kind of far-flung and massive transportation infrastructure in the first place.

Imagine communities in which work, school, friends and family, and food and other everyday goods are available close at hand, within an easy walking distance. Radically de-centralized production processes and serious telecommuting could be vastly augmented, and extended to many more jobs. New community structures would arise—next-generation public libraries, colleges, shops, or community centers, for one thing. Sweden is building such "tele-cottages" nationwide, with built-in childcare and family space. Next we could build in a variety of work areas and gardens hooked into a new neighborhood commons, reclaiming the space that the street and parking lots used to occupy. Everything could be "down the block" from home, or part of a co-housing community's common house. (Perhaps there would be no more "blocks," either!)[17]

Shopping? Neighborhoods and co-housing communities or small businesses could manage collective schedules and maybe a jointly-owned vehicle or two to bring in groceries. Some vegetables and maybe fish you or your neighbors would grow yourselves, intensively and right around the corner. Malls could go virtual, for those who really want them, and provide delivery through a morphed form of UPS or FedEx—a few trucks or carts running on small peripheral roads. There could be trains too—we might as well make use of the corridors and tracks we've already got—when it really is necessary to physically go somewhere else, maybe to the beach a few times a year. New dense neighborhoods could be clustered around the train stops. (Density can be "sustaining" in general. Do we still want to be living in nuclear families? Why not adapt other cultures' practice of adding on living quarters in family compounds for elders and others as time and families change? Wouldn't this, in fact, be a lovely new use for our vast reservoir of suburban lawn space?)

We could promote "virtual travel" too—and when we take *actual* trips, take them long and slow. See the places right in the next town or county: how many globe-trotters, piling on the frequent-flyer miles, have actually explored their own neighborhoods? And, correspondingly, here's a design challenge: how shall we make local travel more exciting? Walk, bike, take a camel, or maybe a blimp…

Earth in Flow

Whole-systems thinking is one way of re-framing our problems all the way down, so to speak. And we must take another large step at the same time. The "system" within which we understand ourselves must now include the whole Earth. It is not simply a matter of redesigning human systems, no matter how radically, as if they were only a kind of backdrop or stage-setting, passive and controllable. Better to imagine the Earth more like a vast living thing itself, in flow in irresistible, immense, and largely mysterious ways. We worry over sea level rises still measured in millimeters, for example, but it turns out that sea level has surged almost a hundred meters (that's 300 feet or so) since the end of the last ice age, a mere 18,000 years ago.[18] Tectonic plate shifts (giving us earthquakes and tsunamis), climate swings, new evolutionary pressures, and God knows what else are actually the *norm*. The real challenge is not somehow better or tighter control of natural processes, but something very different: more deft human *adaptation* to these "flows" of the Earth.

Think of New Orleans once again. After Hurricane Katrina, in 2005, we all learned what ecologists had been saying for some time: that the wetlands and lowlands that once stood between New Orleans and the sea—seventy or so miles of buffer that once would spread out and dilute storm surges—have been wrecked by drilling and re-channeling, as well as by oil and gas extraction from underneath the whole region. The shipping lanes meant to bring bigger ships more readily to the city also served as direct channels bringing storm waters straight into the city. The extent of Katrina's devastation was not "natural," but pre-conditioned by our ecologically heedless ways of building. For sure, then, the city's ecology, as much as the city itself (or rather, as *part* of the city itself), must be "brought back better." But it cannot be brought back invulnerable. No coastal city—in fact no city at all—has that option. The coasts draw us by nature, but by nature they are also places sometimes necessarily swept by high winds and flooded by storm surges. There is always a permeable interface between land, sea, and weather. People have lived in hurricane-prone, over-washed coastal areas since time out of mind, only they didn't live there as if the seas and the sands were just stage-props. Ecosystems evolved to adapt to these flows, and our own building, traditionally, did too.

We must begin to think of coastal life itself in a different key—minor, as it were, rather than major. Low-lying coastal areas and barrier islands call for few permanent residences and only the most resilient or adaptable infrastructure. This is not at all to exclude humans, not at all—but it *is* to invite us to the shores in a different, impermanent, and moveable way. Brittle infrastructures of all sorts—the usual power-lines, hard-surface roads, bridges, tract houses, basements, all the rest—are not a good idea. Instead we could try small, durable, easily-transportable solar power units. Use cell-phone networks (or no phones at all)—nothing hard-wired. Bring in windmills as distinctive as the lighthouses on North Carolina's Outer Banks, the very region where the Wright Brothers came for the first flights precisely for the winds, but which at present has not a single serious windmill. Sandy roads should be our main highways carrying only vehicles built for the beach. Most of us should travel by boat, as it was not so long ago. The outermost regions should be left to the swimmers and campers and fisherfolk, birdwatchers (hurricanes fling in all sorts of uncommon birds) and boaters and houseboaters (who can *move*).

The summer after Katrina, I had the privilege to work with a group of activists and planners along with Louisiana residents and expatriates, re-imagining the future of New Orleans and the Gulf Coast. We began with the stories: loss, pain, disorientation, anger. Terms like "recovery" and "restoration" were in the air. We wanted to affirm and not question people's lives and hopes. Yet, at the same time, a new vision was our mandate. Is a new New Orleans possible? A new kind of city, even?

One person lamented the loss of her little colony of off-season artist-renters on a coastal island. After they fled, a thirty-foot storm surge took out everything. We sympathized. But we also let the story percolate. Artist colonies are expressive, experimental, and *nomadic*…hmm… so, what if the returnees consciously and methodically lived as nomads? What if they went back as long-term, temporary residents? Why couldn't this sort of neo-nomadism be enabled and enriched—legally, economically, artistically, architecturally—and not just in a new New Orleans but all along the nation's, and the world's, hurricane-prone coasts? Whole populations could move inland for the season: what new and intriguing cultural forms could evolve from that? Dwellings themselves could be nomadic. Indigenous nomads developed all kinds of readily-moved or collapsible structures. Elaborate tents? What would it take to build homes that you could just fold back out after the storm? How about buildings—schools, homes, factories—that allow the winds and waters to pass through: first floors that are essentially screened porches or workshops, maybe, allowing rising waters just to flow under the enclosed second level? People at the edge of the sea traditionally built houses on stilts, protected by swales, with open first floors.[19] What new and intriguing things could architects do now?

Someone else mentions houseboats. Another idea: what about a city that *embraces* the waters—in short, a city that *floats?* Houseboats galore; rafts; larger structures, too. When the waters are low, the pontoons may rest on the ground or in the swamps that are in fact the natural state of much of these lands—soaked through, again, rising and no longer sinking. When the high waters come, everything rises. Put in canals, little boats everywhere. Already there are floating cities in Southeast Asia; pontoon architecture is emerging in Holland; there are multiple plans even for ocean-going cities; and certainly there are military contractors and big builders to whom we could always give the challenge of building something new and constructive. Imagine people fishing for crawfish off their porches in a new New Orleans. Imagine Mardi Gras floats that actually float. The charms of Venice added to the sass and sauce of New Orleans. Who says the possibilities of cities are exhausted?

Yes, We Can!

The kinds of changes imagined here are not merely small-scale tinkerings "under the hood" while we continue to take our current expectations and habits somehow as givens. On the contrary, in meeting Thoreau's challenge we must—crucially—*rethink* those very expectations and habits. Tourism, throw-aways, living in beach suburbs or for that matter *any* suburbs, and all the rest: these are not somehow necessities. Work and shopping and enjoyment are *not* necessarily "somewhere else." There is no reason that the average American must continue to spend up to two hours a day in the car, or that we must spend trillions of dollars on roads and road maintenance and therefore only a pittance on public pools, libraries, playing fields, and neighborhoods in general. Nor need we live in dwellings that stay fixed to the ground, especially where the ground wants to be soaked much of the time. Alternative, and in fact, fabulous new possibilities open up the moment we question these apparent verities. So, I would argue, a "new environmentalism" is certainly not a matter of "going back" to some sort of dreary half-life. The way ahead may make today's seemingly so-seductive and unsurpassable life seem, by comparison, only half alive. Maybe *ours* is the dreary half-life? Anyway, so much more is possible!

We can also meet Einstein's challenge. The "means" proposed here are not just further and more desperate applications of industrialism. This new approach to "living green" is not a matter of enacting yet more resource-intensive but cleverer solutions to a specific problem. Attention shifts instead to reorganizing the social system: re-creating neighborhoods, for example, re-imagining who we live with and how work is organized, with multiple advantages and wide ripple effects. We need whole-system views, looking not just at "transportation" by itself, for example, but striving for a whole vision of community with and within the natural world, a vision in which travel is just one small aspect. We should build no more coastal cities which are so "inland" or generic in character that they might as well be in Kansas except for the dikes. *Beyond* the great Mobilization, in short, everything is up for re-imagination and rebuilding at once: neighborhoods, work, food-growing, family structures, houses, wetlands, festivals...everything.

I am not saying that somehow we do not need to mobilize. We *do* need to mobilize. Everything needs to become vastly greener, as soon as possible, and every small step helps. The point instead is that the Mobilization is more like the *last* expression of the outgoing worldview than the first expression of its successor. By the time of our great-grandchildren (yes, we will have great-grandchildren, and yes, they will inhabit a world of their own in which they will not spend all their time wishing they were us) humanity may inhabit not just a new world but a new world*view*. Everything is about to be systematically re-imagined.

Once again, at least, you see that there *are* alternatives a little beyond what we hear in the media and from even the most change-oriented politicians. There is far more room for imagination and improvisation on a global scale. Indeed you can practice it yourself.[20] Stretch, twist, transpose ideas; exaggerate and extrapolate; push beyond incremental changes to qualitative shifts. A truly green world, for instance, will demand a transformed politics—and vice versa. Already people are imagining political communities founded on Affirmations of *Inter*dependence rather than Declarations of Independence: bioregional, deeply participatory and decentralized, spontaneous, festive, varied and multiple in their forms. Go three steps farther: imagine representative assemblies for other beings, say, and/or for future generations. (Seriously: could *you* design such things? Why not?) The Massachusetts Institute of Technology, backed by the United Nations, is now promoting a plan to link the whole globe by putting rugged, dirt-cheap, crank-powered laptops into every village in the world.[21] But what then? Just more pornography or on-line shopping? What might we *do* with such a radically connected world? How about creating new worldwide political organizations based on direct contact among people, and thus ultimately alternative to the United Nations (which is, after all, a union of *nations*) and indeed to the nation-state itself? Permaculturist Bill Mollison proposes a new kind of United Nations in which a "nation" is defined by a shared ethic and culture, where all those sharing an "ethic of earth care" might therefore come together.[22] People are already beginning to connect by watershed, bird flyways, pollution plumes, regardless of the official political borders. Global seed exchanges and gardening forums already exist, and already, according to Mollison, the world has far more organic gardeners than active members of political parties. There are alternative economic summits, bioregional congresses, tribal conferences, garden and farm design groups. Every international bigwig political conference now has its counter-conference. In short, a radically alternative political order is practically here already. Who says that all possible political systems have already been invented?

Religion Gone Wild

Finally, the coming shift also has spiritual dimensions—a side of life not so often explored by environmentalists, while today's religions often return the favor by mistrusting environmentalists right back. But really: here we are, reawakening to the whole Earth, no longer as a mere backdrop, or materials-provider, or "spaceship," but something vaster, more primordial. It's more magical, our *Source* and no mere collection of resources, understood now as an interdependent whole, organically and cyclically linked. All of its beings in a deep way kin. How could all of this not have a spiritual dimension as well?

We are reawakening to ourselves as animals, for one thing. The Mobilization already has us thinking about animal ethics: the industrialized slaughter of billions of our near-kin every year for food. Ethical qualms are rising, and the ecological costs of meat (waste of most of the protein in the feed, water and land degradation) are appalling. But right now, the most we imagine in response to these problems is to reduce the slaughter: mass vegetarianism, maybe, or bio-engineered food grown in factories. Animals themselves slip out of the picture.

Yet we ourselves are animals. We have co-evolved with other animal intelligences. Most traditional cultures recognize other animals as other "nations." Multiple forms of cross-species interchange still go on. Musicians, right now, jam with whales through underwater microphones and speakers, riffing on each others' contributions around a common theme.[23] Designers are already busy planning for "mixed communities" of humans and other species, for genuine co-inhabitation. The whole world is alert and alive in its own ways. Whales pass around half-hour-long songs over thousands of miles underwater. Millions of butterflies, of all things, migrate three thousand miles or more to breed at long-established sites they have never seen before. All life on Earth, according to James Lovelock, works together to maintain favorable conditions for itself on the planet as a whole.

And we ourselves are Earthlings (the literal meaning of the name "Adam," in Hebrew). But the extent of the Earth is barely imaginable to us, and the powers at play, even in the way a sunbeam plays over the trees in the wind, are awesome, mysterious, pervasive. Earth itself, in turn, is just a dust mote in the eye of the solar system, let alone the galaxy, and is in interaction with all of it, constantly absorbing the streaming energies of the sun and dust and rock from comets and asteroids and other planets, while sending some of its own energies back out. Look inward and there are also worlds within worlds, whole galaxies within a single cell, much of it barely understood. When the God of Sinai finally responds to Job's complaints, he does not offer some kind of tedious moral justification for his suffering in typical human terms, as do Job's clueless friends. He merely lifts the curtain on what Thoreau, centuries later, called "that vast, savage, howling mother of ours, Nature, lying all around, and with such beauty..."[24] Ibis swoop through; lions and mountain goats come darting from their lairs; hail, thunder, lightning:

> *Who laid the cornerstones of the earth*
> *when all the stars of the morning were singing with joy...?*
> *Who pent up the sea behind closed doors*
> *when it leapt tumultuous out of the womb,*
> *When I wrapped it in a robe of mist*
> *and made black clouds its swaddling bands...?*[25]

God's message to Job is that the universe is huge, mysterious, and full of glorious energy. Somehow, Job needs to "paint a new picture" of his own relationship to that stunning, God-produced cosmos. Right now, alas, many of our churches seem to think that it is enough of a paradigm shift to just replace the incandescent bulbs in their sanctuaries. Maybe a few of them edge into uneasy questions like "What would Jesus drive?" as if slightly better mileage is the best even God could hope for. It feels like an exhaustion of both imagination and heart: the last cautious sighs of a tired way of thinking, not the first hints of something new. But something new is coming. The religious imagination is already simmering away again, overfull. Interest abounds in the old earth-based religions and in the pagan roots of Christianity itself. Lovelock invokes the Greek Earth goddess Gaia for his theory that the biosphere functions in some ways as a single living being. Evangelicals are beginning to insist upon "Creation Care" with the passion previously reserved for traditional marriage or fetal life. Other Christian theologians reread the prophets and even the Noah and Joseph stories as ecological parables, while some even speak of Earth literally as God's body and reinterpret salvation as a kind of treasuring of all that lives.[26]

Job's God not only speaks "out of the whirlwind" but in the end *is* the whirlwind. There's that hurricane theme again, surely an apt metaphor for the endless and continuing Self-Creation, rushing like a whirlwind through our lives and the cosmos itself. Maybe, just maybe, the natural world is *it*. Not that nature must somehow be shorn from the divine, but rather the exact opposite: divinity, the only kind of divinity there is, is already *here*. Thus, we may be headed toward pantheism—a vision of God everywhere and in everything, God *as* Nature—with an ecological face: a theme both old and startlingly new.

To spiritual traditionalists, all of this may still seem like only confusion and turmoil on the margins of real—that is, traditional—religiosity. Maybe it is. On the other hand, the West's great religious traditions themselves had their origins in the very same kind of confusion and marginality, in the midst of dramatic shifts in world "frameworks" very much like the changes that are coming our way soon. Those changes may still end up regenerating the old religions (though *which* "old" ones is still a question—for, of course, the truly old-time religions are pagan), but then again, just possibly, we may be in line for something truly new. From our present vantage point, on the threshold, we can only say that a world reinventing its politics, its power plants, its cities, and, indeed, its entire mode of life will not hesitate to reinvent its religions too—one way or another. Don't imagine for a moment that the possibilities of religion are exhausted. Everything—yes, everything—is about to go wild.

Notes and References

1. For global and up-to-date information on the state of the environment, go to www.worldwatch.org/. For a well-supported catastrophist reading, see Part I of Lester Brown, *Plan B 3.0: Mobilizing to save civilization* 3rd ed., New York: Norton, 2008.

2. *Climate change 2007*, Report of the Intergovernmental Panel on Climate Change—a global scientific effort established by the United Nations Environmental Program and the World Meteorological Organization, Cambridge, UK: Cambridge University Press, 2007 and on the Web at http://www.ipcc.ch/.

3. Lester Brown, *Plan B 3.0*; Al Gore, *An inconvenient truth: The planetary emergency of global warming and what we can do about it* (Emmaus, PA: Rodale, 2006); and Franz Josef Rademacher, *A planetary contract: Global Marshall Plan for a worldwide eco-social market economy*, Global Marshall Plan Foundation, 2004.

4. The potential for cap-and-trade systems to stimulate green technological innovation is well argued in Fred Krupp and Miriam Horn, *Earth: The sequel. The race to reinvent energy and stop global warming*, New York: Norton, 2008.

5. Bryan Walsh, Why green is the new red, white, and blue. *Time*, 28 April 2008, p. 46. The analogy is elaborated in Brown, *Plan B 3.0*, pp. 203–206.

6. Charles Holliday, Jr, Message from the chief executive. In Dupont, *Sustainable growth 2002 progress report*, Dupont, Inc.: Wilmington, DE: 2002, pp. 2–3.

7. Brown, pp. 177–181.

8. James Lovelock, *The revenge of Gaia: Earth's climate crisis & the fate of humanity*, New York: Basic Books, 2007.

9. Henry David Thoreau, *Walden*, New York: New American Library, 1960, p. 40.

10. Aidan Davison, *Technology and the contested meanings of sustainability*, Albany: SUNY Press, 2001.

11. G. Haxell, "Rare earth elements critical resources for high technology," *United States geological survey fact sheet: 087-02*, on line at pubs.usgs.gov/fs/2002/fs087-02/fs087-02.pdf.

12. A good overview of the hydrogen debate is at http://en.wikipedia.org/wiki/Hydrogen_economy.

13. John Bohannon and Martin Enserink, Scientists weigh options for rebuilding New Orleans, *Science* 309 (16 September 2005), pp. 1808–1809.

14. Lovelock, Chapter 7; and Chris Mooney, Global cooling, *Wired*, July 2008, pp. 128–133. As if these weren't enough, check out http://www.guardian.co.uk/environment/2001/jun/10/globalwarming .climatechange for a plan to use comets and asteroids to re-jigger Earth's orbit to pull us farther away from the heat of the sun.

15. Classic on this theme is William McDonough and Michael Braungart, *Cradle to cradle: Rethinking the way we make things*, New York: North Point Press, 2002.

16. See www.garbagewarrior.com/index.php.

17. Julian Darley, David Room, Celine Rich, *Relocalize now! Getting ready for climate change and the end of cheap oil*, Gabriola, B.C.: New Society Publishers, 2008.

18. See http://en.wikipedia.org/wiki/Sea_level_change, or, for the wiki-phobic, Kevin Fleming, et al., Refining the eustatic sea-level curve since the last glacial maximum using far- and intermediate-field sites, *Earth and planetary science letters* 163 (1998): 327–342.

19. Bill Mollison, *Permaculture: A designer's manual*, Tyalgum, Australia: Tagari Publications, 1988, Chapter 10.

20. For help, see my little book *How to re-imagine the world*, Gabriola, B.C.: New Society Publishers, 2007.

21. David Pogue, Laptop with a mission widens its audience, *New York Times*, 4 October 2007, on-line at http://www.nytimes.com/2007/10/04/technology/circuits/04pogue.html.

22. Mollison, *Permaculture*, p. 508.

23. Jim Nollman, *Dolphin dreamtime: The art and science of interspecies communication*, New York: Bantam, 1990; David Rothenberg, *Thousand mile song: Whale music in a sea of sound*, New York: Perseus, 2008.

24. Henry David Thoreau, "Walking," in Carl Bode, ed., *The portable Thoreau*, New York: Viking, 1964, p. 621.

25. Job 38: 6–9.

26. Lovelock's classic on the Gaia Hypothesis is *Gaia: A new look at life on Earth* Oxford, UK: Oxford University Press, 1979. The Evangelical Climate Initiative is at http://christiansandclimate.org/. For ecological and social-justice-oriented readings of the great Judeo-Christian stories, see Michael S. Northcott, *A moral climate: The ethics of global warming*, Maryknoll, NY: Orbis, 2007. For an introduction to eco-feminist Christianity, try Sallie McFague, *The body of god: An ecological theology*, Minneapolis: Fortress Press, 1993.

Questions for Discussion

1. Some psychologists suggest that we increasingly feel a sense of sadness and loss for the familiar and loved natural environments that are now changing before our eyes. Some call it "global mourning." Australian eco-activist Joanna Macy believes that we are emotionally blocked from effectively responding to environmental crises precisely for this reason: the grief, and fear, and pain of it are so overwhelming that even completely irrational responses (like claiming that there is really no problem at all, or conversely that everything is already so screwed up that there's nothing to do) are actually more psychologically sustainable than facing it and working

out ways forward. Macy holds that the only way to free ourselves to act is first to face the pain, to express it fully, however much it may wrack us. *Then* we are free to act. It certainly has been her own experience. What do you think?

2. What has shaped your current idea of environmentalism? Experiences? Films? Popular media? Reading? (Be specific about each of these: e.g. *what* films?) Are these, on the whole, reliable sources? Why or why not? What is the most familiar form of environmentalism to you? Why? I would guess that some of the ideas in this essay probably surprised you. Why? Why do we not hear about these kinds of ideas in the mainstream media, or in the universities, or from our elected leaders? This question has a variety of answers, by no means all cynical—stick with it.

3. Supposing that the Mobilization wins the day—as it well might, especially if dramatic environmental disasters or abrupt climate shifts occur in the near future—what kinds of changes will occur in everyday life, yours for example? What happens when we are required to radically reduce our "ecological footprint"? (For a useful introduction to "ecological footprint" analysis, see www.footprintnetwork.org/.)

4. Exactly what are the objections to the Mobilization that this essay links to the thoughts of Thoreau and Einstein? Put them in your own words. Do you agree that the Mobilization's "underlying aim is essentially to sustain middle-class, industrial consumerism"? Why or why not? Is it, in fact, "exactly the style of response you'd expect from the system that produced the problem in the first place"? If so, how could we have missed this connection?

5. How might you portray and explain a world that really has "gone wild" in some of the ways this essay suggests? Imagine the sorts of practices, institutions, ways of life—foods, government, arts, medicine, sports, education, child-rearing, etc.—that a radically different world might have. In imagining such across-the-board change, you may want to make use of the "web of culture" concept introduced in this book in the essay by Anne Bolin and Laurence Basirico (Chapter 2). And please remember that by "imagine," I don't mean just a loose sort of dreaminess. Imagination can be systematically practiced: it actually has rigorous methods. Watch for suggestive facts: overtones, hints, clues. Go farther to invite—even force—exotic associations. (Start with a random prompt and then ask what new ideas or associations it provokes when put together with your issue or question: *then* start honing the ideas.) Stretch and twist ideas. Exaggerate and extrapolate. (What's three steps beyond recycling?) Systematically transpose ideas: reverse expected relationships, think opposites. (What would be the opposite of a "weapon of mass destruction"? Some highly visible, dramatic, and unexpected acts of social/environmental transfiguration—a *method* of *mass transformation?* Like what?) And get wild. Welcome even the unlikeliest thought, at least for starters. The key rule of brainstorming (yes, brainstorming has rules too) is: Defer Criticism. Let the ideas percolate before critical shut-down. Take them somewhere. What if Heaven is right here? What if a new house of Congress consisted only of young people speaking for the future? How else could the future be made much more visible in the present? Could there be, say, a space program inspired by the ideas in this essay? What would it look like? And could there be wholly new cultural forms (that is, *besides* foods, government, arts, medicine, and all the rest) that only a totally new way of thinking would suggest? Such as . . . ?

Suggested Readings

Buell, L. (1995). *The environmental imagination: Thoreau, nature writing and the formation of American culture.* Cambridge, MA: Belknap Press of Harvard University Press.

Lovelock, J. (2009). *The vanishing face of gaia: A final warning.* New York: Basic Books.

Rothman, Hal K. (2000). *Saving the planet: The American response to the environment in the twentieth century.* Chicago: Ivan R. Dee.

8

Western Imperialism and Its Legacies

Brian Digre

An appreciation of relevant historical background goes a long way in understanding current world events. Many of the globe's present problems, such as tension in the Middle East and ethnic conflict in Africa, have their roots, to a large degree, in the way in which the nations of the West for centuries have interacted with non-Western societies. This chapter traces the historical developments of these relationships.

As a Peace Corps Volunteer in the Democratic Republic of the Congo during the late 1970s, I taught English and history in a rural high school. On the wall of the school office was an old road map of our region that I often studied before teachers' meetings. I had traveled frequently on the main road connecting the two regional capitals, Mbuji-Mayi and Kananga, but the map showed another important road connecting the cities. My colleagues told me it was now impassable except as a foot trail. Intrigued, I convinced a Peace Corps friend to hike the path with me during one of our school holidays. It took us several days; we spent the nights in small villages with the families of my students.

One beautiful afternoon as we hiked along the trail, we unexpectedly came upon a large road sign bearing the colonial names of the nearby cities and distances to them in kilometers. It was an incongruous sight: the old European sign surrounded by tall elephant grass, on a footpath, listing distances that were really only meaningful if you were driving, to places that no longer bore the names on the sign. At a glance it was an indication of the lack of development, even decline, since independence. But with a deeper look at the Congo's colonial past, the sign might illustrate more about the character of European imperialism and its legacies.

European colonial officials often viewed roads as instruments of economic development. To colonial enthusiasts, they would allow the export of African raw materials and the import of manufactured goods from Europe. Many Africans had different perceptions. They saw in European policies exploitation rather than development. Roads were often built with forced labor, as was the case in the Belgian Congo. It is not surprising, then, that with independence their maintenance was abandoned in many cases.

The forsaken sign and the road also might illustrate the artificial character of colonial rule. In a search for a more authentic identity, many African states chose African names for their cities and new nations upon regaining their independence. The original drawing of the Congo's colonial borders and the total failure of the Belgian administration to prepare the country for democratic self-government bear much of the responsibility for the chaos and civil strife that followed independence. The legacy of imperialism has been among the many challenges to economic development faced by independent African states.

I doubt these thoughts passed through my mind that day, but I do remember that by the afternoon we were hungry and tired as we entered a village three days' hike into the bush. Stopping at a house, we asked whether we could buy some food. The owner's reply indicated both the lasting influence of imperialism and the survival of customary African hospitality. "Pourquoi acheter?"—"Why buy it?"—he replied in French, the language used by Belgian colonial authorities and now the country's national language. Then he set before us a free lunch; indeed, no one along our route off the beaten commercial track would accept money for hospitality.

Chapter Overview

This chapter describes the basic characteristics of the old colonial system, then focuses on the implications of the new burst of Western imperialism that began in the late nineteenth century. It seeks to explain the motives for what became the most rapid colonial expansion in history during this latter period. It examines the effect of colonial rule on different regions of the world and the revolt against the West that followed the Second World War. Finally, the chapter assesses how, even after independence, the legacies of the new imperialism have continued to shape our world.

This discussion is designed to provide a useful historical background for understanding contemporary global issues, especially those relating to developing countries. Far too often, contemporary discourse on events in Asia, Africa, or the Middle East takes place either in a historical vacuum or with references to a hazy skyline of past events. Naturally, this limits the opportunity for informed discussion and makes it difficult to appreciate non-Western perspectives.

It may be useful to begin with some definitions of terms readers are likely to encounter in a discussion of imperialism. Although imperialism and colonialism are often used interchangeably, Edward Said offers a valuable distinction: "'Imperialism' means the practice, the theory, and the attitudes of a dominating metropolitan center ruling a distant territory; 'colonialism,' which is almost always a consequence of imperialism, is the implanting of settlements on distant territory."[1] When one speaks of Western imperialism, Western commonly refers to Europe and the United States although the term is imprecise.[2] Finally, historians have used the term "new imperialism" for the period because it was the second great wave of European expansion to sweep across the globe.

The Old Colonial System from the Late Fifteenth to the Early Nineteenth Centuries

The first wave began with the voyages of discovery by European navigators in the late fifteenth century. These voyages heralded the beginning of the global era of world history and the rise of European domination.[3] Motivated by dreams of easily obtained new riches, a crusading Christian zeal, individual initiative, and national rivalries, Europeans explored the world's oceans and laid claim to vast new lands.

Motives offer only part of the explanation for this European expansion. Technological developments provided the means for domination. Improvements in sailing ships during the fifteenth century produced the highly maneuverable oceangoing caravel. Europeans added cannons to these new ships and borrowed Arab navigational instruments, the compass and the astrolabe. These advances not only made possible exploration of the world's oceans, but also established European naval supremacy.

In the Americas, other European advantages (guns, horses, Indians' lack of resistance to Old World diseases), as well as individual initiatives and internal weaknesses of the Indian states, opened the way for the defeat of the existing Aztec and Inca empires and the beginning of European colonization. In contrast, most of Africa and Asia remained free of direct European rule during this period. Why? In part it was because of the existence of states capable of resisting European advances, but also able to supply European trading demands. In addition, the role of disease was reversed in tropical Africa, where Europeans lacked resistance to yellow fever and malaria.

The old colonial era witnessed growing national rivalries and conflicts among European states over their colonial possessions and corresponding shifts in preeminence. During the sixteenth century the Portuguese established a seaborne empire while they were traveling around the coast of Africa to trade with Asia, while Spain concentrated on colonization efforts in the Americas. In the seventeenth century, the Dutch emerged as the dominant colonial power, displacing much of the Portuguese trade with Asia. By the eighteenth century, Britain and France were locked in a global struggle for colonial supremacy. The valuable sugar-producing islands of the Caribbean and rivalry in North America were at the heart of this competition, but it ranged as far afield as India.

Even though the old colonial era is now distant history, whose significance can be hidden under easy generalizations, the student should remember that the legacy of even the early part of this period is still with us. In South Africa it was descendants of Dutch settlers who advanced the racist ideas of apartheid in the twentieth century; and in Angola and Mozambique the Portuguese fought African liberation movements until the mid-1970s.

The economic philosophy most closely associated with European imperialism during the seventeenth and eighteenth centuries was mercantilism. Advocates of this idea viewed the world in terms of national economic competition, where the purpose of colonies was to strengthen the European states. Colonies were to provide commodities desired in Europe and markets for European manufacturers. European governments jealously attempted to guard commerce with their colonies through trade monopolies, tariffs, and bounties.

Among the many significant consequences of the period, Old World diseases and European greed produced two great human catastrophes. Long isolated from diseases in

Europe, Asia, and Africa, American Indians lacked natural resistance to many illnesses, especially smallpox. This lack of protection, combined with forced labor on plantations and in mines, decimated the Indian population. In most of the Caribbean the indigenous population was virtually wiped out. Throughout the Americas, millions died in this calamity that accompanied the arrival of the Europeans.[4]

This human devastation contributed to the second great evil of the era. Faced with labor shortages on the valuable plantations of the Caribbean, Brazil, and the southern United States, Europeans turned to the frightful traffic in human beings that produced the Atlantic slave trade. From the sixteenth through the nineteenth centuries, Africans were torn away from their homes, brutally transported across the Atlantic Ocean, and forced to labor as slaves in the Americas. Most brought to the Caribbean and southern United States came from West Africa, while those who toiled in Brazil came largely from Angola.[5]

The Europeans who engaged in the infamous trade lived mostly along the coast in forts such as Elmina in Ghana or sailed along the shore purchasing slaves from African rulers and slave traders. Popular images of European slave traders capturing unsuspecting Africans and leading them off into slavery are largely misleading. But this does not relieve Europeans of their responsibility for these crimes against humanity that continued century after century. Modern visitors, black or white, who witness the horrible conditions that existed at Elmina are likely to agree with Ali Mazrui's comment in the video series *The Africans* that it is a place of "infinite sadness."[6]

It also is true that various forms of slavery existed in Africa, but they were fundamentally different from those of the New World. What Westerners often described as slavery encompassed different categories. For example, some were captives taken in war, while others more closely resembled indentured servants. African slaves generally remained part of their communities, too, sometimes marrying into their master's family. One West African saying notes that, "A slave who knows how to serve may inherit his master's wealth."

Finally, it should be noted that firearms played an insidious role in the slave trade. Frequently they were exchanged for slaves, making it difficult for individual African leaders to escape from the traffic. For example, the ruler of Benin, the Oba, at first refused to engage in the slave trade. He soon found that European traders were no longer interested in his country's other goods. As his neighbors acquired firearms through the slave trade, he was obliged to participate.

The Atlantic slave trade reached a peak in the eighteenth century before being abolished in the nineteenth. The end of the trade reflected both the growing moral condemnation advanced by abolitionists[7] and the progress of the industrial revolution, for slavery was not only cruel but increasingly inefficient economically. After Britain outlawed the trans-Atlantic trade in 1807, British ships, which had carried more slaves than those of any other nation in the previous century, were replaced by British naval patrols trying to halt slave runners. The film *Amistad* (1999) portrays this period of the nineteenth century, when slavery persisted in the Americas despite efforts to prohibit the trade from Africa.

The abolition of the slave trade coincided with other events that mark the end of the first wave of European colonial expansion. The American Revolution, and subsequent revolutions in Latin America, appeared to represent the victory of independence over continued colonial rule from Europe. At the same time, mercantilism was being challenged by the free trade arguments of Adam Smith. By the middle of the nineteenth century, European politicians and theorists questioned the need for colonies, arguing that they were too expensive. Remnants of the former colonial empires, of which British India was the most significant, continued to exist. But their future was unclear. Historians have sometimes described this mid-century interval as a period of informal imperialism, or even anti-imperialism. Then, quite suddenly, in the late nineteenth century came the explosion of the new imperialism that would transform Africa, Asia, and eventually the Middle East.

Motives for the New Imperialism in the Late Nineteenth and Early Twentieth Centuries

For much of the twentieth century writers have debated the causes and consequences of this new wave of imperialism. Most have viewed the developing industrial revolution in Europe, the United States, and Japan as the critical force behind the rapid scramble for colonies. Industrial growth created an increasing demand for tropical products, such as palm oil and rubber, as well as minerals. Colonies also appeared to offer potential new markets for Western manufactured goods.

In some cases, Western imperialists suggested a revival of mercantilist policies to justify colonial expansion. Under this rationale European powers, such as France, could impose preferential tariffs and other economic policies on their colonies with the aim of monopolizing their trade. Although British policy makers advocated the contrasting doctrine of free trade, the mercantilist arguments voiced in other countries provided an incentive for the British to preserve potential markets by seizing colonies preemptively.

Perhaps the most controversial economic explanation for the new imperialism was advanced by J. A. Hobson in his 1902 book, *Imperialism: A Study.* He had served as a British newspaper correspondent during the Boer War in South Africa and had become thoroughly disenchanted with the consequences of Western imperialism. He maintained that the inequities of modern capitalist states had created an overaccumulation of capital, and that this excess was the "taproot" of imperialism. He saw the machinations of investors, bankers, and speculators behind the drive for new colonies.

V. I. Lenin, the revolutionary Russian socialist, adopted Hobson's basic argument but transformed it into an even more far-reaching indictment of capitalism. The system's economic contradictions led to the growing domination of banks and trusts, and this developing "monopoly capitalism" exported capital rather than goods. Lenin described imperialism as the "highest stage of capitalism," foreshadowing struggles for the redivision of the Earth and worldwide socialist revolution.

From a historical viewpoint this theory of capitalist imperialism has been criticized for reducing a complex process to a simplistic formula. In fairness to both men, it should be noted that they recognized other causes for the new imperialism but saw them as secondary in importance. Debate over the theory often has reflected the proponents' political passions as much as their scholarly analysis of the subject. Nationalists in developing countries and Western radicals were often attracted to the theory because of its indictment of capitalism; conservatives were inclined to reject it for the same reason.[8]

Apart from the foregoing economic explanations, there were a variety of other incentives for the new imperialism. Non-economic considerations included strategic, political, and cultural motives.

The interest of the British in the Suez Canal and the Americans in the Panama Canal reflected their strategic military concerns as well as their desire for economic benefits. Captain Alfred T. Mahan's widely read book, *The Influence of Sea Power on History* (1890), offered a justification for a strong navy. His argument that control of the seas was a decisive factor in history not only contributed to a naval arms race among the industrial powers but also to the perception that countries needed a worldwide network of coaling stations and naval bases. In their work *Africa and the Victorians: The Official Mind of Imperialism* (1961), Ronald Robinson and John Gallagher advanced the controversial thesis that Britain's interest in protecting the route to India and its consequent involvement in Egypt were the driving forces behind the partition of tropical Africa. Colonies could serve several political purposes as well. They appeared to confer great power status. When Kaiser Wilhelm II demanded Germany's right to "a place in the sun," he was seeking this acknowledgment from Britain and France. Imperial enthusiasts argued that colonies could provide homes for Europe's emigrating surplus population. Although the rationale had some popular appeal, it was both insensitive and inaccurate, for it clearly disregarded the interests of the colonies' populations—and most European emigrants continued going to North America rather than the newly acquired territories.

Economic and political interests were supported by a sense of Western cultural superiority. Arguments were often advanced from national perspectives: the French spoke of their civilizing mission, Germans of spreading their culture, the British poet Rudyard Kipling of the "white man's burden."[9] Today, they sound much alike and equally specious. At the time, they reflected the ideas of Social Darwinism, which in this case was interpreted to mean that the West was entitled to rule less-developed areas. The zeal of Christian missionaries to spread the gospel provided a further moral justification.

The foregoing analysis suggests that a complex combination of motives best explains the roots of the new imperialism. Most contemporary historians are likely to accept such a multi-causal explanation, while recognizing that in individual cases one incentive or another may have been decisive. Many historians (including this writer) also attribute an ascendant role to economic motives. Still, the various explanations for the new imperialism continue to produce controversy.

A satisfactory explanation of the causes of the new imperialism should consider two further perspectives. First, it has been argued that African and Asian dimensions of the new imperialism need more consideration. Leaders in these areas usually resisted, but at times allied themselves with, the imperialist powers, often shaping the direction of the new imperialism. For example, Moshoeshoe, the Sotho king, sought British protection to prevent annexation by the Afrikaners, white South Africans descended from Dutch settlers. At the same time, European "men on the spot," such as glory-seeking French officers in Indochina and West Africa, often acted on their own initiative rather than according to the motives guiding decision makers in Paris.

Finally, in his book *The Tools of Empire: Technology and European Imperialism in the Nineteenth Century* (1981), Daniel R. Headrick argued that the focus on the new imperialism's motives has ignored the means of establishing European domination. The development of modern industrial states allowed governments to spend more than ever before on imperialist enterprises. Medical progress, especially the growing use of quinine to combat malaria, reduced the mortality rates of

Europeans in tropical areas. Advances in military technology, such as development of machine guns, gave Western forces overwhelming superiority. Thus, the real basis of the new imperialism was the growing disparity of power between industrial and non-industrial states.

Africa Partitioned

The most dramatic impact of the new imperialism was the partition of Africa. As late as 1880 most of Africa was still free of European control. Then in just over twenty years, the European powers divided the continent.

One of the major initiators of this mad scramble for territory was Leopold II, the king of Belgium. In Europe he seemed a strange figure for this role, for there he ruled a small state with his power limited by a constitution. In Africa, however, he behaved with brutal greed and the strategic impulse to carve out an enormous personal empire.[10]

He began in the late 1870s by financing a series of expeditions along the Congo River by Henry Stanley, a British-American reporter and controversial African "explorer." Stanley's trips produced unfair treaties providing Leopold with a claim to the area. Even at the time, Europeans viewed these types of agreements as highly dubious because they were often misrepresented to Africans and agreed to by leaders who lacked the authority to make such sweeping commitments. Nevertheless, the assertion of Leopold's claims stirred British concern that they might be excluded from trade in the region.

To settle this question and other growing issues of imperialist rivalry in Africa, the Berlin Conference met in 1884. Representation at the conference contained a tragic irony, for not only were European colonial powers sitting down to decide the future of Africa, but there were no Africans present. The conference satisfied both Leopold and the British by recognizing Leopold's claims but declaring the Congo River basin a free trade zone. It also established a formula for future territorial claims. European countries that controlled sections of the African coast could claim the interior, but they would have to occupy it and inform the other European states. Naturally, this contributed to counterclaims and an accelerating race for territory.

The conference also called for the suppression of the slave trade, but as we have seen, the Atlantic slave trade had already ended. The issue now provided a moral justification for European intervention in East Africa, where a much smaller Arab slave trade had long existed.

If Europeans were concerned about morality, Leopold's Congo soon offered a stinging indictment of Western imperialism itself. He ruled the vast territory, the size of the United States east of the Mississippi, as his personal estate and extracted a fortune from the production of rubber. Draconian punishments, such as cutting off Congolese villagers' hands, were used to coerce workers. The brutality of his regime produced criticism in Europe, such as the writings of E. D. Morel, and by the NAACP in the United States.[11] Eventually, this reform movement, along with resistance in the Congo and declining rubber revenues, led the Belgian government to take control of the colony in 1908 and curb the worst human rights abuses.

The two major European colonial powers in Africa, Britain and France, produced rival plans for partitioning the continent. British imperialists, such as Cecil Rhodes, dreamed of connecting British colonies from South Africa to Egypt. This "Cape to Cairo" vision was driven, in part, by the impractical scheme of constructing a railway line through

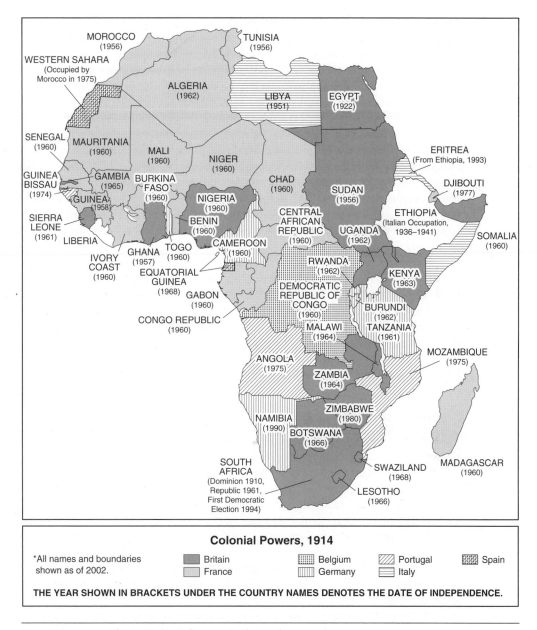

Colonial Powers, 1914

*All names and boundaries shown as of 2002.

Britain Belgium Portugal Spain
France Germany Italy

THE YEAR SHOWN IN BRACKETS UNDER THE COUNTRY NAMES DENOTES THE DATE OF INDEPENDENCE.

FIGURE 8.1   Africa: Colonialism to Independence

British-controlled territory from the south to the north of Africa. In contrast, French army officers pushing inland from bases in west and central Africa raised the prospect of a French African empire extending eastward to the Horn of Africa on the Indian Ocean.

The seemingly unavoidable conflict between these schemes produced the showdown at Fashoda in 1898. There, on the upper Nile in the Sudan, French and British troops met. With a far smaller force and no hope of resupply, the French gave way without a battle. However, the incident soured relations between the two countries and illustrated the tension created between imperialist powers by their colonial competition.

In the face of these European invasions, "Africans did not readily surrender their sovereignty but, rather, resorted to all possible measures to defend it."[12] Thus the Ghanaian historian A. Adu Boahen maintains that confrontation was the most popular response of African leaders to the new imperialism, despite a variety of strategies that included both submission and alliances. Although the Europeans called this approach at the end of the nineteenth and beginning of the twentieth centuries "pacification," it often proved to be the most violent era of the new imperialism.

The common pattern can be seen in West Africa, where Samori Touré bravely fought the French and Yaa Asantewa the British only to be overcome by European military superiority. Even when African courage could defeat European arms on the battlefield, as in the Zulu victory over the British at Isandhlwana in 1879, the ability of the British to deploy the vast resources of their empire meant that the Zulu success was short-lived. The major exception to this outcome was the victory of the Ethiopian emperor, Menelik II, over the Italians at Adowa in 1896. This success, followed by his astute diplomacy, managed to preserve Ethiopia's independence and make it a symbol of liberty to Africans throughout the continent.

Colonial Policies and Their Legacies

Having partitioned the continent, Europeans imposed varying colonial systems. The French system of "assimilation," assuming the superiority of French culture and language, sought to integrate its African colonies into a greater France. For a few select Africans it held out the possibility that a French education could transform them into French citizens. This idea was based on the French revolutionary traditions of equality and universal human rights, but as Basil Davidson notes, it "promised much and meant, in practice, remarkably little."[13]

In contrast, Britain adhered to a policy of "indirect rule." This was predicated on the assumption that African and British societies were so completely different that assimilation was not feasible. Instead the British sought to rule through traditional elites. The preconceptions and ignorance of British officials applying the policy, however, often distorted African political systems.

Trying to apply the policy elsewhere as it worked among the emirates of northern Nigeria, the British sought local leaders, or "chiefs," whom they could use as intermediaries for exercising colonial authority. In some cases this created more autocratic systems by increasing the chosen leader's power, when his traditional authority would have been checked by more democratic institutions, such as the consent of a council or village elders. Elsewhere, as Chinua Achebe illustrates in his novel *Arrow of God* (1964), the British imposed chiefs on societies such as the Igbo where they had not existed before.

Despite the apparent differences, the actual similarities between the French and British systems may be more substantial. Although springing from different assumptions, both ruling methods were based on racist views of European superiority; both were permeated with European privilege; and both pursued economic policies designed to extract African wealth. In both British and French colonies with large settler communities, such as South Africa and Algeria, the settlers attempted to put their own interests ahead of those of the African population.

Frequently it is said that the policies of the smaller colonial powers were significantly worse. We have already noted the brutality of Leopold's colonial policy. As the twentieth century unfolded, Belgian and Portuguese systems could be indicted for providing far fewer African opportunities for a higher education than the British.

One of the lasting legacies of colonial rule in sub-Saharan Africa has been the continued use of European languages. Many African intellectuals have decried this situation and called for more widespread teaching in African languages. The most successful effort in this regard has been the development and use of Kiswahili in East Africa, especially Tanzania.

Elsewhere two important structural considerations have ensured the continued use of the languages of the former colonial powers. At the university level courses are usually taught in European languages, such as English at the University of Ghana. To prepare for the possibility of such study, for which students and their parents everywhere hope, European languages are frequently used in secondary and often primary school. In addition, the colonial borders inherited by the newly independent states often contained ethnic groups with different languages. Despite African objections, the language of the former colonial power has often offered a neutral and practical means of national communication. (See Rosemary Haskell's Chapter 5, "Reading World Literature to Read the World.")

Ironically, access to Western education gave rise to new African voices that challenged the precepts of imperialism. Especially in the British and French colonies, a growing group of Western-educated African spokesmen, such as Pixley Seme of South Africa, J. E. Casely-Hayford of Ghana, and Blaise Diagne of Senegal, turned back upon European imperialists their own ideas, such as liberty and equality.

Yet, before the Second World War, and long after it in South Africa, colonial officials made few concessions to this group and sought to undermine their legitimacy by looking to traditional leaders. Only after 1945 did the group manage to make use of changing international circumstances and growing mass support to effectively challenge colonial rule.

Imperialism in Asia

The combination of incentives that led to the European partition of Africa drew covetous imperialist eyes toward Asia as well. Indeed, in the late fifteenth century it was the prospect of vast wealth to be acquired through trade with the Orient that had lured Columbus to sail West and the Portuguese to travel around Africa to the East.

During that initial wave of European expansion, and for centuries thereafter, China and Japan were sufficiently strong and self-assured to resist Western intervention. Christian missionaries, especially the Jesuits, saw their efforts checked by government opposition and persecution. By the early seventeenth century the Japanese had restricted all contact with the West to a small group of Dutch traders on an isle in Nagasaki's harbor. The Chinese limited foreign trade to Canton and the tiny Portuguese enclave of Macao. So little were they impressed by Europeans that in 1816 the imperial Chinese court sent away the British ambassador without receiving him.

India

In India, too, European influence was largely limited to trading outposts along the coasts for more than 200 years. Then, the decline of the Mughal Empire that had once dominated India and the mid-eighteenth century global conflicts between Britain and France rapidly changed the political situation. The European contenders built up armies of Indian soldiers and sought allies among the Indian princes. By 1763 the French had been defeated, and the foundation of Britain's Indian empire had been established.

During the following century, the British East India Company exercised expanding authority on the subcontinent, while its policies led to growing friction with the Indian population. Indian rulers resented the continuing British absorption of independent states. British intervention in Indian social practices, often deriving from Evangelical Christian impulses, provoked resentment as well.

In this climate of discontent, rumors circulated among Indian soldiers serving under the British that cartridges for their new Enfield rifles, which had to be bitten before use, were greased with both cow and pig fat. Angered, both Muslim and Hindu troops revolted in the Great Rebellion of 1857–58 (referred to by the British as the Sepoy Mutiny—a sepoy being the term for an Indian soldier). The British lost control of much of northern and central India, but they were able to shift troops from other parts of the country and brutally suppress the insurrection.

T. O. Lloyd notes that the uprising strengthened British determination to remain in India. "The earlier idea that Britain's position in India might pass away once peace and tranquility had been fully restored had been dying even before 1857, but the defence of Lucknow and the siege of Delhi killed the idea that the British could ever leave."[14] Thus, the colonial domination Britain had established in India during the eighteenth century was to be carried over into the period of the new imperialism during the late nineteenth century. British concern with protecting their routes to India became a critical consideration in their acquisition of the Suez Canal and in their imperial expansion in South and East Africa.

In the aftermath of the rebellion British officials governed India directly, while the Mughal Empire and the British East India Company disappeared. At the apex of the imperial British administration was the viceroy, supported by the elite Indian Civil Service, drawn largely from British graduates of Oxford and Cambridge. By the end of the nineteenth century, there were fewer than 4,000 British administrators governing a population of almost 300 million.

Suppression of the rebellion had demonstrated that British rule ultimately rested on force, but in practice successful administration of the subcontinent depended on cooperation and acquiescence from important segments of the Indian population. Below the elite British administrators there developed a vast Indian bureaucracy that provided the myriad services required of government. The British also reversed their policy of absorbing princely Indian states and now supported their rulers, seeking a pro-British Indian nobility, who would see their kinship with Queen Victoria, now Empress of India. In the important Ganges valley, the British recognized the zamindars, collectors of government revenue during the Mughal Empire, as landlords. They paid the British administration a set sum but were free to raise the peasants' rent. The deal eventually allowed them to accumulate enormous wealth.

Among the chief economic achievements of British rule in India was the construction of one of the world's most extensive railroad systems. It brought the subcontinent many benefits, such as a greatly enhanced ability to relieve regional famine. But Indian railway construction failed to ignite industrial development as it did in the West. British political pressure undermined the industrial spin-offs that might have occurred.[15]

British political control of Indian economic policy meant that India could not enact tariffs to protect young industries from competition with established British firms. Although in the eighteenth century, India had been an exporter of manufactured goods, especially cotton cloth, Indian handloom weavers could not contend with the cotton mills of Manchester. By the end of the nineteenth century, India had been transformed into an exporter of raw materials. The failure of an Indian industrial revolution at this point, combined with significant population growth encouraged by advances in medicine and public health, contributed to a growing and impoverished Indian peasantry.

In education, too, British policies produced unexpected consequences. In 1835 the British endorsed an educational system based on English, rather than on Indian languages. As a result, in nineteenth-century India there emerged a Western-educated Indian elite studying through college and university levels in English. Children of the wealthy often continued their educations in England.

At first the group favored British modernization of India, but colonial privileges demanded by the British undercut the promises of British liberties. An example of this occurred in 1883 when legislation curbed the power of Indians, who were rising in the civil service, to judge any Briton. Two years later, Western-educated Indians held the first meeting of the Indian National Congress in Bombay. Thus, in 1885, as the Berlin Conference sanctioned the partition of Africa, the organization that would be the chief vehicle for Indian independence was founded.

At first the Congress was designed to advocate Indian interests with the British administration, but by the early twentieth century it was seeking self-government along the lines of the British dominions of Canada and Australia. Ironically, English education and the railway system strengthened a sense of Indian nationalism in place of regional particularism. Yet religion divided and weakened the nationalists. With the Congress predominantly Hindu, and often blind to the concerns of Muslims, the Muslim League was created in 1906.

Southeast Asia

Southeast Asia witnessed an advance of Western imperialism during the nineteenth century similar to that experienced by India and Africa. From India, the British pushed into Burma. The Dutch, building on the foundations established by the Dutch East India Company founded in the seventeenth century, transformed the vast Indonesian archipelago into the Netherlands East Indies.

French missionaries had long been active in Vietnam when mid-nineteenth century persecution of Catholics by the Emperor Tu Duc led to French intervention. Known then as Annam, Vietnam had for centuries been influenced by Chinese culture, while its emperors had recognized varying degrees of Chinese political authority. In the late 1850s and 1860s the French had seized the southern part of the country. From this base, French naval officers initiated campaigns of conquest much as French army officers were doing in West Africa. The Vietnamese looked to China for support, but despite Chinese assistance, by 1885 the French had won control over the entire territory. The French film *Indochine* (1992) examines the contradictions and injustices that accompanied French rule.

The French position in Vietnam led them to establish protectorates over Cambodia and Laos. These protectorates were typical imperialist political arrangements of the era. They were used when the colonial powers believed it was more expedient to rule through the existing governments rather than directly. Together Vietnam, Cambodia, and Laos formed French Indochina, a colonial territory almost 50 percent larger than France itself.

By the end of the nineteenth century other new imperialist powers had appeared. Arriving late, as they did in Africa, the Germans had to content themselves with the northeastern part of New Guinea and islands in the Pacific. The United States wrested the Philippines from Spain in 1898 and then suppressed a determined Filipino struggle for independence. In a situation reminiscent of Ethiopia in Africa, only Thailand (Siam) retained its independence in Southeast Asia.

China

To the north lay the great tempting prize for Western imperialists—China. For centuries the Chinese, confident in their sense of cultural superiority, had rejected European trading and missionary activities. Yet, by the mid-nineteenth century, European military advances had compromised China's ability to resist. At the same time, the ruling Qing Dynasty, often called the Manchus because they had originally come from that northeastern province of China, was in a prolonged state of decline.

The changing dynamics of China's relations with the West were demonstrated by the infamous first Opium War (1839–1842). Western demand for Chinese goods, such as tea and silks, had long exceeded the Chinese demand for European goods. The British sought to redress this trade deficit by the convenient, if unethical, arrangement of selling the Chinese opium grown in India. The Chinese prohibited the importation of opium but with little effect until the appointment of a determined imperial commissioner, Lin Tse-hsu, who seized without compensation the existing stocks of opium in Canton and publicly destroyed them. (See Mathew Gendle's Chapter 10, "Use and Abuse: Drug Use and Drug Commerce in a Global Context.")

Relations between Britain and China deteriorated rapidly. (Actually the British governor-general of India, whose government profited from the opium trade, declared war on China.) British military, especially naval, superiority soon prevailed. By the Treaty of Nanking in 1842, China was forced to pay an indemnity and cede Hong Kong to Britain, open other cities, including Shanghai, to foreign trade, and establish a low uniform tariff of five percent on imports.

This was the beginning of the so-called Treaty System, whereby China was forced to give up much of its sovereignty through unequal treaties extracted at the point of a gun. In 1843 China was compelled to grant Britain, and subsequently other nations, "most favored nation" status, meaning that any trade preferences offered to (or more likely extracted by) one would be granted to all. The following year a treaty with the United States granted all Americans (later extended to Europeans) in China extraterritorial privileges in criminal and civil cases. This meant that an American accused of murder in China would not be tried by a Chinese court but rather by a U.S. consular one.

In the international section of Shanghai, Chinese authority was completely replaced by foreign control. Here, too, one would find that most common baggage of imperialism: racism. In 1924, an angry Mao Tse-tung, future leader of China's Communist Party, would show a Chinese friend who had been studying abroad the infamous sign outside the city's park, "Chinese and dogs not allowed."[16] It was a sign that illustrated the offensive psychological dimension of imperialism which produced a climate of humiliation and sense of inferiority through much of Asia and Africa.

Following further military defeats during the nineteenth century, China was forced to grant territory to France, Russia, Japan, and Germany. Foreign gunboats came to patrol the Yangtze River deep into China's interior. By the end of the century, the scramble for concessions had reached the point where it appeared China would be partitioned as Africa had been. In this climate, the United States announced the Open Door policy, which sought assurances from the other imperialist powers that free trade would be maintained in their Chinese spheres of influence and that China would remain intact. Britain supported this policy, and perhaps it slowed the rush to partition, but its real aim was to protect American business interests.

It is not surprising that under these circumstances Western intervention and influence produced bitter resentment among many Chinese. The paramount political figure in Chinese politics of the late nineteenth century, the resourceful Dowager Empress Tz'u-his (Cixi), was hostile to Western ways throughout much of her ascendancy. An example of this was her support for the Boxer Rebellion in 1899. Members of the Chinese secret society of Righteous Harmonious Fists, commonly referred to by Westerners as the Boxers, began attacking foreign traders and missionaries, Chinese Christians, and eventually the foreign embassies in Beijing. The imperialist powers reacted swiftly, sending a multi-national force to Beijing that suppressed the uprising and inflicted another humiliating defeat on the imperial government.

By the early twentieth century it had become increasingly clear to Chinese reformers in and out of government that Western-style modernization was needed for China to recover its sovereignty. As government officials made half-hearted attempts in this direction, a growing number of Chinese intellectuals called for the overthrow of the dynasty and the establishment of a republic. Their leader, Sun Yat-sen, recognized the connection between democracy and nationalism.[17]

Following a decade of revolutionary organizing and unsuccessful uprisings, the revolt of 1911 finally overthrew the ineffective and despotic Qing dynasty. Yet the new republic that emerged, challenged by rival regional warlords and increasing Japanese intervention, failed to produce a stable and prosperous China. This meant that the struggle against Japanese and Western imperialism would become an important factor in the rise of Chinese communism.

Japan

Across the East China Sea in Japan a very different reaction to Western imperialism occurred during the nineteenth century. American Commodore Matthew Perry's intrusion into Japan in 1853 is frequently cited as initiating an end to centuries of Japanese isolation. Concerned over the treatment of shipwrecked American whaling crews, and seeking ports for resupply and new commercial opportunities for American merchants, Perry demanded Japanese concessions.[18] Under continuing American pressure, Japan eventually agreed to open its markets, a fact whose irony is probably overlooked by most contemporary American critics of Japanese trading practices.

The effect of Perry's visit on Japan's transformation can be exaggerated. It coincided with desires of various Japanese groups, such as merchants, nationalists, scholars, and soldiers, for modernization. The dominance of the powerful Tokugawa shoguns came to an end, and the subsequent Meiji Restoration (1868–1912) proved a period of rapid modernization. New Western ideas contended with Japanese tradition. The Japanese especially sought Western scientific knowledge and technology, swiftly industrializing Japan and building up a modern military.

Then Japan joined the ranks of the imperialist powers. In 1894, much to the surprise of many in the West, war between Japan and China over Korea ended in a decisive Japanese victory. Revealing China's weaknesses, the outcome encouraged the scramble of other powers for Chinese territory. Ten years later the competing imperialist designs of Russia and Japan in northeast Asia led to war.[19] Western observers were even more startled when the Japanese defeated Russian troops in Manchuria and then annihilated Russia's Baltic fleet that had been sent around the world to reverse the military situation.

The Russo-Japanese War and its outcome had many consequences. In Russia, it provoked revolution; in Korea, it led to decades of oppressive colonial domination by Japan. Throughout Asia it demonstrated that the European colonial powers were not invincible. In so doing it gave encouragement to nationalists and drew their attention to the Japanese model of modernization.

Neocolonialism in the Caribbean and Central America

Our survey of the new imperialism has focused on Africa and Asia. It was on these two continents that it produced large numbers of new colonies, directly ruled from Europe. It was in Asia and Africa, too, that the great revolutionary movements against Western imperialism would occur following the Second World War. Yet one should recognize other international developments of the late nineteenth and early twentieth centuries that were similar in character to the new imperialism in Africa and Asia.

In the Caribbean and Central America, and more generally throughout Latin America, the United States asserted its hegemony for many of the same reasons that drew the Europeans to Africa: economic advantages, strategic locations, and a sense of entitlement. Pan-Americanism was used to justify American domination south of the border as Manifest Destiny had warranted westward expansion.

In 1823 the United States had issued the Monroe Doctrine, warning European states against trying to reestablish their colonial empires in the Americas. Until the end of the nineteenth century, British support was needed to give the policy any teeth. Then, with the rise of American industrial and naval strength, and the increasing British preoccupation with interests elsewhere in the world, the United States moved to insist on its predominance in the Western Hemisphere.

The Cuban struggle for independence provided the United States with a cause for war against Spain and an opportunity to increase its influence in the region. In the short Spanish-American War of 1898 the United States handily defeated Spain in the Caribbean as well as the Pacific. Spain was forced to cede the Philippines, Puerto Rico, and Guam to the United States. Cuba became independent, but in reality it was an American protectorate. The Platt Amendment, named for Connecticut Senator Orville Platt, stated that American troops would be withdrawn from Cuba only after the country had accepted a set of conditions limiting Cuban sovereignty in favor of the United Sates. These gave the United States significant control of Cuba's foreign relations, the promise of a naval base (Guantánamo Bay), and the right to intervene in Cuba's internal affairs to maintain "a stable Government adequately protecting life, property and individual liberty."[20]

If the broad terms of the Platt Amendment seemed designed to allow the United States to intervene when it desired, this is indeed exactly what happened. In the early twentieth century, American troops were repeatedly sent to Cuba. They also intervened in Haiti, the Dominican Republic, Nicaragua, Mexico, and Panama. In Panama, the American navy intervened to support the country's independence from Colombia in 1903, but this was not disinterested aid to Panamanian nationalists. Colombia's senate had rejected the financial compensation the United States was willing to pay for rights to a canal zone; the Panamanian revolutionaries quickly accepted the offer.

In 1904 President Theodore Roosevelt issued what became known as the Roosevelt Corollary to the Monroe Doctrine. Whereas the earlier statement had commanded Europeans not to meddle in the affairs of the Western Hemisphere, Roosevelt now claimed for the United States the right to act as a hemispheric policeman in the case of a nation's "Brutal wrongdoing, or an impotence which results in a general loosening of the ties of civilized society."[21]

The "gunboat diplomacy" and marines that symbolized American policy protected U.S. business interests. American investors came to control Cuban sugar cane production, and the United Fruit Company built an enormous banana empire in Central America. The growing industrial demand for rubber created a brutal and destructive system in the Amazon region as it had done in equatorial Africa.[22]

Latin American countries might retain a circumscribed political independence, but economically they had much in common with European colonies in Asia or Africa. They exported raw materials and tropical crops while importing manufactured goods. Critics of the situation denounced it as "neocolonialism," in which independence was a facade hardly obscuring limited sovereignty and retarded economic development.[23] As might be expected, it created popular resentment against "Yankee imperialism" and lasting suspicion of the intentions of the "Colossus of the North."

The Middle East and the League of Nations Mandates

Later generations of Asian and African nationalists would also voice charges of Western neo-colonialism, but in the early twentieth century European imperialism had yet to reach its peak. The climax came during the First World War (1914–1918) and the Paris Peace Conference in 1919. It led to a repartition of Africa, with the Allied powers (Britain, France, Belgium, and South Africa) seizing Germany's colonies. In Asia, Australia and Japan occupied Germany's possessions. Allied leaders attempted to justify their expansionism in altruistic terms, but just as in the earlier partition of Africa, their actions hardly reflected the desires of the colonies' inhabitants.

It was in the Middle East that this high tide of Western imperialism had its most profound consequences for the twentieth and twenty-first centuries. At the First World War's outset, much of the region was still part of the Ottoman Empire, although it had long been in political decline and subjected to imperialist pressures. The empire contained many ethnic groups, of which the two largest were Arabs and Turks, with the Turks forming the political elite. In 1914 the Turkish leaders joined Germany, so the Allies soon looked to fomenting revolution in the now enemy empire and worked for its eventual division.

From its Egyptian stronghold, Britain took the lead in these initiatives. Seeking to win wartime support and to gain postwar territory, British policy makers made three potentially conflicting arrangements. In 1915 they promised Sharif Hussein, the Arab leader in Mecca, a unified and independent Arab state if the Arabs revolted against the Turkish leaders of the Ottoman Empire. The following year British and French officials worked out the Sykes-Picot Agreement, an imperialist arrangement to split the Arab areas of the Ottoman Empire between themselves.[24] Finally, in 1917, the British issued the Balfour Declaration, promising to view with favor the creation of a homeland for the Jewish people in Palestine.[25]

The inherent contradictions of making conflicting promises about the same territory would prove the basis for many of the region's later problems, especially the roots of the continuing Israeli-Palestinian conflict. At the time, the imperialist mindset and urgent wartime pressures largely submerged these future considerations.

By the war's end, two new challenges had arisen to Western imperialism. Following the Russian Revolution of 1917, Lenin's anti-imperialist arguments echoed around the world. Then at the Paris Peace Conference, U.S. President Woodrow Wilson raised a second challenge by advancing the rights of people to self-determination in choosing their own government. Although this principle was originally not intended to apply evenly to all peoples, the Western-educated population in the European colonies recognized its implications. On February 22, 1919, a West African newspaper, the *Gold Coast Leader*, contained a column "The Proposed Repartition of Africa" that argued, "The repartition of Africa is the topic of the hour.... The choice of such a change does not lie with an alien Power but with the people themselves."[26]

Although many European policy makers desired a straightforward imperialist division of the spoils of war, American opposition led to the creation of the League of Nations "mandate system." The Allied powers still gained administration of the German and Arab territories they coveted, but now these lands were to be held in trust for the League, rather than as colonies. This new concept implied some level of international oversight for the territories, and at least some of the mandates were to be prepared for independence.

In the Middle East, the French received the mandate for Lebanon, where they had been the traditional protectors of the Maronite Christians, and Syria, where they now encountered a resentful new Arab nationalism. In response, they drew mandate boundaries that created a large Lebanon at the expense of Syria. Although this new Lebanon had a slight Christian majority in the 1920s, over time this eroded because of a higher Muslim birthrate and greater Christian emigration. Despite a delicate political balance at independence, religious divisions and tensions (along with the repercussions of the Israeli-Palestinian conflict) have been continuing sources of Lebanese political instability.[27]

In Palestine and Iraq, the British mandates also encountered hostility. In the former, the British pursued indecisive and reactive policies toward the growing conflict between Zionist Jewish settlers and the mandate's Palestinian inhabitants. Vacillating between the interests of the two groups, the British proposed a variety of resolutions to their clashing territorial claims. None were acceptable to all.[28] Mounting hostilities finally led Britain to refer the issue to the United Nations after the Second World War. When the UN too proved unable to find a mutually acceptable solution, these conflicts exploded in the Arab-Israeli war of 1948.

In Iraq, British efforts to impose their authority provoked opposition from nationalist, religious, and tribal sources. Critiquing British policies in the London *Sunday Times* on August 22, 1920, T. E. Lawrence (Lawrence of Arabia) observed: "We said we went to Mesopotamia to defeat Turkey. We said we stayed to deliver the Arabs from the oppression of the Turkish Government,…Our government is worse than the old Turkish system. They kept fourteen thousand local conscripts embodied, and killed a yearly average of two hundred Arabs in maintaining peace. We keep ninety thousand men, with aeroplanes, armoured cars, gunboats, and armoured trains. We have killed about ten thousand Arabs in this rising this summer."[29]

Responding to the crisis, the British Colonial Secretary, Winston Churchill, convened a conference in Cairo in March 1921 that would have long-term consequences. Sharif Hussein's son, Faisal, leader of the Arab revolt against the Ottoman Empire and recently driven out of Syria by the French, was made king of Iraq. His prestige and skill helped make him acceptable to many there, but he was an Arab Sunni; and their minority dominated a diverse population that included Kurds and a Shia majority. How Gertrude Bell, a remarkable British expert and official in Iraq, assisted him in consolidating his authority is a fascinating story. It also illustrates the role of British imperial influence. As leading Iraqi tribal leaders promised their loyalty to Faisal, they declared, "We swear allegiance to you because you are acceptable to the British government."[30]

Toby Dodge's 2005 book, *Inventing Iraq: The Failure of Nation Building and a History Denied*, examines Britain's inability to establish a democratic and stable Iraqi state in the 1920s as well as the similarities with the efforts of the United States and its coalition partners from 2003 onwards. The small Iraqi political elite, led by Faisal, "mindful of the need to establish its own legitimacy …, continually demanded greater autonomy."[31] Yet, they remained dependent on the financial support of London and the military support of the Royal Air Force. Facing popular pressures at home, however, Britain sought to reduce expenditures. (For Churchill, Faisal had offered hope of the "best and cheapest solution.")[32] Further, Dodge argues that Orientalist attitudes[33] of the British led them to view the Shia as backward; their religious leaders, according to Bell, were akin to "alien popes."[34] Perhaps not surprisingly many Iraqis remained suspicious of British hegemony and a perceived British desire to control the country's oil resources.

FIGURE 8.2   The Middle East: Territorial Changes, 1918–Present

Revolution in Asia and Africa: Dismantling Empires after 1945

It was after the Second World War that nationalists in Asia and Africa overthrew European colonial rule and regained their peoples' independence in one of the world's great revolutionary movements. The character and pace of decolonization varied from relatively peaceful constitutional transfers of power to protracted liberation struggles, but everywhere it eventually reflected the irresistible nationalist demand for self-determination.[35]

During the Second World War, early Allied defeats and the military experiences of thousands of African and Asian soldiers cracked the image of invincible European colonial rulers. At the same time, Allied leaders appealed, in the name of democracy, for a crusade against Nazi and Japanese tyranny. In August 1941, U.S. President Franklin Roosevelt and British Prime Minister Winston Churchill issued a wartime declaration of principles, the Atlantic Charter, calling for self-government and self-determination. Many African and Asian intellectuals supported this appeal, while recognizing the obvious, if unintended, logic that it must lead to their nations' independence after the war. Further, the significant contributions made to the Allied cause by colonial soldiers and raw materials created a belief that some form of political and economic compensation was due.

In the postwar world (from 1945 onwards), continued European colonial rule encountered pressures from the Cold War policies of the United States and the Soviet Union. Not only were the Soviets actively hostile, but the Americans were increasingly willing to abandon the colonial powers' interests in favor of anti-communist nationalist leaders. At the United Nations, the advocates of colonial liberation grew as former colonies gained their independence and admission. Finally, the nationalist leaders, most with Western educations, successfully turned back on the colonial powers their own rhetoric, both democratic and Marxist.

Asia

India's independence in 1947 was a watershed event in the process. During the interwar years, Indian nationalism, though divided between Hindus and Muslims, had built a growing challenge to continued British rule. Mahatma Gandhi, the spiritual leader of the movement, had provided two critical directions for the nationalists. By appealing to the mass of Indian peasants he had greatly broadened and strengthened the movement, while his tactics of nonviolent civil disobedience undermined Britain's imperialist resolve.

At the end of the Second World War a Labour government, focused on solving domestic social problems, was elected in Britain and finally accepted India's independence as inevitable. The last British viceroy was sent to India to negotiate the subcontinent's partition between a Hindu India and a Muslim Pakistan. The process led to bloody communal fighting, so the joy of independence was tempered by sadness.[36] Yet, throughout Asia and Africa, the enormous implication of India's independence, and the end of the British Raj, was that the days of colonial rule had passed.

At the same time an even more revolutionary challenge to imperialism was unfolding in China. Although the Western powers had gradually conceded many of their privileges to the nationalist Chinese government during the interwar years, expanding Japanese aggression led to war and occupation from 1937 to 1945. This foreign threat forced an end to the civil war between Chinese nationalists and communists. After the Second World War the civil war resumed, and in 1949 the communists prevailed.

The communist victory was based on Mao's astute political combinations of peasant support with guerrilla tactics and the linking of communism with worldwide revolution against imperialism. Mao wrote, "To sum up, it can be seen that our enemies are all those in league with imperialism—the warlords, the bureaucrats, the comprador class [Chinese foremen working for foreign businesses and consulates], the big landlord class...."[37] It was a formula that could be, and was, exported, perhaps with most success in Vietnam.

In French Indochina, Ho Chi Minh led the communist Viet Minh in a determined liberation movement against the French, finally prevailing in 1954. At the time, Vietnam was temporarily partitioned between the communist North and anti-communist South. In the following years the United States was drawn into the renewed fighting in the south because of its Cold War fears of the spread of communism. The eventual communist victory rested in part on Ho's ability, like Mao's, to present the struggle as a national liberation movement against the forces of Western imperialism.

Le Ly Hayslip expressed this idea in *When Heaven and Earth Changed Places*, her autobiographical account of a Vietnamese peasant woman caught up in the war. Addressing part of her introduction to American veterans, she wrote, "For you, it was a simple thing: democracy against communism. For us, that was not our fight at all. How could it be? We knew little of democracy and even less about communism. For most of us it was a fight for independence—like the American Revolution."[38]

Africa

African independence movements formed part of the global revolt against Western imperialism, too.[39] In West Africa, the end of colonial rule was relatively rapid and peaceful. Kwame Nkrumah's remarkable success in Ghana set the pace and then resonated across the continent. Accurately sensing popular opinion, he demanded "Self-Government NOW" and established the new mass-based Convention Peoples' Party. In 1951, the party won a landslide victory at the polls that convinced British officials to release Nkrumah from prison and offer him the position of leader of government business.

Over the next six years, Nkrumah won repeated electoral victories and negotiated the constitutional transfer of power that reached a climax with Ghana's independence in 1957. The British colony had been known as the Gold Coast, but seeking to emphasize its African identity and pride, Ghana, the name of a medieval West African empire, was chosen for the new nation.

The following year, African nationalists from across the continent gathered in Ghana for the All-African Peoples' Conference. In a closing speech, Tom Mboya of Kenya captured the delegates' intentions and determination. In a play on the imperialist "scramble for Africa," he pointedly told the European imperialists, "Africa must be free. Scram from Africa." Throughout western and central Africa this is just what happened in the spectacular outburst of 1960. In that year, Nigeria, Africa's most populous state, gained its independence, as did most of France's African territories. In spite of formal African independence, France maintained strong economic, cultural, political, and military influence in many of its former colonies. Glimpses of this, and the legacies of the French colonial policy of assimilation, can be seen in the West African film *Zan Boko* (1987).

Colonies with significant European settler communities generally proved the most resistant to the growing African demands for democracy and independence. In Algeria, Kenya, and Rhodesia (now Zimbabwe), costly struggles were waged for national liberation. In each case African nationalists eventually prevailed but only after many lives had been lost in futile colonial efforts to preserve settler privileges.

The long and tragic legacy of Zimbabwe's struggle for African majority rule continues to plague the nation today. The intransigent white minority ceded power only in 1980, when its military was stretched to the breaking point. Since then, the country has been ruled by Robert Mugabe, whose initial language of freedom and reconciliation soon gave way to policies of despotism, corruption, brutality, and paranoia over perceived British imperialist intrigue. During a decade of imprisonment under the white minority regime he had become a revolutionary, and then led the strongest guerrilla force fighting for African rights. Notes Martin Meredith, "Once in office, Mugabe continued to use violence to achieve his objectives. Indeed, in later years he was to boast that he had 'a degree in violence.' For Zimbabwe, his rule was to prove ruinous."[40] (See Braye, et al., Chapter 13, for more on Mugabe's rule.)

In 1960, after a tour of Africa, British Prime Minister Harold Macmillan arrived in Cape Town and told the South African parliament that a "wind of change" was blowing across the continent. Unfortunately, it was a message that most white South Africans refused to hear. The National Party, with the overwhelming support of Afrikaner voters, had won control of the white-minority government in the crucial election of 1948.

Afrikaners, primarily the descendants of long-established Dutch settlers, had struggled both to secure control of the land from its African inhabitants, and to overthrow British colonial rule dating from the early nineteenth century. To maintain white power and privileges, the National Party proceeded to impose the system of rigid segregation and brutal exploitation of the African population known as apartheid.

The African National Congress, advancing an alternate vision of racial equality, led the opposition to apartheid through decades of struggle. After demonstrations, civil disobedience, boycotts, an armed struggle, and international sanctions, the South African government was compelled to abandon apartheid. When the country's first democratic election was finally held in 1994, the African National Congress won a convincing victory, and its leader, Nelson Mandela, became president.[41]

For both the country and Africa this election marked the end of the long struggle for political emancipation from colonial rule. However, the political success left much unfinished business. Despite the Pan-African ideals of many African leaders, the colonial borders created by the European partition of the continent in the nineteenth century became the borders of the newly independent African states. As such, they have contributed to ethnic and religious conflicts on the continent, problems that can be seen today in Sudan and Nigeria.

Discontented Asian and African nationalists soon leveled charges of neocolonialism against the former colonial powers and often the United States.[42] The transfer of power was frequently accompanied by elections and the creation of democratic constitutions, but these generally proved fragile foreign instruments. The formal structures of newly independent governments often lacked strong foundations in either their own societies or the colonial experience. Soon most African, and some Asian, states were rocked by military coups d'état. Unfortunately, authoritarian colonial armies proved a more sturdy inheritance from imperialism than constitutions crafted on the eve of independence.

In spite of these limitations, the recovery of African and Asian independence, with its promises of liberty and equality regardless of race, remains a momentous achievement and a dramatic chapter of human history. Following independence, the developing nations have followed alternate paths reflecting their different histories both before and after the new imperialism, as well as their different experiences during the era. With the end of the Cold War, the developing countries have witnessed a renewed search for democracy and new experiments in free market economics. Combined with today's technological revolution, these developments present new opportunities. But they also contain challenges: challenges formed in part by the struggles for independence and the new imperialism.

The new imperialism has remained a controversial topic. Some writers, mostly in the West,[43] have pointed out its benefits, while today more scholars are likely to emphasize its faults. Such a dispute might incline a student to seek a "balanced view," but Professor Boahen points out the fallacy of such a position: "Colonialism definitely did have its credit and debit sides, but quite clearly the debit side far outweighs the credit side. Indeed, my charge against colonialism is not that it did not do anything for Africa, but that it did so little and that little so accidentally and indirectly."[44] It is a perspective Americans should reflect on if they seek a deeper understanding of our global community.

References and Notes

1. Edward W. Said, *Culture and imperialism* (New York: Alfred A. Knopf, 1993), 9.
2. Japan, too, participated in the new imperialism. These countries were at the forefront of the industrial revolution during the late nineteenth century.
3. For a discussion of the early era of European expansion, see G. V. Scammell, *The first imperial age: European overseas expansion, 1400–1715* (London: Unwin Hyman, 1989).
4. Jared Diamond, *Guns, germs and steel* (New York: W.W. Norton, 1997), 210–214.
5. The autobiography of Olaudah Equiano provides a moving firsthand account of the evils of the Atlantic slave trade. Originally published in 1789, it became a popular abolitionist work. For a recent edition see *The interesting narrative and other writings*, rev. ed., Vincent Carretta, ed. (New York: Penguin Classics, 2003). For differing modern perspectives on the Atlantic slave trade, see J. E. Inikori, ed., *Forced migration: The impact of the export slave trade on Africa societies* (New York: Africana Publishing, 1982) and Hugh Thomas, *The slave trade* (New York: Simon and Schuster, 1997).
6. Ali Mazrui, *The Africans: A triple heritage*, (1986), Part 4: Tools of exploitation.
7. Adam Hochschild, *Bury the chains: Prophets and rebels in the fight to free an empire's slaves* (New York: Houghton Mifflin, 2005) offers a stirring account of the British anti-slavery movement set within the broad context of the Atlantic world.
8. D. K. Fieldhouse, *The theory of capitalist imperialism* (London: Longman, 1967) provides a broad documentary survey of the theory and its critics.
9. R. R. Palmer, Joel Colton, and Lloyd Kramer, *A history of the modern world*, 9th ed. (Boston: McGraw Hill, 2002), 622. See Chapter 16, Europe's world supremacy, 1871–1914, for an overview of the new imperialism in this well-regarded history of Europe in its global context.
10. Crawford Young, *The African colonial state in comparative perspective* (New Haven and London: Yale University Press, 1994), 84. Young quotes from one of Leopold's letters to illustrate the covetous eyes he cast not just on Africa but the world: "In Japan there are incredible riches. The treasure of the Emperor is immense and poorly guarded."
11. Adam Hochschild, *King Leopold's ghost: A story of greed, terror, and heroism in colonial Africa* (New York: Houghton Mifflin, 1998) describes the brutality of Leopold's reign and the reformers who exposed its evils.
12. A. Adu Boahen, *African perspectives on colonialism* (Baltimore: Johns Hopkins University Press, 1987), 56.
13. Basil Davidson, *The black man's burden: Africa and the curse of the nation-state* (New York: Random House, 1992), 47.
14. T. O. Lloyd, *The British empire, 1558–1995*, 2nd ed. (Oxford, U.K.: Oxford University Press, 1996), 179.

15. Prabhat Patnaik, "Imperialism and the Growth of Indian Capitalism," *Studies in the theory of imperialism*, edited by Roger Owen and Bob Sutcliffe (Burnt Mill, Harlow Essex, U.K.: Longman, 1972), 213.

16. Stuart Schram, *Mao Tse-tung* (Baltimore: Penguin, 1966), 73.

17. Marie-Claire Bergère, *Sun Yat-sen*, translated by Janet Lloyd (Palo Alto, CA: Stanford University Press, 1998) offers a carefully researched and balanced biography of the nationalist leader and first president of the Republic of China as well as a valuable history of China in the early twentieth century.

18. Relying on the intimidating presence of American warships, Perry's tone in the negotiations ignored instructions that he first try persuasion. Proceeding in a heavy-handed, imperialist fashion, he sent the Japanese white flags, warning that failure to agree to his terms would lead to war and following Japan's defeat the flags would be useful to surrender. Marius Jansen, *The making of modern Japan* (Cambridge, MA: Harvard University Press, 2000), 277.

19. Michael Barnhart, *Japan and the world since 1868* (London: Edward Arnold, 1995), 32–38.

20. Louis Perez, Jr., Cuba: The Platt Amendment, *Imperial surge: The United States abroad, the 1890s–early 1900s* edited by Thomas Paterson and Stephen Rabe (Lexington: D. C. Heath, 1992), 165–166.

21. David Healy, The U.S. Drive to Hegemony in the Caribbean, *Imperial surge*, 87.

22. Tulio Halperin Donghi, *The contemporary history of Latin America*, edited and translated by John Charles Chasteen (Durham, NC: Duke University Press, 1993), 174–176.

23. This general analysis should not be overstated at the expense of the varying roles Latin American leaders played in their countries' economic development.

24. Observed the British Director of Military Intelligence, "We are rather in the position of the hunters who divided up the skin of the bear before they had killed it." Bernard Wasserstein, *Divided Jerusalem: The struggle for the Holy City* (London: Profile Books, 2002), 74.

25. For a full discussion of imperialism and the First World War in the Middle East and Africa, see David Fromkin, *A peace to end all peace: The fall of the Ottoman Empire and the creation of the modern Middle East* (New York: Avon Books, 1989) and Brian Digre, *Imperialism's new clothes: The repartition of tropical Africa, 1914–1919* (New York: Peter Lang, 1990).

26. *Gold Coast Leader*, February 22, 1919.

27. For general overviews of the Middle East during the period see appropriate chapters in Albert Hourani, *A history of the Arab peoples* (Cambridge, MA: Harvard University Press, 1991) and Peter Mansfield, *A history of the Middle East*, 2nd ed., revised and updated by Nicolas Pelham (London: Penguin Books, 2003).

28. Tom Segev, *One Palestine, complete: Jews and Arabs under the British mandate* (New York: Metropolitan Books, 2000) is a readable and controversial analysis of this critical period that asserts Britain pursued a pro-Zionist policy.

29. The *Sunday Times*, August 22, 1920.

30. Georgina Howell, *Gertrude Bell: Queen of the desert, shaper of nations* (New York: Farrar, Straus and Giroux, 2007), 378.

31. Toby Dodge, *Inventing Iraq: The failure of nation building and a history denied* (New York: Columbia University Press, 2005 edition), 30.

32. Howell, 367.

33. Edward Said used the term Orientalism to describe imperialist Western views that were preconceived, oversimplified and critical of Middle East and Asian cultures.

34. Dodge, 68.

35. Prasenjit Duara, ed. *Decolonization: Perspectives from now and then* (London: Routledge, 2004) is a recent anthology of writings by nationalists and historians covering the twentieth century.

36. Stanley Wolpert, *Shameful flight: The last years of the British Empire in India* (Oxford, U.K.: Oxford University Press, 2006) is a new, readable, and controversial account of the independence of British India. Wolpert is particularly critical of how the flawed planning of the last British Viceroy, Lord Louis Mountbatten, contributed to the bloody partition of the British colony into the modern states of India and Pakistan.

37. Mao Tse-tung, Analysis of the Classes in Chinese Society, *Selected works* (Beijing: Foreign Languages Press, 1965–77), 1:19.

38. Le Ly Hayslip, *When heaven and Earth changed places* (New York: Plume Books, 1990), xv.

39. For short accounts of African independence, see David Birmingham, *The decolonization of Africa* (Athens: Ohio University Press, 1995) and Martin Meredith, *The fate of Africa: A history of fifty years of independence* (New York: Public Affairs, 2005), Part I.

40. Meredith, 626.

41. For personal accounts of life under apartheid and the struggle for justice in South Africa see: Mark Mathabane, *Kaffir boy: The true story of a black youth's coming of age in apartheid South Africa* (New York: Macmillian, 1986) and Nelson Mandela, *Long walk to freedom* (Boston: Little, Brown, 1994).

42. Andrew Bacevich, ed. *The imperial tense: Prospects and problems of American empire* (Chicago: Ivan R. Dee, 2003) collects the conflicting opinions of commentators and scholars on the contentious subject of contemporary American imperialism.

43. For a determined, and controversial, defense of Western imperialism, see L. H. Gann and Peter Duignan, *Burden of empire: An appraisal of western colonialism in Africa south of the Sahara* (Stanford: Hoover Institution Press, 1967). Niall Ferguson, *Empire: How Britain made the modern world* (London: Penguin Books, 2004) offers a popular, favorable history of British imperialism that is perhaps more balanced, yet still debatable.

44. Boahen, 108–109.

Questions for Discussion

1. Discuss the legacies of the new imperialism for the developing world. How are the historical experiences of African, Asian, and Latin American countries during that era likely to shape their people's views of the world today? Are Americans generally aware of these perspectives and the history behind them?

2. Compare the characteristics of the old colonial system and the new imperialism. What similarities and differences do you see, and how would you explain them?

3. Evaluate the motives for the new imperialism. Were some more important than others?

4. Explain the term neocolonialism. Why might the peoples of the Caribbean and Central America have felt oppressed by it at the beginning of the twentieth century? Why might people in developing countries feel that way today?

5. What continuing legacies does European imperialism early in the twentieth century have for the Middle East today?

6. What forces account for the successful independence movements in Asia and Africa after the Second World War?

7. Mao Tse-tung and Ho Chi Minh managed to fuse their communist revolutions with the struggle against imperialism. How were they able to do this?

Suggested Readings

See the titles suggested in the "References & Notes," above, for additional readings on colonialism, imperialism, and their continued legacies.

9

Looking at the World Through a Gendered Lens

Feminism and Global Studies

Ann J. Cahill

Defining Feminism

Growing up as the oldest daughter in a large, traditional, Catholic family, I had a probably predictably maternal relationship to my three youngest siblings. From their infancy through their childhood, I spent a significant amount of time caring for them—singing them to sleep, bandaging their scrapes and bruises, and, as I am fond of reminding them now, changing their diapers. I was also, from about the age of fifteen, a feminist. (Believe it or not, feminists—both male and female—can enjoy those personality traits and activities that in our culture are termed "maternal"; by the time you've finished reading this chapter, you should understand why.) One day, a friend of my mother's came to stay with us while she gave presentations to churches and other groups, presentations that argued that feminism was an evil and corruptive set of ideas. Flushed with excitement after one of her talks, she strode into our house one evening and proclaimed to my younger sisters, "All feminists are Marxist, atheist, lesbian witches!"

Well. That's one way to put it.

I tell this story not to focus on my fairly irate reaction to her pronouncement: how dare she impugn my character to my beloved sisters! Rather, I tell it to indicate the various ways in which feminism is defined by different persons and groups, and to make the point that not all of these definitions are equally valid. For example, although my mother's friend felt passionately about the truth of her definition, my very existence contradicted it: I was not a Marxist, an atheist, a lesbian, or a witch.[1] More importantly, I had already read a fairly extensive collection of feminist literature and thought, and her definition just didn't match up with the thinkers with whom I was familiar, and who self-identified as feminists.

But this exchange doesn't address the big question: Just what IS a feminist? More precisely, what is feminism? Our ability to examine critically the claims and insights of feminism is directly related to our understanding of what it is; before we explore it in depth, we have to know what we're dealing with. We should try, therefore, to adopt a definition of feminism that does not presume to know whether feminist politics or analyses are themselves correct or incorrect; we should also endeavor to work with a definition that accurately describes at least a large proportion of those who self-identify as feminists.[2] As you will see shortly, such a definition may at first appear to be difficult to determine, since there are many different types of feminisms, some of which disagree with each other in significant ways. Yet I believe there is a rather simple, objective, and inclusive definition that accurately describes what a feminist is. Here it is:

A feminist is a person who believes the following:

- that women are systematically disadvantaged;
- that such systematic disadvantaging is unjust; and
- that the social context should be transformed so that the systematic disadvantaging is no longer functioning.

There are a few things that are particularly interesting about this definition. First, it does not include any reference to the gender of a potential feminist. Clearly, both men and women could adopt the term as so defined without contradiction.[3] Second, the definition does not indicate precisely how any particular feminist understands or analyzes the disadvantages imposed upon women. In fact, different feminists describe those disadvantages in importantly different ways—which means that their strategies regarding the eradication of gender hierarchies and injustices will also be significantly distinct. Probably the single most destructive misunderstanding surrounding feminism is that it is monolithic; that is to say, that there is "one" feminist way of looking at things, "one" feminist way of describing reality, "one" feminist set of politics. Nothing could be further from the truth. Beyond some generally shared principles, feminists differ greatly.

This definition does not demand that a feminist hold specific beliefs on specific political issues. Despite the portrayal of feminism provided by the dominant mass media, there is no one feminist agenda. Some feminists think we should work toward including more women in existing political structures; others think we should put our time and energy into creating entirely new political structures. Some think we should adopt an ideal of androgyny (that is, that we should aspire to be gender-neutral in our appearance, family roles, etc.), while others argue that we should honor and celebrate some sex-specific abilities and traits. Marxist feminists (and yes, some feminists are Marxists, just not all of them) emphasize structural economic inequities; ecofeminists are concerned with the ways in which our attitudes toward women are connected to our attitudes toward nature and wilderness; and feminist legal theorists explore law as the site of both the liberation and oppression of women.

Yet all of these perspectives are concerned with the matters listed in the definition above: that women are systematically disadvantaged, and they should not be so. It is worth mentioning that the disadvantages that women face are not always obvious or consciously perceived. Indeed, in countries (such as the United States) marked by relative economic privilege and, at least compared to some other countries, by relatively few explicitly sexist laws, the ways in which women are—by custom—rendered unequal to men sometimes need to be pointed out in order for us to realize just how ubiquitous they are. Take, for example, the differences in the way male and female bodies are represented in the visual culture of the United States. There's no law stating that women's bodies must be portrayed as more highly sexualized than men's; or that men should be almost always represented as *doing* something, while women are almost always represented as merely *appearing*; or that women's sexuality needs to be represented as passive, or threatening, or more central to women's identities than men's. Yet these patterns are so absolutely pervasive that many of us tend not to notice them. They both reflect and deepen social norms that damage women's capacities for equal recognition, personally and politically. Other disadvantages abound in the United States: women are disproportionately subject to the possibility of sexual violence, for example, and in many careers remain less well paid than their male counterparts. Obviously, the kinds of disadvantages that women face differ among different cultures; the point I am making here is that the recognition of those disadvantages is a hallmark of feminist thought.

But recognizing those disadvantages is not sufficient. Feminists as a group want to understand their origins, their functions, and their ramifications. Primarily, they want to understand them so that they know how to combat them. At the foundation of feminism, then, is an emphasis on activism. The knowledge that feminism produces is charged with a very specific task: it must help to stop gender inequality. It must help us make the world a better place—assuming that by "better" we mean "more just."

Now some caution is in order here: while this definition is pretty strongly inclusive, it's not without its own history and origin. Although I'm certainly interested in the ways in which feminism has been expressed globally, and the effects that feminist politics has had on women's lives on every continent, my experience of feminism is distinctly grounded in Western culture and ideas. My philosophical and political legacy is marked by such women as Mary Wollstonecraft (who demanded that the emerging humanists in the eighteenth century recognize that women were also persons), Susan B. Anthony (one of the great suffragists of the late nineteenth century, who didn't live long enough to see women in the United States get the vote), and Sojourner Truth (an abolitionist and women's rights activist in the nineteenth century, whose famous speech "Ain't I a Woman?" challenged the racist definition of femininity as weakness and passivity). By the time my feminist consciousness was developing, the so-called Second Wave of U.S. feminism, which challenged the exclusion of women from a variety of public institutions (such as education and business) as well as the oppression they faced in private institutions (such as the family), had waned. Its successes—which are too often ignored and underestimated—provided me with extensive career options, the very real possibility of economic independence, and most importantly, the capacity to think critically about the meanings of gender, sex, and sexuality. However, the successes of the Second Wave of feminism didn't apply equally to all women in the United States, and the opportunities open to me also had much to do with my socioeconomic position (upper class) and race (white). The point I'm making here, though, is that my own engagement with feminist thought and politics was, and is, deeply affected by my cultural situation. What I'm presenting to you here, then, is not a view from nowhere, but an introduction to feminist concepts from a particular cultural, historical, and political perspective.

The Conceptual Tools of Feminism and Global Studies

What does feminism have to do with our understanding of the world as it is today?

Perhaps most basically, feminism can be utilized as a set of analytical tools to discover and interpret basic elements of our global reality. As you've probably realized by now, understanding any given situation or phenomenon in a deep way does not amount to merely gathering nuggets of information. Understanding is a process of organizing information into meaning, which entails articulating relationships among ideas, facts, theories, even emotions.

In this process of understanding, the central questions and concerns of feminism have a dual role. First, they aid in illuminating realities and phenomena that might otherwise be ignored or missed. If one is not concerned about gender inequality, for example, one might not think to wonder why the legislative bodies of a given country are disproportionately populated by men. Indeed, without a sensitivity to gender issues, one might not even *notice* the discrepancy. Second, feminist concepts can serve to explain and problematize those inequalities in rich and profound ways. The lack of women in politics, for example, might be explained away in a superficial fashion with the claim that women just don't like politics. Feminist thinkers would hardly be satisfied with such a vague and difficult-to-prove point. (What, after all, is meant by "women"? All women? Some women? Some women under certain conditions? And what is meant by "like"? Are preferences hard-wired and innate, or are they developed and nurtured, often in conjunction with gender identity?) Instead, a feminist analysis would require deeper, more substantial questions, such as: What kinds of barriers might women in politics face? How do family structures relate to political structures? How do understandings about authority, work, money, and identity intersect with understandings of gender roles?

Note that the feminist questions tend toward the *structural*: they aim to clarify how systematic patterns—those ways of doing things that are so familiar as to be invisible—produce certain outcomes and phenomena. Holding those patterns up to critical examination is the first step in developing the capacity to change them, and thus to change the realities that they produce. Being a responsible global citizen demands precisely this set of skills: the ability to discover and integrate new knowledge, and then to utilize that newfound understanding to effect positive change. The conceptual tools of feminism are crucial to developing those skills.

Collectively, these tools serve to clarify the ways in which women are disadvantaged. They allow us to see, for example, that women have less economic and political power than men, or that they are more subject to certain kinds of violence, or that they are socially devalued by being persistently defined primarily by their sexuality and appearance. These tools also help us to develop strategies to undo those disadvantages.[4] Once you understand some basic conceptual moves that are at the core of feminist thinking, questions that were once unthinkable become opportunities to achieve deeper understanding.

So this discussion will start off with some brief explanations of those basic concepts. Once those are explained and clarified, we will hold them to the test, by applying them to specific global topics to see how they illuminate complex matters in interesting, and intellectually valuable, ways.

The Social Construction of Gender

One of the most fundamental insights that characterizes feminist analysis is the distinction between sex and gender.[5] This conceptual tool questions the degree to which certain traits or characteristics of women are either natural or universal. Feminist thinkers argue that while there do exist certain biological differences between men and women, differences that persist across cultures and societies (differences that constitute the category of *sex*), the typical behaviors and norms that translate into gender roles are culturally specific (and constitute the category of *gender*). "Sex" is dictated by the universal and politically innocent mandates of biology, while "gender" is formed wholly by particular societies, and is widely varied.

For example, that males have testicles and women have ovaries are examples of sex: biological distinctions that we would expect to discover without variation among all human cultures.[6] In contrast, social arrangements concerning childrearing are extremely varied, and while we may see some strong trends across societies, such that women are often (but not always) expected to do the majority of the childrearing, it is crucially important that there is no *biological necessity* to these types of arrangements. Think about the example of breastfeeding, which is often touted as evidence that women are "naturally" nurturing. Of course, in many cultures, breastfeeding is wholly optional and not necessary at all, although there is much scientific evidence that it affords significant health benefits to mothers and infants alike. But even in those cultures where, due to economic circumstances, breastfeeding represents the best or only chance for infant survival, it does not follow that women necessarily must undertake other forms of childrearing. It's fairly easy to imagine a situation where the male primary caretaker simply brings the infant to the mother as needed, and then takes on all other caretaking duties.

Our expectations regarding masculine and feminine roles and behaviors are strongly formed by our cultural context, and despite the fact that our culture often tells us that it is "natural" for men and women to behave in certain ways, research in sociology and anthropology belies this claim. (Check out Chapter Two of this book, "The Joy of Culture," for more on this point). Moreover, gender norms change within a given society: in eighteenth-century Europe, it was common for men to wear wigs, makeup, tights, and high-heeled shoes, clothing that we now associate exclusively with feminine gender roles.

The sex/gender distinction proved to be crucial to Western feminist thought and political action. Because gender is not natural, it is subject to change. In contemporary United States culture, childrearing duties fall largely to women; but now, as we deploy our understanding of gender as socially constructed, we can see that in fact men are perfectly capable of tending to children of all ages. (Indeed, thanks to the miracle of the breast pump, they can even feed infants breast milk!) By distinguishing between sex and gender, feminist thinkers are able to analyze gender roles as telling indications of what a culture believes women and men are (and should be). Most importantly, feminist thinkers explore the effects that these socially-imposed gender roles and norms have on the social equality (or lack thereof) between the sexes; we can wonder, for example, how the disproportionate amount of child-rearing labor that women perform relates to their economic status.[7]

Gender and Other Social Factors

Sex and gender are not the only categories that are relevant in feminist thought. As feminism has progressed, the connections among gender hierarchies and other systems of inequality have become increasingly clear, such that it is now an accepted truism that it is impossible to study gender differentials in isolation from other forms of inequality. This has been a difficult lesson for many feminist thinkers and activists, particularly those whose experience is grounded in privilege related to their economic status, sexual orientation, or race. In the context of United States feminism, for example, white feminists in particular have been consistently criticized by women of color on at least two grounds. First, feminist organizations themselves have, at times, not only not challenged but actually perpetuated other forms of injustice, such as racism, classism, and homophobia. (Betty Friedan's attempt to keep lesbians out of the National Organization of Women in 1969 stands as a classic example.) Second, feminist movements have often failed to recognize the significantly different challenges faced by women who do not fit the white, heterosexual, middle- or upper-middle-class norm.

A particular case illustrates the latter point. In the 1970s, the mostly white feminist movement articulated birth control as a fundamental means to women's autonomy. The right to choose whether to become pregnant—and to terminate pregnancies should they so desire—was a primary political goal. Feminists argued that women had the right not to be pregnant, and that only an individual woman herself had the moral authority to determine whether her own pregnancy should continue. Thus the focus was explicitly on women's right *not* to reproduce, that is, on their right not to be forced to reproduce against their will. Yet, as Angela Y. Davis (1981) wrote, the right not to reproduce was not one that resonated in the same way with women of color as it did with white women. Davis argued that historical and contemporary racism had often resulted in robbing women of color of the right *to* reproduce; forced sterilizations of the poor and high infant mortality rates among African-American women were (and are) primary examples. Moreover, the history of the birth control movement, which significantly preceded 1970s feminist activism, was sometimes directly or indirectly implicated in political attempts to limit the reproductive activity of "undesirable" elements of society—elements often targeted because of their race.

In other words, the shape of the reproductive freedom question for women was directly related to racial inequity (another example of crucial variations that can occur within cultures). Of course, despite the racial and economic differences among women, there is still an underlying dispute here, namely, that of control: the right of women to control their own reproductive activity, whether that consisted of limiting their pregnancies or being free to embark on pregnancies at will. Yet without a significant sensitivity to racial inequalities on the part of the mostly white, mostly economically advantaged women leading the political movement of women's liberation, the experiences of women of color were ignored and repressed—tragically, and perhaps paradoxically, just as experiences of women as a whole had been ignored and repressed in the past.

Other social factors such as sexual orientation and economic class shape what may be labeled as feminist concerns. The right of "career" women to work hardly resonated with working class women, who had always worked; the need to equalize marriage laws did not necessarily speak to lesbian women, who were (until very recently, in a few states) automatically excluded from the institution of marriage. Thus, contemporary feminism often attempts (perhaps, as some say, with limited success) to frame its analysis with an understanding of the complex interplay among several social factors, rather than focusing on gender inequality as an isolated phenomenon.

The Male Generic

Perhaps one of the most well-known aspects of feminist activism relates to a heightened awareness of language and its role in structuring our world. Although such awareness is often dismissed as oversensitive "political correctness," in fact the feminist emphasis on the power and politics of language is supported by a significant amount of scholarship. Most contemporary scholars agree that the ways in which language is used and changed are reflective of current political structures, and while not all are as concerned as feminists are with the ways in which language intersects with gender and sexism, few would argue that the words we choose to describe our reality are irrelevant.

Common usage in English includes the use of the word "man" or "mankind" to refer to the entire human species, as in Mark Twain's famous remark, "Mankind is the only Animal that Blushes. Or Needs to." Such usage is an example of the male generic; Twain's comment is clearly meant to be a statement about all human beings, not just men; and so "mankind" can stand for "men and women." But there is an obvious inequality here, because "womankind" could never—in most cultures—stand for "women and men." What this distinction means is that the category of "man" is large enough to hold a multiplicity of genders, while the category of "woman" is far smaller, and can only hold one gender. This inequality makes sense only if men are understood as *representative* of the human race: they are the "normal" kinds of humans, the "typical" form of the human. In other words, they can be conceived as *generic* (i.e., gender-neutral) humans, as "just people," whose gender is relatively unimportant. Women, by contrast, can never escape their sex, or their gender. They are always particularly female.[8]

The male generic can also take some other, more subtle forms. When we don't know the sex of a person, for example, we tend to refer to that person as male (as in, "if a lawyer wanted to make a motion, he should indicate that desire to the judge"). Some job titles have non-gendered forms that can refer to men or women (such as the word "actor"), whereas their gendered form refers expressly to women who do the same job ("actress"). While the allegedly gender-neutral form can be used to refer to both genders, the gender-specific form is always used for women alone. Thus a group of men and women who act are referred to as "actors" but never "actresses"—in fact, under no circumstances would one refer to a male actor as an "actress."[9]

The philosophical and political problems with the male generic are in some ways fairly simple. The fact of the matter is that women, simply put, are not men. To claim that it is appropriate to refer to a group by using a term that, properly speaking, only describes half of that group, is to make the implicit claim that the named half is more normal, more charac-teristic, or more important than the non-named half. Thus men are linguistically established as the "real" humans, the "normal" humans, the humans who most clearly represent human-ity itself. Women are linguistically established as the Other. In analyzing the male generic, feminism insists that one's sex is just as relevant to a male person as it is to a female person; that using a male standard of being (such that male behavior is the norm for all human beings) inevitably guarantees that female behavior will be constructed as inferior; and that changing our language to reflect a more just parity between the sexes is an important step in constructing that parity.

It's also important to realize that the male generic functions at levels other than the lin-guistic. For years, research on heart disease focused almost solely on men, and simply assumed that what was true about male bodies with regard to heart disease would be simi-larly true for female bodies. It thus took years for researchers to realize that the symptoms of a heart attack were significantly different for women than they were for men. Before that realization was made, women received significantly inaccurate information about how to recognize the occurrence of a heart attack.[10] The male generic is not only unfair; sometimes, it's downright dangerous.

The Devaluing of the Feminine

One of the results of the male generic is the assumption that what men have traditionally done and been constitutes the height of human achievement. Western history books are replete with stories of men fighting, politicking, and inventing. Rarely do those same books delve into the everyday, and not so everyday, accomplishments of women. One of the main goals of feminist scholarship is to assert that women's activities have not only historical, but also political, social, and philosophical relevance. Note that when feminists turn their atten-tion to the more traditional feminine activities (as they do when they argue that quilting, for example, is a form of art), they are not necessarily claiming that women are not qualified or able to perform those activities traditionally reserved to men. To claim that childrearing is a complicated, socially important skill is not to claim that only women can or should do it. Rather, it is to claim that what women have traditionally done has social importance that has been historically denied. Similarly, when Alice Walker (1984) goes in search of her mothers' gardens—artistic endeavors which expressed the deep creativity and spirituality of her ances-tors, even as they were living under the enormously oppressive systems of slavery and Jim Crow—she is not claiming that black women cannot do the more traditionally accepted forms of art that fill our museums. Rather, she is stating that, even when definitions of art excluded the work of black women, still, black women were artists.

Sometimes the devaluing of the feminine takes the form of the suppression of work that women have done because that work was perceived as inappropriate to their gender. Feminist scholars have therefore gone in search of women writers, artists, and thinkers whose work has been systematically suppressed. Recently, feminist philosophers have begun to uncover the significant amount of philosophical work produced by women in the nineteenth century.[11] Alice Walker herself almost single-handedly rescued the work of Zora Neale Hurston, one of the most important figures in the Harlem Renaissance, from obscurity.

In seeking to counteract the devaluing of the feminine, feminists take as their general assumption the principle that women, despite their absence in traditionally recognized canons of knowledge, have shaped our world in strikingly important ways. Feminists, therefore, take an interest not only in what women have traditionally done, but also in the ways in which women have struggled against the constraints of their gender roles. Where women's experiences and even their bodies have been maligned, feminists seek to introduce a celebratory and triumphant note. An excellent example of this desire to celebrate rather than denigrate feminine aspects of being is Natalie Angier's *Woman: An Intimate Geography* (2000), a virtual paean to the wonders of the female body. Works such as this speak to the feminist desire to define women not only as victims of patriarchal politics and discourse, but also as strong, vibrant, challenging figures who have much to teach us, should we choose to seek them out.

Deploying Feminism's Conceptual Tools Around the World: Some Examples

Okay, so now we have some tools under our belt. We're aware that much of our gendered behavior is dictated by culture rather than biology; that gender as a social and cultural factor is deeply intertwined with other factors such as sexual orientation, race, physical ability, age, and socioeconomic status; that women are considered to be more "marked" than men are by their gender, since men have the possibility of being, and being perceived as, simply human; and that the lived experiences and achievements of women are often ignored or suppressed in favor of those of men. How can these insights inform our understandings of global phenomena?

Before we jump into some examples, it's worth noting that feminist inquiry is not always a simple or obvious means of exploring societal issues. In fact, quite the opposite is true. Recognizing the role that gender plays in any given global phenomenon usually serves to render that phenomenon more complicated than it would appear if we simply ignored gender. Moreover, because gender is such a culturally specific factor, any phenomenon related to it cannot be explored outside of a specific cultural context. That means that it's rarely possible to describe any given practice or behavior as inherently or absolutely sexist. Similar practices or behaviors can have quite different meanings when they take place in different social and historical contexts. Looking through a feminist lens does not, and should not, mean jumping to conclusions and judgments about the practices and beliefs of different cultures. Rather, it should slow us down by encouraging us to look more deeply into the systems of meanings that surround gender inequities. What we are after here are not simple answers, but richer understandings of complex phenomena—and, specifically, how gender plays a role in creating the meanings of those phenomena. Things which seem unrelated or insignificant may turn out to be what feminist critics call "gendered" phenomena. In other words, a fuller understanding of them can only be achieved by relating them to their culture's constructions of maleness and femaleness. The examples below show how feminist analysis can achieve precisely these analytical and interpretive goals.

Example 1: Female Genital Cutting (FGC). Our first example demonstrates both the efficacy and the complexity of feminist approaches. It utilizes three of the conceptual tools described above: the notion of gender as socially constructed, the need to understand gender as related to other factors, and the need to highlight the experiences of women.

Female genital cutting (sometimes called "female genital mutilation" or "female circumcision") is prevalent in certain African cultures, particularly (but not only) in Islamic ones. It takes a variety of forms, ranging from the removal of the prepuce of the clitoris, to the wholesale excising of the clitoris (clitoridectomy), to an excision of the clitoris, the labia majora and the labia minora, plus the sewing up of the vagina (infibulation). Procedures are often performed on pubescent or pre-pubescent girls, sometimes with unsanitary instruments, and often impose significant suffering: "Common complications from female genital cutting include shock, bleeding, infection, and—for infibulation—delayed problems such as menstrual pain, urinary tract infections, painful intercourse, and difficulties in childbirth. On rare occasions, complications arising from FGC can even result in death" (Boyle, Songora, & Foss, 2001, p. 526).

The first job of feminist scholarship with regard to FGC has been to bring the very fact of its existence to a scholarly light: to discover an element of women's experience that had until that point been unknown, and to name it as a violation of women's rights. Of course, feminist analysis does not stop there; as both global citizens and scholars, we have a responsibility to delve into the meanings of this phenomenon. But it is here that things get complicated.

On the one hand, a feminist analysis of FGC would almost certainly interpret the practice as a social institution grounded in the belief in women's inferiority, and in particular, in a belief that women's sexuality is dangerous and in need of control. In this case, the social construction of women—particularly beliefs about women's proper sexual roles—results in a painful transformation of women's very bodies. The imposition of FGC often means that sexual interactions will hold no pleasure for women; therefore, sexuality becomes wholly oriented around the twin axes of male pleasure and procreation. Women become merely vessels, and wounded, mutilated vessels at that. From this perspective, FGC seems, at least ethically, a relatively simple matter. Pratibha Parmar therefore insists that cultural relativism is not a sufficient response to it: "This reluctance to *interfere with other cultures* leaves African children at risk of mutilation. If we do not speak out, we collude in the perpetuation of this violence" (Walker & Parmar, 1993, p. 95).

Yet even FGC retains some ambiguity and provokes ambivalent reactions among different groups of people. Or, more to the point, while the ethics of the practice may seem obvious, its cultural meanings are not. They are complicated by, among other factors, the fact that the practice is often supported by the women of the culture in question (see Yount, 2002, pp. 338–339). Such support comes in a variety of forms: mothers insist that the procedure is done on their daughters; the individuals who actually perform the procedure are often women; and there are even examples of adult women voluntarily choosing to have the procedure. Just as (some) women in Western society can be among the strongest proponents of sexism, so too do (some) women in these African cultures genuinely hold that the practice is moral, sometimes religiously dictated, beneficial to the young girl (in terms of her social status and marriage prospects), and overall a positive element of their culture.

It is worth noting here that the existence of patriarchal societies that include women who are committed to perpetuating practices that harm women should not, ultimately, surprise us: no matter how deep the oppression of women is in a culture, it is *part* of that culture, and women are themselves embedded in it. The social construction of gender is deep, intense, and central to individuals' identities. Moreover, given the depth of social construction, it is often difficult to distinguish between enculturation and individual choice or desire. After all, part of the effect of culture is to engender certain kinds of desires and preferences. Finally—particularly in cultures that ostensibly champion individualism and autonomy—few of us want to believe that we are being coerced into certain practices or into complying with certain norms. Instead, we insist that our behaviors are solely reducible to our own independent decision making. So women in Western culture develop a taste for painful shoes, constricting clothing, and dieting practices that are often health threatening; women in cultures where FGC is practiced believe women's genitalia to be ugly, unclean, and worthy of excision.[12] They no more hesitate to take a knife to their daughters' genitals than many parents in the United States hesitate to circumcise their male infants (a wound that, while certainly less damaging than some forms of FGC, is nonetheless medically unnecessary) or offer breast enhancement surgery to their daughters as a high-school graduation present.

Because feminism holds that women's voices and experiences are important to understanding any cultural phenomenon, such perspectives cannot be dismissed. Nor, as even my brief discussion above seems to imply, should they be automatically considered as examples of false consciousness. That is, one should not automatically assume that women's support of such a practice is utterly reducible to their acceptance of patriarchal or misogynist values; it may well have other sources and meanings. This does not mean that a feminist must agree to condone such a practice on the basis that some women in those cultures support it. However, it does mean that any feminist analysis must be able to take their perspectives into account and address them. Thus, when feminists Alice Walker and Pratibha Parmar (1993) set out to explore FGC in several African countries, they insisted on interviewing at length women who both commit and have undergone FGC. Understanding how these women understand the practice is crucial to understanding the practice itself.

Gender is not the only cultural force at work here; political and historical features further complicate the meaning and value of FGC. The history of anti-FGC legislation in Egypt illustrates this point. Since the 1970s, the Egyptian government experienced significant international pressure to take action against FGC, while simultaneously faced with internal acceptance of it. The conflict came to a head in 1994, when CNN broadcast a video of a 10-year-old girl undergoing FGC:

> Swept up in the international uproar, but still immersed in a national culture that generally supported female genital cutting, the Egyptian government floundered. The state's immediate response to the international attention was to arrest the freelance television producer who arranged the filming for damaging Egypt's reputation ... When this action met with more international criticism, Egypt released the producer, arrested the circumcisor, and pledged to pass a law banning female genital cutting. (Boyle et al., 2001, p. 532)

Islamic clerics condemned such a law, and a compromise was reached: the practice would be allowed, but only if performed in hospitals—a position that, obviously, enraged opponents of FGC. After a series of lawsuits and reports, the government finally moved to outlaw the practice altogether; however, in doing so, they attempted as much as possible to "distance themselves from international actors" (Boyle et al., 2001, 533), so as to counter the common perception that "attempts to eradicate female genital cutting are part of a Western conspiracy to undermine Egyptian culture" (Boyle et al., 2001, 533).

This Egyptian example demonstrates how gendered phenomena can be intertwined with other factors, in this case, political and historical contexts. International efforts to eradicate the practice of FGC were not experienced primarily by some members of Egyptian society as attempts to improve the quality of life of women; instead, they were interpreted as yet more evidence of Western arrogance and ethnocentrism. Indeed, given the long history of cultural imperialism experienced by African countries at the hands of colonial nations, such interpretations are understandable and coherent. Thus, in order to face the phenomenon of FGC honestly and effectively, we must recognize the political forces which have historically marked Western relationships with these countries.

Such a recognition does not mitigate or diminish the clearly anti-woman nature of the practice. Indeed, feminist scholarship has clearly shown that FGC is embedded in a set of cultural norms, beliefs, and practices, most (but not all) of which refer directly to women's inferiority. Should we choose to act to change this practice, we must base our arguments against it in a context of an understanding of these norms and beliefs. Moreover, particular solutions must be framed with the individual culture in mind; as M. Mazharul Islam and M. Mosleh Uddin remark, "As female circumcision is a deeply rooted tradition in Sudan, it cannot be eradicated unless the deeply felt beliefs of those who practice it are well understood and a culturally acceptable policy is adopted" (Islam & Uddin, 2001, p. 75).

Given the broad extent of the questions and controversies associated with FGC, success in its eradication may seem somewhat hopeless. Fortunately, we have some examples that contradict such a conclusion. Peter Easton, Karen Monkman, and Rebecca Miles described in detail the process by which a Senegalese village, Malicounda-Bambara, undertook to effect the complete eradication of FGC in their community. The authors note three elements of the success of that undertaking:

> First, the approach was *collective*. It explicitly recognized that families cannot abandon a deep-rooted cultural practice if there is no collective will to change the incentive structures and at least some of the objective conditions that hold it in place.... Second, the strategy adopted was grounded in the *local context* and evoked some of the strongest values and practices of ambient culture—parental love, Koranic piety—to challenge other practices. It came across more as a movement for internal consistency and liberation than as an outside condemnation.... Third, the tactic was *empowering*—that is, while rooted in personal testimony and the transmission of new information, it left resolution and action up to the initiative of each community and its members. It cast the problem of FGC in the larger frame of women's health and human rights—topics of importance to men too. (Easton et al., 2003, p. 451)

Grounded in local and social practices and norms, led by both religious leaders and women intimately familiar with FGC (including the cutters themselves), this movement resulted in thirteen villages agreeing to entirely oppose the practice.

A final word before moving on to our next example. Note that exploring a gendered phenomenon in a culture different from one's own often results in a greater awareness of the role that gender plays in one's own culture. Too often, issues such as FGC are discussed, in both scholarly and political contexts, in a way that implies that the cultures within which they occur are hopelessly backward and primitive in their approaches to women, sexuality, and bodies—and that, by contrast, industrialized and developed countries, such as the United States, are admirably free from such horrific instances of sexism and misogyny. Beware of such (often unconscious) associations. One need only look at the statistics concerning sexual violence to recognize that, daily, in the United States, women's bodies are very much placed at risk.[13]

Example 2: Agriculture. If FGC appears, rather obviously, to be a "women's issue," the practice of agriculture and other forms of food production and management seem far less so. After all, everyone needs to eat, and hunger affects people similarly, whether they are men or women. How can agriculture possibly be understood as a gendered phenomenon?

It's helpful to remember that food is always a central element to any human culture. How food is produced, prepared, served, consumed: these are often highly ritualized and important cultural features. Moreover, they are often persistently gendered, because they are related to that particular culture's construction of maleness and femaleness. In many cultures, gender dictates not only who produces the food, but who prepares it (and how—in contemporary U.S. culture, for example, grilling outside has become a distinctly masculine enterprise). Gender can even shape the order in which food is consumed; in some cultures, for example, the men have their fill before the women have a chance to eat. In others, men and women are forbidden from eating together.

Agriculture—part of a culture's economic institution—is a widespread form of food production, and cultures differ widely in the ways they organize and practice it. Often, however, the labor that is associated with agriculture is distinctly gendered; thus, in an excellent example of the social construction of gender, masculinity becomes associated with certain tasks (plowing, perhaps), and femininity becomes associated with other tasks (harvesting, for example). Barun Gurung and Prem Gurung describe the gendered organization of work among the Kirats of Eastern Nepal:

> Seed management is an important agricultural activity that is considered indoor work. In the traditional scheme of the Kirats, the role of women in managing household seed systems is perceived as synonymous with feminine fertility and, as a result, is classified within the domestic space of the household.
>
> Kirati women play a key role in local seed systems, particularly seed storage, one of the least visible postharvest activities that includes grain storage, food processing, and food preparation. As grains or other crops come in from the fields, women decide what will be stored, processed, and saved for next year's crops. In making these decisions, women concentrate on providing adequate and nutritious food for their families throughout the year. They must

consider factors such as taste and the texture of the food, depending on the meals that will be prepared and whether the food will be fed to children, adults, older people, or particular animals. These decisions are based on considerations that take account of the multiple uses of crops. (Gurung & Gurung, 2002, pp. 241–242)

As the Kirati often experience significant food shortages, it is not difficult to imagine the social importance of this distinctly feminine set of roles and knowledge.

How does understanding the gendered nature of agriculture affect our understanding of it as a global phenomenon? First, let's consider some common trends and movements in global agricultural practice. Of concern to many scholars and activists is the trend toward monoculture, that is, the practice of growing only one crop over a large area of land. When the global demand for a certain crop—say, corn—grows significantly, so does the possibility of replacing varied crops with just one. Another controversy regarding global agriculture is the increased use of genetically modified (GM) crops, that is, crops resulting from seeds that have been genetically altered to resist disease or increase crop health and yield. Both monoculture and the use of genetically modified crops almost always conflict with indigenous methods of farming, and as such, the newer ways often represent the methods (and the economic needs) of industrialized rather than developing countries.

How does agriculture as a site of cultural conflict affect women's lives? Vandana Shiva argues that the logic of industrialized countries concerning agriculture—a logic that values homogeneity, predictability, and a very particular understanding of biology—is inherently opposed to women's ways of working with and on the land. Drawing particularly on examples from India, Shiva marks a stark contrast between the industrial emphasis on homogeneity and the logic of diversity often underlying indigenous women's practices:

> The recent concern with biodiversity at the global level has grown as the result of the erosion of diversity due to the expansion of large-scale monoculture-based production in agriculture and the vulnerability associated with it. However, the fragmentation of farming systems which was linked to the spread of monocultures continues to be the guiding paradigm for biodiversity conservation. Each element of the farm ecosystem is viewed in isolation, and conservation of diversity is seen as an arithmetic exercise of collecting variety.
>
> In contrast, biodiversity in the traditional Indian setting is a relational category in which each element gets its characteristics and value through its relationships with other elements. Biodiversity is ecologically and culturally embedded.... Women have been the selectors and custodians of seed. When they conserve seed, they conserve diversity; and when they conserve diversity, they conserve a balance and harmony. (Shiva, 2008, p. 439)

Shiva argues that the failure on the part of industrialized countries to both recognize and honor women's role in indigenous farming practices can change native gender roles and damage women's status:

> Women's work and knowledge is central to biodiversity conservation and utilization because women work between 'sectors' and perform multiple tasks. Women have remained invisible as

farmers in spite of their contribution to farming, as people fail to see their work in agriculture. Their production tends not to be recorded by economists as 'work' or as 'production' because it falls outside the so-called production boundary. (Shiva, 2008, p. 438)

Women are thus written out of the story of agriculture, and in their absence, their particular knowledge and insight are lost. With that loss comes suffering, particularly to communities whose very existence depends on the biodiversity that goes unrecognized by what Shiva terms "the patriarchal model of progress" (Shiva, 2008, p. 437). "This push toward uniformity … undermines the diversity of biological systems which form the production system. It also undermines the livelihoods of the people whose work is associated with diverse and multiple-use systems of forestry, agriculture, and animal husbandry" (Shiva, 2008, p. 437).

Let me gesture here also, in an exploratory fashion, to another possible consequence, one not explored directly by Shiva in her work. Remember the knowledge of the Kirati women, and the importance of that knowledge for the survival of the community. Isn't it likely that a significant degree of women's social power—the respect with which their voices are met, their ability to weigh in on matters of consequence—is related to their knowledge of seeds? In other words, their knowledge may be directly related to their social status, such that to ignore that knowledge—or to adopt practices that no longer render that knowledge necessary or useful—could seriously undermine women's social position. And indeed, the use of genetically modified crops (whose seeds are often sterile, thus making it impossible to save them for use in the next season) may have precisely that diminishing effect on women. In this way, changes in agricultural practice would not only lead to changes in the cultural infrastructure; they would also potentially render women more powerless and less honored. Such a possibility demands closer exploration and analysis, as a loss of social worth and respect could directly harm women (for example, exposing them to increased violence, or marginalizing them from community decision making).

Scholars have increasingly taken on the task of understanding the value of traditional ecological knowledge—that is, knowledge produced and reproduced within indigenous cultures—and its ability to manage ecosystems effectively (see Turner, Ignace, & Ignace, 2000; Berkes, Colding, & Folke, 2000). This is surely to the good; the environmental damage that has been imposed by monoculture and other forms of agriculture associated with industrialized countries is too large to ignore, and there seems hardly any doubt that new ways of understanding human interaction with land, water, and air are desperately needed. Yet it must not be forgotten that the knowledge most likely to be missed or undermined or even eradicated is that associated with women—and that utilizing feminist modes of analysis can correct for such a bias.

Example 3: HIV/AIDS. The HIV/AIDS epidemic that is faced by developing countries, particularly those on the continent of Africa, has been met with a fair amount of media attention, if not an adequate quantity of medical and financial resources. While efforts to make antiretroviral drugs available to the staggering number of people who need them continue (check out the Web site of the World Health Organization for more details: www.who.int), the need for preventive methods is also clear. AIDS is, after all, eminently preventable, particularly by the consistent use of condoms. And so all sorts of organizations, from NGOs to governments, have launched PR campaigns to encourage the use of condoms. And indeed, given the success rate of condom use to dramatically reduce the spread of HIV/AIDS, one can hardly argue with such campaigns.

However, such campaigns have sometimes been slow to recognize the ways in which gender inequality and sexual norms are related to both the use of condoms and the spread of AIDS (see Aniekwu, 2002). In a subtle way, such a failure of recognition is an example of the male generic. In encouraging condom use, such organizations have sometimes assumed that all sexually active persons in a particular culture are equally empowered to set the terms of any given sexual encounter; they have also, perhaps, assumed that the possibility of multiple partners is equally high among all persons, and that HIV/AIDS is primarily a disease of individuals with multiple partners. If both of these assumptions were true, than a relatively gender-neutral campaign encouraging condom use would make sense.

In fact, however, both of these assumptions often refer more accurately to *men* than to all people. In other words, the allegedly gender-neutral language masks a distinctly gendered set of experiences. In many developing countries, women are not in fact equally empowered when it comes to individual sexual encounters. Indeed, one might wonder if women are so equally empowered in virtually any country on the planet; nor is promiscuity a gender-neutral phenomenon. Take, for example, the country of Nigeria:

> Women now account for 42% of people living with HIV. This increase in the number of HIV positive women reflects their greater biological vulnerability to the disease. It is also a consequence of the social constructions of female and male sexuality as well as the profound inequalities that continue to characterize many heterosexual relationships in Nigeria. Many women find the heterosexual relationship a difficult one to negotiate as strategy for their own safety. Generally, and culturally, sex continues to be defined primarily in terms of male desire with women being the relatively passive recipients of male passions. Under these circumstances, women often do not articulate their own needs and desires and their own pleasure may be of little concern. Even in marriage most women cannot assert their wish for safer sex, for their partner's fidelity, or for no sex at all. As a result their health and invariably that of others are put at grave risk. It is estimated that in parts of Africa 60–80% of women infected with HIV have only had one sexual partner. Though partner change increases risk, most HIV positive women would have been infected through their male spouse or regular partner. (Aniekwu, 2002, p. 32)

In this particular culture, then, wives are expected to be sexually submissive to their husbands; husbands (but definitely not wives) are expected to be promiscuous; and for a wife to insist on the use of a condom would be inappropriate in the extreme.[14] Indeed, even raising the issue—even demonstrating that one knows the meaning of certain words—can constitute a challenge to existing gender norms, a challenge that can render women even more vulnerable: "In many settings, women are not supposed to be knowledgeable about sex, are expected to be passive in sexual matters, and may be less comfortable than men with discussing sexual matters, especially their own sexual satisfaction.... Women who raise the topic with their husbands may be perceived as promiscuous" (Blanc, 2001, pp. 193–194).

In other words, sex and sexuality exist within a social and political context that is already stacked against women, which means that HIV/AIDS is as much a human rights crisis as a health crisis. Women's vulnerability to HIV/AIDS is both biological—it is far easier for a woman to become infected with HIV from a man than the other way around—and cultural. To stop the increasing rate of infections, which are disproportionately experienced by women, it will be necessary to address the unequal power relations between men and women. It is all well and good to spread knowledge concerning condom use, but if sexual and marital norms preclude women from actually applying that knowledge, such that to do so could expose them to violence or social isolation, then the effort is futile.

What is needed here is an understanding of the many complicated ways in which sexuality, including the spread of sexual infections, is a gendered phenomenon. As discussed above, whether one is a man or a woman determines to an enormous degree one's risk of becoming infected as well as one's ability to take steps to prevent infections. It also determines the social ramifications of being infected or having family members who are infected. These social meanings are heavily influenced by other ways in which gender is organized within the particular society. It also becomes clear that gender cannot be separated from other cultural features, particularly economics and the related topic of class. Gender can intensify the burden of poverty, and class can exacerbate the disadvantages of gender, as the following illustration makes clear.

In Zimbabwe, traditional practices forbade women from inheriting or owning land (practices which have persisted despite laws that protect women's property rights). Such practices, combined with a tendency to blame widows for their partner's death from AIDS, have resulted in increasing numbers of women and orphans being evicted from their homes (Izumi, 2006, p. v). Similar stories come from countries such as Tanzania; in the situation described here, whether a widow has had children (particularly boy children, who are more highly valued) can also determine her fate:

> Land ... is traditionally inherited and therefore used by the same clan from one generation to the next. When a young man marries, his father divides the land and gives a portion of the land to the son, who then settles with his family. In the case where a young man dies before his parents, two things normally happen: the widow can use the land, if she has mainly male children, or the widow can be chased away if she has no male children. The children can either go with their mother or remain behind to be cared for by the grandparents. This is done so as to make sure that the plot is under the control of the husband's parents.
>
> If the woman is chased away, then she, and in some cases the orphans too, suffers due to the lack of land. When she decides to return to her own clan, she does not inherit land there either, because the land has already been divided and given to her brothers. This traditional method of land tenure results in women having no land to inherit because the family assumes that when married she will inherit her husband's estate. In cases where the woman is barren, she will be chased away outright after her husband's death, even if they bought the land together. (Katunzi, 2006, p. 64)

Thus, losing a husband to AIDS can cause a woman to be rendered homeless, a vulnerability that does not exist in the same way for men who lose wives.

Indeed, the list of factors that serve to particularize women's experiences of HIV/AIDS seems nearly endless, and can range from economic disparity to social roles to procreative pressures:

> Access to and use of services are sometimes more problematic for women because of economic constraints, restrictions on their freedom of movement, and the double jeopardy of being both a woman and HIV-positive.... Because of their traditional role as caretakers of children and others, women often bear disproportionately the physical and emotional burden of caring for persons in their households who are living with AIDS. In some countries, this problem has likely been exacerbated by reductions in government budgets for social support brought about by economic structural adjustment programs.... Finally, although many HIV-infected women in sub-Saharan Africa intend to have additional children, a partner's desires can override women's childbearing intentions even among those infected women who wish to avoid future pregnancies. (Blanc, 2001, p. 199)

When we approach HIV/AIDS in a gender-neutral way—when "man" is allowed to stand for "human," and "human" is allowed to refer, but implicitly, to the experience of only "men"—all of these particularities, which are each fundamental to any individual's experience, are lost. And, more to the point, the particular ways in which women are suffering and dying are invisible. In asking the question: "How is this experience gendered?" feminism and feminist analysis allow women's lives to show up—which is the first step to ameliorating them.

Example 4: Fill in the Blank. The examples explored above are just that, examples. They are the tip of the iceberg in terms of global difficulties facing women, and are meant merely to illustrate the kinds of analyses that feminist scholarship can produce. Your challenge, as a global citizen, is to explore other topics, including those that do not seem obviously gendered, in terms of their relation to gender and gender inequality. Here are just a few, to prime the pump:

- *Education.* In many cultures, the right to read is a distinctly masculine one, which results in literacy rates that are heavily skewed to men. Yet in the United States and most of the Western world, far more women than men are attending college. How is learning gendered? What are some far-reaching effects of expanding female literacy on a global scale? What might be the long-term effects of lower college attendance by men, in the Western world? (Here's a hint: if you're interested in reducing overpopulation and its negative effects, teach women to read.)
- *Political leadership.* What kinds of cultures tend to accept women as leaders? How do women become leaders even in those cultures suspicious of female authority? When women do achieve political authority, do they employ it in different ways than men? How does the gendered nature of power affect women's political horizons? Should democracies insist on a specific percentage of women in positions of political leadership (as the United States did in post-Saddam Hussein Iraq)?

- *Military.* How does women's participation, or lack of same, affect any given country's military? How are women's experiences of the military affected by gender norms and beliefs (both of their own culture and of the culture where they may be serving)?
- *Health care.* How are medical needs particular to women (for example, prenatal care) addressed in different cultures? How are medical institutions themselves gendered? How can international attempts to improve health care be illuminated by an understanding of gender inequality?

The list is endless—virtually any aspect of global studies can be explored with an eye toward gender. You could, in fact, view every chapter in this book through a gendered lens: colonialism, globalization, religion, environmentalism, the mass media, and so on. Doing so will help you to understand these diverse phenomena in a more detailed, nuanced way.

Conclusion

As a student of the world, you have a daunting task. You seek to learn more about the world around you and your place in it. You seek to understand dynamics and phenomena that seem hopelessly complex. I mean, really: global warming? How are we ever going to understand that one completely?

There are at least two responses to that question. The first takes the form of an answer, and it's a negative one: we're never going to understand global warming, or any other complex phenomenon, completely. We're never going to decide, once and for all, whether men and women are mostly the same or mostly different; we're never going to figure out definitively or completely how to negotiate cultural differences without causing, at the very least, discomfort and confusion; we're never going to unpack all the mysteries of the other-than-human world. Some find this point demoralizing: Why do all this work if we're not going to get anywhere? Others find it liberating; since perfection is impossible, we don't have to worry about being perfect!

The second response takes the form of a refusal, and it refuses the question itself. The point of studying global dynamics is not to come to a complete understanding, not to arrive at a definitive position, not to *solve* anything (at least not in an absolute way). The point of Global Studies is to enrich your understanding of a wondrously messy world so that you can be a more effective global citizen. And being effective does not mean coming up with the perfect idea that will render poverty, or hunger, or gender inequality, or war, obsolete. Being effective means being able to *work toward the better*. To work toward the better—the better means of providing energy, or health care, or education; the better way to interact with the natural world; the better way to view cultural difference as a resource rather than a problem—is to recognize that the world is a constantly shifting set of intricate forces. That everything is in movement means that you will never arrive at a moment when you can safely stop learning. It also means that you don't have to wait until you know everything before you take action—because that day will never come!

To work toward the better, of course, you need to understand the challenges that face the global community. You also need conceptual frameworks that will situate those challenges in relation to a multitude of complex and related factors: history, culture, and the vicissitudes of the material world (just to name a few!). Feminism is one of the frameworks you should have at your disposal. If you believe that women and men should be valued equally; if you believe that one's sex should not serve to reduce one's economic, political, or social possibilities; if you believe that the current state of gender inequality is actively causing suffering; then you have a moral responsibility to understand and ameliorate that inequality. Utilizing the conceptual tools offered by feminism will help you to recognize injustice and expand the possibilities for greater freedom for all women and men. And that sounds like a pretty good job description for a global citizen.

Notes

1. Of course, another response to such a definition could be: what's so wrong with being a Marxist, atheist, lesbian witch? In fact, although that description does not fit the majority of feminists, many feminist thinkers (including myself) do question capitalism, patriarchal systems of religion, and the dominance of heterosexuality.

2. Definitions as a whole are a far more complicated matter than I represent them to be here. Who gets to do the defining, how those definitions are placed within political contexts and dynamics of power, how one determines whether a definition is accurate, and whether definitions are ever useful are all exceedingly complex issues. While not entering into the philosophical quagmire of the problem of definitions, I merely intend to make the point here that one must be critical of the ways in which feminism is defined and represented within the larger political spectrum. In doing so, I encourage you to read feminist thinkers yourself, and base your evaluations of the worth of their thought on an in-depth analysis of it—not upon a conglomerate of commonly-held, loaded, and wrong-headed impressions. Given that feminism often finds itself marginalized politically, the ways in which it is commonly defined are often those that are developed by persons or organizations that oppose it, reason enough to adopt a critical stance.

3. To see some feminist political activism undertaken by men, check out the Web sites of the following organizations: Real Men (www.cs.utk.edu/~bartley/other/realMen.html) and Men Can Stop Rape (www.mencanstoprape.org).

4. A word of explanation is warranted here. This section is particularly concerned with the tools of feminism as it has been taken up in the academic arena. Much feminist activity occurs beyond the walls of educational institutions. In fact, feminist activism preceded formal feminist scholarship, and it was the political activism of the 1970s women's movement in the United States that inspired the academic discipline of Women's Studies. (Of course, as long as there has been patriarchy, there have been individuals who have questioned its logic and moral authority [see Spender, 1982]. It is only within the last thirty-five years, however, that feminist scholarship has been formalized within the academy and recognized as a valid and valuable way of generating knowledge.) Feminist activism includes a host of tools that are not discussed at length here, ranging from political lobbying to nonviolent resistance to consciousness-raising. Out of this feminist movement came questions that demanded new forms of inquiry, new interpretations of knowledge, and new means of gathering knowledge. And so, almost forty years after the Second Wave began, we have academic fields such as feminist sociology, feminist literary theory, feminist economics, and feminist international policy. Women's Studies, as its own distinct discipline, draws on these and many other fields. Feminist academic inquiry, then, is a complex and complicated affair, representing a wide variety of methodologies, concerns, and issues. Yet it is distinguished from many other academic fields in that it is fundamentally beholden to a spirit of activism. As esoteric as feminist scholarship can get, it must always serve a purpose it holds in common with feminist activism: to understand and to stop gender inequality.

5. This distinction is controversial in contemporary feminist thought; many feminist philosophers argue that the two categories are linked in important ways, and that even the allegedly neutral, biological

category of "sex" is undergirded by gender inequality. For more on this matter, see Gatens (1996) and Butler (1993). Feminist sociologists and anthropologists often claim that even the category of "sex" is only loosely based on biology, and is primarily used to reinforce and perpetuate so-called "natural" differences. Nevertheless, I include the distinction in this discussion because it emphasizes the general suspicion with which feminist thinkers tend to approach any claims concerning gender that are based on an uncritical reference to "nature."

6. That's what we would expect, and as a broad generalization, we would be correct. However, the growing scholarship on intersexed individuals—that is, persons born with ambiguous genitalia—throws even this generalization into doubt (see Preves, 2003). Even the biological category of sex is not nearly as clear-cut as we tend to assume.

7. Becoming a mother can be an expensive proposition. In many economic structures, mothers earn lower wages than non-mothers, thus rendering them more economically dependent on either other individuals or the state (see Self, 2005).

8. Race can work in a similar fashion in contemporary U.S. culture. For example, black politicians are sometimes met with suspicion because of fears that they will represent only black voters. Rarely is a white politician accused of representing only white voters; just as men are often constructed as gender-neutral, white people are often constructed as race-neutral.

9. There are a few cases where informal references to jobs can be gendered masculine; think, for example, of the persistent use of the term "male nurse." Such gendering highlights the rarity of the situation: we expect men to be doctors, not nurses (and—not coincidentally—we consider doctors to be more proficient, more important, and better paid than nurses). Note that this gendering indicates a lack of status on the part of the man in question, so strongly that the very term "male nurse" seems to ask the question, "Why isn't he a doctor?"

10. See Hayes (2007).

11. Check out Margaret Atherton's classic work, *Women Philosophers of the Early Modern Period*, on this topic (1994).

12. And let's not make the mistake that it's only non-Western cultures that have such an image of women's genitalia. Cosmetic surgeons in the United States now offer procedures that promise to endow women's genitalia with a more youthful appearance; one can even choose to have a hymen reconstructed, allegedly to mimic the state of virginity (see Boodman, 2007).

13. The U.S. Bureau of Justice reports that in 2005, 176,540 women in the United States experienced sexual assault; in the same year, 15,130 men were similarly victimized (Catalano, 2006).

14. Contraception of any kind is often a fraught topic in many marriages. Indeed, researchers have discovered that many women in the developing world practice contraceptive methods without telling their male partners that they are doing so: "Women's secret use of contraceptive methods is one of the clearest examples of the potential consequences of unequal power in sexual relationships. Women may practice contraception secretly for several reasons: Their partners may disapprove of contraception, their partners may desire more children, or they may have difficulty speaking about contraceptive use with their partners....Although only a few quantitative estimates are available, a recent review estimates that secret use among women accounts for between 6 and 20 percent of all contraceptive use (based on studies in sub-Saharan Africa)" (Blanc, 2001, p. 197).

References

Aniekwu, N. I. (2002). Gender and human rights dimensions of HIV/AIDS in Nigeria. *African Journal of Reproductive Health 6*(3), 30–37.

Angier, N. (2000). *Woman: An intimate geography*. New York: Doubleday.

Atherton, M. (1994). *Women philosophers of the early modern period*. Indianapolis, IN: Hackett Publishing Company.

Berkes, F., Colding, J., & Folke, C. (2000). Rediscovery of traditional ecological knowledge as adaptive management. *Ecological Applications 10*(5), 1251–1262.

Blanc, A. K. (2001). The effect of power in sexual relationships on sexual and reproductive health: An examination of the evidence. *Studies in Family Planning 32*(3), 189–213.

Boodman, S. G. (2007, March 6). Cosmetic surgery's new frontier: Procedures popularized in L.A.'s 90210 come to D.C.'s 20037. *The Washington Post*, March 6, p. F01.

Boyle, E. H., Songora, F., & Foss, G. (2001). International discourse and local politics: Anti-female-genital-cutting laws in Egypt, Tanzania, and the United States. *Social Problems 48*(4), 524–544.

Butler, J. (1993). *Bodies that matter: On the discursive limits of "sex."* New York: Routledge.

Catalano, S. M. (2006, September). Criminal victimization, 2005. *Bureau of Justice Statistics Bulletin*, http://www.ojp.usdoj.gov/bjs/abstract/cv05.htm.

Davis, A. Y. (1981). *Women, race and class.* New York: Random House.

Easton, P., Monkman, K., & Miles, R. (2003). Social policy from the bottom up: Abandoning FGC in Sub-Saharan Africa. *Development in Practice 13*(5), 445–458.

Gatens, M. (1996). *Ethics, power and corporeality.* New York: Routledge.

Gurung, B. & Gurung, P. (2002). Addressing food scarcity in marginalized mountain environments: A participatory seed management initiative with women and men in Eastern Nepal. *Mountain Research and Development 22*(3), 240–247.

Hayes, S. (2007, April 3). Heart disease in women: A Mayo Clinic specialist answers questions. http://www.mayoclinic.com/health/heart-disease/HB00040. Mayo Foundation for Medical Education and Research.

Islam, M. M. & Uddin, M. M. (2001). Female circumcision in Sudan: Future prospects and strategies for eradication. *International Family Planning Perspectives 27*(2), 71–76.

Izumi, K. (Ed.). (2006). *The land and property rights of women and orphans in the context of HIV and AIDS: Case studies from Zimbabwe.* Cape Town, South Africa: Human Sciences Research Council.

Katunzi, P. (2006). Land of our own. In K. Izumi (Ed.), *Reclaiming our lives: HIV and AIDS, women's land and property rights, and livelihoods in Southern and East Africa: Narratives and Responses* (pp. 64–65). Cape Town, South Africa: Human Sciences Research Council.

Preves, S. (2003). *Intersex and identity: The contested self.* New Brunswick, NJ: Rutgers University Press.

Self, S. (2005). What makes motherhood so expensive?: The role of social expectations, interdependence, and coordination failure in explaining lower wages of mothers. *Journal of Socio-Economics 34*(6), 850–865.

Shiva, V. (2008). Democratizing biology: Reinventing biology from a feminist, ecological, and Third World perspective. In A. M. Jaggar (Ed.), *Just methods: An interdisciplinary feminist reader* (pp. 433–445). Boulder, CO and London: Paradigm Publishers.

Spender, D. (1982). *Women of ideas and what men have done to them: From Aphra Behn to Adrienne Rich.* London and Boston: Routledge and Kegan Paul.

Turner, N. J., Ignace, M. B., & Ignace, R. (2000). Traditional ecological knowledge and wisdom of Aboriginal peoples in British Columbia. *Ecological Applications 10*(5), 1275–1287.

Walker, A. (1984). *In search of our mothers' gardens: Womanist prose.* San Diego: Harcourt Brace Jovanovich.

Walker, A. & Parmar, P. (1993). *Warrior marks: Female genital mutilation and the sexual binding of women.* New York: Harcourt Brace & Company.

Yount, K. M. (2002). Like mother, like daughter?: Female genital cutting in Minia, Egypt. *Journal of Health and Social Behavior 43*(3), 336–358.

Questions for Discussion

1. One of the main distinctions used by feminism is the difference between sex and gender. Assuming that by "gender" we mean "culturally specific behavior and practices," what are some aspects of gender as experienced in current United States society? In other words, what behavior and traits are considered "masculine" or "feminine"? Are you aware of the different ways other cultures construct gender? If so, what are they? What kinds of gendered behavior in contemporary United States society might be considered as appalling to people of other cultures as FGC is to United States citizens?

2. Consider some of the assignments that you will complete in your Global Studies class. How might the insights of feminism help you to complete them in a more effective manner?

3. Assume that you don't know whether women are disadvantaged in a given society or not. What kind of questions would you need to ask in order to find this out? Now apply those questions to our society. In your (thoughtful!) opinion, are women disadvantaged in contemporary United States society?

4. What are some concrete ways in which our society indicates that women's activities, particularly their work, are less valued and valuable than men's? If you set out to construct a gender-equitable culture, how would work be structured differently than it is in current U.S. culture?

5. Has this article changed your opinion of feminism? Why or why not?

Activities

These activities are designed to explore some of the fundamental concepts of feminism, particularly the notion of gender as socially constructed. As you undertake them, articulate what other cultural dynamics are at work, and how the activity might be different if undertaken in a different culture. For example, the first activity involves going to a toy store. How would the activity be different in a culture where toys are mostly handmade rather than store bought?

1. Find a local toy store. Do a walk through the store to get a sense of what is available and how sex-stereotyped the toys seem. Consider the organizational structure (are toys organized by age? gender? content? size?). Ask for help choosing a gift (make up your story in advance). When asked whom the gift is for, answer "a newborn," or "a three year old" (i.e., don't mention gender) and see how long gender takes to come up. Notice what questions the clerk asks you. You might try to select a cross-stereotype gift (a doll for a boy, or an army truck for a girl) and note any reactions. (You don't actually have to buy the toy, of course).

2. Do a matrilineal family tree: that is, trace your family back through your female ancestors (your mother, your mother's mother, your mother's mother's mother, etc.). Find out as much as possible about these ancestors by interviewing any who are alive, researching family documents, and researching public documents. How were these women's lives affected by gender? How did the opportunities for women change across the generations? What aspects of these women's lives would be considered historically important by current standards? How do gender norms affect your ability to find out information about these women?

3. Choose a chat room on the Internet that you find fairly interesting. Spend a half-hour each night, for three nights, talking with the other members—but choose a different name for each night. The first night, speak as yourself; the second, speak as if you were a member of the opposite sex; and the third night, attempt to speak in such a way so as not to divulge your sex. Do you notice any differences in the way you speak, or in the ways people speak to you? The Internet is often lauded as a place where bodily differences such as sex are rendered irrelevant; is this true? In what ways?

4. Interview three women of different generations (for example, a woman in her 80s, a woman in her 50s, and a woman in her 30s) who have had children. Ask them about their experience of childbirth. How do these differing experiences reflect different ways of understanding women and childbearing? How do they reflect other cultural changes that have occurred? (Be sure that you choose women who are willing to speak at some length and in some detail about their experiences!)

5. Go to a large bookstore. Go through the magazine section, and compare how many covers are devoted to men, and how many are devoted to women. Can you notice some differences between the way women and men are presented (what they tend to be wearing, the way they're sitting, their expressions, etc.)? While you're at it, and if they have any, compare the number of pornographic magazines catering to men with the number of ones catering to women. What do your discoveries tell us about representations of male and female sexualities?

Suggested Readings

Banaszak, L. A. (Ed.). (2006.) *The U.S. women's movement in global perspective: People, passions, and power.* Lanham, MD: Rowman & Littlefield Publishers.

Ferree, M. M. & Tripp, A. M. (Eds.). (2006.) *Global feminism: Transnational women's activism, organizing, and human rights.* New York and London: New York University Press.

Hesford, W. S. & Kozol, W. (Eds.). (2005.) *Just advocacy?: Women's human rights, transnational feminisms, and the politics of representation.* New Brunswick, NJ and London: Rutgers University Press.

Moghadam, V. M. (2005.) *Globalizing women: Transnational feminist networks.* Baltimore, MD: Johns Hopkins University Press.

Ricciutelli, L., Miles, A., & McFadden, M. H. (Eds.). (2004). *Feminist politics, activism & vision: Local and global challenges.* London and New York: Zed Books.

10

Use and Abuse

Drugs and Drug Commerce in a Global Context

Mathew Gendle

Drugs Around the World: The Challenge of Cultural Relativism

Throughout time and place in history, the use, abuse of, and commerce in, mind-altering substances has been central to the human experience. For thousands of years, cultures around the globe have used naturally occurring plant and animal products to ease physical and mental pain, commune with the spirit world, and alter consciousness for recreational purposes. The intentional ingestion of mind-altering drugs appears to be a fundamental part of being human, and some form of drug use has been incorporated into most cultures, both past and present. Interestingly, the use of mind-altering substances is not unique to humans; numerous species of animals are known to seek out and intentionally ingest intoxicating plant products (Siegel, 2005). Therefore, it appears that drug use has an origin that is deeply primal, and is not solely a product of human existence. Indeed, Ronald Siegel (2005) has suggested that humans' seemingly unstoppable quest for intoxicants should be considered similar to our motivational drives for food, sleep, and sex.

As a general rule, however, access to food, potable water, clothing, and shelter are considered the four basic needs of human survival. Yet, given the scope of drug use and drug commerce around the world, one could argue that ready access to psychoactive compounds is also a basic human need. Indeed, individuals addicted to alcohol, cocaine, methamphetamine ("speed"), and opioid drugs (such as heroin, morphine, and oxycodone) routinely forgo the four basic human needs in order to maintain access to their drug of choice, which suggests that the individual drive toward intoxicated states (and the desire to stave off the negative effects of drug withdrawal) is very powerful. The staggering size and scope of the domestic and international commerce in psychoactive compounds provides evidence of the centrality of drugs in the human experience. For example, opium is essentially the sole agricultural product of Afghanistan; 3,400 tons of the drug were produced there in 2002 alone (McCoy, 2003). Additionally, U.S. Drug Enforcement Agency agents have estimated that marijuana is the single largest cash crop in the United States, surpassing common foodstuffs such as corn, wheat, and soybeans (Schlosser, 2003). In 2005, the United Nations' World Drug Report estimated that the annual global commerce in drugs was worth roughly 320 billion U.S. dollars, a figure that the report notes is larger than the individual gross domestic products of almost 90% of the world's nations.

Although drugs are often viewed in either a positive or negative light, psychoactive compounds themselves are neither inherently benevolent nor harmful. Rather, it is the cultural context in which these substances are used that creates either the positive or negative connotations surrounding a particular drug. Because each culture decides what drugs and uses of these compounds are acceptable, the approval and prohibition of different psychoactive compounds varies widely across cultures and history. Consider alcohol, which has been banned by several Protestant and Muslim religious traditions, but simultaneously serves as a holy sacrament in the Catholic Church. Many other compounds, including DMT (one of the active ingredients in Amazonian ayahuasca), peyote, and marijuana are similarly positioned as being revered as a sacred part of a religion by one culture, and banned from use by another.

Prohibitions of, or permissions for, the use of different psychoactive substances are not limited to those compounds ingested within the context of a religious belief system. For thousands of years, coca leaves (the plant from which cocaine is derived) have been chewed by inhabitants of the Andean region of South America. As described by Streatfeild (2001), chewing coca leaves provides increased energy, reduces fatigue and hunger, and allows individuals to work longer in oxygen-deprived mountain regions. To help stave off altitude sickness, coca tea is often provided to newly-arrived visitors to the Andes. Cocaine is also frequently included as an active ingredient in balms and other medicines produced and used throughout South America. Because chewing coca leaves slowly releases the cocaine contained within the plant tissue, the user receives a low, steady dose of the drug that does not produce a strong euphoric "high." Therefore, coca chewing is unlikely to lead to extensive abuse or addiction, and these oral methods of cocaine ingestion are often legal and widely utilized in Peru, Bolivia, and other countries in the region. In fact, Streatfeild (2001) suggests that coca use in South America is quite similar to caffeine use in the U.S. and Europe. Both are utilized as mild stimulants that provide a "pick me up" throughout the day, and assist fatigued workers in completing their labors.

This, of course, is in contrast to the cultural norm of cocaine use in the United States and much of the rest of the world. To most citizens of the United States, cocaine is known only as an infamous drug of abuse, associated with psychological addiction, feelings of intense pleasure, and, often, with various criminal activities. Outside of traditional South

American settings, cocaine is used primarily as a recreational drug that is considered quite distinct from caffeine. In recreational settings, which may often be categorized as "abusive," cocaine is isolated from the coca leaves, and inhaled or injected, rather than administered orally in whole-leaf form. This direct administration of the active compound from the coca leaf produces levels of cocaine in the blood and brain that are much higher than those produced by coca chewing. These increased levels in the brain are directly responsible for cocaine's powerful psychological effects. Because of cocaine's significant potential for recreational use and abuse, it is nearly universally illegal and demonized in cultures that do not share its traditional context of use.

Despite the fact that the use of psychoactive compounds appears to be fundamental to the human experience, patterns of drug use and commerce are inherently intricate and difficult to study. These patterns are culturally unique, change over time, and deeply shape cultural traditions, values, and social organization. These complexities are magnified whenever different cultures interact over drugs, be it through one culture accepting or prohibiting the drug-based traditions and habits of another, or through commerce in psychoactive substances themselves. Together, these features make the long-term consequences of cultural patterns of drug use fundamentally unpredictable, and the decision to consume, ban, or trade a drug by one culture often results in significant and unanticipated outcomes for other societies or cultural groups.

Drug use and culture exist in a multifaceted relationship that is both reciprocal and complex. In order to understand the interactions between culture and drugs, one must adopt a way of thinking that is culturally relative and breaks down ethnocentric barriers that would otherwise prevent an objective understanding of widely variable cultural practices. For example, groups of nomadic reindeer herdsmen in Siberia follow traditions that involve the ritualized consumption of hallucinogenic fly agaric mushrooms by high-ranking shamans, who believe that the fungi can facilitate communication with the spirit world (described by Knipe, 1995). Because the psychoactive ingredients of the mushrooms are excreted in the urine of those who ingest them, the urine of the shamans is often collected and consumed by lower ranking members of this society, who then enjoy the mind-altering effects of the fungi.

I suspect that many readers will find the idea of drinking urine to be repugnant. Human urine is generally sterile, yet many cultures have a very strong norm that explicitly prohibits the consumption of human waste. Disgust regarding the notion of drinking urine stems from these cultural taboos, rules, and norms, and is not based on any absolute rule that governs all people or a fundamental notion of what is "right." As described by Basirico and Bolin (Chapter 2), all of us are saddled with ethnocentric "cultural baggage" that influences the way in which we view the practices of other cultures. Our cultural norms often lead us to assume that the beliefs and practices of our native culture are indeed "normal," i.e., generally acceptable and universally practiced, while the different practices of others are aberrant. Ethnocentric patterns of thought are dangerous because they promote the reflexive condemnation of behaviors (such as the drinking of a shaman's urine) that are different from our own.

Indeed, many of the views regarding the acceptability of one culture's drug tradition to another are rooted in ethnocentric thinking. During the fifteenth and sixteenth centuries, Spain was a pre-eminent world power. Using what the monarchy believed was absolute authority from God, explorers were dispatched to Asia, and then the New World. Because the inhabitants of Central and South America were not Christian, and engaged in religious and cultural practices unfamiliar to the Spanish, the early explorers ethnocentrically assumed that these groups were uncivilized brutes that could be exploited or killed as the Spaniards saw fit. One of these unfamiliar cultural practices was tobacco smoking, which the Spanish quickly labeled as an evil vice (Gately, 2001). Although New World civilizations had rich and extensive traditions of smoking tobacco in a variety of religious, medicinal, and recreational contexts, smoking of any type was unknown to Europeans prior to their arrival in the Americas (Gately, 2001). As described by Gately, the religious climate of the Inquisition fostered visual iconography that depicted Satan as an ethereal, smoke-like being that emerged from the orifices of the possessed. This religious imagery was combined with the perception that smoking was the habit of the "savage" inhabitants of the New World, and native Europeans were aghast when early explorers returned from the Americas with a smoking habit. As retold by Gately (2001), sailor Rodrigo de Jerez was jailed by the Inquisition for three years for the seemingly innocuous act of smoking in public. Although tobacco smoking was eventually popularized throughout Europe by the Spanish royal court, the continent's initial reaction to this new habit was entirely a consequence of their own ethnocentric ideology regarding the religion and cultural practices of the peoples of the New World.

As a globally-minded thinker, one must move beyond ethnocentric attitudes, and consider different cultural practices from a viewpoint of cultural relativism, as described in Chapter 2 by Basirico and Bolin. Such a view resists the outright condemnation of unfamiliar cultural practices, treats them respectfully, and attempts to understand customary practices by connecting them with the context of their native culture. A cultural relativist also temporarily suspends the judgment of another culture's *customs* until a fully-grounded understanding has been obtained. Culture and history are so complex, indeed, that we must tread carefully, realizing that the features of an alien culture may have several hidden causes, and even more unanticipated effects, than the novice observer can grasp. Historians can tell us still more about the difficulty of explaining the present in terms of the past, and of predicting the future based on either the past or the present.

The novice observer, indeed, may find the idea of drinking a shaman's urine to be disgusting, if not profane. However, a culturally relativist view of this urine consumption would consider the behavior within the broader social context of the practice. Specifically, fly agaric mushrooms are rare in the harsh Siberian climate (Knipe, 1995). Therefore, their ingestion is limited to high ranking members of the culture, specifically the shamans (Knipe, 1995). Because urine contains the psychoactive compounds from the mushroom, the cultural practice of urine consumption provides an economical method through which lower ranking members of this society can obtain the mind-altering effects of the mushrooms.

Similarly, most of my students were surprised to learn about the traditional methods of coca use in South America. Because of the usage patterns that are typically observed in United States culture, they often assume that anyone using cocaine daily must be enslaved to the drug, and regard the user in the negative light by which United States culture stereotypically portrays victims of cocaine addiction. When I discuss this with my students, I often ask them (following Streatfeild's lead) if there is really any functional difference between traditional South American coca use and the daily ingestion of caffeine in the United States. My students' typical answers to this query demonstrate real-world ethnocentric thinking in action. "Of course it's different," my students usually respond. "Caffeine is in everything, but cocaine is a dangerous and illegal drug!" My students often seem quite willing to condemn the very idea of daily coca chewing, without first stopping to consider how the South American tradition might differ from United States patterns of use. They do not stop to think about the fact that many daily caffeine users (including many children!) experience withdrawal when caffeine intake is stopped, yet heavy caffeine use is not stigmatized by United States culture. This failure to consider different cultural contexts of drug use can be attributed to the United States cultural norm of demonizing the use of some drugs (such as cocaine, heroin, and LSD) through social norms that are disseminated and enforced *via* the mass media and public educational programs, while at the same time allowing, or perhaps encouraging, the use of other drugs (caffeine, tobacco, and alcohol).

By utilizing a culturally relativistic view that is free of ethnocentrism, one can approach this cross-cultural comparison and realize that the cultural traditions of coca leaf chewing and caffeinated beverage consumption are much more similar than they are different. What most readily distinguishes them are the cultural beliefs and assumptions about what sort of drug (and how much and in what setting) is an appropriate compound to use as a daily stimulant or for recreational purposes. Individuals raised in parts of South America where coca chewing is common often find the United States demonization of cocaine absurd, much in the same way most of my students consider ridiculous the characterization of caffeine as a psychoactive compound that can produce states of drug withdrawal.

Examining our attitudes toward coca chewing and the shamanic use of fly agaric mushrooms are but two ways of illustrating how a culturally relative worldview can promote the understanding of complex cultural behaviors. When one thinks about drug use in a way that is free of ethnocentrism and is culturally relative, two general and wide-reaching themes regarding drug use across cultures become apparent. First, the relationship between drugs and culture is multidirectional in nature. The historical use of drugs within a culture often directly shapes the current drug-related practices of that culture. At the same time, cultures develop unique laws, rules, and norms regarding the use of drugs in both recreational and religious contexts. Second, because traditions of drug use are so widespread and culturally variable, conflicts will invariably arise regarding drug use when distinct cultures interact. These interactions can be complex, and are related to economic, political, and diplomatic motivations. Because drugs are inherently valuable, they have often been utilized as generators of wealth and as instruments of foreign policy. Interestingly, the utilization of drugs as economic or diplomatic instruments has sometimes led to foreign policies where the methods of achieving geopolitical goals that involve drugs are directly at odds with national moral, religious, or public health norms.

Drugs Have Shaped Culture, Just as Culture Has Shaped Drug Use

Peyote and the Native American Church

Without question, the relationship between drugs and culture is complex and bidirectional. Throughout history, there are many examples of drug use acting as a fundamental mechanism to shape culture. One such case is the Native American Church (NAC), which was formally incorporated in 1918. As described by Knipe (1995), the consumption of peyote has long been a part of the religious traditions of the indigenous peoples of modern-day Mexico and the southwestern United States. Peyote is a spineless cactus whose flesh contains mescaline, a potent psychedelic. When eaten, peyote produces profound visual disturbances and alterations in consciousness which are interpreted within a spiritual context by the members of the NAC. The NAC does not sanction the recreational abuse of peyote, and approved consumption is limited to heavily structured and ritualized peyote ceremonies. The belief system of the NAC is quite interesting, as it mixes Native American shamanic traditions with old world Christian practices. This synergy is the result of decades of persecution of the practitioners of the peyote tradition at the hands of Christian European immigrants. As European-Americans forcibly took over native lands, they attempted to prohibit the ancient peyote tradition, deeming it evil and barbaric. Realizing that the Christian European-Americans could not be driven away, the peyotists resolved to incorporate their belief system and religious practices with those of Christianity. As stated by Knipe (1995, p. 149): "Peyotism, at least for its practitioners, provides an ethnic identity distinct from the dominant American culture without compromising local beliefs and practices. Peyotism is the source of Indianness, as opposed to tribalism."

Despite this synergy, peyote traditions continued to be persecuted by the increasingly dominant European-American laws and belief systems. As described by Knipe (1995), the NAC was founded by peyotists in order to use the First Amendment of the U.S. Constitution (which guarantees freedom of religion) as a shield against further attacks by Christian leaders as well as various governmental authorities. The NAC struggled to maintain its religious freedoms throughout most of the twentieth century, a battle that became increasingly difficult when the federal government formally criminalized peyote use and possession. However, in 1970, the NAC won a hard-fought battle, and was able to have ritual peyote use by members of the NAC excluded from the federal Drug Abuse Prevention and Control Act. As a whole, the history of the NAC provides a fascinating example of how drug use can be essentially responsible for creating a novel set of cultural beliefs and traditions.

Caffeine and the Eight-to-Five Workday

A fascinating example of drug use and cultural interactions may be found in the role played by caffeine in the emerging industrial society of the Western world. Take a moment to ponder the many ways in which caffeine is an integrated part of the modern first world. Millions of people start each day with one or more cups of a caffeinated beverage, and a considerable percentage of these caffeine users will exhibit signs of withdrawal if consumption is halted. Caffeinated products, ranging from soft drinks to candy bars, are ubiquitous in restaurants and grocery stores. Caffeine is perhaps the only psychoactive drug in the Western world where use by children is not only accepted, but often actively promoted.

In their book *The World of Caffeine*, authors Bennett Alan Weinberg and Bonnie K. Bealer (2001) provide a compelling and surprising argument for why caffeine is such a central component to Western industrialized societies: caffeinated beverages were one of the driving forces behind industrialization itself. Weinberg and Bealer point out that before the industrial revolution, Western economies were primarily agrarian, and manufacturing was performed on a small scale. These lifestyles allowed for a lax view of time, where work schedules aligned with natural cycles of sleep and wakefulness. This lackadaisical attitude toward time was likely reinforced by the fact that drinking water was often unfit for consumption, and most of the potable beverages available (such as beer and wine) were alcoholic. Historical records suggest that enormous quantities of alcohol were consumed each day by men, women, and children throughout Europe, which would have (of course) resulted in the populace living in a perpetually inebriated state. As such, the precise measurement of time was not of paramount importance, and clocks that were accurate to the minute did not become common until well into the 1600s. These dramatic improvements in the precision of timekeeping coincided with the widespread cultural adoption of caffeine-containing beverages throughout Europe (which resulted from yet another complex web of cultural developments and interactions that spanned the globe). Weinberg and Bealer posit that the advent of accurate clocks and caffeinated beverages created a "perfect storm" that promoted large-scale industrialization. Precise timekeeping allowed for the widespread coordination of industrial efforts and worker schedules, and caffeinated drinks such as tea and coffee replaced the once heavily consumed alcoholic beverages. The stimulant properties of caffeine made possible the scheduling of lives around inflexible industrial timetables (such as shifts in a factory), rather than by the individual's own natural biological rhythms. Caffeinated beverages also functioned to stave off physical and mental fatigue produced by laboring for long hours, often under inhumane conditions. From this, Weinberg and Bealer conclude, perhaps a bit too emphatically, that: "There is a sense, therefore, in which the combination of the clock and caffeine may have been essential to the development of modern civilization, and it may not be going too far to assert that the modern world, at least as we know it today, could neither have been envisioned nor built without this combination to make it possible" (p. 126).

This is a far-reaching conclusion, indeed. Just try to imagine modern industrialized society without any caffeinated beverages, and no way to tell time save the movements of the sun, stars, and other heavenly bodies. The temporal precision that guides and articulates Western civilization would likely grind to a halt. The modern first world industrial ethos of rising before dawn and engaging in work and leisure activities well into the night would be made more difficult without the stimulating effects of caffeine. It is interesting to note that as United States and European societies become more rapidly paced, caffeine use (through such new and diverse routes as energy drinks, caffeine pills, and caffeinated bottled water) increases as well. Thus, it appears that caffeinated beverages may be an important brick in the cultural foundation that has supported the development and maintenance of the industrialization of the Western world.

Drug Prohibition in the United States

Just as drug use can mold culture, culture also shapes the use of psychoactive compounds. This causal relationship often occurs through the placement of cultural prohibitions on the use of certain psychoactive compounds, usually in response to a perceived or actual societal harm caused by the drug(s) of interest. In most societies, these prohibitions are enacted as formal laws and criminal codes, which are then enforced by the government itself. However, such restrictions may also be promoted through condemnation by religious authorities (e.g., the prohibition of alcohol consumption by certain Protestant and Muslim faith groups), or through informal social organizations such as Straight Edge.

For a moment, let us consider a nation where essentially all psychoactive drugs are legal and widely available without prohibition. Heroin, cocaine, and amphetamines can be obtained by anyone, without a prescription or age limitation, at any pharmacy. Morphine and hypodermic syringe kits are available for purchase through mail order catalogues. Analogues of modern over-the-counter cure-alls typically contain dangerously high quantities of alcohol and opium. Even certain soft drinks and pediatric medicines (such as toothache drops and infant soothing syrups) are formulated with significant doses of opium, caffeine, and/or cocaine as part of the recipe. Thousands of this nation's citizens, many of whom are upper-class professionals, are addicted to cocaine, morphine, and opium (Hodgson, 2001; Streatfeild, 2001). Could such a scenario actually have occurred? My students are often shocked to learn that this nation is not fictional, and the country I am referring to is not The Netherlands. It is the United States at the dawn of the twentieth century.

So, how could this have happened? And how could the United States have gone, in much less than a hundred years, from what was essentially an "anything goes" drug free-for-all, to a country that has some of the most stringent anti-drug laws in the industrialized world? The answer lies in how United States culture responded to the unbridled drug use and availability I have just described. The nineteenth century was a golden age in medicinal chemistry, when psychoactive plant alkaloids including morphine, caffeine, and cocaine were first isolated from their sources (Hodgson, 2001). These isolate compounds were initially thought to be medically valuable, and were soon put to use in therapeutic contexts that ranged from the miraculous (e.g., use of morphine as a post-surgical pain reliever) to the absurd and outright dangerous (e.g., cocaine as a treatment for morphine dependency; Hodgson, 2001; Streatfeild, 2001). Initially, the medical community's general understanding of the long-term dangers of drug use was incomplete and misinformed, and cocaine and several other compounds were touted as cure-alls by many eminent medical professionals including Sigmund Freud (Streatfeild, 2001). However, as both the medical community and the lay public came to understand the dangers posed by these drugs, social and political movements to regulate or ban many of these compounds began to emerge and coalesce.

Initially, regulation from the United States government took the form of the Pure Food and Drug Act of 1906, which forced manufacturers of tonics and cure-alls to list all ingredients on the product label. Soon after came the Harrison Narcotic Act of 1914, a tax act which effectively criminalized non-medically supervised use of cocaine, opium, morphine, and heroin. In the decades that followed, additional legal measures were put in place to regulate the use of other drugs such as amphetamines and marijuana. These legislative efforts culminated with President Richard Nixon initiating the federal "War on Drugs," in 1972, which set into motion the federal policy of broad drug criminalization still present in the United States today. Interestingly, however, this trend may be slowly reversing at the local and state level, as there is increasing regional legislative activity to decriminalize personal use and possession of marijuana, as well as to reduce jail sentences for certain drug offenses.

Race, Social Class, and Drug Legislation

As much as we might like to think that drug prohibition in the United States is solely an outcome of the government's desire to protect individual citizens from personal harm, this is often not the case. Drug laws in the United States have frequently been a convenient instrument through which the government has enacted social control over minority groups. One of the first drug laws in the United States at any level was enacted in San Francisco in 1875. This law, which explicitly prohibited the smoking of opium in dens, was drafted in reaction to large numbers of Chinese immigrants who now populated the city. Specifically, this law sought to limit the patronage of opium dens by white women, who were thought to be enticed by Chinese men into vice, sexual immorality, and addiction (Hodgson, 2001; Streatfeild, 2001).

Racial motives also underlay the movements in the United States to criminalize cocaine and marijuana. The social pressure to include cocaine in the Harrison Narcotic Act came not from concerns regarding the health of the populace, but from racism and fear-mongering (Streatfeild, 2001). During the early 1900s, popular media reports frequently focused on the supposed danger posed to society by African Americans under the influence of cocaine. Sensationalistic articles (such as an infamous piece published in the February 8, 1914 edition of *The New York Times* entitled "Negro Cocaine Fiends are a New Southern Menace") drummed up fear that African Americans under the influence of the drug were violent and frequently sexually assaulted white women (Streatfeild, 2001). Similarly, the Marijuana Tax Act of 1937 was enacted largely because of inflammatory rumors that marijuana was being used extensively by Mexican immigrants, who were also supposedly predisposed to violence and the corruption of children and "upstanding and pure" white females (Schlosser, 2003; Streatfeild, 2001).

Unfortunately, racially motivated drug legislation is not unique to the past in the United States. It is very much alive in the present penal code for drug offenders. During the 1980s, the use of freebase cocaine (known as "crack") became common throughout urban areas. Crack was attractive to residents of poor, inner-city neighborhoods because it was cheap, easy to obtain, and produced a profound psychological high when smoked. As crack use became more common, its use was sensationalized in much the same way that powdered cocaine had been in the early 1900s (Streatfeild, 2001). The popular media created a frenzy whereby crack was fingered as the cause of many urban crimes, particularly those supposedly committed by minority groups, as well as being labeled as a particular danger to children (Streatfeild, 2001). As a consequence, federal criminal sentences for the possession of crack were enacted that were much more severe than those punishing the possession of powder cocaine (Streatfeild, 2001).

During the "crack epidemic" of the 1980s, physicians in urban hospitals began to notice that mothers who tested positive for cocaine at the time of delivery often gave birth to children with a wide spectrum of developmental complications. Ignoring the possibility that these problems could have resulted from the use of other drugs (such as tobacco and alcohol), poor nutrition, a lack of health care, or any number of other environmental variables, cocaine use was quickly demonized as a scourge of pregnancy and the cause of "crack baby" syndrome (Streatfeild, 2001).

Rather than attempt to understand the complex socioeconomic causes of maternal substance abuse, those in authority laid the blame for the "crack baby" phenomenon squarely on the behavior of the addicted mother. Crack was described by writer Charles Krauthammer (1989) as "the most effective destroyer of the maternal instinct ever found." Substance-abusing mothers from economically disadvantaged and minority backgrounds became viewed as transmitters of poverty from one generation to another, through the intellectual deficits that they were purportedly passing on to their children. Such thinking led to various attempts to reduce the incidence of "crack babies" through any means necessary, including forcing addicted mothers into protective custody (presumably to reduce access to drugs during pregnancy) and charging substance-abusing women with a myriad of criminal deeds, including child abuse, criminal mistreatment of a child, child neglect, reckless endangerment, and distribution of drugs to a minor. Some "concerned" citizens' groups (using such web addresses as www.cracksterilization.com and www.cashforbirthcontrol.com) went as far as to offer cash (up to $200) to addicts in exchange for temporary or permanent sterilization.

The fact that such groups thought that addicts were likely to remain compliant to any birth control regimen underscores how little they understood or cared about the unfortunate psychosocial condition of these troubled women. Nor did these groups focus their efforts on sterilizing pregnant women addicted to nicotine or alcohol, two legal drugs then known to pose hazards to unborn children, with a usage rate during pregnancy many times that of cocaine. This finding further suggests that the war against "crack babies" was strongly influenced by sociocultural biases, and provided a convenient excuse for the targeting of low socio-economic status minority women by the welfare reform policies and "war on drugs" of the Reagan and (first) Bush administrations (Humphries, 1999; Litt & McNeil, 1997). Indeed, it has been suggested that the "war on drugs" championed by Presidents Ronald Reagan and George H. W. Bush was not so much a quest to improve public health, as it was a political smokescreen designed to: 1) divert attention away from the dangers of legal drugs and the powerful political lobbies that support their commerce; 2) place blame on substance-abusing minorities rather than on complex social problems that have no simple or immediate solution, [and in so doing] 3) make the government appear proactive in the face of a national "health crisis"; and 4) justify the legal oppression of poor and minority groups through increased policing and prosecution (Neuspiel, 1996; Siegel, 1997). Thus, the "war on drugs" can be viewed as an instrument designed to enact social control over oppressed groups that might otherwise have been a threat to rebel against the political "status quo" (Neuspiel, 1996).

The cases previously described are but a few of the many examples of how culture influences drug use. Perhaps they also show how particular phenomena—in this case, drug use—can channel, or allow to converge, a culture's dominant values, attitudes, and beliefs. Prohibitions placed on drug use that are designed to target specific ethnic or cultural groups are often a consequence of close-minded, or at least limited, thinking regarding the reasons for, and consequences of, drug use within a particular culture. Although we would like to assume that laws forbidding drug use are enacted to protect personal and public health, this is often not the case. Indeed, the British gin acts of the 1700s as well as the widespread prohibition of absinthe in Europe at the turn of the twentieth century had very little to do with the dangers to personal or public health posed by these alcoholic drinks. Instead, these laws reflect upper-class prejudice towards the economic, social, and political demographics of the people who were likely to consume large quantities of these beverages (Conrad, 1988; Warner, 2002). The criminalization of LSD by the United States government in 1970 can also be viewed as a reaction to the "hippie" movement, which posed a considerable threat to the dominant political and social order in the United States during the late 1960s.

Drugs and Relationships Between Cultures

Although drug use does play a central role in individual cultural development, it is also important to recognize how it may modify interactions between cultures. Given the frequent use of drug prohibitions as a mechanism to legitimize the centrist thinking of those holding economic, political, and social power within individual countries, one should predict that such attitudes would also influence how one nationality or culture will interact with another. Throughout history, the use of drugs has very much colored the relationships between cultures, the consideration of which invokes this chapter's second theme of interest. As the examples discussed previously show, the prohibition of drugs is often based more on how race, socioeconomic class, gender, and religion are perceived by those in power, rather than on absolutist notions of morality or public health concerns. Similarly, the international commerce of drugs has been shaped not only by health and moral positions, but also by economic and foreign policy objectives. Indeed, drug commerce has frequently been used as a powerful implement of foreign policy, even under circumstances where such policy is directly at odds with an individual nation's laws, collective moral positions, or government programs designed to improve public health.

Drugs have, in these contexts—imperialism, colonialism, and globalization— helped to define interactions between cultures. Given the fundamental drive that humans exhibit in seeking out psychoactive compounds, it makes sense that drugs of all types have played a central role in trade throughout world history. When studying the many ways in which the international drug trade has shaped national and cultural trajectories, one quickly discovers that the international commerce of drugs often has far-reaching and unforeseen consequences that bridge space and time. World economies are staggering in their complexity and even one small perturbation to any system or interaction can result in significant changes in functional outcomes.

During the last 500 years, the global drug trade may be conceptualized as one of several economic "engines" that have driven imperialism and colonialism; two processes that were central in the initial creation of global networks of commerce and trade. As discussed by Brian Digre in Chapter 8, "Western Imperialism and Its Legacies," imperialism can be generally defined as the attitudes of a dominant culture being employed in a geographically distant territory, while colonialism can be thought of as the establishment of settlements in such a territory for the purposes of economic gain. According to Digre, the first wave of European imperialism and colonialism began with exploration of the New World during the latter part of the fifteenth century. Through the use of advanced weapons and technology and by taking advantage of accidental circumstances (such as the introduction of Old World diseases and internal strife within several New World societies) European explorers overtook the native civilizations of the Americas, and claimed these lands as their own. The Europeans worked quickly to establish profitable industries, such as mining and agriculture in the New World. Some of the most important agricultural products of early American colonies were drug-containing plants, specifically coca and tobacco.

Europeans Discover Coca and Tobacco

It is interesting to note that at the time of the "golden age" of European exploration, few recreational psychoactive compounds were widely used across the European continent. Alcohol use was, of course, quite common, and opium was utilized medicinally for its pain-relieving properties. Additionally, several members of the potato family (including datura, nightshade/belladonna, mandrake, and henbane) were employed to produce altered states of consciousness. These plants produce poisonous compounds that, when taken in small doses, induce profound hallucinatory states and stupor (Knipe, 1995). It is thought that the modern cultural image of witches riding on broomsticks originated in the historical tradition of Renaissance-era witches self-applying these plant extracts vaginally, using a wooden staff, to experience supernatural visions of flying and demonic sexual encounters (Knipe, 1995). However, Europeans had essentially no drug traditions beyond the three just described. As mentioned earlier in this chapter, the very idea of smoking plant matter to obtain altered psychological states was completely unknown to them.

This, of course, all changed as the Americas were opened through exploration, and Europeans came into contact with the wide variety of drugs unique to the New World (including coca, tobacco, cacao/chocolate, peyote, ayahuasca, and ebene). Interestingly, the cultural trajectory of the rejection and then eventual incorporation of the use of many of these drugs in European culture evolved repeatedly in the same way. Initially, European explorers and religious figures rejected New World drug traditions. Because these practices were unknown, different, and were the custom of "savages," who were not Christian, they were therefore ethnocentrically assumed to be demonic and/or inferior. Because one of the primary purposes of early European exploration was to produce wealth, New World drug traditions were often co-opted for commercial purposes. For example, in Peru, the Spanish realized that coca could be a money maker, and quickly set to cultivating coca and selling it to the native Incans, as well as other groups throughout South America (Streatfeild, 2001). The Spaniards also provided coca as a stimulant and appetite suppressant to malnourished and overworked natives who were functionally enslaved in silver and mercury mines (the profits of which benefited the Spanish monarchy and the Catholic Church) throughout Peru and Bolivia (Streatfeild, 2001).

Despite early European religious and cultural taboos against the use of drug-containing plants like tobacco and coca, some early explorers did eventually partake, and quickly became aware of their pleasurable effects. As accounts of the positive effects of New World drugs reached Europe, interest was piqued in the often bored upper class of society, and demand for export was created by elite members of European aristocracy who wished to experience these exotic goods. Much like today's celebrity-obsessed culture in the United States, European society in the 1500s was infatuated with the royalty and upper class, and anything being done or consumed by the top echelons of society was immediately deemed desirable and fashionable by the rest of the populace. Through this mechanism, certain New

World drugs such as nicotine (tobacco) came to be popularized in Great Britain as well as other countries throughout Europe. The resulting increase in demand meant that a large-scale export source for tobacco to feed Great Britain's growing habit needed to be found, and it was, in the form of the British colony of Virginia.

As described by Gately (2001), the Virginia Company, which was initially chartered in 1606 as a moneymaking operation for the British crown, survived only because of tobacco. The original intended purposes of the Company (including mining metals and various non-tobacco agricultural concerns) quickly and summarily failed in the swampy climate of Jamestown, and it initially seemed as though the presence of a permanent British settlement in Virginia would not last. However, in 1612, an enterprising colonist named John Rolfe began studying and experimenting with different methods for growing and curing tobacco. After several years of work, Rolfe created a unique flavor for Virginia-sourced tobacco, and tobacco from the Jamestown area quickly became prized throughout England. Between 1618 and 1629, tobacco exports from the Virginia colony increased more than 7400%, and the wealth and prosperity of the colony was thus ensured.

Unfortunately (as discussed by Gately, 2001), tobacco cultivation is quite labor-intensive, and there were simply not enough workers in the colony to keep up with demand. This labor shortage triggered the import of African slaves (a practice that was soon extended to other labor-intensive crops), a truly dark chapter in world history, with wide-reaching effects. Not only did institutionalized slavery on Virginia tobacco plantations cause unspeakable hardships to those taken against their will from their native Africa, it also radically altered the interactions of native African groups with one another (see Chapter 8 by Digre). In Africa, slavers frequently traded alcohol, tobacco, firearms, metal tools, and other manufactured goods for slaves. As these goods were in high demand, many African peoples took up slaving, and traded fellow Africans captured from weaker or rival groups. With ready access to firearms through trade, the slaving Africans held a distinct upper-hand over the groups they preyed upon, which were often politically and socially weakened or destroyed by the trade.

Because African slaves were proven to be an economically viable source of labor for tobacco cultivation, African slavery was later expanded to the production of cotton, sugar cane, and other labor-intensive agricultural products throughout European colonies in the Americas. Therefore, the collective suffering of millions of African slaves has its roots partly in the popularization of tobacco as a recreational drug in Europe. Indeed, the unfortunate and enduring legacy of racism against people of African origins in the United States, Colombia, Haiti, and other former slave-holding areas can also be attributed, in part, to the growth of tobacco consumption during the early 1600s.

In 1618, no one could have predicted that the development of Virginian tobacco would spawn a global economic, political, social, and public health juggernaut that, over the course of the next 390 years, would simultaneously produce great wealth, unspeakable suffering, addiction, and countless deaths worldwide from cancer and emphysema. Because humanity is globally connected in such fundamental, but also in such complicated ways, individual economic, political, or social actions can produce long-term outcomes that are utterly unpredictable.

China, Great Britain, and Opium

But perhaps the most infamous example of the impact of drug use and drug commerce on an imperial foreign policy involves the so-called Opium Wars of the nineteenth century. The long-term consequences of these wars, fought between Great Britain and China, are often downplayed by Western historians. Yet, there is no doubt that these cultural interactions have been central in the development of China's current attitudes toward the Western world. As described by Jack Beeching in his detailed book *The Chinese Opium Wars* (1975), these conflicts were primarily about resource allocation and the accumulation of wealth, and provide a case study of the disaster that can occur when two fundamentally ethnocentric cultures clash. During the 1800s, the British Empire was the world's preeminent military and commercial superpower. Great Britain commanded a strong and well-equipped navy, and controlled colonies and influenced nations around the world. Much of the Crown's wealth originated in the trade of global commodities, and was organized through state-held commercial entities such as the British East India Company. This British economic and military might cultivated an attitude of cultural superiority and arrogance, particularly within the context of interactions with non-Western nations.

One of Great Britain's most important trading partners during the nineteenth century was China, thanks to heavy British demand for Chinese goods such as porcelain, tea, and silk. At this time in history, China was ruled by the Ch'ing Dynasty, who claimed that their power was bestowed upon them by the heavens. To the Chinese, the world outside of their nation's borders was ethnocentrically assumed to be backwards and barbaric, and they found little value in foreign inventions and commodities. To this end, the Chinese maintained a policy of isolationism, and tried to limit interaction with foreigners as much as possible. These anti-foreign ideologies made the British trade with China difficult, particularly because the Chinese displayed little interest in imported British goods. The British soon found themselves in the unenviable position of having a trade deficit with China, and were forced to pay for Chinese items with silver. This was not a viable long-term economic strategy (as the British treasury would quickly be depleted), and British merchants were pressured to find other goods that could be traded directly for tea and silks. Opium was soon found to be this commodity.

Although the Chinese emperor had banned the importation and sale of opium several decades earlier, British merchants now began smuggling ever-increasing amounts of the drug (sourced from Bengal) into China. This, of course, rapidly changed the economic fate of the British, and contributed to a staggering rate of opium addiction in China. In response to the continued pressure of opium imports in the face of formal state prohibition, the Chinese engaged the British in a series of diplomatic and trade skirmishes, to which the British responded repeatedly with armed force (actions collectively known as the First and Second Opium Wars). Initially, the Chinese did not fear the British empire's military might, as they were convinced that they were the superior culture. However, as British land and naval forces used their advanced military technologies (such as steamships) to destroy coastal settlements and eventually capture the city of Canton, the Chinese were forced to subject themselves to the foreign empire's commercial will. The armed actions of the British smashed the doors of China wide open for trade, and opium importation to China was eventually legalized.

As previously suggested, the Opium Wars provide a unique study of the perils of ethnocentrism. Both the Chinese and British were convinced that theirs was the superior culture, and each group felt that the other could be bullied into doing as the other wished. Just as the Chinese often referred to the British as "barbarians" and held their customs in great distain, so the British also treated the Chinese as inferior. Indeed, the Chinese, because they were convinced that their methods of warfare were superior, and would easily prevail, were the ones to initially confront the British. During the Second Opium War, the British destroyed the Summer Palace, in Beijing, which held extensive priceless cultural artifacts and was a visual symbol of the power and wealth of the Chinese dynasty. This action was done explicitly to humiliate and punish the emperor for failing to cave in to British demands. Even the act of opium importation itself can be viewed as deeply ethnocentric. By forcing the commerce of a highly addictive drug on an unwilling state, the British demonstrated that the welfare of the Chinese people was less important to them than the economic gain of the Crown.

The long-term effects of the Opium Wars were widespread. Extensive war reparations and ransoming by the British emptied the Chinese treasury, awarded Great Britain unparalleled commercial access to China, and gave the island of Hong Kong to the British. The economic, political, and social impacts of the wars severely crippled the already weak Ch'ing Dynasty, and left it vulnerable to pressures from internal political strife and rebellions. Additionally, years of heavy opium importation left China full of addicts, and firmly cemented large-scale drug trading in the region, which increasingly involved the Chinese themselves (Brook & Wakabayashi, 2000). Along with several other historic events in the region (such as aggressive Japanese imperialism in the 1930s), the consequences of the Opium Wars have resulted in China deeply distrusting foreign nations, particularly those with trade or commercial interests within its borders.

One of the most interesting, yet also the least obvious and perhaps most unanticipated, effect coming from the Opium Wars is the fact that Britain's military actions during this period indirectly increased African slavery in the United States. As described by Beeching (1975), Britain outlawed the trans-Atlantic slave trade in 1807, and at the time of the Opium Wars, British warships were patrolling the west coast of Africa to enforce this prohibition. As tensions in China escalated, some naval vessels were re-assigned from this duty and dispatched to engage the Chinese. This, of course, made it easier for slave ships to enter the open Atlantic from the African coast, bound for the Americas with their human cargo. This is yet another example of how an event occurring in one area of the globe can have profound and unanticipated consequences in other parts of the world. Although we often fail to realize it, humans are deeply connected across both time and space, and seemingly small actions can have large and widespread effects.

U.S. Foreign Policy in the Twentieth Century

Illustrations of these unpredictable effects from unlikely causes can be observed in modern international relations, where politics, economics, and cultural views on drug use are tightly enmeshed. In the last 40 years, the relationships between the United States, Colombia, Nicaragua, and Afghanistan have provided illuminating examples of the fundamental entanglement of these three themes.

It has been said that those who forget history are doomed to repeat it. While the shape of the interaction has changed, drug-based military interventions with an overarching commercial intent continue to occur. In 2008, the United States is perpetuating a more than thirty-year-old international "war on drugs." Initiated by President Richard Nixon in the early 1970s, this "war" is based on a two-part strategy of capturing and prosecuting the domestic users and distributors of illegal drugs, while simultaneously using military, economic, and political strategies to reduce the production of illicit substances abroad. Although the international component of the "war on drugs" may have begun with the best of intentions, the actions of the United States suggest that there may be more to the international "war on drugs" than simply stopping the production of these illegal substances.

Drugs, Oil, and War, by political analyst Peter Dale Scott (2003), presents a compelling argument suggesting that U.S. drug interventions in Colombia, Afghanistan, and Southeast Asia have been, and continue to be, at least partially intended to further American geopolitical interests, rather than for their stated purpose of cocaine and opium eradication. Scott has noted that all three of these geographical regions share three commonalities: 1) extensive drug production and exportation; 2) large oil reserves; and, 3) current or past U.S. military interventions designed to stabilize local political systems. From his analysis, Scott concludes that the "war on drugs" isn't about drugs at all, but is instead designed to promote and assist governments in oil-rich geographical areas that are friendly to the United States. Without a doubt, the world's oil supplies are being stretched, and as demand for this finite resource increases, so will conflicts over the control of dwindling petroleum reserves. The United States has long decried imperialism in the name of obtaining natural resources, and Scott argues that the "war on drugs" allows the United States to engage in military interventions that are publicly framed as anti-narcotic, but that are really in support of friendly capitalist governments who will provide ready access to a region's oil wealth.

Colombia.   For example, consider the long-standing "war on drugs" operations in the South American country of Colombia (as described by Streatfeild, 2001, and Scott, 2003). Despite the expenditure of millions of dollars on anti-cocaine military interventions in Colombia, this country continues to be a significant producer of cocaine and opium (used to make heroin) sold in the United States. By nearly any statistical measure, the "war on drugs" in Colombia has failed to reduce drug use or drug-related crime in the United States. Yet, the United States continues to pour large sums of money into this unsuccessful battle every year. Why? Scott suggests that these interventions are intended to influence the victor of the long-running Colombian civil war, and notes that because Colombia has expansive petroleum reserves, the winner of this contest will have a significant impact on future world oil markets. In this way, a well-intentioned anti-drug foreign policy has been derailed by geopolitical concerns.

Today, there are three main groups involved in the Colombian civil war. The first is the internationally recognized official government of Colombia, which champions the ideals of democracy, capitalism, and free trade. Several independent paramilitary organizations, such as the United Self-Defense Forces of Colombia (or AUC) fight (or have fought) in support of the formal state government, and have been linked to massacres of civilians and numerous other human rights abuses during the conflict. Although the AUC is said to have formally demobilized in 2006, it is widely assumed to still be engaging in clandestine political activities in Colombia. The second group of note is a guerilla organization known as the Revolutionary Armed Forces of Colombia (or FARC). FARC is a neo-Marxist group that wishes to install a socialist government in Colombia that would oppose the influence of multinational corporations on Colombia's economy and prevent the privatization of natural resources, such as oil. Because of their tactics, both the AUC and FARC have been formally listed as terrorist organizations by the U.S. Department of State. Like many civilian military groups around the world, both the AUC and FARC have historically obtained a considerable portion of their funding through the support and protection of the drug trade (in this case cocaine, much of which is ultimately sold in the United States). Financing military operations is a very expensive undertaking, as soldiers need to be quartered and salaried, weapons need to be purchased, and transportation arranged. Involvement in the drug trade is often a simple way for clandestine groups like FARC and AUC to raise large amounts of capital quickly, money that can then be used to support military activities.

Based on the group's political ideologies, it is clear that the United States has a vested interest in defeating FARC, as recent American foreign policy has typically focused on fostering democracy and free-trade in underdeveloped nations around the globe. As mentioned earlier, Colombia claims vast petroleum reserves, and a government friendly to free-market capitalism will be necessary in order for U.S. oil companies to have access to these reserves. Unfortunately, the conflict in Colombia does not have a simple "good guy vs. bad guy" structure, and supporting the Colombian government means that by political connection, groups like the AUC and their dealings in cocaine are also being supported. This is extremely problematic, as it puts United States foreign policy objectives at odds with the American government's professed moral and public health goals of the "war on drugs" at home. From his analysis, Scott concludes that that inconsistency has been solved by a United States military policy which labels the FARC as terrorist "drug runners" and focuses the resources from the "war on drugs" on military actions against FARC, including extraditing and prosecuting paramilitary leaders captured by the Colombian government, while leaving the in-the-field operations of paramilitary groups like AUC largely unmolested. These tactical decisions imply that in regards to United States policy, long-term international economic development and the promotion of governments friendly to the United States have taken priority over stemming the tide of drugs smuggled out of Colombia.

The complexity of this issue is further heightened by the reality that economically motivated decisions to support groups like AUC are sometimes made by private United States corporations as well as by the government. For example, in March 2007, the United States Department of Justice announced the completion of an investigation that uncovered extensive and illegal monetary contributions to the AUC from the United States banana producer, Chiquita Brands International. Between 1997 and 2004, Chiquita made over 100 cash payments to the AUC (totaling over $1.7 million) as part of a protection racket involving their banana production operations in Colombia. So, by purchasing Chiquita products during this time, United States consumers were unknowingly helping to finance a paramilitary group recognized as a foreign terrorist organization and indirectly supporting international cocaine trafficking. Yet again, seemingly unrelated events, such as a single consumer choice in a local grocery store, and the operations of a Colombian paramilitary organization are, in fact, linked.

Throughout the twentieth century, several other public and well-documented incidents—many of which are described in University of Wisconsin-Madison Professor Alfred McCoy's brilliantly researched book *The Politics of Heroin* (2003)—have repeatedly demonstrated that United States foreign policy is sometimes conducted so that geopolitical self-interest trumps professed domestic moral positions about drugs. On several occasions, the United States has found itself unintentionally aligned with international drug producers and smugglers while it attempts to achieve certain political or economic outcomes.

Nicaragua.   Consider the role played by the United States (and recounted by Streatfeild, 2001) in Nicaragua during the 1980s. At this time, Nicaragua was ruled by an anti-imperialist Marxist group known as the Sandinistas. Several organizations that professed democratic ideals (collectively known as the Contras) opposed the Sandinistas' authoritarian rule and hoped to overthrow them through the use of force. This philosophical position earned the respect of United States President Ronald Reagan, who was fearful of communist or even socialist movements overtaking South and Central America. Likening their struggle to that of the American founding fathers, Reagan promoted his government's financial and military support of the Contras. However, like the AUC and FARC, the Contras funded their operations partly through the traffic of cocaine, largely into the United States. This reality was brought to light through the careful investigative journalism of Gary Webb (of the *San José Mercury News*) who demonstrated that the Central Intelligence Agency (CIA) knew that the Contras were importing and selling cocaine in the United States, and presumably did little or nothing to stop it.

Afghanistan.   Yet another example of the strange and unintentional alliances formed between the United States government and drug producers and traffickers can be found in Afghanistan. The United States has long held a crucial stake in the politics of Afghanistan, partly because of its geographical location near the oil-rich Middle East. As discussed earlier, the United States has no formal interest in obtaining oil through traditional imperialism. Instead, one of its long-standing foreign policy objectives is the support of friendly state governments that are open to trade in areas holding critical natural resources, such as oil. As such, the United States has a long history of involvement in Middle Eastern affairs, given the petroleum wealth of this region. During the late 1970s and 1980s, Afghanistan was considered a critical strategic buffer between the Soviet Union, the Persian Gulf, and rich Middle Eastern oil fields. Following the September 2001 attack in the United States by the radical terrorist group al Qaeda, Afghanistan came to be viewed as a potential harbor for Islamic fundamentalist groups who planned to violently oppose capitalism and Western access to the area's petroleum wealth.

Back in 1978, before the "9/11" factor was added to the mix, the government of Afghanistan had been overthrown in a military coup that installed a Marxist style of government. Resistance from the Afghan populace (who shared a history steeped in tribalism and was opposed to the new government's reforms) was immediate, and armed uprisings soon followed. In 1979, the then-Soviet Union (the U.S.S.R.) invaded Afghanistan to support the Marxist coup. This invasion marked the beginning of the nine year Soviet-Afghan war, which pitted the Afghan government and Soviet forces against the mujahedeen resistance movement. The United States and other Western powers were horrified by the idea of a Soviet controlled Afghanistan, but could not intervene directly, because—in the context of the "Cold War"—such a military action could be viewed as a dangerously confrontational attack on Soviet interests. Instead, the United States and other nations provided financial assistance, weapons, and training to the mujahedeen.

Keeping with the pattern we have seen several times already, the mujahedeen financed some of their operations through the cultivation and sale of opium. As documented by McCoy (2003) and discussed by Scott (2003), financial support and political protection of the mujahedeen by the United States facilitated the growth of a large opium production and distribution network that, once constructed, was not easily dismantled. After the final withdrawal of Soviet troops in 1989, Afghanistan was plagued by violent infighting among factions that once comprised the mujahedeen. Much of the funds used to finance this ongoing warfare continued to come directly from opium cultivation, which by the early 1990s had become the primary engine of the Afghan economy. By 2001, a group known as the Taliban had gained control of much of Afghanistan, and set up a radical Islamist state, despite continued opposition from a group of former mujahedeen members known as the Northern Alliance. Opium was utilized as the primary source of state revenue, with the Taliban taxing harvests, heroin refiners, and exports (McCoy, 2003). Despite international eradication and diplomatic efforts, opium production flourished under the Taliban, and Afghanistan soon was the source of nearly all heroin worldwide. Although the Taliban formally banned opium cultivation in 2000 for political reasons, members of the Northern Alliance continued to grow opium poppies in vast quantities to support their continued military actions against the Taliban. McCoy has likened the ban to "economic suicide" because the Afghan economy and the Taliban itself were weakened considerably with the loss of the country's primary agricultural product.

Following the events of September 11, 2001, it became clear that Al Qaeda operatives were being sheltered in Afghanistan and supported by the Taliban. Given the orchestrated attacks on the United States by al Qaeda, as well as the need for long-term political stability in the Middle East, the United States and other NATO (North Atlantic Treaty Organization) nations responded with force. In October 2001, the NATO alliance attacked Afghanistan, and swiftly removed the weakened Taliban from formal power. Immediately following the first steps of the NATO invasion, the Taliban revoked the prohibition of opium cultivation, and funded their operations against NATO and its allies from the proceeds of the opium trade. One of these allies was the Northern Alliance, which viewed the NATO attack as an opportunity to rid Afghanistan of the Taliban. NATO forces greatly valued the participation of the Northern Alliance in the conflict, as it meant that fewer NATO troops had to be put in harm's way during operations in Afghanistan. However, much like the Taliban, the Northern Alliance was funding their campaigns through opium cultivation, and the United States was again put in the position of having to choose between a political victory and a victory in the "war on drugs" (McCoy, 2003; Scott, 2003). As had occurred so many times before, the United States decided to look the other way while its allies produced massive quantities of drugs, a considerable amount of which was refined into heroin and ultimately exported to the United States.

As of 2009, NATO and Northern Alliance forces continue to fight the Taliban in Afghanistan, and both the Taliban and Northern Alliance operations remain funded through the opium trade. Although the United States and other nations have invested millions of dollars on anti-cultivation efforts in Afghanistan, the country produces record opium harvests each year and exists as the overwhelming primary source for the world's opium. Thirty years of warfare, environmental destruction, drought, and poor fiscal planning have left the national economy of Afghanistan almost entirely dependent upon opium cultivation. This dependency, combined with uneven efforts to halt cultivation, suggest that Afghanistan will continue to be the world's single largest producer of opium for many years to come.

From all of this historical data, McCoy (2003) concludes that the government of the United States, like the British before them, has a history of complicity in allowing extensive drug commerce by geopolitical allies around the world. Covert operations in Southeast Asia, Colombia, Nicaragua, and Afghanistan that were intended to provide support for friendly political entities fighting against Marxist regimes have had the unfortunate and unpredicted outcome of dramatically increasing the world's supply of heroin and cocaine. While McCoy's research suggests that at no point did United States agents directly engage or assist in drug manufacturing or distribution, ample evidence indicates that governmental organizations (such as the Central Intelligence Agency) were aware of the drug operations of their allies, and chose to ignore them. In so doing, a choice was made where the support of "friendly" political groups in areas with geostrategic importance became viewed as more important than winning the "war on drugs."

Drug Proxy Armies and Foreign Policy

Foreign policy itself is not the only thing influenced by attitudes toward drug use. The means and instruments by which foreign policy goals are implemented and achieved may also be shaped by drug production, distribution, and commerce. Again, it is sometimes the case that societies that traditionally oppose drug use find themselves politically supporting producers and suppliers, if such support facilitates particular foreign policy objectives. Although the use of mercenary and stand-in proxy forces in armed conflict has been a long-time occurrence throughout world history (see *Licensed to Kill* by Robert Young Pelton [2006] for an excellent analysis of this phenomenon), the international commerce in illegal drugs has produced a distinct form of these warriors: the drug proxy army. As discussed by Peter Dale Scott, in *Drugs, Oil, and War,* (2003), drug proxies can be thought of as non-state military groups (such as guerilla warfare organizations) that fight in alliance with a formal nation (hence, the proxy) and are funded in whole or in part by drug profits. Indeed, by this definition, the AUC in Colombia, the Contras in Nicaragua, and the mujahedeen/Northern Alliance in Afghanistan can all be viewed as drug proxies for the United States. Scott suggests that the use of drug proxy groups can be viewed as a method to engage in conflicts where the direct deployment of large numbers of formally recognized troops would be either diplomatically dangerous (e.g., the situation in Afghanistan in the late 1970s) or generally unpopular (e.g., military interventions to gain political influence over Colombian oil reserves). Ethnocentric attitudes regarding proxy armies are particularly noticeable in the United States' recent partnership with the Northern Alliance to fight the Taliban in

Afghanistan. Although many Americans believe in the overarching tactical and political goals of military operations in Afghanistan, few want to sacrifice the lives of the many of their own country's soldiers who would undoubtedly be killed in a fully dedicated pursuit of these objectives. The use of proxy armies partially solves this problem by replacing a significant number of NATO soldiers with Afghan citizens, thereby transferring some of the casualties to the Afghans themselves. Of course, this reduced death toll of United States soldiers comes at a steep price. By training and supporting drug proxies, the United States is facilitating opium production and export on a gigantic scale. Additionally, members of the Northern Alliance may come to view themselves as being "used" by the United States, which will only further fuel resentment and anti-American sentiment in the region.

It is fascinating that the concept of the drug proxy has come full circle during the 200-plus years of United States history. Indeed, the Continental Army that fought the British and won American independence can itself be considered a drug proxy army for France. As described by Gately (2001), the colonists used tobacco to secure a loan from France to help finance the revolution. Because France and England were bitter enemies, and France hoped to see British influence decline in North America, this arrangement resembles, in a general sense, several more modern drug proxy arrangements.

Conclusion

In this chapter, I have attempted to explore some of the mechanisms through which drug use and the commerce in drugs have radically affected human existence. The examples that I have chosen are but a small set of many possible historical occurrences: it is clear that drugs have played a broad and important role in shaping human cultures and, indeed, significant parts of world history. What lessons, if any, can we conclude with? First, we might conclude that drugs are neither inherently good nor bad. The set and setting of the use of a drug within a particular cultural context determines whether a drug will be revered or condemned by that culture. Second, humans universally appear to seek out experiences that alter conscious experience. These experiences may come from behaviors such as fasting, chanting, the infliction of ritualized pain, or deliberately-induced physical exhaustion. However, many cultures have incorporated drug use into their accepted practices as means through which consciousness can be altered. Third, as a consequence of this powerful drive to alter consciousness, drugs are universally valuable commodities. It is no accident that coca leaves, tobacco, chocolate, and alcohol have all been utilized as currency in different historical and cultural settings. This universal value also means that drug commerce can be harnessed as an easy source of financing for terrorism and clandestine military activities, and also employed as a potent foreign policy instrument. Social or moral norms regarding drug use and commerce are often displaced in these contexts by broad geopolitical and ideological positions. Fourth, because psychoactive substances are valuable, the processes of obtaining drugs, engaging in drug commerce, and attempting to prohibit such activities will continue to be widespread cultural characteristics, and will often lead to violent conflict. One needs only to look at the history of drug criminalization in the United States, be it the prohibition of alcohol by the 18th amendment, or more recent "wars" fought by the Drug Enforcement

Agency (DEA) against cocaine, to see how such legal action spawns violence. Fifth, drug use and commerce often connect people and events in complex ways across place and time, challenging the analytical and interpretive skills of anthropologists, historians, economists, and political scientists. Finally, and perhaps most importantly, the centrality of drugs and the ascribed meaning of various alterations in consciousness within individual cultural practices (such as religion) create strong ethnocentric and culturally-centered belief systems that often condemn dissimilar cultural ideologies. For example, the hippie movement of the 1960s was denounced by the mainstream United States population primarily because of the social and political beliefs of the hippies, which were intrinsically associated in the minds of the general American public with the excessive use of marijuana and LSD.

Knowledge of the diversity of drug use across humanity should encourage us all to think in more culturally relativistic ways about what (and who) defines acceptable and unacceptable behavior, and how these definitions are constructed. What may be one group's key to the spirit realm is another's condemned instrument of Satan. In the case of alcohol, what is one individual's holy sacrament is another's deepest sin. Because all people are bound by the "cultural baggage" of their upbringing and native culture, we are all predisposed to the assumption that our ways are right, and that the ways of an "other" group must be wrong. But this dualistic view is a simplistic illusion of our own making. There are no inherently universally "correct" patterns of sexual behavior, physical appearance, food preferences, or—indeed—of drug use. All of these things are cultural constructs, which we, as members of different societies, internalize and often abide by. When we come to recognize these tendencies inherent in our thinking, understand their origins, and step out of their restrictive boundaries, we can begin to truly witness, understand, and appreciate the enormous diversity of human culture that surrounds us.

References

Beeching, J. (1975). *The Chinese opium wars*. San Diego, CA: Harcourt Brace Jovanovich Publishers.

Brook, T., & Wakabayashi, B. T. (2000). *Opium regimes: China, Britain, and Japan, 1839–1952*. Berkeley: University of California Press.

Conrad, B. A. (1988). *Absinthe: History in a bottle*. San Francisco, CA: Chronicle Books.

Gately, I. (2001). *Tobacco: A cultural history of how an exotic plant seduced civilization*. New York: Grove Press.

Hodgson, B. (2001). *In the arms of Morpheus: The tragic history of laudanum, morphine, and patent medicines*. Buffalo, NY: Firefly Books.

Humphries, D. (1999). *Crack mothers: Pregnancy, drugs, and the media*. Columbus: Ohio State University Press.

Knipe, E. (1995). *Culture, society, and drugs: The social science approach to drug use*. Prospect Heights, IL: Waveland Press.

Krauthammer, C. (1989, July 30). Children of cocaine. *The Washington Post*, p. C07.

Litt, J., & McNeil, M. (1997). Biological markers and social differentiation: Crack babies and the construction of the dangerous mother. *Health Care for Women International, 18*, 31–41.

McCoy, A. W. (2003). *The politics of heroin* (Rev. ed). Chicago, IL: Lawrence Hill Books.

Neuspiel, D. R. (1996). Racism and perinatal addiction. *Ethnicity and Disease, 6*, 47–55.

Pelton, R. Y. (2006). *Licensed to kill*. New York: Crown Publishers.

Schlosser, E. (2003). *Reefer madness: Sex, drugs, and cheap labor in the American black market*. New York: Mariner Books.

Scott, P. D. (2003). *Drugs, oil, and war*. Lanham, MD: Rowman & Littlefield Publishers, Inc.

Siegel, L. (1997). The pregnancy police fight the war on drugs. In C. Reinarman & H. S. Levine (Eds.), *Crack in America* (pp. 249–259). Berkeley: University of California Press.

Siegel, R. K. (2005). *Intoxication: The universal drive for mind-altering substances.* Rochester, VT: Park Street Press.

Streatfeild, D. (2001). *Cocaine. An unauthorized biography.* New York: Picador Press.

U.S. Department of Justice (2007). Chiquita Brands International Pleads Guilty to Making Payments to a Designated Terrorist Organization and Agrees to Pay a $25 Million Fine. Press release. Accessed on August 4, 2008 at http://www.usdoj.gov/opa/pr/2007/March/07_nsd_161.html

Warner, J. (2002). *Craze: Gin and debauchery in an age of reason.* New York: Random House.

Weinberg, B. A., & Bealer, B. K. (2001). *The world of caffeine.* London: Routledge.

Questions for Discussion _____

1. In this chapter, the author presents an argument suggesting that drug use and commerce have played an important role in shaping human culture. Can you think of any other events (such as the rise of the Internet) that have played, or are likely to play, a similar role in cultural development?

2. Early in this chapter, the author discusses the practice of lower-ranking members of groups of Siberian herdsmen collecting the urine of shamans, for the purposes of drinking it to obtain the psychoactive effects of the fly agaric mushroom. Why do you suppose many cultures place a prohibition on the consumption of human secretions?

3. Can you think of reasons why U.S. culture generally accepts the use of caffeine, alcohol, and nicotine, but condemns the use of other drugs, such as marijuana and LSD?

4. Should members of the Native American Church be allowed to consume peyote as part of their religious tradition, even though such consumption is illegal for the rest of the citizens of the United States? To what degree should the law protect the religious beliefs and practices of different groups? For example, should members of the Fundamentalist Church of Jesus Christ of Latter-Day Saints (FLDS) be allowed to practice polygamy and marry underage children because it is part of the group's religious traditions?

5. Do you agree with the author's assertion that humans possess a universal drive to alter their own consciousness? Why or why not?

Suggested Readings _____

Huxley, A. (1990). *The doors of perception;* and *Heaven and hell.* New York: Perennial Library, Harper and Row.

Norton, M. (2008). *Sacred gifts, profane pleasure: A history of tobacco and chocolate in the Atlantic world.* Ithaca, NY: Cornell University Press.

Tracey, S. W. & Acker, C. J. (2004). *Altering American consciousness: The history of alcohol and drug use in the United States, 1800–2000.* Amherst, MA: University of Massachusetts Press.

11

Navigating Religion in the Global Context

Jeffrey C. Pugh

Introduction

In September of 2005 the Danish newspaper *Jyllands-Posten* published twelve editorial cartoons critiquing Islam through various graphic styles, including portrayals of the Muslim prophet Muhammad. One of the most controversial cartoons was a picture of the Prophet, with his turbaned head depicted as a bomb. The newspaper's publishers argued that Islam was being treated just as any other religion would be in a secular, democratic society and that religion was fair game for satirical treatment, but the content was deemed extremely offensive by, and to, Muslims in Denmark and around the world. In the ensuing response to these cartoons, riots broke out worldwide that left more people dead in Nigeria than in any other country in in the world.

The line that stretches from Copenhagen, Denmark to Lagos, Nigeria is invisible, yet firm, as the world reveals itself to be far more connected and yet, far more fragmented than we realize. For example, the controversy generated by the Danish cartoons reverberated around the world as Danish embassies were burned in Syria, Lebanon, Iran, and elsewhere in the Middle East. As I was writing these words in the summer of 2008, more Danish embassies had just been set ablaze, still in response to these cartoons.

Critics of the cartoons found them reflective of a condescending and arrogant mindset in the European world. The drawings were, they said, typical and representative of the attitudes of an imperialistic West which, in both its religious and secular orders, wants to colonize the Islamic world culturally and politically. The cartoons were interpreted as nothing less than a smear campaign against the Muslim world and the religion of Islam. Though we may be perplexed at such attitudes, we need to understand what drives them because, for many Muslims, it is Islam that is perceived to be under attack, and when people are threatened, they will fight back. How we are able to negotiate these emerging religious tensions is going to determine the world we, and our children, inhabit.

The "Danish Cartoon Story" is only one small snapshot of the world in which we now navigate our way. It is in this world of rapid globalization that we find a curious phenomenon: those who resist the lures of the global economy and the identities that come with it often appeal to religion to strengthen their rebellion.[i] And this response is characteristic not just of the worldwide resistance to globalization; it is also the case that the appeal to religious identity drives many of the world's conflicts and difficulties. From Darfur to Iraq, Sri Lanka to Beirut, there seems to be an endless stream of daily conflicts concerning religion that carry profound implications for how we find our way forward in the world.

Religious conflict, of course, is as old as humans; what we experience today is nothing new. What is more interesting than just the fact of the conflict, however, may be the reality that we live in a time when the challenge of religious conflicts offers us the opportunity to create the space for developing a new imaginative view, even vision, of humanity and its faith communities. We will explore this later; however, first I want you to consider some of the reasons why religion exercises such power in the world today and how various conflicts emerge from and between, and even within, religious communities.

The Disappearing God: Is Religion Relevant in the Western World?

Religion in the West, that is, in the post-industrial countries of North America, Europe, and Japan, has generally moved out of the center of concerns about public life. Though it is true that we find many expressions of religion in America in our public life, these are usually expressions of a civil religion. This form of faith revolves around the American mythology of being a Christian nation. "In God We Trust" is found on our coins, but we do not order our financial structures on religious belief. We may have our Presidents invoke God's name as they close speeches with the words "God bless America," but this is a religion of the lowest common denominator. Religion along these lines is what serves to bind us to our common heritage as Americans.

The most dominant form of religion in America has been moved into the realm of private life and belief. Given the character of American individualism most of us think of religion as a private matter, something between a person and his or her God. Sometimes the public expression of religion can stir great debate exactly because so many believe it is a private matter.

---

[i]For further analysis of this tension, see Braye, et. al., in Chapter 13 in this volume, which addresses Benjamin R. Barber's "Jihad vs. McWorld" formulation of the conflict between "tribal" and "global" forces.

Those countries where religion is tightly bound to government, and where religious disputes are a way of life make us nervous, because our belief in what constitutes freedom means we are free from the tyranny of religion that would force everyone to follow a particular doctrine or belief. We find those countries where religion centers on public life difficult to comprehend, and sometimes this limitation blinds us to other cultural features—ethnic, economic, familial—that may be entwined with religion.

People of the United States exist in a society that has a long history of making space for the freedom of the religious believer, without religion dominating society. The freedom of religion in United States society is both freedom of, and freedom from, religion—at least, for most people. We actually live in a secular culture, which is also a contested fact of our lives today. This is a tension that is constantly being debated, but the precedents have been established in our Constitution. This heritage makes it difficult for us to completely grasp the hold religion has on some people, particularly beyond our shores.

However, our religious complacency and secular comfort were jolted following the events of September 11, 2001 as we strove to understand and interpret what had happened. Some scholars called this moment a "clash of civilizations," and framed the events in such a way as to tell the story of a long-term struggle between the West and Islam. As subsequent history suggests, it would appear that this was the way some of our political elites viewed the situation, especially with the framing of "The War on Terror."

The fact that religion was added to the mix only underscored the threat many felt, for citizens of the secular world had perhaps believed that as technology and knowledge grew, as human beings "progressed," the need for religion would disappear. We were living in a situation in which religion had been relegated to the private and interior dimensions of life. We saw ourselves as children of the Enlightenment and the habits of thought that have emerged from the past three centuries have conditioned us to believe that we had taken the forces of chaos that religion unleashes and had tamed them. No one need die anymore over whose doctrine or God was true or better. As humankind reached its full adulthood we could acknowledge, even tolerate, religion, but we did not have to allow it to command us how to establish the political and social orders we built. The fact that others might find these attitudes condescending did not really occur to us.

Western history, rooted in Europe, had narrated to us that it was religion that fueled some of the worst conflicts and killed more people than any other aspect of humankind. Or, at least, this was the story we accepted. Further examination would show that politics and the desire for power fueled much of the conflict after the Reformation and subsequent break up of Christendom in the sixteenth century, but religion helped these forces to mobilize people in order to further political aims.[1] Because religion was such a ready tool for exploitation, however, many felt that it was best to be rid of something that created so much conflict and appealed to people's private interpretations of scripture. It would be better, we assumed, to order society according to things everyone could agree on, things that offered empirical evidence for belief. Religion was meant to disappear behind the fences that the secular order constructed to secure power for itself. Rationality and science would be our new guides into the world and we would not have to concern ourselves with the vagaries of private revelation.

Until relatively recently, religion has been ignored by the West as a significant force shaping the world. Having relegated religion to a relatively private role, Westerners failed to take account of the fact that it is not an isolated and private practice in much of the world, but an inseparable part of people's public lives. Western secularists reject the authority of sacred texts or leaders, but many other world cultures accept their authority as binding, and structure political and social lives around them.

This tension between religion and secularity has global implications that will continue to shape the way different cultures and nations relate to one another. Religion, in fact, performs incredibly complex functions in societies and cultures around the world, constructing human consciousness and identity in ways many people find mysterious and impenetrable. Understanding religious motivation and consciousness and how human beings internalize their world is therefore important to our comprehension of the entire world.

Shaping Our Inner and Outer Worlds

The celebration of secularity that the Western world embraced has now exploded into apocalyptic nightmares of falling skyscrapers and exploding suicide bombers. The slow domestication of religion in the West is not the reality that shapes other people in the world. We now live in a time when we will have to learn how to negotiate communities and claims that are foreign to us. And this is true no matter what the ground or position we occupy on this planet. The Muslim in Mecca contemplating life in the United States has the same difficulty understanding a society that orders itself without religion that many in the West have when reflecting on theocratic life in parts of the Muslim world.

These complexities point to the difficulty of assessing any global conflict or situation without a broader understanding of the intersection of religion and culture. Religion, as an aspect of culture, works to help construct the worldviews and realities that people believe. In Chapter 2 of this book, "The Joy of Culture," you may read in detail about the "web" of culture, which shows how humans construct worldviews and identities, and how these are connected with a particular culture's institutions and with the values, beliefs and attitudes embedded in those institutions. But for our purposes it is enough to keep in mind that we exist in a web of relationships that have shaped us to understand the world in certain ways. Society is constructed in such a way that it is meant to be taken for granted. We create meaning, order, language, and culture on the basis of traditions that have shaped generations and often these traditions resist questioning. This is as true of the technological societies of the developed world as it is of tribal cultures in South America.

The world that we have created thus has the power of being a "fact," a concrete reality that we should not question. It is very difficult for us to accept the idea that our very ability to think in certain ways and patterns has been a part of this shaping, but it has. This does not mean that new ideas and concepts cannot become a part of our reality, only that our ideas of what the world should look like have become so powerful that alternative worldviews will meet heavy resistance when we are confronted with them. One interesting aspect of our awareness about the ways in which we construct the world is that now we do have the opportunity to navigate our religious differences. In the realization that religion shares in the same historical processes that create human culture we can find a freedom to imagine religion differently and this opens up some possibilities for religious dialogue. We will have more to say about this presently.

Religion has been a part of this process of shaping worldviews, but it is also different in that it possesses a distinctly powerful role in shaping who we understand ourselves to be. So much of what we label as "religion" is the attempt to root our selves and all extensions of our selves found in family, tribe, nation, or state within the realm of the absolute, or transcendent, reality. Once our lives are rooted within this notion of the absolute, anything becomes possible in the name of God: even the death and annihilation of all others who don't share our view of God or the absolute. We seldom find the gods on the side of our enemies, after all.

In locating our lives in the realm of the absolute, our actions, the way we live our lives, often become justified on the basis of transcendent command. God thus becomes employed for privileging my—or your—tribe, community, and culture. One can easily see the delusions that follow from this mindset, because now we interpret our lives on the basis that our culture is not rooted in the contingencies of history, but located in the demands of the absolute, no matter whether you call that "absolute" thing God, Allah, or something else.

This special kind of "absolutism" also reveals another of religion's unique dynamics in social construction: the connection between religion and exclusion. If religion translates human action into the realm of the sacred and provides an order for a society, then whatever threatens the religion must be an agent of darkness, or chaos. Thus religion carries the potential of creating in the minds of some a bipolar world of those who are good and those who are not. Depending on the social location of your culture, society, or nation there are some religious communities that call for a more exclusionary stance against the onslaught of the unbelievers and infidels.

This desire for purity, to draw the boundaries between the pure and the impure, constitutes one of the most insidious marks of religion. It divides the world up into two categories, the forces of light and the forces of darkness. It should go without saying that the forces of darkness are usually the ones who disagree with us. Religion constructs its boundaries so tightly, however, that we seldom see the ways in which our own communities may follow the darkness.

The insidious nature of this boundary construction is seen most clearly in the very logic of purity itself: "The 'will to purity' contains a whole program for arranging our social worlds—from the inner worlds of our selves to the outer worlds of our families, neighborhoods, and nations. It is a dangerous program because it is a totalitarian program, governed by a logic that reduces, ejects, and segregates" (Volf, 1996, p. 74).[2] This is one of the inner dynamics that drives some religious communities.

In the dichotomy of the pure-impure we find the delusion, the lie of our own purity, our own innocence. This delusion allows us to proceed with impunity to visit violence on those who threaten us. The attraction of religion is that we can be both idealistic and nationalistic at the same time. It allows us to believe that we have cast off evil and are impenetrable to its colonization.

This principle, once enshrined into our social worlds, means that religion becomes transmuted into cultural morality. Social arrangements and political structures that are historically conditioned and contingent enter into the realm of the sacred. What follows is the justification for violence when you feel your religious identity under attack. This is what religion can do; it divides life, persons, the world, into the spheres of the sacred and the profane, the spiritual and the secular, the saved and the damned, and, perhaps most insidiously, the

FIGURE 11.1 *Source:* Joe Heller/Green Bay Press–Gazette

good and the evil. The exclusions and the brutalities we visit upon others can be excused because *they* are not the "chosen ones." Because it works in the area of the absolute, religion allows for anything in the name of the good. Simplistic dualisms, without a rigorous self and cultural examination, can create the conditions on the ground for any kind of atrocity in the name of the good.

The will to purity is another inner dynamic that drives global religious conflicts and the actions of the religious extremists, but it also may be the Achilles heel that ultimately makes religious extremism a very weak force for the long haul. Once the contagion of the pure versus the impure takes hold, it infects people and nations.

An example of what I mean can be seen in the relationship between Osama bin Laden and the central figure in the Iraq insurgency, Abu Musab al-Zarqawi. A Jordanian, Zarqawi converted to militant Islam and global jihad and found himself in 1989 in Afghanistan, the front for the war against the Russian occupation. After a series of travels that led him to meet many of the leaders of al Qaeda and to become trained by them, he ended up in Iraq, leading some of the most gruesome attacks against both the United States forces and the nascent Iraq government. These attacks were so indiscriminate that the leadership of al Qaeda sent a message to Zarqawi not to alienate the Shi'ite population of Iraq. He regarded the Shi'ites as apostates and did not heed the call to moderation. His answer to this call for moderation was to plan the destruction of the Imam al-Isqari Mosque in Samarra, one of Shi'ite Islam's most sacred shrines (Juergensmeyer, 2008, pp. 210–11).

Zarqawi himself would be killed by a United States attack in June of 2006, but the animosity he sought to foment between Shi'ite and Sunni Muslims in Iraq illuminates the principle that when the notion of purity becomes central in religious communities, religious violence may not be too far behind. Sometimes this violence will be trained on your own community when the "true believers" disagree with the existing social order. This notion of cleansing the earth of the impure or unrighteous is found in many of world religions' sacred texts. But when those who consider themselves pure fall upon their supposedly less-pure co-religionists, it truly does become the case that a house divided against itself cannot stand.

When Worlds Come Undone

Such internecine strife in the name of religious belief makes it clear that it will be very difficult, though not impossible, to question those forms of life the culture and self take when they are formed around such a powerful force. Religion shapes us so powerfully because of the narratives it offers us. Humans are in some ways narrated creatures, whose worlds are shaped by the stories that we heard as we grew up. These stories, many of them religious in origin, locate us in the world. Conveyed by trusted elders, these stories tell us who we are and who our people are. In the telling of these stories, religion legitimates all social arrangements in society for those who believe. The actions we take, the beliefs we hold, our very place in the cosmos, all these things are located in an authority beyond the relativities of history. Religion establishes an order that guides and instructs its adherents. This is the ideological power of religion.

So, if my religious community tells me stories that the land I live on has been given to us by God, or if I have been told that God has chosen my tribe or people above all others, then this is the reality that I accept and live within. For example, one of the most powerful narratives in the world today comes from the story of Abraham, found in the religions of Judaism, Christianity, and Islam. This story narrates the identity of Judaism and Islam to a remarkable extent, and influences Christian identity in distinct ways as well. Even in a secular society, these stories acquire a power to shape our lives and place us in the world in such a way that to be disconnected from these narratives means a loss of self.

When we do begin to question the most fundamental aspects of our lives, then, the resultant anxiety triggers significant resistance from those who find meaning in the prevailing orders. This anxiety is most often produced when we encounter those whose stories may differ from the ones that shaped us. When we find ourselves confronted with other worldviews and realities and religions we often resist those whom we consider "Other" to us.

Fear of others has been present in the dynamics of religion from the time we first gathered around fires in caves to tell the stories that formed us. When foreign ideas challenge the part of our cultural identity that is tied to the sacred, the results can be extremely powerful. Religious and cultural identity combine to create conditions that can cause us to commit atrocity in God's name: "Such sacralization of cultural identity is invaluable for the parties in conflict because it can transmute what is in fact a murder into an act of piety" (Volf, 1996, p. 37). Suicide bombers and Crusaders alike share this attitude of demonizing those who do not subscribe to their worldview.

This bipolar worldview of the pure and impure, the sacred and the secular, also causes religious violence to be a reality the global community must face. Feeling threatened, religious adherents in some parts of the world push back in such a way that they reject modern society precisely *because* it is so secular. This rejection has created cultures of violence in religions as diverse as Judaism, Islam, Christianity, Hinduism, Buddhism, and Sikhism. Mark Juergensmeyer, who wrote the book, *Terror in the Mind of God: The Global Rise of Religious Violence* (2003), says that religious extremists share three common characteristics:

> First, they have rejected the compromises with liberal values and secular institutions that were made by most mainstream religious leaders and organizations. Second, they refuse to observe the boundaries that secular society has imposed around religion—keeping it private rather than allowing it to intrude into public spaces. And third, they have replaced what they regard as weak modern substitutes with the more vibrant and demanding forms of religion that they imagine to be a part of their tradition's beginnings. (p. 225)

When the society we have constructed feels as if it is coming apart, when what has structured our lives seems to be slipping into chaos, when the order we were familiar with dissipates in front of our very eyes, we look for reasons. In heavily religious communities, these types of evil are seen not as the work of social forces only; they are interpreted as spiritual forces also, that must be resisted, because evil *cannot* have the final word. When our worlds are threatened, there is a cosmic battle between good and evil at work. The great irony of our age is that both the secular and religious communities can often feel exactly the same way about one another. Until this polarization is overcome, we face a difficult future.

Worlds Colliding: When Religions Conflict

Let us look briefly, then, at some places where the conflicts seem to be the most acute. Take the global struggles between Islam and the West mentioned earlier. In part this can be seen as push back against the inroads that Western society has made into societies of the Middle East. The impact that the West has had in the world has been borne by a number of factors, some cultural, some market based, and some political. As previously argued, one of these political factors stems from the fact that the Western world has created, through centuries of debate and struggle, societies that do not incorporate religion into their culture in anything other than a nebulous and vague way. In America this has resulted in one of our bedrock assumptions about the role of religion in society—the separation of church and state.

In many parts of the Islamic world, especially those societies where clerics exert significant power, this cardinal principle of Western society is seen as a potential threat. What many in the West fail to grasp is that for many Muslims, this encroachment of the West upon their lives is not just secular; it is in some way also Christian. Because religion is inconceivable as something separate from society, many Muslims have difficulty understanding how a "Christian" society can allow the separation of God from culture. Why should religion be separate from the governing powers of society if the governing powers are following God's will laid out in holy scripture? The fact that the West doesn't honor its religious heritage is problematic for many in strongly religious countries. Oddly enough, it is also a problem for many of the most fervently religious in the West because they desire that their countries be brought under the rule of the righteous.

We can say that because clerics feel their power being threatened they use religion as a tool of control, but this interpretation fails to do justice to the deeper realities present when religion shapes a community. For many in the Islamic world, secularity is a corrosive influence on religious devotion. They see the results in our cultures of the separation of religion and society and are horrified. We, conversely, see the results of religious influence in their culture and are horrified for a whole other set of reasons.

Another perspective that affects some Muslim thinking is the reality that the type of modernity we are offering the Islamic world is regarded as toxic. In Iraq, for example, one of the quietly stated goals of the United States invasion of 2003 was to bring the blessings of democracy to the Middle East. If democracy could just take root in Iraq, it might spread to other nations in the region and the area could be freed from the religious extremists who oppressed the societies in which they lived. At least this was the hope of a small group of thinkers who believed that the region could be transformed if only it would adopt democracy.[3]

But what form of democracy did the United States offer? In the eyes of many, democracy was as godless as the Communism that the Soviet Union had offered the region in an earlier era. This was because Islam, the dominant religious community in the area, was viewing the situation through different sets of lenses. Their perspectives have been colored by the history of European colonialism in the Middle East, especially after the fall of the Ottoman Empire.

After the fracturing of the Ottoman Empire, the European powers, at the close of World War I, sought control of land in the Middle East and created nations, such as Iraq, where none had previously existed. (See Brian Digre, Chapter 8 in this book, "Western Imperialism and its Legacies," for more information about the formation of the modern nation of Iraq.) Thus, in the form of political ideologies and economic power, a secular nationalism, imposed by outsiders with different historical and cultural roots, rearranged the boundaries of large parts of the Middle East. This was seen as corrosive to the religion of the region. Why would anyone want a government where God did not establish the laws? This history, stretching back to the post-1918 period, strongly influences the relationship between the West and Middle East today.

The secular basis of government that the Western powers want to establish is anathema to many in Muslim culture. When Osama bin Laden issued his *fatwa* in 1996 against the United States and the European West, he was directing his fire at what he saw as cultural colonialism and a new Crusade against the Islamic world. This struggle against the growing secularism of government has already been engaged in the Middle East in places such as Egypt with the Muslim Brotherhood, and in Iran with the Iranian Revolution of 1979, when a religious order was established. This rebellion against secular values is true of many other countries around the world, some examples of which we will see shortly. There were many elements in these countries prepared for revolution and even assassination to accomplish the destruction of the secular order and the establishment of a transnational Islamic world. This desire for a united Islam flies in the face of those who believe that religion must not be a part of public life in a significant way.

The ground for democracy in the West had been prepared precisely because we had had centuries of secular power wielded on the authority of something *other* than God's command. But this secular government is seen as polluting and corrosive by those who are committed to Islam and to the forms of law and governance that they believe Islam should take in the Muslim world. These same critics also, more seriously, regard the West's idealistic desire for "freedom and democracy" in the Middle East as an assault on their very identities. The intersection of religion with other institutions of culture, particularly politics and government, creates the conditions for profound mistrust and misunderstanding.

The case of Iran provides us with an instructive perspective because it represents the only instance in which a specifically religious government has been established in the region. It also represents the intersection of colonialism, Western secularity, and Islamic diversity. The flashpoint for the struggle between religion and the secular order in Iran occurred in 1979, with the overthrow of the Shah of Iran by the Muslim activists loyal to the Ayatollah Khomeini. This marked the first time in recent history that a Muslim movement had overturned a government patterned after the secular nationalism of the West.

The establishment of Islamic government in Iran signaled an important shift in the relationship between the West and the Middle East, but it was also indicative of what was taking place among Muslims. This revolution, which still affects us today, was brought about by the Shi'ite branch of Islam, which itself opposes the majority branch of Islam, the Sunnis. Thus, the role of religion in the worldwide struggle of Islam with the secular West can sometimes hide the divisions within Islam itself. Take the case of Iran and Iraq as an example. While many think of Islam as monolithic, or at best as a group with just two major segments, the Sunni and the Shi'ite, there are even more lines of fracture underneath the surface of which we are often not aware. All these factions are heavily involved in the ongoing relationships between these two countries.

The principal division, however, into Sunni and Shi'ite, arose upon the death of Muhammad, when a decision about his successor had to be made. Some Muslims took the position that the new leader should be elected from the community as a whole. As a result, Muhammad's close friend, Abu Bakr, became the first caliph of the Islamic nation.

Other Muslims believed that the leadership of the nascent Muslim community should have come from the Prophet's own family. These Muslims felt that the leadership of the Muslim community should have passed to Muhammad's cousin and son-in-law, Ali. This dispute set the conditions for centuries of conflict within Islam because Shi'ite Muslims follow a line of Imams who, they believe, have been appointed by virtue of their descent from the Prophet Muhammad. From this initial division over political and spiritual leadership, many other threads of Islam spun out regarding law, spiritual practices, doctrine, and other matters.

In Iran, Shi'ites constitute the majority of the population. One reason why Iran was such fertile soil for the revolution against the secularizing forces in the Middle East was that Shi'ite Muslims are part of a tradition that respects the clerical leadership, and sees world history in terms of a narrative that tells the story of a great Imam, yet to appear, who will be a spiritual and political leader, much as Muhammad was. During the time when this great ruler is not physically present, or remains hidden, his power resides within the mullahs, or Shi'ite clergy. This was the reality guiding the Iranian clerics when the Pahlavi regime assumed control of Iran in 1925 after the end of the Qajar dynasty, and held it until the overthrow in 1979.

In Iran, the previous ruling family before the revolution of 1979 was headed by the Shah, whom the Western powers preferred, not least because of the arrangements made with him to protect their economic interests. The Shah's family had no claim on the lineage of the awaited twelfth Imam, but the Muslim cleric Ayatollah Khomeini did. The clerics in Iran had been a powerful force in that country for some time, but revolutionary fervor was also stoked by another religious belief. In the Shi'ite understanding, the Imam who is hidden will—at the end of history—reappear as the Mahdi, or the Messiah, who will overthrow the forces of darkness and institute a reign of justice and freedom.

Khomeini himself never claimed this title. But because the narrative had structured the thinking of Shi'ites and, as mentioned previously, because human beings are profoundly shaped by the stories they embrace, the cultural conditions were primed for a new Islamic renaissance that would awaken the region to the dangers represented by secularism. In the Shi'ite mind, the Shah and those who installed him were evildoers. Though this is a complex story involving geopolitical concerns, it is undeniably the case that the Shah was aided in his ascension to the throne by the CIA in 1953, which is just one of the events that increases the suspicion of American motives in the Middle East.

When the United States helped to overthrow the democratically elected prime minister of Iran, Mohammed Mossadegh, and reinstall the Pahlavi regime, it left an impression in the minds of the mullahs, who saw the United States as the "Great Satan." From their perspective, the political order that was brought to them by the Shah of Iran was the perspective of the infidel. The ensuing secular captivity of Iran warranted resistance and overthrow in the minds of the religious leaders and Khomeini brought it in religious form.

Through a series of events driven mostly by political and religious narratives that had shaped the culture of ancient Persia, the Islamic Republic of Iran was established in 1979. Since then, it has undergone several changes, but the ongoing struggle between more moderate elements and the hard-line Muslim clergy has not been between a secular and religious form of government, previously represented by the Shah and Khomeini, respectively. Now, the conflict is over how strictly Muslim law will be enforced in the new order. In this new situation, Iranian nationalism has been fused with Shi'ite political and religious ideology. The state and mosque are intimately connected. This is the exact opposite of what a secular government would look like. Religious belief in this way has become rooted in the state apparatus in Iran to an extent neither seen nor desired by the Western world.

These conflicts have affected the Muslim community in significant ways, and cannot be ignored when trying to negotiate our way forward in Iraq as well as Iran. The percentages of Sunni to Shi'ite Muslims in Iraq are inverse to the Islamic world as a whole. While Sunnis constitute the majority of Muslims (85%) worldwide, in Iraq they are a minority. Shi'ite Muslims, who were not aligned with Saddam Hussein's government, make up about 65% of Iraqis.

In the aftermath of the 2003 Iraq invasion, various splinter groups of these communities formed inside Iraq to fight for political influence. Sunni sects, such as al Qaeda of Iraq, have driven these conflicts and numerous others seeking to take back power the Sunnis enjoyed under Saddam Hussein's regime. The Shi'ite Muslims, for their purposes, have sought to settle old scores, including the execution by Saddam Hussein of 48 major Shi'ite clerics, including Mohammad Baqir al Sadr, father-in-law of one of the most powerful clerics today in Iraq, Muqtada al Sadr, a leader of Twelver Shi'ism. These various factions, vying for political power, all have different religious perspectives on Islam. To deny that the religious shadings do not influence events within Iraq is to ignore a major source of ongoing conflict.

Resistance Is No Respecter of Religions

Islam is not the only religion to shape the global community, and religious conflict is not solely driven by the religious-secular conflict. Other religions and agendas also participate in the global conflicts we see today. This is one of the reasons why grasping the role of religion in the world is so vital to our understanding. Sometimes the conflict is not between religions, but within religious communities. One such skirmish is found within Israel as it struggles with its fervently religious communities over the direction of the government. Those who are most militant decry the fact that Israel is regarded as a secular state. Their desire is to reinstitute the biblical state of Israel, complete with adherence to biblical law, the Torah.

In this regard, they have a family resemblance not only with Muslim militants, who also want religious law, the Sharia, to be the guiding force in social and political structures, but also with certain fundamentalist Christians in the United States who desire and work for the institution of biblical law to rule their country.

The presence of religiously motivated communities in Israel has led to violence in the past and is likely to in the future because religious believers feel so much is at stake in their struggles. One of the most horrific moments that Israel experienced was in 1995 when a Jewish activist, Yigal Amir, assassinated the prime minister of Israel, Yitzhak Rabin. He was driven by God, he said, to kill Rabin for his policies regarding the Palestinians in Gaza and the West Bank. Amir was later to say that he had been influenced by the teachings of militant rabbis who believed that such an assassination would be justified by the idea of "pursuer's decree" in Jewish legal precedent (Juergensmeyer, 2008, p. 62).[4]

This assassination symbolizes a massive problem facing the Middle East, because as moderate as Yitzhak Rabin may have been, there are religious extremists on all sides driven by the type of cultural dynamics mentioned earlier in this chapter. One concern that drives these communities revolves around a Jerusalem site sacred to the three Abrahamic religions. For Muslims, the site is known as Haram al-Sharif, the place where Muhammad is said to have ascended into heaven. Presently, this site houses the Dome of the Rock and is one of Islam's holiest shrines.

The conflict comes because this part of the city of Jerusalem is also sacred for devout Jews as the place where they seek to rebuild the Temple first built by Solomon, rebuilt upon Israel's return from Babylonian exile, and then destroyed by the Romans in 70 CE. The theology of some segments of Judaism regards this area as crucial for the start of the messianic age. In order for the Messiah to come and the world to be redeemed, the Temple must be rebuilt precisely where the Dome of the Rock now stands. Some of the most fundamentalist groups of Christians in the United States also believe this.

Thus, for certain Christian and Jewish devotees, to ensure the Messiah's appearance, one of the holiest Muslim places must be destroyed. Indeed, the matter is taken so seriously that numerous plots to blow up the Dome of the Rock have been uncovered over the years. Religiously fueled riots have broken out in this area, some leading to serious political consequences. There have even been attempts by Christian fundamentalists to blow up the Dome of the Rock, because they believe that Jesus cannot return to earth unless the Temple is rebuilt.

Tensions concerning religion and the political order also exist outside the Middle East. For example, over the last several decades, in Latin America, many Christians appealed to their faith as justification for their opposition to oppressive ruling oligarchies who blocked political change. This movement, called Liberation Theology by its followers, sought to connect a Marxist-style analysis of societal problems with a fairly Catholic expression of Christianity, in order to make claims that the Christian Gospel called for the liberation of those who were oppressed by the ruling powers. The most radical theologians, including some priests, advocated armed struggle if government oppression against the people turned deadly. However, most of those who took this theological turn advocated peaceful means of conflict resolution. Many of those who engaged in this religious movement suffered the violence of the ruling powers, notably the Archbishop of El Salvador, Oscar Romero, who was assassinated in 1983 while celebrating mass.

For a period of about two decades, this theology of liberation was the only effective resistance to the ruling elites who sought to control events in countries as diverse as Argentina, Brazil, Bolivia, El Salvador, and Nicaragua, among others. These elites were trying to ensure that the wealth and resources of their countries stayed in the hands of a small number of people. In Latin America, the Catholic Church was one of the few institutions strong enough to stand up for the powerless against regimes established by the European colonial powers in the nineteenth century. In reality, however, the part of the church that did support the position of the the poor was often in conflict with the official stance of the Roman Catholic Church. Though the threat was not a loss of religious identity such as we find in the struggle against the dominance of secular society, religiously centered identity empowered the resistance of many in the church against the ruling oligarchies.

Latin America was not the only place where Roman Catholicism experienced conflict with political authority. This was also the case in Poland right before the 1989 fall of Soviet-backed Communist government in that country. The Polish Solidarity movement, led by Lech Walesa, started the ball rolling, but the Poles were able to withstand the Communists' efforts to break them because the Catholic Church provided the movement with a legitimacy that mobilized millions of their countrymen to support and stand behind the labor movement. The Polish-born Pope, John Paul II, brokered relationships between the church and Solidarity that led to the ultimate demise of Communism in Poland. Religion had an enormous influence in this conflict.

There are religions other than the three Abrahamic traditions that experience conflict and tension. In northern India, for example, the Sikh religious community has for decades engaged in armed struggle with the forces of the secular state of India as well as with Hindu activists associated with the Bharatiya Janata Party (the BJP, or Indian People's Party). This conflict was guided, for many years, by one of the most revered figures in certain Sikh circles, Sant Jarnail Singh Bhindranwale, who would set in motion one of the bloodiest periods in Indian history.

He rose to power in the Punjab region of India, but advocated a strong religious nationalism that called for Sikhs not to lose their identity to either secularism or a resurgent Hinduism. This religiously based stance was problematic to the ruling party of India, then led by Indira Gandhi. In response to a series of events that led Bhindranwale to sequester himself in 1984 in the most revered site of Sikh faith, the Golden Temple of Amritsar, the government of Gandhi sent in troops to storm the Temple and, as a result, over two thousand people were killed, including Bhindranwale. This disaster was followed by the assassination of Gandhi herself later that year at the hands of her Sikh bodyguards. Both events inflamed a religious conflict that still simmers between Hindus and Sikhs.

Even in the United States, we find religiously powered resistance that spawns violence. This resistance exists within violent and extremist groups such as the Christian Identity Movement, which believes the world is locked in a struggle between the forces of good and evil. In the minds of people belonging to such groups, evil is represented by the federal government of the United States.

This is one reason why the Christian terrorist, Timothy McVeigh, chose the Murrah federal building in Oklahoma City for his 1995 attack. It represented all those governmental forces of moral decay and irreligion that religious extremists feel are destroying the United States. The fact that this attitude mirrors the Muslim terrorist mindset should give us pause. The extremists of many religions would see the other believers as completely antithetical to followers of the "true" religion, yet each side would employ the same violent means to initiate the reign of God on earth. In this great conflict—necessary for cleansing the world of unrighteousness—the notion of a coming apocalypse factors into the religious ethos they have embraced. Because this is a battle between nothing less than good and evil, the stakes are enormous.

The reality of the situation is that both the Muslim and Western worlds struggle to understand one another. Muslims struggle to understand other Muslims, and Hindus struggle to understand Sikhs; Jews try to understand Muslims, and Christians seek to understand other Christians. The divides we face are complex and multifaceted, but they exist both among and within various communities and present us with challenges as we seek a way forward. Indeed, one of the greatest challenges before us is that some religious communities don't want, or know how, to understand others. Sometimes this isolationism is tied to doctrinal or creedal differences, but more often it relates to conflicts generated by tribal competition for resources and to strife over tribal identity.

In the African Context: Nigeria and Darfur

One example of how religious conflict can create turmoil in societies is found in a country mentioned earlier, Nigeria. One place to start might be the village of Yelwa in central Nigeria. This area was colonized by Islam in the first surge of Muslim invaders in the eighth century CE, but they could only go so far because of a tsetse fly band that extended across the continent of Africa, making movement south impossible due to sleeping sickness disease. This meant that Muslim influence was concentrated to the north of this line for quite some time. South of this line, other religious communities emerged. The conflict in this village is between Muslim merchants and herders of the Jarawa tribe located in the northern part, and the Tarok and Goemai tribes, which are predominantly Christian, located in the southern part.

For years the Christians had denied citizenship rights to Muslims, relegating them to second-class status. This created a great deal of tension and resentment between the different groups, but this would soon boil over to open conflict between tribes. In February of 2004 as the Yelwa congregation of the Church of Christ of Nigeria were praying, they were set upon by a group of Muslims and savaged. When the attack was over, many were dead and the church was decimated. Two months later, groups of Christians rampaged against the Muslim community, killing hundreds of Muslims and burning Mosques and homes.

This event, which unleashed months of violence in the region, is only a microcosm of a larger conflict that has enveloped not only Nigeria, but also the entire central band of Africa. Part of this territory, northern Nigeria, has one of the oldest and most established Islamic communities in Africa. The African Islamic communities were galvanized by the Iranian revolution in the late 1970s and northern Nigeria was no exception to this, but alongside this growing resurgence of Islam, another faith community—Christianity—was experiencing its own growth. Much of this growth was due to high birthrates and aggressive evangelism. The expansion of the Christian religion in Nigeria has been so explosive that "the demographic and geographic center of global Christianity will have moved by 2050 to northern Nigeria, within the Muslim world (Griswold, 2004, p. 43).

This is the reality that Nigeria will be coming to grips with in the future. Different religious communities will be in competition for scarce resources of food and water, and the geographic boundaries that worked to separate them previously are eroding. The struggle between the two religious communities is not the only reason why this area is so symbolically instructive of what is taking place more generally in the rest of the world. The other reality is that some of the greatest struggles are also taking place within religious communities. In these struggles to define themselves religiously, people ask the question, "Whose Islam, or whose Christianity, ends up structuring society for the rest of the community?"

Religions seldom exist in monolithic blocks, but are incredibly diverse among, within, and between faiths. In the Nigerian context, Pentecostal Christians exist with Orthodox Christians, and Sunni Muslims exist with Shi'ite Muslims. There are different ways of understanding their faiths within all these variations. Add to this the reality that traditional African religion still has a powerful influence in many of these communities and shows up in the lived practices of the believer. As an example of this, there are reports of persons drinking the ink used by schoolchildren to write out the words of the Qur'an because it would mean the Word of God held holy power, accessible by the ingestion of the ink. This syncretism, or blending together of elements of various practices, is a profound mark of many traditional cultures in general.

These dynamics are also found in the midst of Africa's other challenges, which do involve land, water, and survival. In Darfur, for instance, we see all these features present. Situated in the western part of Sudan, Darfur exhibits the reality that religion is inextricably bound to ethnic identity and the abuse of governmental power. The situation there is complex because of the religious divisions present. The recent troubles began in 1983 in the Sudan, when then-President Gaafar Nimeiry began a campaign for Sudan to adhere more strictly to Islamic law. This precipitated a two decades long civil war between the Arab Muslim North and the Southern Sudan, where Christianity, or, in some places, animism, is the majority religious practice. The Christians, of course, objected to having Sharia law imposed upon them.

The troubles in Darfur were heightened in 2003 with a rebellion launched against the Arab dominated government in Khartoum. The grievance was that the government was oppressing non-Arabs and neglected Darfur. The government responded by attacking the rebels and unleashing Arab militias, the Janjaweed, on the region. The result has been catastrophic there. This conflict is not as simple to define as the earlier conflict, however, because most of the violence has been done by Muslims against other Muslims.

In an article in the *New York Times* of August 22, 2004, Marc Lacy, reporting on the struggle in Darfur, recounted the following scene. A meeting was held in a village about six miles from the Chad border and at this meeting a dozen sheiks gathered to explain their views of the violence. The Africans sat on one side and the Arabs clustered on another. Lacy relates the event by saying that the Arab sheik spoke first and said the conflict could be resolved without outside involvement if everyone would simply follow the principles of Islam. The Qur'an, he claimed, stated that Muslims should talk about and discuss and solve their problems together. Then he proceeded to question the religious convictions of some of the combatants, particularly the convictions of those Muslims who were African rebels.

At this point in the proceedings, an African sheik spoke and questioned the devotion to Islam of those in the government-backed militias who attacked his people. He said he had searched for a divine reason for all the death and destruction and could accept only the notion that it was ultimately God's will; perhaps they were being punished, he said (Lacy, 2004). This incident illuminates the reality that the same religion can affect different parties involved in conflicts, but that tribal and ethnic identities will also color the way that the religious precepts are employed. As we have seen, religion participates in social structuring, along with other components of culture, but this participation is always contextual, existing within the web of relationships that define society.

One of the problems with this social construction, however, is that the religions so interpreted will inevitably assert universal status, making claims on the adherents that transcend time and place. In other words, for the religion to function effectively as a comprehensive identity in a culture it must stake a claim that it possesses a unique status in the world. The religious belief cannot, under any circumstances, be seen as conditioned by social and historical location because that would mean a dissolving of religious commitment, and the erosion of religious and social authority. This erosion is just what is being fought against in many parts of the world. In Darfur we can detect the consequences of this by looking at the fact that religion is used to shore up tribal and ethnic identity in opposition to those who are ethnically different, even though they share the same religion.

Is There a Way Forward?

These are only some of the many examples of how religion will continue to influence the world for quite some time. When personal and cultural identity are tied to the dynamics that exist in religion, the type of concerns we have raised in this chapter become more difficult to deal with because, for the believer, the stakes can sometimes be much higher than for the nonbeliever. One of the difficulties that confronts us as we move forward is how to respond to these tensions between religion and society. To find the way ahead is going to mean that we have to respond in several different ways to the rising of religious influence in various parts of the world.

The present world situation is now—at least in some regions—loaded with animosity between religious rebellion and secular pretension. Those who see the benefits of secular society and fear the consequences of religious influence find it hard to figure out how to make a space for religious practice that has any public or political significance in society. Though these secularists may seek to accommodate the religious believer, what they are concerned with is precisely the gravitational pull and power of "the absolute," discussed earlier in this chapter, that drives some religious expressions. This Newtonian force is in danger of pulling all of society into its orbit because the most fundamental expressions of religion find any accommodation with the prevailing order to be a threat. To accommodate to the secular order means an erosion of religious identity. In this instance, the creation of alternative faith communities existing within the social order can fulfill the need to protect identity.

The danger comes, however, when those who feel religiously disenfranchised seek to legitimate their religious beliefs through political power. Oftentimes, the ruling political orders bring this response on themselves because they have become corrupt and neglect the call to reform. Rebellion then becomes more attractive to those who are on the margins. Because religion functions as such a powerful shaper of cultural and individual identity, it is religious movements and institutions that have the ability to resist the forms of governance seeking to destroy the space for particular religious beliefs and practices.

What is taking place today in the world transcends the global jihadists; it goes to the heart also of many other cultures and religions. How will space be created for religious communities to co-exist in the global context? How can those who feel they are under attack by the relentless forces of secularism, such as the consumerism that contemporary capitalism generates, fight back against the power that shapes their lives with such alien values? How will claims between devotees of various religious communities be negotiated? How will reconciliation take place? How do we deal with the claims to land in Israel that some religious texts animate in the minds of their believers? Who gets to define what home looks like?

The response to what threatens us will not be without appeals to violence and everlasting holy war by those elements who find their meaning in the notions of sacred war. Oddly enough, this notion of eternal conflict also drives some secularists as well. Religious communities find their counterparts in the secularists who also seek to define matters in terms of war so as to keep populations mobilized against external threats. Locked in their dance of mutual destruction, these secular fighters too may pull the rest of the world into their visionary framework, seeing no other possibility than dominance by one order or the other. The "Cold War" of the long post-1945 era provides the most powerful example of such an essentially secular quest for world dominance.

Where can we find hope, then, that the conflicts engendered by strong religion can be negotiated? Curiously enough, one recent example helps us to enlarge our imaginations to entertain the idea that creative ways are possible when the will to peace becomes stronger than the will to order. The example comes from another religious conflict, one which fueled strife for decades in Northern Ireland. The roots of this conflict extend back to the sixteenth century, to the time when Protestant immigrants from Scotland arrived to protect British colonial interests. In the following centuries, the English, and the Protestants, consolidated their power, much to the chagrin of the Catholics, who had been in Ireland since the days of Saint Patrick. In the twentieth century, this conflict took an increasingly violent turn as the country was partitioned into independent Irish "Catholic South," and the "Protestant North," which was officially loyal to the British Crown.

The "Troubles," as the long conflict between Catholics, and Protestants aligned with Great Britain, was named, came to an important crossroads in Derry on "Bloody Sunday," in 1972, when thirteen Catholic protesters were killed by British troops. Direct British rule was then imposed, and continuing violence flared between the Catholic IRA and its two main opponents, the British army and the Protestant inhabitants of Northern Ireland. Most people on both sides believed the situation was intractable and that no resolution could be found: "You cannot negotiate with terrorists" was the official British mantra. The situation was an incredibly complex one, where religion had long served to solidify personal and community identities and interests. Yet, on April 9, 1998, Good Friday, a peace agreement was finally concluded that began a long and heavily negotiated path toward peace in Northern Ireland.

The reason this came about is that space was created for the majority of participants to feel as though both their political interests were being protected *and* their religious identities were being respected. The "extremist" fringes of the dispute, represented in part by Protestant minister and polarizing political figure Ian Paisley, had been marginalized to such an extent that they could not derail the agreement.[5] In later years, the path was opened for Ian Paisley to participate in the new government, and in his inclusion he actually shared power with Catholics such as Martin McGuinness, former member of Sinn Fein.

This is not to say that Paisley himself was ever able to completely overcome a lifetime of prejudice, but enough space was created by the peace process that his religious followers could accept the new definition of the relationship between religion and politics in Northern Ireland. The way forward was accomplished by enormous patience and the willingness to not respond in kind to terrorist attacks. This restraint alone took immense discipline and repeated efforts at building trust between parties. But this trust was built not just within the official political structures, but also in the civic community of "ordinary people."

Can such initiatives work in other parts of the world where religious conflict has produced situations that defy solution? In fact, Marc Gopin in his book, *Holy War, Holy Peace: How Religion Can Bring Peace to the Middle East* (2002), argues that religion itself can bring peace to the Middle East, especially in the conflict between Israelis and Palestinians. Incorporating the view that religious texts, myths, metaphors, laws, and values are a subset of cultural formation, he suggests we use these elements to uncover what moors persons to their cultural contexts and to turn those very elements into the means of conflict resolution.

In this way of approaching things, the road forward does not just exist in political negotiation, but in cultural negotiating of religious identity as well (Gopin, 2002). It is doubtful that we will be able to rely on existing political structures or leaders alone to foster a healing cultural process. Such a process must be dedicated to finding space and time for draining the anger and fear of those who feel threatened when their own religion struggles to create, or maintain, its foothold in the global community. We will have to find alternative ways of negotiating the terms of our common life. This will entail creative ways of responding to the concerns that presently drive the world.

Such creative opportunities beckon where religions themselves become sources of peace amidst conflict, but this is no easy road. Still, it is already happening in some places: for example, the Parliament of the World's Religions, where inter-faith dialogue and debate take place on a global scale, with worldwide conferences attended by thousands of people. The next conference will be in 2009 in Melbourne, Australia and will "educate participants for global peace and justice" through exploring the types of issues that we have been reflecting on in this chapter. Such things as religious conflict and globalization, creating community and cross-cultural networks, and addressing religious violence, are on the agenda.

The Web site of the Parliament suggests it will support "strengthening religious and spiritual communities" by providing a special focus on indigenous and Aboriginal spiritualities. But it will also be seeking to facilitate cooperation between many different religious communities; crafting new responses to religious extremism; and confronting homegrown terrorism and violence.[6] This is but one example of ways that religions can address what appear to be intractable issues. The good news is that other organizations are now seeking to address the same problems.

One such is a group of Jewish, Christian, and Muslim scholars, who comprise the Scriptural Reasoning Society. At academic gatherings and in their local communities, persons from the Abrahamic faith traditions are committed to reading their sacred texts and having forthright and honest discussion about religious belief and identity. There is a strong commitment in this community to existing together in the world without using violence as a way of maintaining cultural identity. It is this type of initiative that offers promise for those who seek to find in their religion the resources not for exclusion, but embrace.

Another example is the Institute for Interreligious Dialogue, established in 2000, following the efforts of Iranian President, Mohammad Khatami. Though some may see this as solely a propaganda arm of the Iranian government, people of faith should not allow their governments to cut off dialogue with other religious communities. The point is that even though there may be official places that the political order establishes or supports for public dialogue and discussion, the type of honest exchanges that can lead to religious mutuality will often occur in both official and non-official contexts. In this way spaces are created that may allow religious communities to find common ground with one another.

After the events of 9/11, new possibilities have arisen because believers in many religious communities have realized that humankind is standing at a moment of profound opportunity. We can not learn how to merely exist with one another, but also how to respect and support one another in a world that is increasingly shrinking. It has only been in the last century of humankind's cultural evolution that we have been brought so close to one another's faiths.

At this moment in our cultural evolution we cannot rely solely on secular governments, whose approach to religion is often one of manipulation or fear, to dictate how the religious communities will negotiate the power of identity and cultural formation. The world's religions will have to step up and lead the global community to an awareness that religious tensions, claims, and conflicts can be constructively addressed and resolved.

Perhaps it may be the case that, as we learn more of one another's faith communities, we will acquire a compassion bordering on communion with one another that can guide our way into the future. This will not be accomplished by the political order primarily, but by a community of persons who dare to think in new ways about how we can honor religious identities.

These are significant challenges and it will take a long view to see fruition. It may take centuries to overcome centuries of cultural conditioning. I have mentioned only some of the initiatives, but there are many. Some attract little public attention, but are having a big impact. In mosques, synagogues, temples, and churches, people of good faith are seeking ways not only to tolerate, but also to honor and respect, the religious commitments of others. This task will take enormous discipline and patience, especially when the extremists respond with violence. But it is not impossible.

Notes

1. The student who is really interested in this history might want to read William Cavanaugh's "A fire strong enough to consume the house: The wars of religion and the rise of the state," *Modern Theology*, 11: 4 (October 1995), pp. 397–420. Cavanaugh makes a compelling case that the so-called wars of religion served the state's desire to take power from religious institutions and thus served as a narrative of control for the establishment of the modern nation-state.

2. I discuss the issues of absolutism in religion and the tension between the pure and the impure at greater length in *Religionless christianity: Dietrich Bonhoeffer in troubled times* (2008). London: T. & T. Clark, pp. 75–77.

3. This was not one of the most publicly stated goals because of the problems behind fighting wars for ideology; but it was influential inside the White House in 2002. This agenda was set forth by a group known as the neo-conservatives and was described in a document called the Project for a New American Century. This document can be accessed at http://www.newamericancentury.org/ Last accessed 15 November, 2008.

4. In this text, Juergensmayer details even more conflicts than I have mentioned here.

5. Paisley is an interesting person, partly because he was both the founding member of the Free Presbyterian Church of Ulster and co-founder of a political party, the Democratic Unionist Party. In his person he embodied many of the intractable difficulties faced by people in Northern Ireland. Religious identity combined with political identity served to create in him the notion that he was standing on God's side in his fight against the Irish Republican Army. Later, after he became part of the peace process, and took on the role of First Minister of Northern Ireland, his views changed somewhat. For a fuller account of this fascinating story, see Steve Bruce, (2007), *Paisley: Religion and politics in Northern Ireland*. Oxford, UK: Oxford University Press.

6. The Web site for this event is at http://www.parliamentofreligions.org/index.cfm?n=8 Last accessed 16 November 2008.

References

Gopin, M. (2002). *Holy war, holy peace: How religion can bring peace to the Middle East*. Oxford, UK: Oxford University Press.

Griswold, E. (2008, March). God's country. *The Atlantic Monthly*. 40–55.

Jyllands-Posten Muhammad cartoons controversy. http://en.wikipedia.org/wiki/Jyllands-Posten_Muhammad_cartoons 28 May 2009.

Juergensmeyer, M. (2003). *Terror in the mind of God: The global rise of religious violence*. Berkeley: University of California Press.

Juergensmeyer, M. (2008). *Global rebellion: Religious challenges to the secular state, from Christian militias to Al Qaeda*. Berkeley: U of California P.

Lacy, M. (2004, August 22). In Sudan, hunger and hunted alike invoke the prophet. *The New York Times*.

Volf, M. (1996). *Exclusion and embrace: A theological exploration of identity, otherness, and reconciliation*. Nashville: Abingdon Press.

Questions for Discussion

1. Do some research on the cartoons mentioned at the beginning of the chapter. How have they been received in the Muslim world? Why do you think the response has been so intense? How might you respond if your religious leader were attacked in a similar manner? Would your reaction differ from the reaction of the Muslim world? Why?

2. Pugh makes the argument that religion in the West has accommodated itself to secularism and no longer influences in any profound ways the key cultural institutions of society, such as economics or politics. Do you agree or disagree with this assessment? Why?

3. In this chapter, Pugh makes reference to the ways that narratives, or stories, shape how we think about the world and our place in it. What are some of the stories that have shaped you? Are there religious stories that have shaped you? Family stories? National stories? How do you think someone growing up in another culture is shaped to believe their stories are true as well? For example, think about the Muslim story of the Twelfth Imam, The Mahdi, who appears at the end of time as a representative of God's plan. Is this different from the story of Jesus coming back at the end of time that many Christians believe in? Do both stories shape the consciousness of their hearers?

4. Did you find the author's arguments convincing about the division between the secular and religious cultures? Why or why not? How much do you know about the historical development of the separation of church and state in the West? Can you give examples from your own life that would strengthen your argument?

5. Do some research to point to places where religion may be making a positive impact on the global community. For example, did religious belief play any role in the Truth and Reconciliation Commission in South Africa? Do a Web search to find organizations or individuals who are working to promote religious pluralism and to encourage relationships among several religious communities. Can you find any inter-religious dialogue that seeks to establish positive relationships among religious communities? Do you think religion is a more positive or negative force in the world?

Suggested Readings

Clausen, C. (2007, Winter). America's design for tolerance. *Wilson Quarterly*. 26–32

Haught, J. (1995). *Holy hatred: Religious conflicts of the '90s*. Amherst, New York: Prometheus Books.

Mitchell, C. (2006). *Religion, identity and politics in Northern Ireland: Boundaries of belonging and belief*. Aldershot, UK: Ashgate Publications.

Rosenblum, N. (Ed.) (2000). *Obligations of citizenship and demands of faith: Religious accommodation in pluralist demouncies*. Princeton, NJ: Princeton University Press.

12

Global Politics and Global Issues

Where Do You Fit?

Laura Roselle, Robert G. Anderson, Kerstin Sorensen

Many students today want to understand how to contribute positively to the solution of global problems and want to take advantage of the world of opportunities that awaits them after graduation. Many events and many trends—for example, civil war in Sudan and Sri Lanka, the global slave trade, United States involvement in Iraq and Afghanistan, the world economy, environmental degradation—are important to many college students. However, some believe that, while they want to participate in world affairs, "politics" is not for them. But global politics coordinates behavior in the world and you must understand it if you want to help shape world affairs and solve world problems. If you think about it, politics is really about making things happen, and that means that politics can be about creating a different and perhaps better world. "Politics" refers, of course, to how governmental policies are made and implemented; but it has a broader definition as well. Politics describes the interactions among people who have both authority and power. Politics, then, shapes the lives and relationships of all people within the purview of that authority and power: in the workplace, in the local community, and at state, national, and global levels. Politics is, among other things, about who gets what. So, even if you see yourself as an "un-political" person, with no strong party-political or ideological identity, you will, whether you like it or not, be affected by what happens in the political world.

Without a doubt, political action has changed the world. Just consider ending legal slavery, securing the vote or other rights for women, the promotion of human rights for victims of genocide or dictatorships, or international actors coming to agreement on environmental or arms control or international economics. None of these actions would have been possible without people challenging the status quo and envisioning a better world for themselves or future generations. In addition, domestic politics often has ripple effects across national borders, occasionally even years after events have happened. Just think about the Civil Rights movement of the 1950s and 1960s in the United States and how it inspired renewed activism in South Africans' struggle against apartheid, a system of legalized racial segregation that ended in the early 1990s. While this is an example of a monumental change in world political history, changes on a smaller scale also affect, and are influenced by, global politics.

Political action and political theory, then, are instrumental in shaping our world, and our views of that world. This chapter attempts to illuminate some aspects of world politics by answering the question: "What characterizes global politics in the twenty-first century?" Many United States citizens seem to assume that international relations fundamentally changed with the events of 9/11 in the United States. Citizens of countries outside the United States however, have a different opinion. This chapter assesses changes in international relations over a longer period of time, focusing on the various types of political actors in the global system and the challenges prominent in the world today. States, international organizations, non-governmental organizations (NGOs), religious groups, terrorist cells, and ordinary citizens all have a part in our increasingly complex system. This chapter describes these different actors and identifies the importance of interests, ideas, perceptions, and power in the world today. The chapter also covers the role of international law, how scholars and politicians have studied and understand international relations theory, and new communication processes and technologies. These topics allow us to conclude with some perspective on the politics of addressing pressing global problems and pursuing global opportunities. In short, politics is central to the resolution of the world's most pressing difficulties, and this chapter will show you how a better understanding of international politics can enrich your understanding of the current problems facing the global community.

States as Political Actors

When most United States college students think about global politics, they often think about the actions of countries or states around the world. This is understandable when you consider the information which appears in the newspaper or on the nightly television news. You will notice that states are the "actors," or chief agents, in many news stories. For example, a story might say: today the United States agreed to meet with the United Kingdom to discuss common interests in Europe. There are a few things to notice here. First, "states" are, in this context, countries, not states as in the fifty states of the United States. There are more than 190 states in the world today as recognized by the United Nations. Second, states are not inevitable. What does this mean? It simply means that states are not the only way to organize global politics. In fact, states are relatively young entities. Most international relations scholars date the emergence of states to the Treaty of Westphalia in 1648, which closed the Thirty Years' War in Europe. City-states, empires, and other types of political arrangements were the norm before the development of states as we think about them today.

The emergence of states from the 1600s on was characterized by the consolidation of groups—often associated with nations—with a set of common interests related to security. Here it is important to distinguish between states and nations. When studying global politics, scholars make the distinction in the following way: States are political entities based on territory. Nations are groups of people who consider themselves to have a common culture, history, language, or other distinguishing characteristics. As you can see, a nation may reside in a state—such as in Japan where, for the most part, there is one cultural nation in one political territory or state. But, you can also have a nation whose boundaries cut across a number of different states. The Kurds in Iraq, Turkey, Iran, and Syria are an example. They consider themselves to be one nation (or people) that resides in different states. What is important to realize here is that as the state-centered international system developed over time, the match between nation and state was (and is) not perfect. And as you would imagine, this discrepancy can cause problems.

A significant development in the history of international relations was the creation of new states during the twentieth century, particularly after World War I and World War II. After both of these conflicts, new states were created—some based on national groupings and some based on other considerations. The development of states in Africa, for example, is a clear example of states being created without regard for national or tribal groupings. In essence, most African states gained their independent status based on a common desire for liberation from colonial oppression and domination—not on a common shared nationalism or sense of identity. Brian Digre's Chapter 8 explains some of these imperial legacies.

Most modern African states achieved independence in the post-WWII era with boundaries and indigenous populations created by the interests and needs of their former colonial rulers—interests and needs that seldom accommodated or consolidated the historical, political, cultural, ethnic, or geographic dynamics of the subjugated African peoples. Division of ethnic and tribal groups by artificial political boundaries was the rule, not the exception in most of colonial Africa. Post World War II independence offered few changes to these artificial lines of separation between historically and culturally similar African peoples—contributing to many of the conflicts today in places such as Kenya, Sudan, Uganda, Congo, and Rwanda. It is no surprise, then, that the late twentieth century witnessed an avalanche of state conflicts and collapse in Africa and elsewhere; this disorder was at least partially associated with unresolved colonial divisions of peoples whose cultural and ethnic identities and traditions were not successfully integrated or incorporated into the new independent states.

While there have been many examples of these, and other, state failures, the state structure itself has been relatively stable over time. Central to the stability and authority of the state system is the principle that the state—as a political entity—is *sovereign* in terms of its territorial authority. Sovereignty means that there is no overarching authority to tell states what to do. As you can probably surmise, in an international system in which states interact with others, there will be constraints on the extent of those states' freedom of operation and limits on their expressions of sovereign power. But the bottom line here is that there is no overarching political or legal authority with coercive (or military) power that can force a state to do something it does not want to do. One example of the principle of sovereignty is the case of the United States mining the harbors of Nicaragua in 1984. Nicaragua took the United States to international court and won, but the United States simply refused to recognize the jurisdiction of the court. There is not much to be done in this—and other similar cases—where a state asserts its sovereign "right of refusal."

The principle of national sovereignty includes the right of each state to determine the extent and definition of its obligations to other states, and the rights and freedoms conceded to subunits within its geographic boundaries. While a Universal Declaration of Human Rights was produced in 1948 as part of the initial process of creating a post-WWII international organization—the United Nations—this Universal Declaration was merely a recommended standard or gauge—not a legal requirement—for determining the rights and freedoms provided citizens of individual nation-states. But the promotion of universal political, social, and economic rights depends on the acquiescence of states to these international standards.

In the twentieth century, powerful state actors, especially the United States and the then-Soviet Union (USSR), repeatedly challenged each other for global strategic military and economic advantage. The two states differed significantly on the form and regulation of international trade, the role of the state in defining human rights and freedoms, and on the appropriate responses to the many national, ethnic, and religious liberation movements which emerged in the post-imperial world. But until the dissolution of the Soviet Union at the end of the twentieth century, most scholars described global politics as a process that focused on the dominance of the traditional state, which was essentially the continuation of a pattern of state consolidation and centralization of political power that had begun around 1648.

Rules and Organizations for the Engagement of States

As you might expect, as states first became important international political actors, an international system that coordinated state interaction was gradually established, or emerged, as new needs had to be met. *Diplomacy* provides one set of rules about how states should interact, for example. There are special rules for the behavior of and communication between diplomats. These rules set out consistent and shared expectations about the behaviors of political leaders, diplomats, and states. States, for example, designate particular individuals as diplomats who are charged with communicating on behalf of the state. Traditionally, because diplomats have been the international communication conduits, their travel and safety have been assured and they have been granted what is called diplomatic immunity. Diplomatic immunity means that diplomats are protected in the "host" country from lawsuits and legal prosecution. Specific rules about how to conduct diplomacy and how to maintain appropriate decorum evolved as a means to reduce the possibility of miscommunication or misunderstanding.

Important to diplomatic relations between and among states was the development of *international organizations* (IOs) in which states are the primary actors or players. The United Nations (UN) is one such international organization. In the General Assembly of the UN, for example, states send representatives to discuss issues of relevance to the world, such as global warming, the rights of indigenous peoples, gender equality, global poverty, hunger, disease, homelessness, lack of employment, and economic opportunity. Other international organizations can be found in Figure 12.1. These international organizations are based in

Examples of International Organizations	
Organization	**Headquarters**
United Nations	New York, New York
World Trade Organization	Geneva, Switzerland
World Health Organization	Geneva, Switzerland
The World Bank Group	Washington, D.C.
International Criminal Court	The Hague, the Netherlands
Organization of American States	Washington, D.C.
Organization for Security and Co-operation in Europe	Vienna, Austria
African Union	Addis Ababa, Ethiopia
European Union	Brussels, Belgium
Asia-Pacific Economic Cooperation	Singapore

FIGURE 12.1

various cities around the world and take up a wide range of important global issues. As with many organizations, international organizations often come to have a structure and a culture that distinguish them from other IOs. So even as international organizations are composed of state actors, there are often IO staff members who become linked to the success of the organization itself. Such organizational identities and loyalties can certainly complicate the clarity and efficiency of national and international policy and action on the world stage.

Non-state Political Actors

While this chapter emphasizes the ongoing importance of the state in global politics, it is also important to understand the changing global political landscape in the twenty-first century, mainly by highlighting the important roles of many new *non-state actors*. On the one hand, international institutions have established infrastructures and rules, or procedures, that facilitate the interaction of states on the international stage. On the other hand, a big change has occurred with the increasing number of non-state actors. There are international organizations with states as actors, to be sure, but there are also growing numbers of non-governmental organizations (NGOs), religious groups, terrorist cells, and even individuals and corporations, that play significant roles in the global arena.

Organizations for Non-state Actors

Non-governmental organizations (NGOs) are made up of non-state groups or individuals. Amnesty International, for example, is an NGO. Amnesty International operates in over 80 countries and seeks to promote human rights in the global community by researching and publicizing violations and pressuring governments and others to fight against the violation of human rights. According to its mission statement, Amnesty International seeks to "stop violence against women, defend the rights and dignity of those trapped in poverty, abolish the death penalty, oppose torture and combat terror with justice, free prisoners of conscience, protect the rights of refugees and migrants, regulate the global arms trade."[1] Other examples of NGOs include: the Women's Federation for World Peace, the World Council of Independent Christian Churches, Médecins Sans Frontières (Doctors without Borders), Operation Smile, Anti-Slavery International, and the World Wildlife Fund International. Although difficult to count, scholars suggest there are tens of thousands of NGOs worldwide. Some groups seek a role at international organizations' meetings as they present expertise on particular issues and help give voice to people all over the world. Others work solely at the grassroots level to serve people in many places.

Another type of non-state group that some say is increasingly important in global politics today is the *religious group*. One example might be the Taliban. The Taliban is a fundamentalist group of Muslims operating principally in Afghanistan. Members of this group believe in an extreme form of Islam that includes the barring of women from education and work outside of the home. The Taliban has used violence to consolidate power in certain areas and is now fighting the state or national governments of Afghanistan and Pakistan, and the NATO (North Atlantic Treaty Organization) forces (a large number of which are from the United States) which support that government. No one elected the Taliban in Afghanistan and they do not represent the government of Afghanistan, but the group is an important player in Afghan affairs, both domestic and foreign. This situation illustrates what we mean when we say that a non-state actor has a significant role in international relations.

Finally, the role of *individuals* in global politics should not be overlooked. Of course, political leaders, through their decisions and actions, can make a significant difference in the course of world events. For example, President George W. Bush's decision to go to war in Iraq has significantly affected the shape of international relations. Nelson Mandela, the first President (1994) of post-apartheid South Africa, is another example of a political leader who has shaped his own country's future and, many would argue, the moral climate of the rest of the world. Consider, in addition, the following list of powerful individuals who have affected, or continue to shape, the course of world events: Joseph Stalin, Mao Zedong, Franklin D. Roosevelt, Winston Churchill, Adolf Hitler, Fidel Castro, Robert Mugabe, Nouri al-Maliki, Hugo Chávez, and Hamid Karzai.

But it is one thing to say that political leaders shape international politics. What about people like you or your classmates? One particularly important question that many students ask is: Can I affect what happens in the world? And the answer is: yes! As discussed at the end of this chapter, ordinary individuals can shape the world in a number of different ways. To do so, it is important to learn as much as possible about how the global political system works. This includes understanding the causes which encourage global actors to argue, fight, and cooperate. Some of these causal factors are national and state interests, ideas, perceptions, and power.

Key Concepts Related to Cooperation and Conflict: Interests, Ideas, Perceptions, and Power

Global politics is about relationships characterized by conflict *and* cooperation among the many actors identified in the first part of this chapter. You can surely think of examples of both conflict and cooperation. The war in Iraq is one example of a conflict, but so are disagreements among states on trade or environmental regulations, protests by citizen groups at World Trade Organization (WTO) meetings, or the use of suicide-bombings, and other violent events. Conflicts are marked by dispute(s) over perceived interests, processes, policies, or outcomes. Conflicts can be violent or non-violent, easily resolved or intractable, multi-dimensional, or focused on a narrow issue, and related to resources or ideas.

Cooperation is evident when peace treaties are signed, astronauts and scientists from a number of countries work together on the international space station, or when environmental agreements are implemented. It is marked by actors working together to find a solution to a problem or conflict. Cooperation is marked by non-violence, and usually involves communication, negotiation, and compromise. There is no assumption here that all actors will get everything they want or that the outcome will be equitable or fair. One side may give up more than another, for example.

One of the ways that scholars have studied global politics is by focusing on what makes cooperation or conflict more or less likely, and this involves a deeper look at what scholars call *interests, ideas, perceptions,* and *power.* These concepts are central to our understanding of global politics.

Interests can be envisioned as what motivates a state to behave in a particular way. Certainly many scholars would say that states as actors in the global political system are first concerned about, or are interested in, their own survival or security. So survival is assumed by many to be a state interest. That does not mean that states cannot cease to exist: Czechoslovakia became the two states of the Czech Republic and Slovakia on January 1, 1993, and the Union of Soviet Socialist Republics (the USSR or Soviet Union) became the 15 states of Armenia, Azerbaijan, Belarus, Estonia, Georgia, Kazakhstan, Kyrgyzstan, Latvia, Lithuania, Moldova, Russia, Tajikistan, Turkmenistan, Ukraine, and Uzbekistan in December 1991. Still, most states attempt to maintain their territorial and political integrity. They wish to continue to exist.

In addition to state survival, there are other state interests as well, including economic or other cultural values regarded as vital by the state. A state's leaders, for example, may claim that it is in the state's interest to pursue a particular policy because by doing so the state will increase its economic resources or enhance certain values, beliefs, or practices central to the state's culture. Take, for example, the creation of the Organization of Petroleum Exporting Countries (OPEC) in 1965 by states that wanted to pursue their economic interests of maximizing oil revenues. These states continue to meet today to coordinate the supply of their oil. Or take the example of France's cultural policy that seeks to promote the French language, arts, and culture around the world as a counterpoint to French perception of American cultural dominance.

As you can see from the examples above, ideas are extremely important to understanding global politics because *ideas* shape how people understand the international system and their own interests. For example, political leaders who have the idea that cooperation will lessen the likelihood of conflict may behave differently—that is, make different policy decisions—from political leaders who believe that cooperation only makes a nation-state more vulnerable. Understanding that ideas matter is central to understanding global politics today. These ideas include those about how states do and should behave, about how economic systems do and should work, about the importance of particular political systems such as democracy, and about the goals of global interactions. Competing or contradictory ideas about these important areas may impede cooperation and increase (or catalyze) conflict. This chapter will turn to some of the fundamental ideas associated with global politics in the section on international relations theory.

Directly related to the concepts of interests and ideas is the understanding that *perceptions* often matter when thinking about conflict and cooperation. Perception implies that certain leaders of states, groups, or individuals may understand—or see, or feel—the same events as having different causes, or results. Perception implies that psychological processes are involved in, and affect, how global politics work. For example, leaders may—in addition to acting on the biases created by their own personal and idiosyncratic cognitive frameworks—make decisions based on perceived historical examples. And the historical examples on which they choose to focus matter greatly. In the United States, the historical lessons of Munich in 1938 (associated mainly with British appeasement of Germany before World War II) and the Vietnam War (associated with any number of lessons, including the dangers of protracted conflicts, the need for the use of massive military power once committed to war, and the challenge to domestic policy posed by an unpopular war) have been applied to conflicts such as those with Grenada, El Salvador, Nicaragua, Panama, Bosnia, Kosovo, Kuwait, Afghanistan, and Iraq.

Finally, it is important to understand something about the role of *power* in the international system. Power generally refers to the resources or capabilities that a state possesses that enable it to influence or coerce others in the international system. It is often divided into *hard power* and *soft power*. Hard power consists of military capabilities (the number of guns, bombs, people in the armed forces, and so on). More military power, for example, may allow a state to get its way through threat of, or actual use of, force. This equation explains the tremendous escalation in military arsenals during the twentieth century, in particular. The history of the development and proliferation of nuclear weapons also clearly shows the perceived importance of hard power in global politics. Why have some countries, such as India, North Korea, Pakistan, and Israel, pursued the development of nuclear weapons? It is because they believe that having such weapons will make them more secure. Security comes from the mere *threat* of using nuclear weapons against unfriendly states and was, in fact, the basis of the long-standing Cold War policy known as "deterrence." Not all states think this way, however. For example, South Africa, Kazakhstan, Belarus, and Ukraine have given up nuclear weapons, believing that the weapons cannot be used without jeopardizing their own survival and the survival of the world.

Soft power, on the other hand, refers to cultural power. For example, a state whose culture is seen as attractive or appealing may be better able to convince others to agree with its policies. Joseph Nye, a famous international relations scholar, argues that soft power is based on three components: a state's "culture (in places where it is attractive to others), its political values (when it lives up to them at home and abroad), and its foreign policies (when they are seen as legitimate and having moral authority)."[2] So, soft power involves the belief that a state's ideas are right, good, and/or attractive. One important point to note is that there are those who argue that real power does not come from being able to force others to do something they do not want to do, but from having the ability to foster or create consensus on an issue. This "cultural power" may indeed set the stage for the creation of such a consensus.

International Law—Its Range and Limitations

Many of the concepts discussed above are relevant to an increasingly important area of global politics—*international law*. Any complex political system eventually incorporates some form of legally binding governance procedure to assist in the formal regulation of behavior—if for no other reason than to avoid complete anarchy and provide a foundation for acceptable means of predictable and peaceful interaction between members. In the case of global politics, over hundreds of years, states have produced a semi-voluntary framework of international rules, regulations and law based on a variety of sources—including conventions, treaties, customs, general principles of law, and judicial decisions and teachings of highly qualified jurists and scholars. Interest, ideas, perceptions, and power all have been central to the development of international law.

Consistently, however, students—and many others—seem to wonder if international law is really law! If international law applies only to states—and specifically only to matters about which states voluntarily agree to be bound—how important, influential and real is such a legal system? Such skepticism about international law generally arises from a perspective that most of global politics takes place in an environment of global anarchy—where independent sovereign states selfishly contend for unilateral advantage. To some degree, this observation has merit. But such a perspective tends to emphasize the conflicts between states in the international system—to the exclusion of the amount of substantive cooperation taking place between states in efforts to enhance commerce, travel, research, health, sport and cultural activities, and educational opportunity.

An additional concern often expressed is that international law possesses only weak and rarely used formal court systems—with no reliable and permanent police force to enforce legal decisions. But are courts and police the real reason people decide to obey laws? Yes—domestic law is universally enforced within the context of highly institutionalized police and court systems. But what is often overlooked—even in analyses of domestic law—is the fact that most people comply with the domestic law not because they are forced to do so, but because of the expectation that in doing so, they will receive positive reciprocal behavior from their peers. In addition, most people in most states regard "the law" as basically legitimate and believe that it should be obeyed. While international law may lack the highly institutional court structure, and the fulltime enforcement agents of domestic law, it still benefits from the fundamental belief of many that abiding by the law usually produces helpful and predictable interactions among consenting parties. International law also benefits from the commonly shared voluntary acceptance of legal norms, and of the principle of legitimacy, that will—on the whole—produce compliance and positive outcomes. So it seems fair to say that international law is really law—or at least very close to law as it is defined domestically.

State Dominance in International Law

Many argue that almost all international laws, rules, and regulations have been produced to protect or preserve the interests of only state actors—usually focusing on the interests and needs of the most economically and militarily powerful states at the time the actions were taken. While many non-state global actors have been active for centuries, most international law recognizes the state only as the primary legal entity with international legal standing.

State dominance in international law relates to the previously discussed concept of state sovereignty. Each state is the sovereign of its legal domain (all matters relating to actions within its geographical borders, and all matters related to its interactions with political entities beyond its borders). Each state is accountable to no supranational sovereign authority above the state. And this legally translates into the fact that each state retains all rights and legal standing on matters related to its actions, citizens, resources, and economic interests unless it voluntarily concedes some of its sovereign right and legal standing through an internationally recognized agreement process—usually some form of treaty or other international agreement. This process means that all states have similar juridical equality and are—for the most part—bound only by the laws, rules and regulations to which they have consented.

As far as an executive authority to enforce international law, there is no centralized or permanent police force mechanism under international law. But this does not mean that there is no way to enforce international law! States rely heavily on "horizontal enforcement mechanisms," which include public condemnation of illegal behavior, suspension of political or diplomatic relations with an offending state, or application of unilateral or multilateral economic sanctions. Most international organizations have adopted specific enforcement powers, such as expelling a non-compliant member from the organization. The Security Council of the United Nations even has the power to use coercive measures against states to compel compliance with its decisions—including the use of force, as demonstrated in recent years by Security Council measures against Somalia, Iraq, and Sudan. But again, there is no permanent enforcement agent for every international law decision.

In most cases, because states willingly submit to international law, compliance is voluntary and states abide by the decisions of the specific court. In more serious situations, such as cases involving accusations of human rights abuse, genocide, or aggression, accused individuals and states often resist the decisions of the international judicial body making the decision. In such cases, it becomes the responsibility of member states of the organization to provide the needed personnel and support to ensure legal compliance—often a slow and ineffective process for making offending states abide by international judicial decisions, as repeated United Nations peacekeeping efforts in Sudan clearly demonstrate.

International Law and Non-state Actors

Other global actors—including inter-governmental organizations (IGOs), non-governmental organizations (NGOs), subnational governments, individuals or groups, businesses and corporations—obtain international legal standing only as the state agrees to recognize their standing beyond the state's domestic legal system and its existing international legal obligations. While individuals have no international legal status to sue another state, since World War II, numerous treaties have been ratified and courts formed to prosecute individuals accused of major violations of human rights, such as genocide. Current examples include the formation of special international tribunals created by the United Nations to bring to justice individuals associated with human rights atrocities in the Balkans and Rwanda.

The International Criminal Court (ICC) —which came into existence in 2002—also has the power to bring indictments against individuals accused of genocide, crimes against humanity, and war crimes. Jurisdiction of the ICC applies only to states signing the treaty (the Rome Statute) that created the ICC. So far, 108 states are signatory to the treaty— although some major state powers have refused to ratify the treaty for various reasons— including the United States, China, and Russia.

One example illustrates the conflict between the ICC and the principle of state sovereignty. On March 4, 2009, the ICC issued an indictment for the arrest of the president of Sudan, Omar al-Bashir, on charges of war crimes in the western region of his country known as Darfur. This is the first time in the history of international law that a "sitting president" of a recognized nation-state has been indicted by an international legal entity. The Sudanese president refused to surrender to the arrest warrant and said that the ICC has no jurisdiction over him or his actions and the indictment is politically motivated by the United States and other western nations seeking to interfere in the affairs of Sudan. President Bashir openly defied the warrant by making trips to Egypt, Eritrea, Libya and Qatar in the last weeks of March 2009. He made these trips to Arab neighbor countries with the understanding that they would not arrest him and turn him over to the ICC. Only Jordan and two other tiny Arab League members, the Comoros and Djibouti, are parties to the ICC Charter. Most Arab states support President Bashir and reject the ICC's arrest warrant.

The ICC is supplemented by a growing number of *ad hoc*, regional, and very specialized dispute resolution institutions, such as the Dispute Settlement Body of the World Trade Organization (WTO), the European Court of Human Rights, and The International Criminal Tribunal for the Former Yugoslavia—just to mention a few examples. States may also submit disputes for *ad hoc* arbitration if both parties to the dispute are willing.

Beyond the ICC, inter-governmental organizations (IGOs)—including the United Nations, the European Union, and NATO—have significant international legal standing and members of these organizations are legally bound—through formal treaty ratification— to assume specific obligations and accept the authority ceded to these organizations. Recent history documents the legal authority of these organizations to address significant global issues (especially in situations of aggression, human rights abuse, terrorism, and the spread of nuclear weapons), but critics are quick to point out that the actual outcomes of many IGO actions vary significantly in quality, level of commitment, and substantive effectiveness—as Sudan, Iran, and Iraq illustrate. Nonetheless, IGOs rank second only to states in their international legal standing. And, as the European Union seems to demonstrate, more states on a regional level are willing to concede major aspects of their national sovereignty to a supranational semi-sovereign entity, to advance more successfully their individual national interests.

Non-governmental organizations (NGOs)—such as Greenpeace and Amnesty International—regularly act transnationally, not limiting to a single state or region their advocacy on a variety of topics. These highly influential NGOs have yet to be extended the formal international legal status even approaching that of states. Nor have the NGOs been given formal standing in international judicial forums, with the exception of some cases heard at the level of regional organizations. But because they now operate largely outside the direct control of the states from which they originally hailed and are receiving limited formal status at some international decision making conferences, some juridical experts believe NGOs will eventually have an expanded international legal presence, especially in the areas of human rights and environmental law.

While significantly impacting, and impacted by, global politics, transnational businesses and corporations generally have only very limited standing in public international judicial and dispute resolution bodies, even when they may be the main parties involved in a dispute. In international law, disputes involving corporations are framed as disputes between their countries of origin. This was the case in a recent World Trade Organization matter that was contested between the United States and Brazil, even though, in fact, the dispute was really between two large oil companies. The increasingly global nature of corporate giants makes it harder and harder for any single state to regulate them—creating a situation where the corporate community itself is becoming a real source of growing global political power.

Based on the previous discussion, it should be clear that while states are under pressure from other groups and from the forces of globalization, they are and will remain the primary focus of international law. In the absence of a centralized body empowered to make laws binding on the international community, states are the "legislators" of international law mainly through their involvement in the creation of treaties and their historical roles in forming customary international law.

As this brief description of the role of international law in global politics indicates, one should not expect today's most pressing global problems to be resolved principally through an international legal system. Because international law is designed primarily to regulate relations between states, it is very limited in controlling what happens within the states themselves, where, unfortunately, so many human tragedies are staged. What states do to their own people (if not limited by treaty ratification) has, historically, not been the domain of international law. This absence of regulation of the internal lives of sovereign states, however, may not necessarily stop their near and distant neighbors from unilaterally or multilaterally acting "preemptively" to prevent a domestic situation from escalating into an event that will affect broader global security. But internationally, the practice of preemptive action is very controversial and often does not produce the expected result—as the world's responses to the United States-initiated Iraq invasion in 2003 indicate.

International law should be viewed simply as another very specific tool that can positively affect global politics where agreement on the obligations, interests, and needs between and among states is clear and specific. Actually, there are many areas of agreement, especially in matters related to trade, the environment, scarce resources, the sea, outer space, diplomatic relations, use of force, and human rights. And if international political actors—especially the leaders of the world's most powerful states—are willing to make the commitment, international law can play an increasingly important role in resolving existing disputes, preventing an escalation of conflict, deterring potential threats to peace and security, bringing international criminals and terrorists to justice, and protecting the environment and advancing human rights. More political will within individual states to empower the international legal system to act more independently and broadly is the needed prerequisite to enhanced international legal remedies for global problems. An example of such "political will" can be found in the late March 2009 actions of Spanish courts, which, at the request of several international human rights groups, proposed an international investigation into allegations that high-level officials in the administration of President George W. Bush in the United States had violated international law by providing the legal framework justifying the torture of prisoners at Guantánamo Bay, Cuba. The meaning and power of this example, however, is modified when we note that most United States legal experts said that such warrants, if issued, would be mainly symbolic, not practical, and that it was almost a certainty that the United States officials would not be arrested if they did not leave the United States. And yet, Spain has been a leader of international efforts to expand the scope and reach of international law. For example, it was a Spanish magistrate, Baltasar Garzón, who, in 1998, originally indicted the former Chilean dictator Augusto Pinochet for human rights violations.

International law creates a semblance of order through uniformity of action generated by the law itself. But always, people and groups may perceive events and actions on the international stage differently. Perceptions, indeed, may spring from a particular theoretical perspective, which includes—among other things—a set of assumptions about the relative importance of different values, aspirations, and beliefs. The next section addresses some of these different theoretical perspectives and their role in international relations.

The Role of Theory in International Relations

Differences in worldviews or theoretical perspectives affect which issues or problems we focus on (or find worthy of study), the methods we use to study them, and consequently, what we consider knowledge. The multitude of actors involved in international relations contributes to the complexity of competing worldviews and explanations that make up the field of international relations. It may seem puzzling to you that scholars and students of international relations can look at the same facts, yet draw different conclusions from them. For example, there is no *single* theory that can explain conflict and cooperation in international relations. Scholars working in the tradition of the school of thought called *realism* explain international relations in terms of a struggle for power; thus, they highlight conflict between actors (states). Another school of thought, called *liberalism*, emphasizes the role played by international law and norms, and international organizations, thus stressing cooperation among actors. Fundamental to these (or any) theoretical perspectives is the difference in worldviews, i.e., how each theory views human nature, the nature of the international system, and the potential for stability or peace in the system.

As there is a rather close connection among international relations scholars, think tanks, and policy makers, scholarship in international relations can and does influence domestic and international policy and law. There are many examples of how international relations scholarship has influenced international relations. From what you have learned so far, can you think of an example? As a student of international relations, you would learn about many theoretical perspectives and their variants. Indeed, a single theory may have several strands. For example, one strand of *liberalism*, the democratic peace theory, posits that democratic states, while as warmongering as other political systems (e.g., authoritarian states), do not go to war with one another. So far, there are no historical cases that challenge this theory. Why do you believe democratic peace theory has held up so far? What might some of the reasons be that democratic states do not fight wars with one another? You might try to tie your thinking on these questions back to a consideration of interests, ideas, or perceptions, in the preceding section.

Other theories in international relations that have gained importance in the field are *constructivism* and *feminism*. Often referred to as alternative theories, they challenge many of the assumptions underpinning the traditional realist and liberal perspectives. *Constructivist* scholars are particularly interested in how ideas, interests, and identities are created and evolve over time, and how these ideas, interests, and identities shape state behavior. Indeed, constructivists have been particularly effective in explaining the role of norms in shaping humanitarian military intervention, and in elucidating how non-state actors (such as international organizations) may shape states' interests and behavior.

Feminism, with its many variants, has, despite great resistance in the field, made inroads into international relations. While there are significant differences between the strands of feminism, they have in common a critique of the traditional perspectives' exclusion of women and gender[3] in studies of international relations. They address some of the consequences that the absence of gender awareness has had, and continues to have, for theory and the practice of international relations. An example of how 'bringing women and gender' into the field of international relations has influenced global politics can be seen, for instance, in the area of development assistance. During the last ten to fifteen years, inter-governmental organizations such as the World Bank, the International Monetary Fund, the United Nations, the Inter-American Development Bank, and the European Union, have begun to 'mainstream' gender issues and consider how their policies affect men and women differently in developing countries. Indeed, many organizations now have gender action plans to deal with gender inequalities both within their own organizations and in their work with developing (and developed) countries. In an effort to support economic opportunities for women and spur economic growth, the World Bank is now integrating a gender perspective into its policies in sectors such as energy, transport, agriculture, and finance: areas that traditionally have not considered gender differences.

The push to integrate a gender perspective on mainstream issues has come from various domestic and international actors, with the international women's movement as the major actor. The involvement of women from this broad movement in a multitude of activities, many related to a large number of UN world conferences since the 1970s, has been pivotal in pressing for change and calling upon governments and international development agencies to integrate women into the development process.

A gender perspective has become important to IGOs because they have found that the gendered structure of society has affected the implementation of global policies and the human rights of women around the world. For example, in Africa, approximately 80% of agricultural work is done by women. Hunger alleviation, therefore, must be understood within this context. If women are not included in the development of international programs, there is little chance that programs attempting to address food shortages, for example, will be effective. Or take the concept of 'missing women' presented by Nobel Prize winning economist Amartya Sen, who refers to the worldwide deficit of 100 million women because of the sex bias which governs the allocation of resources in the planning and delivery of healthcare. Women who should be here are not—they are 'missing'—because girl babies, and adult women, are not given adequate nutrition and medical treatment, or suffer other kinds of neglect or even abuse.[4]

Perhaps most important to point out in a discussion about competing theories in international relations, is that there are consequences for the differences in perspectives because each theory views the world, and potential solutions to global problems, differently. The policy prescriptions coming out of the *realist* and the *liberal* perspectives are, as you can imagine, quite different. How might they differ in their views on issues such as diplomacy, nuclear proliferation, human rights, or poverty? Why?

The United States in the World Today

A chapter on the United States and global politics would not be complete without a discussion of the effect of what, for many United States citizens, is the date when global politics took center stage—September 11, 2001. Suddenly, for these Americans, the violent conflicts and complex politics of a largely remote and not well-understood twenty-first century world arrived on United States shores with dramatic force and unprecedented psychological impact. Many claimed that a world shaped since the end of World War II by United States economic and political dominance had been turned upside down and redefined. The seemingly invincible global supremacy of United States national power was both challenged and shaken as the country entered wars in both Afghanistan and Iraq that have now lasted for several years. Some fear the shape of a new post-9/11 world.

But despite the claims from some in the United States about the beginning of a new global world order marked by 9/11, global politics today has developed through a long and gradual political process with its roots deep in the economic, military, legal, ideological, and social decisions made after World War II, and often only grudgingly altered in subsequent decades. Initially, these post-1945 decisions, grounded in the laws and principles of national sovereignty and the supremacy of the state, defined and imposed a new twentieth century global *status quo* dominated by a relatively few economically and militarily powerful states. This *status quo* has been challenged by an increasing number of non-state actors, perhaps making the concept of a "global community with a foundation of rights, freedoms, and obligations designed to promote the basic common good" hold more relevance and importance for twenty-first century global politics than might have been perceived in the last century. It is clear that a number of states and non-state actors think that this is the case, and there has been global movement on an expanding range of issues. Some of these major issues are listed here:

- traditional state conflict and reconciliation
- non-state generated conflict and terrorism

- racial, ethnic, gender, religious discrimination, exclusion, even genocide
- proliferation and possible use of weapons of mass destruction (nuclear, biological, chemical)
- widespread poverty, hunger, disease
- environmental degradation and future ecological sustainability
- economic and cultural globalization, and the global economic collapse of 2008
- an information and technological "global access explosion"

As central as "responding to 9/11" or "winning the war on terror" might seem to the future enhancement of long term global or United States security and prosperity, these specific goals must be placed in the larger and more complex dynamic of "expanded global politics." We know that perceptions matter, for example, so it is important to understand how other states in the world view the United States. In a 2006 Pew Global Attitudes study, for example, "majorities in Indonesia, Turkey, Egypt, and Jordan [said] that they [did] not believe groups of Arabs carried out the Sept. 11, 2001 terrorist attacks."[5] BBC polls taken in the last few years show a negative global view of the United States: "positive views of the US eroded from 2005 (38% on average), to 2006 (32%), and to 2007 (28%); recovering for the first time this year [2008] to 32 per cent."[6] The election of Barack Obama has shifted these numbers somewhat, at least initially. These global perceptions are not trivial. Today, global politics is marked by an environment in which not even the world's wealthiest and militarily strongest states can consistently motivate or coerce other global actors to support and supply the resources needed to achieve their interests. Sometimes hard power is not enough.

As the United States has learned in its war on terror and 2003 invasion of Iraq, eliminating non-state terrorist cells, capturing or killing their leaders, and reconstructing the political, economic, and social foundations of even one state requires more than "massive military shock and awe"—or the expenditure of trillions of dollars. The complexity and interrelationship of events and actors in global politics today make both the formulation and execution of a successful political strategy to ensure future security and prosperity a multi-layered, multi-actor, preferably consensus-based, long-term process that extends decision making, resource sharing, and risk taking beyond the traditional political patterns of nation-state interaction. And while the state remains the major political, economic, and social power in global politics today, it is not without multiple non-state challengers to its primacy. These non-state challengers—often disposed to violent action—include, among others, religious groups, groups without religious affiliation, those who might profit from the business of selling chemical, biological, and nuclear weapons on the black market, and pirates on the high seas.

As this chapter demonstrates, challengers to traditional state politics have grown in number, influence, and power in the late twentieth and early twenty-first centuries. As these non-state challengers have increased, the global political system has expanded almost exponentially beyond a system dominated by a few economically and militarily powerful western states at the end of World War II to almost 200 recognized states with vastly different historical, geographic, demographic, and resource profiles and capabilities. Mix into this expanded list of state actors a diverse array of newly empowered non-state actors—terrorist cells, religious or environmental groups, transnational organizations and corporations, international non-governmental organizations, international governmental organizations, corporate and freelance media of all forms, dedicated individuals determined to make a global difference (such as Bono)—and global politics seems to be an almost anarchic competition between endlessly diverse and largely incompatible interests and ambitions.

But global politics—today and in past generations—is a dynamic, not a static process. To move beyond seeing just anarchy and conflict among the many actors in modern global politics requires envisaging the world and the role of multiple global political actors from a new perspective. The basic concepts of this chapter offer a framework for understanding this seemingly impenetrable complexity. If we have basic concepts and a working knowledge of theory, we should be able to make sense of what's happening, at least in an elementary fashion. Indeed, our attempt in this chapter is to offer insights into how the global political landscape has evolved in the post-World War II world; how the traditional state system has been forced to incorporate the input of many new actors and technologies affecting global politics in the twenty-first century; and how observers can better understand and assess the nature of cooperation and conflict in the world today.

The Politics of Addressing Pressing Global Problems and Pursuing Global Opportunities

So where does that leave the individual student? Where do you fit into global politics and how can you have a voice in addressing important problems or questions? Perhaps the most important message of this chapter is that you are already enmeshed in global politics because all action is political action and all thought is political thought, at least in some sense.

While you may not think of your daily life in political terms, most of our everyday actions are, in fact, political. Take something as basic as what food to choose for dinner, which clothes to buy, where to buy them, and so on. These decisions, whether or not you are aware of it, are affected by global politics (in terms of trade agreements, regulations of food stuff, labor laws, and so on). In addition, the domestic economy is inextricably linked to the global economy, as the 2008 market collapse has shown. Individual states cannot alone address the causes of, or provide the cures for, the whole of this economic downturn. Effective responses will include the work of international and non-governmental organizations as well as both large and small corporations. Recent economic and financial problems suggest that state *interests* must be broad in scope and have challenged the *idea* that trade without regulation is always the best course. The crisis also clearly shows how important *perception* is at the individual level. Your belief about what will happen in the global economy, and the beliefs of millions of people, will shape consumer spending and investment behavior, and these things, in turn, will have global repercussions. Your future livelihood and the potential to be economically secure are affected by what happens in global politics. And your ability to connect with, and participate in, global politics is now much greater than it was for your parents and grandparents, mainly because of the communication revolution which has taken place since the advent of the Internet.

Communication and Making Connections

Just as international law connects and regulates the actors and their actions around the world, so communications of all sorts can shape world politics in ways that would have been difficult for your grandparents and great-grandparents to have predicted. Many younger people today may not fully comprehend how much our ability to communicate has changed in the last 100 years. If you look at the timeline in Figure 12.2 you will notice that it has only been in the last one hundred years or so that the mass media—newspapers, radio, television, and so on—have become a part of our world. The computer, for example, has been around for general public use for less than three decades. And if you think about it, there is no doubt that this technology, and its availability, have changed global politics in a number of ways. Our increasingly sophisticated communication technologies, coupled with greater speed and ease of travel, have helped groups and people around the world to more easily and efficiently share ideas, organize themselves, and raise money.

- The first commercially successful transatlantic telegraph cable was successfully completed on July 18, 1866.
- Edison received U.S. Patent 223,898 for his incandescent lamp in 1880.
- Wilbur and Orville Wright's first airplane flight, 1903
- Alexander Graham Bell makes the first transcontinental telephone call to Thomas Watson from New York to San Francisco, 1915
  - Cellphones sold commercially, 1983
- Records, used to record sound, were invented in 1877 by Thomas Alva Edison.
  - The long-playing record (the LP) was invented in 1948 by Columbia Records
  - Music CDs commercially available since the 1980s
  - MP3s commercially available in 1998
- The first radio news program was broadcast August 31, 1920 by station 8MK in Detroit, Michigan.
- The first talking movie presentation, 1910
- Television commercially available since the late 1930s
  - VCR since the 1970s
  - Cable since the 1970s
  - TiVo since the late 1990s
- Photocopier invented, 1937
- Personal Computers, 1980s
  - Public Internet access, 1990s
  - Facebook first launched, 2004

FIGURE 12.2 Communication Timeline

Some argue, in addition, that technology such as the Internet, for example, can facilitate the spread of democracy and that it has diffused power in the international system from a narrow elite governing class at the "top," down through the hierarchy of power to the rest of us, at the bottom. You can, for example, exercise political power by joining groups instantly online and by "meeting" people (if only online or onscreen) from around the world. New communication technologies have facilitated the growth of NGOs, and if you want to join a group that is concerned about environmental issues, with members from around the world, you can. You are now constrained neither by state borders nor by political elites, nor by the expense and difficulty of travel.

All is not rosy, however, as there is a large, and in some places increasing, disparity between those who have access to new communication technologies and those who do not. What advantages do those have who *do* have access to enhanced communication technologies? This is an important question to ask. With new technologies and enhanced communication abilities come questions about how people will make use of these. With more available information comes the need to learn to discern what is credible and what is not, and to determine what is important and what is not. These new technological abilities bring with them new obligations, indeed, and make it less easy for us to avoid global politics. You—and all of us—will need more skills than ever to understand and, perhaps, to act upon, the deluge of information at our fingertips. Chinedu "Ocek" Eke's Chapter 6 and Jean Schwind's Chapter 3 advise readers how to approach *all* texts carefully.

Your Place in Global Politics—or the "Who Cares?" Question

It is one thing to *understand* that your life is a part of the global political world and that your opportunities to communicate and participate are greater than those afforded past generations. Some people, however, want to go further than this understanding and want to actually change at least part of the world they live in. And because states are not the only political actors in the global system, if enough people take action, they may well be able to affect global politics. Actions by United States students during the 1990s illustrate this point. While becoming aware of the exploitation of labor in sweatshops in developing and developed countries (indeed, as close as in New York City), and then understanding the role that their own schools played in supporting this system of exploitation, students began to demand change. They looked for a greater acknowledgement of responsibility by their schools for the conditions under which their college's licensed apparel—T-shirts, hats, and so on—were made. Concerns about healthy, fair, and safe working conditions were of great importance to these students, and they became involved in the anti-sweatshop campaigns that stretched across the country (and into Canada) to stop the shoe and shirt companies from using the labor of people in conditions which most United States citizens would regard as barbarous.

The anti-sweatshop movement is only one example of how a group of non-state actors, in this case a broad and diversified social movement including a large number of students, may effect change in the world. Similarly, recent anti-slavery movements,[7] often giving support for actions to end not only sweatshop abuse, but also human trafficking, sexual slavery, and child soldiering, reflect how non-state groups (NGOs) and individuals can co-operate to help solve global problems.

So: is becoming a political activist the only way to effect change and make a positive difference in the world? No, not necessarily. There are a multitude of ways in which you can use your talent (or develop one!) to participate in global politics. Perhaps you love writing? Then contributing articles to your university newspaper might be a way for you to increase awareness about a topic you feel strongly about, be it immigration, racism, genocide, human trafficking, global warming, or any other matter of public concern. Doing internships or volunteering for organizations such as NGOs, on or off campus, is another way to get involved. At the same time, you could be developing communication and leadership skills, as well as gaining knowledge and a greater understanding of the connections between and among domestic and international matters. So, whether you are interested in the arts, sports, social justice, medicine, food, foreign cultures, the environment, animals; whether you want to support human rights, religious freedom, or environmental awareness; sharing your time, talent, ideas, and expertise may lead to an enriching experience in the realm of global politics.

At a minimum, understanding the basics of global politics which have been presented in this chapter may help you to grasp how events in the world can—and will—affect you and your life. And, of course, you may choose to become more actively engaged with global politics by using technology to connect with friends around the world, by staying informed about world events, and even, eventually, by choosing a particular career path. Global politics, as a field of study, challenges us to understand the identities and roles of various global actors; the large number of world organizations and their purposes and ways of operating; the many causes of world conflict; and the wealth of opportunities for international cooperation. In the absence of this understanding, we are unlikely to be able to make sense of the world, or of our place in it.

Notes

1. http://www.amnesty.org/en/who-we-are/about-amnesty-international 2 June 2009.
2. Joseph S. Nye, Jr. Think again: Soft power. *Foreign Policy*, 1 March 2006. Available at Yale Online, http://yaleglobal.yale.edu/display.articl?id=7059
3. Gender is usually regarded as socially and culturally constructed, whereas "sex" is regarded as a biological given, though even these distinctions can be blurred. See Ann J. Cahill, Chapter 9, "Looking at the World Through a Gendered Lens: Feminism and Global Studies," for a more detailed discussion.
4. See Sen's article, "More than 100 million women are missing." *The New York Review of Books*. Dec. 20, 1990. Vol. 37, No. 20. Available at http://www.nybooks.com/articles/3408 2 June 2009.
5. http://www.pewglobal.org/reports/display.php?ReportID=253 2 June 2009.
6. http://www.worldpublicopinion.org/pipa/articles/views_on_countriesregions_bt/463.php?ib=btvoc&pnt=463&nid=&id= 2 June 2009.
7. See, for example, Elon University's "End Slavery Now" Web site to learn more about the coalition's activities on campus to end slavery: http://www.elon.edu/e-web/students/endslavery/about.xhtml.

Questions for Discussion

1. Choose an important current event that illustrates a global conflict. Who are the major actors? What interests, ideas, and perceptions have played roles in the conflict? What has been done to try to resolve this conflict? What might you do to contribute to a solution?

2. Pick an international non-governmental organization (NGO) and research its mission and history. What individuals played a major role in the organization? What was the organization's most important success? Its most disappointing failure? What do the success and failure tell us about global politics?

3. What do you believe to be the most important *soft power* assets of the United States?

4. Do you believe global politics would operate differently if the majority of state leaders were women? If so, how? What evidence supports your claim?

5. Identify two ways in which global politics touches your daily life. How might these interfaces affect your personal and career life choices?

Suggested Readings

International Relations Texts

Goldstein, J. S., & Pevehouse, J. C. (2006–2007). *International relations* (7th ed.). New York: Longman.

Mingst, K. A., & Snyder, J. L. (2004). *Essential readings in world politics* (2nd ed.). New York: W.W. Norton & Co.

Nye, J. S. (2007). *Understanding international conflicts: An introduction to theory and history* (6th ed.). New York: Longman.

Other Works on Global Politics

Allison, G., & Zelikow, P. (1999). *Essence of decision: Explaining the Cuban missile crisis* (2nd ed.). New York: Longman.

Elshtain, J. B. (1995). *Women and war.* Chicago, IL: University Press of Chicago.

Enloe, C. (2000). *Maneuvers: The international politics of militarizing women's lives.* Berkeley: University of California Press.

Finnemore, M. (1999). *National interests in international society.* Ithaca, New York: Cornell University Press.

Gilpin, R. (2000). *Challenge of global capitalism.* Princeton, NJ: Princeton University Press.

Gruber, L. (2000). *Ruling the world.* Princeton, NJ: Princeton University Press.

Huntington, S. (1996). *Clash of civilizations and the remaking of world order.* New York: Simon & Schuster.

Jervis, R. (1976). *Perception and misperception in international politics.* Princeton, NJ: Princeton University Press.

Katzenstein, P. (1996). *Culture of national security.* New York: Columbia University Press.

Keck, M., & Sikkink, K. (1998). *Activists beyond borders: Advocacy networks in international politics.* Ithaca, NY: Cornell University Press.

Keohane, R., & Nye, J. (2000). *Power and interdependence* (3rd ed.). New York: Longman.

Krasner, S. D. (1999). *Sovereignty: Organized hypocrisy.* Princeton, NJ: Princeton University Press.

Milner, H. (1997). *Interests, institutions, information.* Princeton, NJ: Princeton University Press.

Nye, J. (2004). *Soft power: The means to success in world politics.* New York: Public Affairs.

Peterson, V. S., & Runyan, A. S. (1999). *Global gender issues.* Boulder, CO: Westview Press.

Pettman, J. J. (1996). *Worlding women: A feminist international politics.* New York: Routledge.

Ruggie, J. (1998). *Constructing the world polity.* New York: Routledge.

Spruyt, H. (1994). *The sovereign state and its competitors* Princeton, NJ: Princeton University Press.

Tickner, A. J. (1992). *Gender in international relations.* New York: Columbia University Press.

Wendt, A. (1999). *Social theory of international politics.* Cambridge: Cambridge University Press.

13

"Jihad vs. McWorld"

Benjamin R. Barber Revisited

Stephen Braye, Rosemary Haskell, and Thomas Arcaro

Introduction: Finding Frameworks for the World's Multeity and Unity, Change and Stasis

This essay comes last in the book because it attempts to make the parts of the whole cohere: it tries to put everything together while acknowledging that the pieces must also fly apart. This last chapter, then, may perhaps help us to see the world and its inhabitants both synthetically and analytically. This over-ambitious goal is worth our last shot. "'Jihad vs. McWorld': Benjamin R. Barber Revisited" proposes, in fact, that the amazing variety of peoples, places, ideas, values, attitudes, and beliefs which span the globe can be addressed methodically. It also suggests that such diversity and complexity can be interpreted—that is, can be made sense of—within a containing framework. We can, in fact, pick our own terms, and metaphors, for the world's multeity in unity. Some people will signify this tension between the many and the one with such terms as *e pluribus unum*, or, more metaphorically, "a Pandora's box," or even as a "box where sweets compacted lie," as George Herbert's seventeenth century poetic line has it.[1]

Picking a metaphor or two, indeed, is what Benjamin R. Barber does in his very influential 1992 essay, and, later, in the 1995 book of the same name: *Jihad vs. McWorld: How Globalism and Tribalism Are Reshaping the World*. This is the dyad he uses as an interpretive tool for making meaning out of what we usually see as an increasingly "globalized" world and, at the same time, as an increasingly fragmented and fractured one. His own

All are but parts of one stupendous whole,
When body, nature is, and God the soul ...

Look round our World; behold the chain of Love
Combining all Below and all above,
See plastic Nature working to this end
The single atoms each to other tend ...

Nothing is foreign, Parts relate to whole;
One all extending all-preserving Soul
(Alexander Pope, from "The Essay On Man," qtd.
Barber, 1996, p. 156).

metaphors—the Golden Arches of spreading western-style capitalist consumer culture set against the "holy war" of the struggle of "Jihad,"—offer a place to start and an argument to consider. Barber helps nascent global citizens—and some fully-fledged ones—consider what they should think and do in the face of a world which, while apparently racing towards a "globalized" unity, seems, at the same time, to be enriched, fractured, or exploded, depending on your point of view, by "tribalizing" forces.

Needless to say, Benjamin Barber has not been alone in attempting to understand a world where unity and diversity co-exist, and where movement and stasis are tense partners. The challenge of both these apparent paradoxes has a long and respectable philosophical, political, religious, and indeed scientific history. Barber himself notes (1996, pp. 156–157) that the English Enlightenment poet Alexander Pope argued for the essential harmony and order of a complicated and packed world in his long poem *An Essay On Man* (1731).

And, long before the founding fathers of the United States of America worried about how to stabilize the witches' brew of people from many lands, state loyalties, and federal centrality with their "*e pluribus unum*" motto, others had considered the paradox of the "many and the one." The "Presocratics" (i.e., the scientist-philosophers living and working before Socrates, who died in Athens, in 399 B.C.) tried to find a unifying frame, or principle, for the variety of physical phenomena they observed. Was that basic principle fire, as Heraclitus suggested? Was it water (Thales)? Was everything made of some version of air (Anaximenes)? Was it four elements, governed by attraction and repulsion (Empedocles)? How, they asked, can we explain not only the *variety* of the physical world, but also its constant *change?* It was Heraclitus who told us that we cannot step into the same river twice; atomic theory has told us since that we cannot even step into the same Honda Civic twice. In fact, present day "scientists"—whom Heraclitus and Thales and the other Presocratics would have recognized as philosophical kindred spirits—struggle with the same old problems.[2] Is "String Theory" not just one more attempt to account, in a final and inclusive push, for multiple forces operating at the same time? Does it not also try to allow for the tension between change and stability? These opposing pairs—the many and the one, change and stasis—are still, apparently, fundamental to our interpretive struggle with the physical universe.

For us, in Global Studies, however, those who try to explain multeity and unity, or change and stability, tend to be social scientists of some kind: economists, sociologists, anthropologists, and their colleagues. Barber's "global" studies of the early-to-mid 1990s lie within that broad field, as do those of Thomas L. Friedman, Jeffrey D. Sachs, Joseph Stiglitz, George Soros, Peter Singer, and George Ritzer, among others.[3] We focus here on Barber's work, which has helped to set the terms for our analysis of a world both beset and energized by contesting forces. Sometimes, the need to explain "what's happening" on a global scale seems particularly urgent. Perhaps we are going through an "urgent" phase now, at the end

As we confront our global community and the many global problems we face daily, we can feel overwhelmed fairly quickly. Bombs are going off in some parts of the world, people are starving in other parts, ancient hatreds are leading to killing after killing, and governments are arguing over nuclear power, national borders, and the environment. All these problems can seem impossible to understand and even harder to address. Yet we want to be responsible global citizens; we want to make a positive impact on our world. So how can we work to understand this cacophony of events in order to enact what we believe and value most?

of the first decade of the twenty-first century. If so, we need thinkers and writers, such as Barber, Friedman, and others, to help us advance in this project of understanding and explanation, or, as Barber calls it, "the journey of the imagination" (1996, p. 291).

One way of framing the world's change and variety, proposed by German philosopher Friedrich Hegel (1770–1831), was to see human history and actions through the lens of what is called the *dialectic*. As discussed in the discipline of philosophy, the Hegelian dialectic begins with the *thesis*, a thought that is put forward with some conviction, in the attempt to address a major issue or problem. Upon reflection, it is realized that the original thought is lacking in many ways. This perception leads us to the *antithesis*, the opposing force that is offered in contrast to the original idea. These two positions are clearly seen in a debate format, where ideas are explored in a point-to-counterpoint style. In a debate, though, the tension between the two is not resolved. One side wins; one side loses. For Hegel, however, these opposing forces are temporarily reconciled in a step called *synthesis*, where oppositions lead to a new thesis, which in turn generates a new antithesis. Thus, for Hegel, change is a constant.

We see this dialectic consistently playing out in human history. For a moment, think of the forces that shaped the world in the twentieth century. The rise of industrialization in the nineteenth century and the growing dominance of a bourgeois ruling class over a landless proletariat were explained by Marxist, Leninist, and other "left-wing" or "socialist" theorists. These theories were adapted to explain, among other things, the Bolshevik Revolution of 1917. In the post-World War II years, two opposing forces, capitalism and communism, struggled to control the world. The nuclear capabilities of the United States and the then-USSR, or Soviet Union, threatened a "hot" war, which did not materialize. However, the "Cold" War, manifested on the one side by the United States and the West, with the Soviet Union and China on the other, pitted two inherently expansionist forces against each other in a struggle that, it was argued, would leave the world dominated either by communism or capitalism. Instead, Hegel's idea of *synthesis* prevailed. With the collapse of the Soviet Union in the early 1990s, the struggle ended with neither side winning the "war," and a synthesis of these two forces developing. We can see this manifested today in the United States and China. Faced with an economic crisis, our capitalistic system is adopting many socialist practices to deal with the recession (government intervention to provide massive "bailouts" for foundering banks, investment firms, and automobile manufacturers, for example). China, once the epitome of isolationism and "command economy" communist-style economics, celebrates its free-market style economic growth as the nation becomes a major player in the global marketplace.

Today, globalization is a powerful force in this cacophony of events. When we talk about a range of topics—contemporary slavery, climate change, or fair labor practices, for example—we are exploring globalization and its impact on our world. Driven by international economies and information technology, globalization is the interaction and integration of people, governments, and corporations across traditional national boundaries, usually into international corporations (e.g., Sony, Honda) or governmental alliances (e.g., European Union, NATO [North Atlantic Treaty Organization]). This integration influences the world's cultures, including their economic and political institutions, and even our view of the natural world we all inhabit.

Like the Cold War forces mentioned earlier, globalization is inherently expansionistic. Capitalistic businesses are predicated upon profit and steady growth, and once national markets have been saturated (think of the expansion of McDonalds or Wal-Mart throughout the United States), these businesses must move across national borders to continue growing. This growth, however, influences a great deal more than just the businesses available to people across the world. All aspects of culture are affected, leading to what may be an unintended outcome of globalization, what George Ritzer, in his 1995 book of that title, called *The McDonaldization of Society*. Ritzer takes up half of Barber's paired metaphor in some detail. Just as Barber uses "McWorld," so Ritzer uses "McDonaldization" to signal, among other things, the homogenizing effects on the world of American-style (i.e., United States-style) consumer-capitalism.

Ritzer argues that contemporary society is coming to function more and more like a fast food restaurant, as it becomes more managed and controlled by "outside"—i.e., non-native—entities, whose chief allegiance is to the "bottom line" of the account ledger. He claims there are four basic components of McDonaldization. Globalization fosters *efficiency*, minimizing the time actions take. Our push for advanced technology reflects this need. Doing things faster means being able to do more in "less" time, enabling us to do more in the time we have. This encourages the idea that faster is better. The idea of *calculability* means valuing quantity over quality. McDonaldization works to provide more at a lower cost, ignoring the variable of quality, judging satisfaction by measuring how much you have and how little you paid. *Predictability*, the third component, means providing the exact same service and product in the same way every time, no matter where that service is provided. In order to promote predictability, globalized companies value highly repetitive, routine tasks, minimizing creativity and variation. *Control*, the last component, attempts to remove the human element in the equation, replacing human workers with technology, when possible, and minimizing worker independence, when it is not.

Globalization, then, can be defined as a force which homogenizes highly diverse cultures so that the same products may be marketed to many different people, leading to the greater sales which signal the success of a consumer society. For Barber, McWorld is the establishment and integration of a global community driven by economic and technological development. This phenomenon resembles what Friedman, in his "updated and expanded" second edition of *The World Is Flat: A Brief History of the Twenty-First Century*, (2006), considered a "flattening" or leveling of the playing field of economic competition. The forces of "McWorld" ignore national boundaries and obliterate local and regional cultures in favor of a global market, bringing its formerly disparate components together. As Friedman says, "the flattening of the world means … that we are now connecting all the knowledge centers on the planet together into a single global network" (p. 8). McWorld depends upon free trade, shared technology, a global supply chain, and limited governmental regulation in order to create the common global markets essential to its success. The 1993 North American Free Trade Agreement (NAFTA) and the European Union, the hugely-expanded descendant of the post-World-War II "Common Market," were important to the development of McWorld, because they boosted the freedom of movement of goods, services, capital, and people across national borders.

The problem for globalization, however, is the tenacity with which highly diverse cultures value their differences, and the expression of their individuality through what we call *tribalism.* Tribalism includes the sense of oneself as a member of a group formed around a unique identity. This identity separates the members of one group from those of another. Tribalism can be predicated upon one or more of many defining cultural features: for example, religion, race, ethnicity, art, leisure, economics and politics, with all the associated differences among beliefs, values, attitudes, aspirations, and cultural practices. The people of the United States frequently realize tribalism, for example, through sports. Our passion for specific sports, and our identification with specific teams, are expressions of our tribalistic tendencies. For reasons we don't always understand, a significant part of our identity can be tied up in our connection to a specific team or school. Every football Saturday, Memorial Stadium in Lincoln, Nebraska, becomes the third largest "city" in Nebraska, the temporary home of the approximately 89,000 people watching the University of Nebraska football team. Stadiums in Tennessee, Michigan, and Ohio each bring together over 100,000 people to cheer for their own teams. The Red Sox hate the Yankees. The Redskins hate the Cowboys. Duke hates Carolina—and the feeling is mutual. We may not understand it, but this identification with a team can influence who we hang out with, who we like and dislike, and how we spend certain parts of our lives.

This tribalism may be relatively harmless, as when people check to see if their college teams win or lose. It may develop toward those who sometimes wear paraphernalia from their team, a T-shirt, jersey, or hat. Even then, we understand that this hat-wearer is a "fan," showing a normal and healthy enthusiasm for his tribal identity. Think, though, how we start to look at this behavior if the hat-wearer escalates his expressions of identification with his team. He might become one of those people who *always* wear clothes with their team logo and who display license plates, posters, stickers, seat cushions, and all kinds of things that announce their identification with their team. They plan weddings, vacations, and weekends around their team's schedule. Their moods change as their teams win or lose. They get depressed, perhaps even violent, after a painful loss—and euphoric after a big win. At this point, we may see their identification as unhealthy, comment that the person is "crazy" about their team, and start to wonder at the wisdom of their team identification. Some observers have seen such passionate team loyalty as a form of "proxy" warfare, indeed, where fans dress for battle at the Saturday game and experience the day's contest with the intense emotional and even physical involvement that might accompany an actual military engagement.

You can quickly see how this tribalism, as Barber has suggested, serves as a counterpoint to globalization. Tribalism, or tribilalization, privileges separation, even while it unites privileged members around selected identifying marks. Globalization wants to erase these distinguishing markers, to promote our collective identity through traits we share across cultures.

Barber: "What I have called the forces of Jihad may seem then to be a throwback to premodern times: an attempt to recapture a world that existed prior to cosmopolitan capitalism and was defined by religious mysteries, hierarchical communities, spellbinding traditions, and historical torpor. As such, they may appear to be directly adversarial to the forces of McWorld. Yet Jihad stands not so much in stark opposition as in subtle counterpoint to McWorld and is itself a dialectical response to modernity whose features both reflect and reinforce the modern world's virtues and vices—Jihad *via* McWorld rather than Jihad *versus* McWorld" (1996, p. 157). Where in the world may we find illustration of Barber's explanation of these two forces and their relationships to each other?

Locating *"Jihad"* and *"McWorld"*

Since Barber published his 1995 book, some events highly illustrative of his thesis have occurred. For example, in 2001, from remote locations in the Afghan countryside, Osama bin Laden and others used cell phones and the Internet to plan a series of attacks in the United States, culminating in the attacks of what we now call "9/11." Not long after, bin Laden and his group, Al Qaeda, released a video of the leader himself, one that had been produced and directed with advanced technological equipment and expertise. This video was left at the offices of Al-Jazeera, a television company based in Qatar, one of the Persian Gulf states. Created five years earlier, in 1996, as the first Arabic language television station, Al-Jazeera was available on five continents, due to an increase of satellite technology and a cooperation agreement they had signed with CNN, owned by AOL-Time Warner, one of the largest communication corporations in the world. These international connections allowed almost instant transmission of this video to the world, over television and the Web, reaching over 7 million viewers in the first week. In the video, bin Laden, wearing what appears to be a Timex watch, condemns the Western world, its culture, and modernity; in other words, he condemns the same modern culture and civilization that produced and shared the technology which enabled him to plan the attack, produce the video, and communicate with the rest of the world.

This portrait of the al Qaeda leader illustrates perfectly Barber's theory (see box) that Jihad is brought about via—courtesy of—McWorld. He argues elsewhere that the two forces, Jihad and McWorld, are certainly antagonistic. But he also claims that they are mutually reinforcing: "Jihad not only revolts against but abets McWorld, while McWorld not only imperils but re-creates and reinforces Jihad" (Barber p. 5). McWorld, at the time a nascent movement towards globalization, was promoting common markets and universal information technology, while Jihad, fostering tribalism and its sub-national identifications, was fracturing the geopolitical landscape of the late twentieth century. Ultimately, Barber argued, the struggle between these forces would alter the ways we perceive, and act in, our world.

Look around you right now. Check the labels on your clothes. Where do they come from? How do they get from where they are made to you? And why does it happen this way? Look at the technology that surrounds you. How many pieces of technology can you find made in Japan or China? Visit a local Starbucks. Where do their coffees and teas come from? Imagine the transportation system that enables all these things to get to your door. How many times today have you texted a friend, called on your cell phone, or accessed the

Globalization and tribalization are both powerful forces, if Barber's 1995 argument is correct. Using Barber's terms as lenses to look through, we can perhaps get that "Necker Cube" effect, beloved of social scientists, where we do a double-take and wonder if we are looking at a picture of a candlestick or at a picture of two ladies with large noses facing each other, or both. The Jihad/McWorld pairing puts us off balance enough to give us a quick glimpse of our world as it does *not* usually appear to us.

Internet? How many parts of the world are you connected to right this minute? Yes, for this brief moment, the forces of McWorld seem to be winning. But wait a minute....

The idea of Jihad may be a bit more difficult to grasp, perhaps because we do not daily feel its impact. For Barber, the term "Jihad," meaning "struggle" in Arabic, represents the conflict between the traditional and ancient forces of tribal culture and identity with the forces of globalization. Jihad favors individual cultures, practices, and beliefs, reaffirming separate and unique identities. It resists integration with other cultures, striving to maintain separate religious, political, and cultural institutions. When threatened by the invasion of global cultures and practices, Jihadic forces react fearfully, often actively, in order to assert their identity and legitimacy. It's no surprise that when we consider Jihad-style forces, or even the word "tribe," we look far away for examples. We may think of the time when the Taliban ruled Afghanistan in the late 1990s, and when many of their restrictive practices against women, and men, were presented as attempts to "protect" the laws of Islam from western-style reinterpretation and corruption. Or we may look to the often violent uprisings in the 1990s in central and eastern Europe at the demise of the Soviet Union. These uprisings reflected ancient tribal differences, and the unwillingness to compromise those shared identities for the sake of peaceful nation-states.

Now turn your eyes, however, to examine the United States in the twenty-first century: the "English-only" movement, the conviction that English should be the official and "only" language of the United States, reflects the perceived threat that other languages spoken in this country might endanger the legitimacy of "our" very own language. Is this not a sign of a tribalizing force? Note, also, that the very technology brought to us by McWorld may serve to keep us networked *only* to a select few "people like us." Not everyone can afford to use the Internet, the telephone, or even the motorcar—even assuming these things are available. As relatively prosperous students and professors, we are accused, and accuse ourselves, of living in a "bubble" of privilege. And we may react negatively when faced by outside forces that threaten to burst that bubble. In fact, we may work hard to keep McWorld at bay. Jihad is probably closer to home than we had realized.

Now pick up any copy of the *Wall Street Journal, Denver Post, New York Times* or any local, national, or international newspaper to see both of Barber's forces, in various guises and relationships, at work. You will, on at least a few days in just about every month, find news about terrorist attacks in India, Pakistan, and Iraq; economic recovery plans constructed by the G-8 and the European Union; contaminated food in China raising health concerns throughout the world; and the Palestinians, Georgians, and Kurds campaigning for separate

Jihad has much to do with the ways we think about ourselves and our world. Clearly, we all struggle with our tendency to be ethnocentric, given that the limits of our ability to perceive and experience the world limits correspondingly our ability to make sense of it.

homelands. You will also hear that Turkey wants entry into the European Union, while some in Europe resist her entry; that Americans want low-cost Hispanic labor and a more secure Mexican border. Meanwhile, North Carolina and South Carolina fight over water rights in the context of global climate change. Brazilians are told to quit burning down the rain forest so that the whole world can breathe more easily; and the Sudanese are told by "the international community" to stop the "genocide" in Darfur. In short, we see how "Jihad," as an ethnocentric force, can limit people's participation in the affairs of the rest of the world.

The Wars in Afghanistan and Iraq

The wars in Afghanistan and Iraq represent the most important struggle—at least to people in the United States—involving the forces of Jihad and McWorld today. On the one side, we have the forces of McWorld, looking for secure resources and new markets, while attempting to limit the chaos caused by terrorists in the region. The spread of McWorld depends upon the flow of natural resources from and to all parts of the globe, and clearly the current global machine depends upon oil and gas in order to thrive. United States interests in the Middle East, and the variety of conflicts at work there, reflect our dependence upon these resources. The oil-supply problem, and the impact this continues to have on the industrialized world, demonstrates how much the global market can be influenced by nation-states controlling a vital commodity. The global community hopes to bring stable, open governments to the Middle East as a way of promoting peace as well as securing the inexpensive energy supply necessary to a strong global economy. On the other hand, according to Vali Nasr and Daniel Consolatore, in the paragraphs which follow, the very intervention of "United States as McWorld" may have triggered a new wave of Jihad-like energy not only in the Middle East, but also in Afghanistan. In the third of

The tension Barber represents between the two concepts of Jihad and McWorld can help us make some sense of world affairs. We may be able to recognize what motivates people to act in such different ways. But what use is this understanding to us? How does Barber's "Jihad vs. McWorld" pairing help us understand today's global community and the problems we need to address? Let's look in more detail at some situations, and events, where these two forces appear to be operating.

these paragraphs, Barber himself argues that NATO intervention in the Balkans released forces the opposite of "democratic."

- Vali Nasr argues in "When the Shi'ites Rise" (2006) that the United States/United Kingdom invasion of, and the subsequent regime change in Iraq have triggered a renaissance of Shi'ite power, not only within Iraq but across national borders. Affected states include just about everyone in the region: Iran, Jordan, Syria, Lebanon, and the Gulf States. The old Sunni/Shia balance of power has been profoundly affected by the "globalizing" force of the pursuit of "democracy for all." McWorld triggers Jihad, according to this view of things. Juan Cole makes approximately the same argument in "A 'Shi'ite Crescent'? The Regional Impact of the Iraq War" (2006).

- Barber's chapter, "Jihad Within McWorld: 'Transitional Democracies,'" was written well before the Iraq war of 2003, and even before the Afghan adventure of 2001. Nevertheless, the chapter may help us to understand the global/tribal dynamics in Iraq and Afghanistan, and the fragility of the democracy which, it is claimed, is the ultimate goal. Barber's own illustration, however, lies in the Balkans, the states which emerged, or re-emerged, in the wake of the collapse of the Soviet empire in 1991–1992. The wars attending the disintegration—or re-tribalization—of the resilient and somewhat independent communist state of Yugoslavia illustrate, Barber argues, the "paradoxical interface of Jihad and McWorld" (1996, p. 195). He describes these states as "'transitional' or 'emerging democracies,' which, though certainly emerging from communism and in transition to somewhere, are for the most part neither democratic nor very likely to become so any time soon" (1996, p. 195). Since Barber wrote these words, NATO forces have fought in the Balkans (1999) against the ultimate tribal horror: the so-called "ethnic cleansing"—or mass killing—of Muslims in Bosnia and Serbia. In spite of that disaster, history's answer to Barber's 1995 argument about "transitional democracies" has been, essentially, "Yes, it was a distant prospect; democracy in the Balkan states *is* pretty fragile still; but it's alive and promises to become stronger."

- Daniel Consolatore, in a recent article, gives us another updated version of Barber's model of Jihad vs. Mc World. This time it is at work in Afghanistan. Consolatore, in "The Pashtun Factor: Is Afghanistan Next in Line for An Ethnic Civil War?" (2006), lays out in grim detail the revival of the Taliban in the wake of their initial defeat at the hands of the United States and its allies in 2001–2002, and the subsequent reconfiguring of old tribal alliances:

> When major combat ceased the top Northern Alliance warlord-generals—like the brutal Uzbek Rashid Dostum, the Tajiks Ismael Kahn and Mohammed Fahim, and the Hazara Karim Khalili—found themselves in powerful ministries of the provisional government. Predictably, the Pashtun population was wary and less than enthusiastic to see these developments, and even the rise of the Pashtun Karzai and inclusion of many Pashtuns in the new government didn't put fears of being dominated by a coalition of the other groups entirely to rest (p. 111).

Both Nasr's and Consolatore's analyses may be illuminated by Barber's model, which helps us to see that, at the interface of the Jihadic and McWorld forces, democracy may be a casualty, not a prize; other, unforeseen, events may spin off from the encounter. We might note, too, that history has not yet told us how Mr. Karzi's fragile transitional democracy in Afghanistan will fare.

In spite of the explosiveness of these encounters between globalization and tribalization, we might argue that the forces of McWorld want peace in the Middle East and in Afghanistan in order to limit disruptions to the global network. The international political community argues that much of the world's terrorism is planned in the remote parts of Afghanistan and Iraq. Terrorism in any form is anathema to the international supply chain and free trade. While there are many reasons for the United States to fight a war on global terrorism, one much desired outcome is a secure global marketplace, where goods and services can be reliably exchanged. By limiting terrorism to small corners of the globe, the forces of McWorld can hope to develop stable markets across the rest of the world.

So who would want to resist these McWorld forces, forces which are attempting to bring people together in peace? Anyone threatened with the loss of their culture and of its related identity, is one answer. We must remember that Iraq was formed from afar after World War I, mainly by British and French politicians who, for the most part, had never visited the region. (See Brian Digre's Chapter 8, "Western Imperialism and Its Legacies," in this volume, for more about this example of imperialist nation-building and map-making.) In attempting to bring together three areas, Baghdad, Basra, and Mosul, the imperialists also brought together peoples with significantly different cultures, religions, and languages, which were identified with different segments of the map: Kurds in the north, Sunnis in the central region, with Shi'a in the south. As a result of this imperialist allotrope of globalizing pressure, these peoples, proud of their identities, have suffered much, and have even died defending their unique differences. Their differences, indeed, shaped their experiences under Saddam Hussein's regime in the late twentieth century. As a result, the United States' own attempt to discover ways to develop a democratic socio-political system that can guarantee and protect these differences has proven to be challenging.

Finally, in this section about Iraq and Afghanistan, let's briefly consider the proposition, implicit in the recent foreign policy decisions of the United States, that bringing democracy is a primary good, trumping all others, and the goal of spreading democracy justifies the attendant military intervention, tremendous civil upheaval, and the shedding of blood. Barber argues—as we have seen—that democracy is promoted neither by globalizing nor by tribalizing forces. Democracy is the goal for us, he says, in the face of, or perhaps beyond, these forces: "Thus in Rwanda, or in East Timor or in Haiti, we perhaps misconceive the challenge when we ask how to partition or internationalize or pacify a disintegrating country; perhaps the real challenge is how to make it democratic. Democracy is, to be sure, already the sought-after final outcome for those trying to rescue the planet: but it must also be the guiding principle going in" (1996, p. 291).

China and the Olympics: Beijing, Summer 2008

The Olympics held in Beijing in 2008 can be seen as the force of McWorld continuing to push across all national boundaries. China, probably the best example of a nation-state reflecting the principle of Jihad, is "opening up" to western-style economics as it attempts to "modernize" and increase its stature in the global community. Notice China is not doing this by exporting Chinese culture to the rest of us. No, it is doing this by giving up the political and economic system it has depended on for at least half a century. Holding a successful Olympics would help the world to see that China is "just like the rest of us," a modern culture ready to partner with the global community in the twenty-first century.

At the same time as China was welcoming foreign tourists for the Olympics, it was imposing strict visa requirements, which, according to the Chinese government, were to insure a safe Olympics. These requirements led to the rejection of thousands of visa applications, many from foreigners who had frequented the country in the past. These restrictions were finally eased, to some degree, when Chinese businesses complained that company representatives from throughout the world were unable to enter the country to place orders for the upcoming holiday season.

China's rapid economic expansion has come at quite a cost to the environment. Pollution has become the leading cause of death in China, China has surpassed the United States as the leading producer of greenhouse gases in the world, and nearly 500 million people lack access to clean drinking water. China admitted to the scope of the problem by replacing "normal" lax environmental regulations with strict ones, in an attempt to clean the air around Olympic venues. But history tells us that no country in the world has become a major industrial power without creating a massive amount of environmental damage. Many developed countries are putting pressure on the Chinese to limit their air pollution, which affects life in the air and water throughout Southeast Asia. But many developing countries wonder what yields to the "old" industrial nations the moral high ground, given their own history of environmental destruction. Do the Chinese have the right to devastate their environment, the way Europeans and Americans did centuries before? Or does newer knowledge and understanding of our environment mean that we must *all*, now, measure economic development against the damage to nature that it will bring?

Zambia: A Personal Experience

A recent trip to Zambia, spending time in both the capital, Lusaka, and rural western Zambia, Kaoma, gave one of the authors of this chapter an up-close perspective on how these two forces—Jihad and McWorld—shape this part of southern Africa.

Driving from the Lusaka airport into the city, one is confronted by a number of large billboards, focusing on virginity and abstinence. This seems strange in a country where about 1/5 of the adult population is HIV positive, where there are 600,000 orphans, many of whom are HIV positive, and where 70% of the population is under 25 years of age. It would be easy to conclude that Jihadic tendencies, either Zambian religion or other parts of the local culture, would play a major role in the push towards abstinence. But that is not the case. Instead, the long arm of McWorld, in this case, the arm of the United States and the Bush administration, pushes the case for abstinence. The Global Gag Rule, the U.S. restriction on international family planning, fosters the Zambian stress on abstinence. This U.S. policy denies any foreign organization receiving U.S. family planning assistance the right to use any funds, including their own, to engage in abortion-related public policy debates or legal abortions. In Zambia, where abortions are legal, Planned Parenthood of Zambia refused the terms of the gag rule, and lost nearly one-half of its $5 million budget. The government, desperate for family planning assistance, promotes abstinence in the attempt to get any U.S. family planning funding it can.[4]

Drive around the outskirts of Lusaka, the capital city of over 1.2 million people in a country of 10 million, and you can see the impact of urbanization, part of the McWorld movement from a rural to urban culture. Many adobe and thatch huts dot the countryside, most occupied by displaced farm families. Too often, you find communities of pre-teens, no adults in the community at all, created when parents who can no longer afford to care for their young children abandon them in the countryside. These children are food insecure, scrounging daily to survive.

In the world of a college professor in the United States, the Internet is everywhere. We complain when we cannot get good cell phone service—and say that we must be in the backwoods somewhere. In cafés in the United States, the author, Stephen Braye, had access to multiple free networks. Zambia, in fact, has a strong cell phone service in its cities, especially Lusaka, where everyone has a cell phone. Travel 300 miles west to Kaoma, however, and you leave McWorld behind. The cell phone purchased in Lusaka from a Zambian phone company gets no signal. Forget about Internet access. Even in Lusaka's Internet cafes, the Internet service was spotty and the computers painfully slow. Do not waste your time trying to upload even one picture or download a single song from iTunes. The people in Kaoma were aware laptops existed, and a few outsiders had them, but no natives of the village owned one, nor did they expect Internet service any time soon. The world's events seldom intruded upon their daily lives.

One of the major problems facing Habitat for Humanity-Zambia was the cost of concrete for building houses that would withstand the rainy season, while providing a safe sleeping environment for Zambian children, too often victims of deadly snake bites while sleeping. The cost of the concrete has doubled in the last year, which is surprising, given that Zambia has a number of large concrete manufacturers who supply concrete throughout southern Africa. The problem? The World Cup, to be held in South Africa in 2010. Given the many stadiums that are being built or refurbished in anticipation of the event, the additions to airports, the roads built or re-built, and the new hotels needed to handle the many visitors coming for the event, the price of concrete has increased dramatically in the past year. NGOs like Habitat have been severely hurt in their attempts to provide low cost housing across southern Africa, mainly because of the diversion of the concrete from housing to World Cup events.

In terms of the vast African continent, Zambia, at around 10 million people, is sparsely populated, and only slightly larger than the state of Texas. Yet, drive from Lusaka, in the central part of the country, through Kafue National Park, the second largest park in the world, to Kaoma, in the western province, and you see barriers those of us in McWorld rarely see. The few routine greetings learned in Lusaka no longer worked in Kaoma. The language, though similar, was distinctly different, as were the customs. Even the very important three part handshake, a sign of respect to Zambians and their culture, altered in the move to Kaoma. These cultural differences, separated by physical but not political boundaries, show the distinct cultures that resist the uniformity of McWorld.

Zimbabwe: Tribalism Dial Set at "Self-Destruct"?

In another part of southern Africa, Zimbabwe's condition toward the end of the first decade of the twenty-first century demonstrates the toxic result of one iteration of "Jihad vs. McWorld" strife, still unresolved. Zimbabwe, once the British colony of Rhodesia, gained its independence in 1980. Robert Mugabe, former heroic freedom fighter against a white-supremacist Rhodesian government, and now elected national leader, pledged to turn swords into ploughshares. He would, he said, create a prosperous and equitable society, free of the racism of the former white-settler colony. But now, about three decades later, his country, shaped so profoundly at its birth by the global force of imperialism, lies in ruins, with civil society all but dissolved, rampant inflation, and the institutions of education and health care all but defunct. One-party rule has become the norm, and after nearly thirty years in power, Mr. Mugabe resists almost all electoral pressure.

Mr. Mugabe's response to his country's ills—until just before the time of going to press—had been to refuse all international calls for political reform, and all offers of outside aid. He continues to blame the United Kingdom, Zimbabwe's old colonial ruler, and the United States, for his country's condition. In Fall 2008, for example, he claimed that a dangerous cholera epidemic was the result of a United Kingdom plot. Mugabe and his government have turned inward to an extent difficult to predict in the hopeful years of the early 1980s. Early in 2009, however, Mr. Mugabe requested international aid, but only if he could use it freely, with—essentially—no strings attached.

Looking at Zimbabwe through Barber's lens, we can see that the tensions among a hermetically-sealed national identity, the perceived force of the old colonial power, and the pressure of the Western world in general, have produced stalemate. In an interesting twist on the Jihad vs. McWorld model, other leaders of African countries—mostly former colonies too—for many years demonstrated their own form of tribal loyalty by refusing to criticize Mugabe, their fellow freedom-fighter. Their shared identities in the struggle for independence against (mainly) the United Kingdom bound them together in this long-running struggle against a postcolonial "McWorld." As the crisis inside Zimbabwe has deepened, however, that kind of tribalism has shown signs of weakening. (An Associated Press article by Michelle Faul, filed from Johannesburg, South Africa, on December 22, 2008, reported: "Also stepping up pressure, the Roman Catholic Bishops' Conference of Southern Africa called for Africans … to isolate Mugabe entirely." The same article informed its readers that the Botswana Foreign Minister, Phandu Skelemani "called for African nations to close their borders with Zimbabwe, saying it would bring Mugabe down in just a week or two.") The dire straits of the country have driven a wedge between Mugabe and at least some of his old regional allies, leaving him and his people in almost total isolation. The world outside looks on, but Jihad and McWorld seem at loggerheads here, with no happy ending in sight.

Namibia Since Independence: Beyond Jihad and McWorld?

In contrast with Zimbabwe, the former German and South African colony of Namibia (old name: Southwest Africa) seems to have triumphed against the threats posed by both Jihadic and McWorld forces.

So we see how the forces of Jihad and McWorld may not only shape events; the pairing may also help us to interpret those events, situations, and even the actions of people themselves. Sometimes, we can see a "third way," something resembling Hegel's "synthesis," beyond the two antagonistic forces, as demonstrated by events in Namibia. The possibility of this "third way" should encourage us to modify our sometimes too-simplistic responses to the complexities of many current world problems. A few examples and talking points follow.

The first post-independence leader of Namibia, Sam Nujoma, made some choices which lifted his country above the tribal fray and away from resentment against the Western world of the old imperial powers. He chose English as the official language in a country of many competing tongues; he embarked on productive partnerships with, among others, the United States of America, for trading and other economic benefits.

Unlike other post-independence African rulers, such as Julius Nyerere, Hastings Banda, Kenneth Kaunda, and (still) Robert Mugabe, Sam Nujoma did not cling to power for decades after independence; nor did he create a one-party quasi-dictatorship. Elections were held, and a new leader came to power after his third term as President. Indeed, the South West Africa People's Organization (SWAPO) remains in power in Namibia, but Hifikepunye Pohamba, the new Namibian President, is providing stable leadership that is sensitive to the nation's diversity.

Namibia, in spite of its devastating encounter with HIV/AIDS, is a model of a "new" country transcending the dangerous mix of Barber's two forces, which seem to turn particularly lethal in the postcolonial setting.

Talking Points

Exporting Democracy

If the United States wants to export democracy throughout the world, it must understand the relationship between democratic forms of governing and Jihad and McWorld. Neither force assumes a specific form of government. McWorld can function with any form that minimizes interference in economic activity. Jihad expects self-determination, no matter the form it takes. But, as Barber points out, neither force fosters democracy in any way.

However, Barber's chapter, "Securing Global Democracy in the World of McWorld," illustrates how difficult, but also how necessary, it is to "secure democracy" in "modern conditions." Barber says of *Jihad vs. McWorld* that "the first and last and only lesson this book can teach is that until democracy becomes the aim and end of those wrestling with the terrors of Jihad and the insufficiencies of McWorld, there is little chance that we can even embark on the long journey of imagination that takes women and men from elementary animal being ... to cooperative human living" (1996, p. 291).

The Successes and Failures of McWorld

McWorld's success is measured by the accumulation of wealth and economic opportunities, not human rights and access to equal opportunity. A global community dominated by McWorld essentially alters the governing structure from a nation-state to, in essence, a corporate empire. If nation-states continue to exist, they do so to keep "petty" interference (e.g., global strife and natural disasters) from disrupting international commerce. Keep in mind, though, that, unlike nation-states, McWorld does not promote or protect the welfare of its people. Instead, it works to promote consumption and protect profit. We need to make sure we understand the implications for humanity of a global community dominated by profitable enterprises, instead of not-for-profit nation-states.

McWorld often looks fairly appealing. Economic growth means more money, more consumption, new buildings, and the latest technology. But look at the issue for a second from the perspective of the Chinese. What beliefs and values are we sharing with them through McWorld? China now has around 2000 Kentucky Fried Chicken restaurants. A new one opens every other day. McDonald's has well over 1000 locations, with new ones opening every week. What does this mean to the Chinese and their culture? Are these the values and beliefs that define United States culture and thinking? Is it our goal to make Beijing the fast food capital of the world? Who ultimately shapes the future of Beijing: corporate CEOs or the people of China?

The Successes and Failures of Jihad

On the other hand, Jihad is grounded in exclusion, and not much interested in equality, either. There is an isolationism associated with Jihad that tends to promote authoritarian forms of government, not democracy. If organized into nation-states, Barber's Jihadic—isolationist and inward-looking—cultures may use the governing structures of those states to preserve and strengthen certain practices in order to protect them from outside influence. Taliban rule in Afghanistan manifested a good example of this reinforcement, with strict social restraints placed on women, and men, in the name of religious purity, becoming the laws of the state. These laws—anathema to most Westerners—then attained parity with the laws of other sovereign states. Still, secular Westerners should be wary of rejecting religion-based governments out of hand. (Remember that "advanced" western European democracies, such as Sweden and the United Kingdom, have "state" churches.) As Timothy Samuel Shah and Monica Duffy Toft say in their article "Why God is Winning," (2006), "The spread of democracy, far from checking the power of militant religious activists, will probably only enhance the reach of prophetic political movements, many of which will emerge from democratic processes more organized, more popular, and more legitimate than before—but quite possibly no less violent. Democracy is giving the world's peoples their voice, and they want to talk about God" (p. 29). Perhaps "fusion" politics are occurring here, to overcome the binary pattern of Barber's two-sided model?

It may be that the desire for the so-called tribal identity provided by religion has indeed fused, in some places, with the democratic impulse. Is this an area of human experience where the attempt to secure democracy has succeeded, but without wiping out tribal identity through McWorld-style homogenization? Look to Turkey, for example, where the secular state is paramount to the nation's post-1923 identity, when Kemal Ataturk set the country on the road to a "modernization" which meant growing westernization and secularization. Islam is the religion of the huge majority of Turks, but the law forbids the public use of Islamic symbols. Even the headscarf cannot be worn by women in schools nor in the Parliament. France's longstanding anticlericalism has had a similar impact, where the movement toward democracy and secularism started by the French Revolution has had to find a way to accommodate the indigenous Roman Catholicism of the majority.

Barber's "Jihad" appeals to those wielding the power, certainly, but makes no attempt to satisfy those excluded from the privileged community. Minority views within the nation-state or culture are squashed, and laws are created to promote obedience to the "group," often by denying people their individual rights. This Jihadic process may also mean rejecting a role in the global community. Sadly, Jihadic cultures too often have used their isolation and inaccessibility to commit violent actions against minority groups within their own borders. In 1975, the Khmer Rouge closed the Cambodian borders in order to "purify" and protect the culture from outside influence. This action allowed them to kill 1.7 million Cambodians, about 20% of the population, without interference from the outside world. And at least 100,000 Kurds were killed in the Anfal campaign, in 1987: the Iraqi government's attempt to erase Kurdish life from rural northern Iraq. Can the world live with these kinds of actions? Do we want Jihadic communities, so isolated and disconnected from the rest of us, to act out whatever philosophies they choose?

Ultimately, we have to deal with the movement to a single connected world, if for no other reason than because we understand today how we all share the same ecosystem. We understand that burning the Brazilian rain forest has environmental consequences for the entire world and that deciding the future of the rain forest is not a decision to be made solely by a single culture or nation-state. We also have to recognize that national boundaries do not restrict people as they have in the past. We routinely travel outside the United States to many parts of the world, and we must face the fact that what occurs throughout the world directly and indirectly influences our lives. Trains bombed in Madrid and attacks on the city of Mumbai affect the global community, not just the people of Spain and India. We must also deal with the fact that diseases do not respect national boundaries, and that global travelers can spread a disease from one part of the world to another in a single day. We just cannot live isolated from the rest of the world.

Such considerations mean that our lives and livelihoods are inextricably bound with those from around the world. The future of the global community determines the future of

In the end, what does all of this analysis mean to us? Can we use the knowledge produced by our understanding and application of Barber's "Jihad and McWorld" dyad to help us improve the world? What kind of world do you envision developing in your lifetime?

our planet, and our lives are parts of that planetary society, even though we may not always realize it. Acquiring as much knowledge as we can from many different perspectives may help us in the end to make informed, rational decisions about global problems that may seem far removed from our everyday lives. But we will be better off still if we have an interpretive framework to help us to synthesize the complicated data with which we have to deal. Barber's interesting Jihad vs. McWorld dichotomy certainly provides two axes along which to plot the events, trends and phenomena of life at home and abroad.

It is the application of this knowledge that will determine where we go from here. Do we have the right or the responsibility to intervene in Darfur? How do we address global warming together? What role does the United Nations play in establishing international laws to promote the welfare of all people in the world? How does this knowledge shape the way we vote in national and local elections, so that we act responsibly in the global society? How do we act in our local communities? What kinds of cars do we drive, what products do we consume, and where do we invest our money? Our responses to each of these questions will shape the beliefs and values promoted throughout our lifetimes, hopefully beliefs and values we have developed after careful consideration of a wide range of perspectives and ideas. Recognizing our role and responsibility in the global community through concepts like McWorld and Jihad can help us make better decisions about some complex problems.

Can We Do As Well As Barber, Friedman, et al.? Some Student Voices

Hopefully, discussions regarding global forces such as Barber's Jihad and McWorld help us understand how much we have to explore in order to move from our limited ethnocentric view of the world to that of a responsible world citizen. This movement is not a direct one, from A to Z, or even from A to B. Instead, it is an uncertain and sometimes recursive route through new material, new information, and new-old ways of thinking. If we rely only upon what we already know, and if we do not seek out productive modes of thought, be they new or old, we will remain trapped within our limited world. We then may fail to develop the tools we need to address complex global problems. As one Elon University Global Studies student explained:

> The most influential outcome of taking the Global Experience class is the expanding of my outlook on life. I came to Elon [University] believing that I had an open mind and could see the perspectives of others, but I was really trapped in a state of dualistic thinking.

Getting outside this dualism is a major first step towards becoming a global citizen, to dip your toe into the ocean of global problems and all the responsibility that comes with this knowing. As another student put it:

> I wrote in my first paper that I am guilty of sometimes being lazy, complacent, or self-centered. I am guilty of skipping right over the "World News" and "U.S. News" sections in the newspaper to get to the far more interesting stories about celebrities and television shows.

This is intellectually a much easier way to deal with global problems. We minimize their impact on our life, thinking about other things that do not make us question our own ideas and beliefs in any depth.

Learning, though, requires this depth of thought, this exploration of difficult, murky problems that resist easy solutions. And while we often try hard to convince ourselves that we truly do care about the personal life of a celebrity we will never meet, we find our greatest satisfactions, and frustrations, in playing with complex ideas and concepts which will lead us to address global problems. This shift opens up to us a world we barely knew existed and challenges us to think for ourselves and act upon this thinking. It parallels our move from home to college, the move from seeing the world through the perspective given to us (most often by parents, culture, and friends) to creating one of our own. Doing so, while scary and challenging, also energizes and empowers us as we learn to take control of our own lives.

As another Global Studies student related:

> The Global class was a new experience that introduced me to foreign ideas. I have never been one to read the news and stay educated on current global issues, especially ones that do not seem to apply to my life. Global Studies has forced me to explore different religions and lifestyles, as well as face the harsh facts of global issues. My eyes were opened to many foreign affairs, along with different conflicts that directly influence me. For the first time, I became interested in politics. With the election taking place in November, [2008], I was introduced to varying opinions on both the conservative and liberal sides that I had never considered. This was the first time that I allowed myself to become involved in a political situation, and I was shocked by the intense emotion that many students used to convey their opinions. I was offended and excited by many political statements, but most of all I was able to open my mind to accept opinions on both sides of the argument. This was a very influential time in my life as a student, and beyond, as I was finally able to create my own opinions, rather than rely on my parents' beliefs.

Indeed, we cannot let ourselves and others down by accepting simple or easy solutions just because they make for "neat and clean" papers, where in five to ten pages we can get from a statement of the problem, to a solution. We need to take the time to argue through the various perspectives available to us, to see if our accumulated knowledge can provide for better responses and solutions than we currently possess. This can be most frustrating when people are dying or starving or suffering throughout the world. We do not want to wait; we want to act. We want to decide what to do right now so we can quickly resolve the problem. Global problems resist such simple solutions. We have laws in every nation making slavery illegal; yet slaves exist throughout the world. We agree that we want to protect the planet which makes our life possible; yet we drive billions of miles each year, consuming millions of barrels of oil. Powerful thinking takes time, the time to weigh different options, recognize the consequences of various ways of acting, and develop a clear sense of what makes some ways of acting better than others. As yet another student expressed it:

> This increased awareness is the first step to making a change and has made me realize how passionately I feel about making a positive difference in the world. Now I am faced with the problem of choosing what crisis to confront, what actions to take, and how to best connect my education and future career with my passion. These new questions have created a whirlwind

of ideas, directions, and uncertainties which I hope to sift through, develop or discard, explore or abandon. As I continue through college, I hope future classes will introduce me to new concerns, varying perspectives, and innovative solutions.

This is the challenge facing global citizens: deciding how to act in the face of limited knowledge and uncertainty, remaining confident that as we gain new perspectives we will be able to devise better and better solutions. The best news of all is that, once we pop this bubble, once we get beyond seeing the world as black and white, we start a journey that will engage us for the rest of our lives. We can use what we know to develop better ways of responding to the problems we will encounter:

> I realize that I have a long way to go. I have one more semester in my freshman year, three more years in my undergraduate experience, and an entire lifetime after graduating, and I expect that in all of those stages, I will continue to develop and learn. And the more I learn, the less I will likely feel that I know, because each new piece of knowledge opens up a number of new venues for exploration. This class has been just a stage in what I hope will prove to be a lifetime of exposure to new people, places, and ideas.

Last Thoughts about Our Need for Other People's Interpretive Perspectives in the Field of Global Studies

The students' voices we have heard show that the journey to world citizenship is just that: a series of steps along a road that will become a lifetime's trek into the unknown. But we can make sense of new experience—of the as-yet unknown—by reaching into our toolkit. That toolkit should contain our own knowledge, formed from a rich diversity of information; and our own ideas, values, and principles, shaped by thought and experience. In the toolbag, also, should be other people's ideas, information, and the knowledge they have created. Still more valuable, perhaps, are the thinkers who offer us "big ideas," or "encompassing interpretive frameworks." We have mentioned, in addition to the primary focus on Barber's ideas, the work of Friedman, Sachs, Stiglitz, Ritzer, and Soros as examples.

This chapter has tried to show how useful such an inclusive framework for thought can be. Barber's model is flexible enough to allow new examples to be fitted within it; tough enough to withstand opposition; and dynamic enough to respond to changing world situations. In his 2002 article, for example, "Beyond Jihad vs. McWorld: On Terrorism and the New Democratic Realism," Barber himself retrieves his old model for use in a post-9/11 context. Last word? Start collecting and assessing *other* "big ideas" about the world. Perhaps even go out and create your own Global Studies frameworks, which will inevitably be some kind of synthesis, at least in part, of other people's work. With luck and energy, your own contributions may be as helpful and stimulating as those we have examined here.

Ultimately, the work we do with our toolkits is up to us, individually and collectively. Think about your place in your world at this moment, and the "work" you do every day. You are going to put this book down and initiate hundreds of actions, from brushing your teeth, to buying a cup of coffee. How are these actions, how is this "work," a part of your journey to global citizenship? Do you leave the water running as you brush? Do you choose "fair trade" coffee and cups made from recycled paper? Do you *think* about your actions, considering how they may reflect what you have learned and believe? Are you conscious of the consequences of your actions and do they reflect what you believe and value most? Hopefully, the voices offered in this chapter, and throughout this book, will help you figure out why and how to enact your beliefs and values, and to develop your ability to explore and improve our world.

Acknowledgments

The authors gratefully acknowledge the following students of Stephen Braye, who allowed their writing to be used in this chapter: Mara Bollenbacher, Mary Kate Hinshaw, Kelly Little, and Wendy Mallette.

Notes

1. Herbert, G. (1972). Vertue. In *The metaphysical poets* (pp. 127–128). Ed. Helen Gardner. London: Penguin Books.
2. For a concise and illuminating guide to the Presocratics, see *The Greek Philosophers*, by Rex Warner. (New York: New American Library, 1958).
3. Barber, Friedman, Ritzer, Sachs, Singer, Soros and Stiglitz have written extensively, since the early 1990s, about the nature and worth of the economic and other cultural forces associated with globalization. See Suggested Readings below.
4. The so-called "gag rule" has had a chequered career, in fact. Officially called "The Mexico City Policy," the "rule" was instituted under President Reagan in 1984, reversed by President Clinton in 1993, reinstated by President George W. Bush in 2001 and rescinded once again by President Obama, on 24th January, 2009.

References

Barber, B. R. (2002). Beyond Jihad vs. McWorld: On terrorism and the new democratic realism. *The Nation*, January 21. Vol. 274, Issue 2, 11–18.

Barber, B. R. (1992). Jihad vs. McWorld, *Atlantic*, March, Vol. 269, Issue 3, 53–62.

Barber, B. R. (1995). *Jihad vs. McWorld: How globalism and tribalism are reshaping the world*. New York: Ballantine Books.

Cole, J. (2007). A 'Shi'ite crescent'? The regional impact of the Iraq war. *Current History*. January 2006. Rpt. in *Annual editions: Developing world 07–08* (pp. 82-87) 17th Ed. Ed. Robert J. Griffiths. Boston: McGraw-Hill.

Consolatore, D. (2006). The Pashtun factor: Is Afghanistan next in line for an ethnic civil war?" *The Humanist*, May/June. Rpt. in *Annual editions: Developing world 08–09* (pp. 110–112). 18th Ed. Ed. Robert J. Griffiths. Boston, MA: McGraw-Hill, 2008.

Faul, M. (2008). Britain, U.S. step up pressure on Zimbabwe's Mugabe. Associated Press. December 22, 2008. http://www.wral.com/news/national_world/world/story/4185645/.

Friedman, T. L. (2006). *The world is flat 2.0: A brief history of the twenty-first century*. New York: Farrar, Straus and Giroux, 2006.

Nasr, V. (2006). When the Shiites rise. *Foreign Affairs*, July/August. Rpt. *Annual editions: developing world 08–09* (pp. 92–99) 18th Ed. Ed. Robert J. Griffiths. Boston, MA: McGraw-Hill, 2008.

Ritzer, G. (1995). *The McDonaldization of society: An investigation into the changing character of contemporary social life*. Thousand Oaks, CA: Pine Forge Press.

Shah, T. S., & Toft, M. D. (2006). Why God is Winning. *Foreign Policy*, July/August. Rpt. in *Annual editions: Developing world 08–09* (pp. 29–31). 18th Ed. Ed. Robert J. Griffiths. Boston, MA: McGraw Hill, 2008.

Questions for Discussion _____

1. What is the mascot for your college or university? What images are associated with this mascot? How 'sacred' are these images,? That is, how seriously do students (and faculty?) treat them? Reflect on why your team mascot is so important to so many people.

2. Barber's argument suggests that both forces, "Jihad" and "McWorld", are threats to democracy. Do you agree? Explain how this claim might work, first with tribalization and Jihad and then with globalization and McWorld. Can the argument about the threat to democracy be true for one force and not the other?

3. Choose two items from the Suggested Readings or References for this chapter. Read them. Write about, or discuss, the contributions they make to your understanding of globalization and/or tribalization.

4. Look around for evidence that Barber's (and Ritzer's) "McDonaldization" may be occurring. Then consider the *why* of this phenomenon. For this exercise, first list some evidence that globalization *is* occurring. After you have established a list, give some explanation as to *why* these bits of evidence exist. For example, *why* is it that your shirt was made in Honduras? What social, political, and economic forces created this situation?

5. Many words ending in "*-ization*" are processes. In this chapter, these key processes are globalization and tribalization: McDonaldiz*ation* and Jihad*ization*. Who, or what, controls these processes? How do you know? Toward what end point might these processes be tending?

Suggested Readings _____

Barber, B. R. (2000). Can democracy survive globalization? *Government & opposition*, Summer, Vol. 35, Issue 3, 275–301.

Easterly, W. (2007). *The white man's burden: Why the west's efforts to aid the rest have done so much ill and so little good.* Harmondsworth, UK: Penguin.

Friedman, T. L. (1999). *The Lexus and the olive tree.* New York: Farrar, Straus and Giroux.

Hegel, G. W. F. (1991). Ed. Allen W. Wood. Trans. H. B. Nisbet. *Hegel: Elements of the philosophy of right* (Cambridge Texts in the History of Political Thought). Cambridge, UK: Cambridge University Press.

Ritzer, G. (2004). *The globalization of nothing.* Thousand Oaks, CA: Pine Forge Press.

Sachs, J. D. (2005). Can extreme poverty be eliminated? *Scientific American*, September. Rpt. in *Annual editions: Developing world 07–08* (pp. 10–14). 17th Ed. Robert J. Griffiths. Boston, MA: McGraw Hill, 2007.

Sachs, J. D. (2006). *The end of poverty: Economic possibilities for our time.* Harmondsworth, UK: Penguin.

Singer, P. (2000). *A Darwinian left: Politics, evolution and cooperation.* New Haven: Yale University Press.

Singer, P. (2002). *One world: The ethics of globalization.* New Haven: Yale University Press.

Soros, G. (2002). *George Soros on globalization.* New York: Public Affairs.

Soros, G. (2002). *Open society: Reforming global capitalism.* New York: Public Affairs.

Stiglitz, J. (2003). *Globalization and its discontents.* New York: W.W. Norton.

Stiglitz, J. (2006). Social justice and global trade. *Far Eastern Economic Review*. March. Rpt. in *Annual editions: Developing world 08–09* (pp. 47–49). 18th Ed. Roger J. Griffiths. Boston, MA: McGraw Hill, 2008.